How Roosevelt Failed America in World War II

ALSO BY STEWART HALSEY ROSS

Strategic Bombing by the United States in World War II: The Myths and the Facts (McFarland, 2003)

Propaganda for War: How the United States Was Conditioned to Fight the Great War of 1914–1918 (McFarland, 1996)

How Roosevelt Failed America in World War II

STEWART HALSEY ROSS

McFarland & Company, Inc., Publishers
Jefferson, North Carolina, and London

LIBRARY OF CONGRESS CATALOGUING-IN-PUBLICATION DATA

Ross, Stewart Halsey.
　　How Roosevelt failed America in World War II / Stewart Halsey Ross.
　　　　p.　　cm.
　　Includes bibliographical references and index.

　　ISBN 0-7864-2512-1 (softcover : 50# alkaline paper) ∞

　　1. United States — Foreign relations —1933–1945.　2. United States — Politics and government —1933–1945.　3. Roosevelt, Franklin D. (Franklin Delano), 1882–1945 — Millitary leadership.　4. Neutrality — United States — History — 20th century.　5. Capitulations, Military — United States — History — 20th century.　6. World War, 1939–1945 — Diplomatic history.　7. World War, 1939–1945 — United States.　I. Title.
E806.R84　2006
940.53'2273 — dc22　　　　　　　　　　　　　　　2006010929

British Library cataloguing data are available

©2006 Stewart Halsey Ross. All rights reserved

No part of this book may be reproduced or transmitted in any form or by any means, electronic or mechanical, including photocopying or recording, or by any information storage and retrieval system, without permission in writing from the publisher.

On the cover: photograph of FDR ©2006 Clipart.com; flag background ©2006 Comstock Images

Manufactured in the United States of America

McFarland & Company, Inc., Publishers
　Box 611, Jefferson, North Carolina 28640
　　www.mcfarlandpub.com

I dedicate this book to my dear grandchildren.

Madison
Alec
Ian
Sam
Myles
Anne
Jake
Hailey
Benjamin
Ellie
Wisdom
Jade

Acknowledgments

My first debt of gratitude is to the information staff of the Darien Library, Darien, Connecticut. Without these bright, patient, and conscientious people digging up books and papers for me, my research task would have been far more difficult: Carole Braunschweig, Janet Davis, Mary Freedman, Kim Gabert, Sandra Lahtinen, Mary McPherson, Gretchen Naylor, Blanche Parker, Terry Ritchie, and Judy Sgammato. Thank you for your indispensable contributions.

I must also thank reference librarians Indu Arya, Phebe Kirkham, and Fran Sauer of the New Canaan Library, New Canaan, Connecticut, for your help as well in my research.

To my fourteen-year-old grandson, Sam, a personal thanks for the many orders you placed for me with "Amazon.com" for out-of-print books—hard cover and very good condition, please.

And my son, Robert, thank you for your many helpful comments as the book progressed.

My partner and wife of fifty-three years, Judy, continues to inspire me. I love you dearly.

Contents

Acknowledgments	vi
Preface	1
Introduction	5
1. FDR's Undeclared War in the Atlantic	15
2. FDR's Personal Fifty-Destroyers-for-Bases Deal	23
3. Lend-Lease: To the Brink of War	30
4. Charles A. Lindbergh and the America First Committee	38
5. FDR's Expendable "Three Small Vessels"	55
6. Pearl Harbor: FDR's Monstrous Conspiracy	60
7. FDR's Tomfoolery: Unconditional Surrender	85
8. FDR Ignores *Die Schwarze Kapelle*	103
9. Treasury Secretary Henry Morgenthau Jr.'s Scorched-Earth Plan	120
10. Roosevelt: Feeble and Dying	135
11. Was Adolf Hitler Planning to Attack the United States?	150
Epilogue	177
Appendices	
A. President Grover Cleveland's "Toothache," 1893	179
B. The Zimmermann Telegram, January 17, 1917	181
C. Woodrow Wilson's Fourteen Points, January 18, 1918	182
D. The Portentous Lie of Ambassador Henry Morgenthau, Sr., 1918	184

E.	Conspiracy in President Woodrow Wilson's White House, 1919–1920	191
F.	Key Excerpts from the Nye "Munitions Hearings" Report, February 24, 1936	195
G.	America First Committee: Principles and Membership, 1940	200
H.	The Atlantic Charter, August 14, 1941	201
I.	Key Excerpts from a Charles A. Lindbergh Speech, September 11, 1941	203
J.	United Nations Declaration, January 1, 1942	206
K.	U.S. Mustard Gas at Bari, Italy, 1943	207
L.	Memorandum by Henry Morgenthau, Jr., on the Scorched-Earth Plan	209
M.	The Potsdam Declaration, July 26, 1945	213

Notes	215
Bibliography	235
Index	241

Preface

"We will not participate in a foreign war, and we will not send our Army, naval or air forces to fight in foreign lands outside of the Americas, except in case of attack."[1]
FDR, September 11, 1940

"Of course, we'll fight if we're attacked. If somebody attacks us, then it isn't a foreign war, is it?"[2]
FDR, confided to his staff, October 30, 1940

"Well, the old man has gone, a man who never told the truth if a lie would suffice."[3]
General Douglas MacArthur to Brig. General Bonner Fellers, on FDR's death, April 12, 1945

In 1996 I published a book about Woodrow Wilson's presidency, *Propaganda for War: How the United States Was Conditioned to Fight the Great War of 1914–1918*. By the time I had finished my research, I had concluded that it had been a monumental mistake for America to have gone to war against Germany in April 1917. British propaganda in the United States had helped convince "the man in the street" that the war had been started by Germany, intent on her alleged long-cherished plan to dominate the earth, and that Americans were fighting the cause of small and weak nations against the ruthlessness of a bully. Both premises would be proven false once the fog of war was lifted.

Woodrow Wilson, while publicly exhorting Americans to be neutral, privately leaned from the start toward the Allied cause. He supposedly held at bay the growing forces calling for war against Germany because he was uncertain the nation was ready. In March 1917 publication of the secret Zimmerman Telegram was considered proof of Germany's duplicity. In February, the *Reichsmarine* resumed unrestricted submarine warfare and in mid-March three American ships were torpedoed with loss of life.

Whether it was the fateful Zimmermann Telegram or the three American merchantmen sunk by German U-boats that pushed the president over the edge is not known. The only certainty is that is was Woodrow Wilson who put America into the war.

This book traces the activities of another determined president, the Germanophobe Franklin Delano Roosevelt, similarly intent on taking America into a European war. Unlike Wilson, whose electorate had been "conditioned" beforehand, Roosevelt had an electorate that was overwhelmingly isolationist. Beginning in October 1937, in his "quarantine-the-aggressors" speech in Chicago, he indicated to the world the direction in which he was taking the United Sates. Using all the strings of government like a skillful marionetteer, and with the guile of a seasoned politician, Roosevelt slickly manipulated American public opinion. Like Wilson, who also professed American neutrality, FDR after September 1939 engaged in patently warlike acts, open and clandestine, to antagonize Germany.

When purposefully provocative acts in the Atlantic by the U.S. Navy did not draw the fangs of *Kriegsmarine* submarines, and FDR was unable to trigger the war he wanted in Europe, he then turned to a back door: Japan. Japan depended almost entirely on U.S. oil imports, and when FDR embargoed oil in collusion with Great Britain and the Netherlands, Roosevelt's alternate enemy was forced to seek other sources. To unify a nation still nearly 90 percent noninterventionist despite strident and insistent anti–Axis propaganda, Roosevelt played his most ambitious card, Pearl Harbor. The December 7, 1941, assault was pronounced a "sneak" attack and four days later Adolf Hitler declared war on the United States. Roosevelt finally had his sought-after war with Germany.

The subject of this book is Roosevelt's prewar and wartime presidency, covering his successful efforts to bring a sorely polarized America into World War II. It includes details of his far less successful efforts as commander-in-chief during the war and planning for the postwar period. Between the lines, the book illustrates the power of an American president in wartime, whether in a "manufactured" war or otherwise.

On the issue of FDR's instigation and foreknowledge of the attack on Pearl Harbor — almost certainly the most controversial section of the book — I have drawn on the authoritative archival research and personal interviews with surviving U.S. Navy cryptographers of Robert B. Stinnett in *Day of Deceit: The Truth About FDR and Pearl Harbor* (2000). He has written that he was able to obtain through Freedom of Information Act requests "an extraordinary number of documents" that covered previously unknown facts. He has written that "more than 200,000 documents and interviews" have led him to his conclusions. He disposes of the myths that the Japanese task force that struck Pearl Harbor was under radio silence from the time it departed its assembly area in Hitokappu Bay on November 24 to its fly-off of its aircraft on December 7, 1941, and that U.S. code breakers had been unable to break the Japanese naval code prior to December 7. We now know for certain that the British, Dutch, and Nationalist Chinese were reading the encoded messages. For example, Stinnett included a facsimile copy of an FBI report, formerly Top Secret, that states: "The U.S. Navy did break the Japanese military [naval] code prior to the attack on Pearl Harbor and this directly contributed to the United States victory at Midway Island and in Japanese Admiral Yamamoto's being shot down in the Pacific."

I have included a chapter on Franklin Roosevelt's fatal illness, which I consider a defining element of his character. He knew he was dying, yet he decided to run for a fourth term, consulting no one. With his loyal Secret Service detachment, he pretended he was in rugged good health during his notorious drive through New York City's five boroughs just before the 1944 election. This was hubris, plain and simple, and the nation suffered for it. It is a lesson the electorate must never forget.

My research for the last chapter, was intriguing, particularly in light of the recent discovery of a German plan to attack and invade the United States as early as 1903. German historian Holger H. Herwig claims that the evidence of this plan was in the German military archives in Freiburg in the form of 1,500 handwritten pages. Much of the handwriting, Herwig has insisted, matches that of four famous German military figures of the period: Admiral Alfred von Tirpitz, Admiral Otto von Diederichs, Count Alfred von Schlieffen, and Major Erich Ludendorff. The detailed plan was an idiotic scheme that could scarcely have been successful. Its compilers, according to Herwig's handwriting analyses, belied their reputations as Germany's foremost military planners. I treat the subject ambiguously, because there is much evidence on both sides of this issue, and I chose to let readers judge for themselves.

Noteworthy among works of a similar nature critical of FDR's integrity, decision-making, and arrogation of extraordinary wartime powers are Charles Austin Beard's *President Roosevelt and the Coming of the War 1941* (1948); Harry Elmer Barnes's *Perpetual War for Perpetual Peace: A Critical Examination of the Foreign Policy of Franklin Delano Roosevelt and Its Aftermath* (1953); John Toland's *Infamy: Pearl Harbor and Its Aftermath* (1982); and John Costello's *Days of Infamy — MacArthur, Roosevelt, Churchill: The Shocking Truth Revealed* (1994). None of these authors had the benefit of the eye-opening findings of Stinnett, however. Anne Armstrong's thorough *Unconditional Surrender: The Impact of the Casablanca Policy upon World War II* (1961), is considered the most authoritative source on this subject.

Introduction

"I am half American and the natural person to work with you. It is evident we see eye to eye. Were I to become Prime Minister of Britain we could control the world."[1]
                    Winston S. Churchill to Franklin D. Roosevelt

"You know I am a juggler. And I never let my right hand know what my left hand does.... I may have one policy for Europe and one diametrically opposite for North and South America. I may be entirely inconsistent, and furthermore I am perfectly willing to mislead and tell untruths if it will help win the war."[2]
                    Franklin D. Roosevelt to Henry
                    Morgenthau, Jr., May 15, 1942

Two historians, separated by a half-century, while acknowledging President Franklin D. Roosevelt's lies and cover-ups before and during World War II, have absolved him for these underhanded tactics in what both considered the strategic interests of the nation.

Thomas A. Bailey in 1948: "Franklin Roosevelt *repeatedly deceived* the American people during the period before Pearl Harbor. When he warned them against the aggressors, he was branded a sensationalist. When he pointed to perils of storm-cellar neutrality, he was branded an interventionist. When he urged adequate armaments, he was branded a warmonger. He was faced with a terrible trilemma. If he let the people slumber in a fog of isolation, they might well fall prey to Hitler. If he came out unequivocally for intervention, he would be defeated in 1940, or shelved for a candidate more willing to let the masses enjoy their fool's paradise. If he was going to induce the people to move at all, *he would have to trick them....* The country was overwhelmingly noninterventionist to the very day of Pearl Harbor..." (emphasis added).[3]

Robert B. Stinnett in 2000: "...I felt a sense of outrage as I uncovered secrets that had been hidden from Americans for more than fifty years. But I understood the agonizing dilemma faced by President Roosevelt. He was forced to find *circuitous means* to persuade an isolationist America to join in a fight for freedom. Many Americans had chosen isolationism to shelter their young from the horrors of another war, and believed that Roosevelt would not 'send their sons to fight in foreign wars'" (emphasis added).

An entire generation of Americans grew up knowing only one president, Franklin Delano Roosevelt. The 1930s were the heyday of radio and FDR used this medium to his advantage. His "fireside chats"[5] gave him a remarkable tool with which to hoodwink Americans. He skillfully manipulated the press and bent it to his support. He was a habitual liar and a slick propagandist.

He ran a covert, undeclared war in the Atlantic against German submarines while professing American neutrality; bypassed the Congress by personally arranging delivery of fifty old U.S. Navy destroyers to the Royal Navy; brought America to the brink of war with Lend-Lease; then purposefully put an economic stranglehold on Japan that necessarily brought the Pearl Harbor attack in response.

Once he got the United States into the European war through Japan's back door, his "unconditional surrender" edict lengthened the war and caused tens of thousands of needless GI deaths. FDR mulishly refused to recognize the existence of an underground organization in Germany that was seeking an armistice with the U.S. and Great Britain. In 1944, when he was feeble and dying, he secretly spent more time recuperating from illness than on duty in the White House. He self-importantly, some would say stupidly, sought a fourth term; by 1945 his cardiac specialists were straining to keep him alive.

Millions of serious Roosevelt haters saw through his hypocrisies and deceit. "He lied us into the war"[6] became their favorite phrase. As far as they were concerned, three terms were one too many for any president and four, unacceptable. They never bought into his New Deal, claiming—correctly—that FDR's legislation was not what levered America out of the depression; it was World War II. They were galled even by FDR's elitist accent, which they were convinced was feigned.

In the United States, disillusionment with the Great War began shortly after the conflict ended. As patriotic passions cooled, the monumental lies created by Britain's and America's propagandists were exposed to the light, one by one. England had not gone to war to defend the neutrality of Belgium and to preserve the honor of Great Britain; England had gone to war because of an unwritten agreement to come to the aid of France if France went to war with Germany. The infamous British Bryce Report[7] that supposedly proved systematic German brutality during its sweep through Belgium — which played so well in the United States— was nearly all claptrap. There turned out to be not a shred of evidence that German soldiers routinely cut off the hands of Belgian boys (so that they could not fire guns) or the breasts of women. As for the atrocities committed routinely by heartless U-boat commanders, they, too, were wild exaggerations; no less an authority than the commander of U.S. naval forces in the European theater said so.

A calm assessment of the wartime hysteria in the United States—associated with sabotage and sedition by presumably ubiquitous German spies and agents—showed only a handful of indictments and fewer sentences. A year after the Armistice a renowned New England judge declared that it that it was his best judgment that "more than 99 percent of the pro-German plots never existed...."[8]

Henry Morgenthau, Sr., U.S. ambassador to Turkey, wrote a bestselling book which included the sensational disclosure of a Potsdam Crown Council meeting on July 5, 1914, ostensibly to ready Germany for the war to come a month later. The meeting never took place. It was a cruel hoax with far-reaching consequences (Appendix D). "Sole German guilt" as emblazoned in Article 231 (Appendix D) of the vindictive Versailles Treaty no longer held water once the immediate postwar correspondence between conniving Russian and French diplomats was made public by a mocking communist Soviet Union. Indeed, a strong case could be made, if guilt had to be apportioned, that Russia's hands were bloodiest, for that nation was the first to mobilize its vast armies, and in 1914 mobilization meant war.

Even America's thirty-two months of "neutrality" became suspect when the powerful pro–Allied biases at the highest levels in the government, business, the press, and the clergy were viewed objectively. In fact, as with Franklin D. Roosevelt in 1940, Woodrow Wilson piously proclaimed "neutrality" while he covertly aided the Allies. While he hypocritically declaimed he was keeping America out of the war, Wilson had privately told his confidant, Colonel Edward M. House, as early as August 30, 1914, that Germany must not be allowed to win. "If Germany won," Wilson pontificated, "it would change the course of our civilization and make the United States a military nation."[9]

Postwar, the Senate refused to ratify the Versailles Treaty or to permit the U.S. to join the League of Nations. Wilson's "make the world safe for democracy" rang hollow and most Americans viewed wartime slogans, motion pictures, and posters as strident propaganda that misled them. The hot fires of rabid patriotism had quickly cooled.

In 1935 Congress passed the first Neutrality Act,[10] specifically to keep America out of war by prohibiting the nonneutral practices that had prevailed during the 1914–1917 period. It called for the president to declare, at the outbreak of war between two or more foreign nations, an embargo of arms and munitions to all belligerents. Further, a second clause stated that the export of such materials in American shipping was prohibited. It had a time limit of two years, after which it was passed again by a wide majority in both Houses. In 1936 and 1937 the Neutrality Act was stiffened with a "cash and carry" proviso applied to all other goods.

It was not until FDR's surprisingly belligerent "quarantine speech" in Chicago on October 5, 1937, that the president openly announced a shift in American policy, from neutrality to "nonbelligerency," as Winston Churchill framed it. The speech was aimed at Japan in its war with China, but also at Germany and Italy. Roosevelt talked about "homicides raging over the world, destroying all the works of civilization." He warned: "War is a contagion whether it be declared or undeclared.... We are determined to keep out of war.... We are adapting such measures as will minimize our risk of involvement but we cannot have complete protection in a world of disorder...."[11]

In a national poll taken in February 1937, the question was: "If another war like the World War develops in Europe, should America take part again?" Ninety-five percent of the responders said no. In April 1939, the sample was asked: "If England and France should go to war against Germany, do you think this country should declare war on Germany?" Again, ninety-five percent said no. A year later, after eight months of war in Europe, people were again asked: "If the question of the United States going to war against Germany and Italy came up for a national vote in the next two weeks, how would you vote: go into the war or stay out?" Eighty-six percent of the responders said "stay out." In August, 1941 another poll showed only a small slide. The question was: "If you voted today on the questions of the United States entering the war now against Germany and Italy, how would you vote — to go to war now, or stay out?" Seventy-five percent of the responders wanted their country to remain on the sidelines. When asked about war with Japan, seventy-six percent responded negatively.[12]

At the outbreak of hostilities in Europe on September 1, 1939, First Lord of the Admiralty Winston S. Churchill wrote to the president, seeking to enlist America in the war against Germany. He also suggested a system of private communication, to which the American president enthusiastically agreed. Churchill later wrote candidly: "My relations with the President gradually became so close that the chief business between our two countries was virtually conducted by these personal interchanges between him and me."[13]

Later in September FDR called a special session of the Congress to amend the Neutrality Act. He suggested that it was "a shameless and dishonorable fake" to suggest that "any person in Washington has ever suggested in any shape, manner, or form that remotest possibility of sending the boys of American mothers to fight on the battlefields of Europe." America is neutral, he insisted, "and does not intend to get involved in war."[14]

Under the cloak of a bogus neutrality, Roosevelt strove mightily to provoke Germany to strike the first blow that he could use as his pretext for a declaration of war. He secretly sent U.S. Navy destroyers into the Atlantic, first to snoop around for the Royal Navy in its desperate fight against German U-boats and then to actively engage them. The *Kriegsmarine* never took the bait, and only after the war was it learned that Hitler had categorically directed his commanders not to sink U.S. ships to avoid giving FDR his motive for war against Germany. At the same time, the president quietly transferred to the British some fifty Great-War-vintage destroyers that had been rusting in U.S. Navy Yards, in exchange for 99-year leases of British bases from Canada to the Caribbean. Members of Congress first learned of this action — a clear contravention of Geneva protocols and, arguably, an act of war — when they read it in the newspapers!

Next was an even more blatant action by the president but this time its scope was so encompassing, it was necessary to involve the Congress. It was likely a bright wag in the White House who came up with the term Lend-Lease, and when the bill was introduced in the Congress, it was labeled House Resolution 1776. Its disingenuous title was "An Act Further to Promote the Defense of the United States." The Lend-Lease Act, submitted to Congress on January 10, 1941, asked for $7 billion in credits to nations whose defenses were considered vital to the United States. Those members of Congress who fought the bill pointed out correctly that if passed Lend-Lease marked the transition of the United States from peace to war. Lend-Lease became law on March 11, 1941.

The passage of the Lend-Lease Act was a watershed for the president. His actions showed that he considered the U.S. as being in the European war, albeit "unofficially." However, FDR's many campaign promises, especially the unambiguous pledge in the Democratic Party's platform of 1940 not to take America's sons into foreign wars, temporarily hamstrung him. He could not enter the war "officially" until Germany made an "unprovoked attack." This was the origin of his secret naval war in the Atlantic, anticipating that U-boats when pressed would defend themselves by shooting first, or he could convince Americans that they had done so.

That same month, Roosevelt unveiled a series of actions, clandestine and public, each one of which was either a direct violation of international law or was a provocative near-war act. Damaged British warships would be repaired in U.S. Navy yards and U.S. Army Air Forces reconnaissance planes began patrolling the North Atlantic from bases in Newfoundland. In April, work was begun secretly on a U.S. supply base in Iraq; the U.S. Navy began coordinating its movements with those of the Royal Navy; and protocols were set up for secret communications between the two navies. The president unilaterally extended out to 26 degrees west latitude, more than 2,000 miles east of New York, the proclaimed boundary of the Western Hemisphere, in which area U.S. men-of-war would aid the Royal Navy. Greenland was occupied by American soldiers, all the German and Italian consulates in the United States were ordered closed, and U.S. troops relieved occupying British forces in Iceland and made that a base as well.

By the fall of 1941, however, Roosevelt was stymied. He had run out of ideas how to get into a formal, declared war with Germany. He had done everything "short of war" that could be done. "He had no more tricks left. The hat from which he had pulled so many rabbits was empty.... The front door to war in Europe seemed to be closed and barred."[15] But there was a back door as well — in Asia. Relations with Japan were bad and the Roosevelt administration was seeing to it that they were getting worse. There was a belief among most American military officials and diplomats — soon to be dispelled with great violence — that Japan would be easy pickings if push came to shove and then to war. Roosevelt thought so, too. If Japan went to war with the United States, these same people figured, Germany and Italy under their Triparte Pact would declare war against America. They were right.

The first clear evidence of FDR's intent to wage war with Germany by purposely starting a war with Japan — the polls and the electorate be damned — came earlier. On October 10, 1940, Secretary of the Navy Frank Knox sent for Admiral J. O. Richardson, commander of the Pacific Fleet, then based in Pearl Harbor.[16] Knox told Richardson that the president wanted a blockade of Japan's maritime traffic to North and South America by a patrol of American warships in two lines — from Hawaii to the Philippines and from Samoa to the Netherlands Indies. This wall of navy warships would stretch across the entire western Pacific, making it impossible for Japan, a nation that imported nearly all her raw materials, to reach any of that region's sources of supply. In particular, Japan imported 98 percent of her oil from the United States. It was a blockade that Roosevelt was proposing, plain and simple, and an out-and-out act of war. Richardson vigorously opposed the idea, telling Knox that the Japanese would sink the entire Pacific Fleet if the United States attempted to implement such a harebrained scheme. Roosevelt passed for the moment, but Richardson became a marked man and following their next face-off, FDR relieved him of his command.

There would be two other ideas from Roosevelt intended to incite a first strike by the Japanese that would give him his war: his "pop-up cruisers" scheme and the strange voyages of "three small vessels" just days before the Japanese attack on Pearl Harbor (Chapter 5). In April 1941, Roosevelt told his Chief of Naval Operations Harold "Betty" Stark to dispatch some cruisers in the direction of the Far East: "I just want to keep them popping up here and there and keep the Jap guessing." He didn't mind "losing one or two cruisers," he said astonishingly, but "wouldn't want to chance losing five or six."[17] That wild scheme, too, was quashed, this time by a jittery State Department and Admiral Husband E. Kimmel, the Pacific Fleet commander. Kimmel told FDR that the pop-up cruisers idea was "ill-advised and will result in war if we make this move."

Despite almost unanimous disapproval of the idea, Roosevelt stubbornly went ahead, dispatching cruisers on three separate occasions into Japanese home waters.[18] One of the most provocative sorties was a mission that took two U.S. cruisers into the strategic Bungo Strait southeast of Honshu that separates the home islands of Kyushu and Shikoku, a key operational zone for Japanese Imperial Navy warships. It was roughly equivalent to the Japanese sending warships to patrol in the vicinity of the Statue of Liberty in New York Harbor. On the night of July 31, 1941, Japanese fleet units detected the sound of propellers entering the Bungo Channel. Destroyers dispatched to investigate the incursion sighted two cruisers that slipped away under cover of smoke when challenged. The Japanese naval ministry registered a formal protest with U.S. Ambassador Joseph Grew in Tokyo.[19] That same month, the president proposed sending an aircraft carrier loaded with Lend-Lease aircraft for the Soviet Union to a Siberian port, through North Pacific waters close to Japan. Kimmel wrote Stark that any such aircraft carrier deployment was "tantamount to initiation of a Japanese-American war."[20] All of these machinations showed a ruthless side of FDR's character and a willingness to sacrifice American lives to his own clandestine ends.

Roosevelt figuratively replaced his map of Europe with one that showed the North Pacific and the Japanese home islands, with Hawaii and the great U.S. Navy base on Oahu, east and south in the Central Pacific. If Japan were sufficiently provoked — and the United States had been upping the ante for more than a year, ending with an oil embargo in collusion with Great Britain and the Netherlands— of necessity she would strike out at her oppressors. To the Dutch East Indies, to Borneo, to Malaya and strategic but "impregnable" Singapore, to the Philippines? Or to Pearl Harbor, to knock out the U.S. Pacific Fleet to allow Japan to roam freely across the Pacific, imposing its ballyhooed Greater East Asia Co-Prosperity Sphere, creating "Asia for the Asians"? It was some 3,000 miles from Imperial Navy anchorages around Japan to powerfully defended Pearl Harbor.

Then came "the leak."[21] On December 4, three days before the Pearl Harbor attack, a bold headline in the *Chicago Tribune* announced: FDR's WAR PLANS. The scoop was also front-page news that morning in the *Washington Times-Herald*. The story disclosed what the president had been denying for so many months: he was planning to go to war with Germany. Included in the article was a word-for-word copy of the previously Top Secret document, Rainbow Five,[22] and a copy of FDR's authorization letter for the preparation of the war plan. Rainbow Five called for an army of ten million, half of which would form an expeditionary force to attack Germany in 1943.

The New York Times got the story second-hand and ran it on page three the next morning. It included the comments of Stephen T. Early, Roosevelt's press secretary, who would neither confirm nor deny the story but pointed out that even during times of peace it was the duty of the Army and Navy to plan for emergencies.

Quotations from Rainbow Five made fascinating reading for some; others felt deep foreboding. Choice quotes included these:

> Forces deemed necessary to defeat the Axis forces in the field would include five field armies including 215 divisions (infantry, armored, motorized, airborne, mountain and cavalry) with appropriate supporting elements.
>
> If our European enemies are to be defeated it will be necessary for the United States to enter the war, and to employ a part of its armed forces offensively in the Eastern Atlantic and in Europe and Africa.
>
> Germany and her European satellites cannot be defeated by the European powers now fighting against her.
>
> It is estimated that the transportation of this number of men [five million], over a period of one year, would require 7,000,000 tons of shipping, or 1,000 ships, and that to maintain such a force in the theatre of operations would require about 10,000,000 tons, or 1,500 ships.

In the Congress there was a coterie of Roosevelt haters, not all of them Republicans, who were always on the lookout for material to denounce him and his actions. The leak was a fine opportunity for them to flagellate the president for his obvious duplicity. They all remembered his carefully selected words in Boston on October 29, 1940, on the eve of the election that would make him the first three-term president. "While I am talking to you mothers and fathers," he had intoned, "I give you one more assurance. I have said this before, but I shall say it again and again and again: Your boys are not going to be sent into any foreign wars."[23] To the Congressmen and many Americans, Rainbow Five had made a confirmed liar out of the president.

As might be imagined, Army, Navy, and War Department officers were furious. Who was the leaker? The definitive answer has eluded historians ever since. Major Albert C. Wedemeyer, who wrote the final document, was a prime suspect, but the FBI was never able to gather sufficient evidence to make a case against him. What about Franklin Roosevelt, the only administration official with a genuine motive? He had much to gain by infuriating Hitler. In fact, Hitler in his declaration of war against the United States on December 11 referred to newspaper reports of Rainbow Five as one reason.

Three days after the leak, when Japan attacked Pearl Harbor, the issue and the identity of the culprit became academic. There was a war to win.

1

FDR's Undeclared War in the Atlantic

> *"Firmly ensconced in the driver's seat, Roosevelt would have been less than human if he had not welcomed the Greer incident with open arms.... He obviously read too much into the Greer affair in his shoot-on-sight speech. The destroyer-submarine attacks and counterattacks in themselves were not proof that Hitler had serious intentions of enslaving the New World."*[1]

President Roosevelt's first scheme to incite Germany into attacking the United States was based on a covert undeclared war in the Atlantic Ocean. This pseudo-war was fought between the U.S. Navy and the German Kriegsmarine, between U.S. destroyers and German U-boats. FDR expected that aggressive actions by American naval forces would bring retaliation by German submarines in the form of sunken destroyers and drowned U.S. sailors, hopefully inflaming a passive electorate. More importantly, Roosevelt reasoned, an angry Adolf Hitler would be driven to declare war on the United States. This last premise would turn out to be wishful thinking. In 1947, the U.S. Navy Department released a set of captured German documents (Führer Conferences on Matters Dealing with the German Navy 1941) that showed unambiguously that Hitler had consistently restricted his U-boats in 1941, at the height of FDR's private war, to avoid an overt act of war with the United States.[2]

Senator Gerald P. Nye's mid-1930s "Munitions Hearings" (Appendix F), pointing to "merchants of death" and their bankers in the United States and elsewhere as a principal cause of war, had been the first hesitant step in exposing America's "military-industrial complex." A spate of popular books and articles on the same theme followed.

Americans, already disillusioned with what the Great War had brought to America — unpaid debts by the English and French, legless veterans on tiny swivel-wheeled platforms propelling themselves with their knuckles, and the failure of Woodrow Wilson's making "the world safe for democracy"—became firmly convinced that their country should stay neutral if another European war should erupt. Roosevelt knew the attitudes of the electorate, but he did his work clandestinely.

Meanwhile, the Neutrality Act of 1935 was enacted by the Congress, followed by a revised Act a year later known as the Second Neutrality Act. These two laws effectively straitjacketed the United States, forbidding the sale or transport of munitions and associated hardware to countries that were at war. In 1937, the Third Neutrality Act became law, loosening the strictures of the earlier Acts. Henceforth, such raw materials as lead and copper that obviously could be turned into munitions were allowed to be sold by U.S. companies to warring nations, provided their buyers paid cash and shipped them in their own bottoms. This Act lasted two years.

FDR's next step along his desired road to war with Germany was his initiation of a disingenuously-named "neutrality patrol" inside American waters at the end of September 1939. It would not be long before "neutral" U.S. destroyers were directing Royal Navy men-of-war and Royal Air Force anti-submarine aircraft to the locations of U-boats their lookouts had seen on the surface or their sonars had picked up underwater. At the same time, entirely contrary to international law, the president arbitrarily extended what he called a "neutral zone" from 300 to 1,000 miles out to sea for the entire western hemisphere. Belligerents were warned not to trespass inside what became known as FDR's "Chastity Belt." On April 11, 1940, FDR arbitrarily extended the line further east. The new line "was more than 2,300 sea miles from the American coast at New York and only 740 sea miles from the coast of Europe at Lisbon ... something like four-fifths of the Atlantic ocean was declared to be part of the western hemisphere in which American naval forces would shadow German warships and at once report their position to the British. No justification of any sort will be found anywhere in international law for thus extending a security zone or for putting it to the uses to which it was thus arbitrarily put."[3]

On July 8, 1941, U.S. forces landed in Iceland. A year earlier, the Canadians and the British had occupied the island which had become a vital transfer point on the convoy route across the North Atlantic. Since then, London and Reykjavik had been discussing the possibility of replacing the British troops there, who were needed elsewhere, with an American contingent. America hesitated, and Roosevelt did not act until Hitler announced the extension of his war zone as far as the west coast of Iceland and there were signs that Germany might attack the island.

On August 14, 1941, FDR met with Churchill at Argentia Bay, off the coast of Newfoundland. Roosevelt was aboard his favorite U.S. Navy warship, the heavy cruiser USS *Augusta*; Churchill arrived on the Royal Navy battleship HMS *Prince of Wales*.[4] The meeting was later referred to as the Atlantic Conference. Among the issues discussed were the prime minister's unhappiness over America's diversion of supplies to the Soviet Union following Germany's attack, at the expense of Great Britain, and he sought redress. Churchill also wanted a face-to-face opportunity to lobby FDR for U.S. entry into the war as a full-fledged belligerent. Roosevelt hedged, repeating his preference for an undeclared war: "I may never declare war; I may make war. If I were to ask Congress to declare war, they might argue about it for three months."[5] FDR also made two serious commitments that he kept secret when he returned to the United States: to send American troops to the Azores in the mid-Atlantic where a German attack was expected and to issue an aggressive ultimatum to Japan that Cordell Hull wrote in his memoirs had "shocked him."

The communiqué that summarized the meeting's agreements was appropriately called the Atlantic Charter (Appendix H); it omitted all the significant disagreements and commitments made secretly by Roosevelt and Churchill. Read critically, the Charter was a laundry-list of platitudes, yet it later formed the basis for the Charter of the United Nations (Appendix J). The document also served as splendid propaganda, however, and a copy of it, bearing the facsimile signatures of Roosevelt and Churchill, was put on exhibit in Washington's National Museum. It was exquisitely framed and illuminated like an ancient manuscript, where visitors could gawk at what was presumed to be one of history's most important documents.

Three years later, during a press conference on December 20, 1944, following the president's return from the Big Three's Teheran Conference, he was asked about the Atlantic Charter. Had the agreements reached with Stalin had any impact on it? The second and third clauses had unambiguously declared that the contracting parties "desire to see no territorial changes that do not accord with the freely expressed wishes of the peoples concerned and that they respect the right of all peoples to choose the form of government under which they will live; and they wish to see sovereign rights and self government restored to those who have been forcibly deprived of them." These two pledges went out the window in deference to Stalin's demands.

The newsmen could scarcely believe what the president then proceeded to tell them. There had never been a complete Atlantic Charter, Roosevelt said evenly, and went on to the amazement of all in attendance: "It was just a press release. It was scribbled on a piece of paper by him and Churchill and Sumner Welles and Sir Alexander Cadogan. It was just handed to the radio operators aboard the British and American warships to put on the air as a presidential news release." It was revealed later that Stephen Early, FDR's press spokesman, had distributed it on his own with the facsimile signatures of Churchill and Roosevelt affixed.[6]

What about the document hanging in the National Museum? An inquisitive New York *Daily News* reporter asked the curator, who told him that it been loaned to the Museum by the Office of War Information (OWI), America's overt propaganda arm. OWI, it turned out, had printed about a quarter of a million copies and distributed them nationally and internationally.[7] The new exhibit in the National Museum was promptly taken down.

On September 5 came the *Greer* incident, the first "shooting" encounter between a U.S. Navy warship — the destroyer USS *Greer*, a reconditioned four-stacker of the type transferred to the Royal Navy in exchange for British bases — and the *Kriegsmarine* submarine *U-652*.[8] The *Greer*'s mission that day had been, as far as could be publicly ascertained, "innocent" — to deliver mail, high-priority freight, and eleven military passengers to Iceland. A British reconnaissance plane on patrol had located a submarine on the surface some miles directly ahead of the destroyer as it plowed through the seas, and blinkered this information to the ship. There was discussion among the officers of the *Greer* whether she should simply "trail and report" — or take more aggressive action.

In the event, the destroyer acquired the submarine on her sonar and proceeded to follow the submerged, slow-moving U-boat as the RAF patrol plane circled overhead. As far as the U-boat commander knew, his submarine was under attack by a hunter-killer team; his sonar picked up the propeller noises from the *Greer*, and he knew there was also at least one airplane in the vicinity, the one that had driven him underwater. Just before the reconnaissance plane headed back to its base, it dropped its load of antisubmarine bombs. Undamaged, the U-boat rose to periscope depth for a quick look around.[9] No airplane could be seen, only the sub's lone pursuer, a destroyer that could have been British or American. The *Greer*'s commander had skillfully maintained a bows-on track as he followed the U-boat, to present the smallest possible silhouette for a torpedo. Arguably, *U-652*'s commander had never seen either the U.S. flag or the large U.S. Navy hull markings; his first priority was the safety of his ship and crew, and his subsequent actions reflected this.

The deadly cat-and-mouse game continued for about four hours, with *U-652*'s commander coming briefly to periscope depth from time to time to check on the whereabouts of his relentless pursuer and the *Greer* patiently tracking her prey with sonar. With the air inside the U-boat increasingly foul and its batteries running down, the "mouse" finally turned on the "cat," firing one and then a second torpedo, both of which missed. The *Greer* responded by dropping a pattern of depth charges. Before she ended the hunt, the *Greer* made a final pass over the approximate position of the submarine, releasing an even larger pattern of depth charges. No oil slick or wreckage was observed, and the *Greer* resumed her mission.[10]

The president indulged himself regarding this first destroyer-vs.-submarine encounter in a blistering fireside chat on September 11. In a long (2,700 words) and repetitive speech, he said matter-of-factly that the attacker was the submarine and that it had committed "piracy, legally and morally." The Nazis were "international outlaws." His speechwriters dug into their sack of useful metaphors for further amplification: German U-boats in the Atlantic were rattlesnakes. "When you see a rattlesnake poised to strike," Roosevelt pontificated, "you do not wait until he has struck before you crush him." This was a call for a preemptive war, but he skirted that issue; remarkably FDR said "war" only once in his chat. Concerning the USS *Greer*: "In spite of what Hitler's propaganda bureau has invented, and in spite of what any American obstructionist organization may prefer to believe," Roosevelt blustered, "I tell you the blunt fact that the German submarine fired first upon this American destroyer without warning, and with deliberate design to sink her.... We have sought no shooting war with Hitler."[11] As far as the president was concerned, the mere presence of serpents in waters which America considered vital to its defense was an attack. Subsequently, the Navy Department refused to give a copy of the log of the *Greer* to the Senate, using as its excuse the well-worn dictum of "national security."

Roosevelt then gave a strained, not-quite-factual history lesson to his radio listeners to bolster his case. He went back to John Adams' presidency, stating that Adams "had ordered U.S. warships to attack 'European [French] ships of war' that were ravaging American commerce." (FDR refrained from saying that Congress had formally authorized Adams to act). Similarly, Thomas Jefferson ... had ordered American warships to attack 'the corsairs of the nations of North Africa.'" (This undeclared war of 1801–1805 by the United States ... had followed a formal declaration of hostilities by the Pasha of Tripoli).[12]

Roosevelt moved on to invoke the legacy of Woodrow Wilson and one of his ill-starred Fourteen Points (Appendix C) — "freedom of the seas."[13] "It is the Nazi design to abolish freedom of the seas," he gravely intoned, putting fear into the hearts of his listeners "...with control of the seas in their own hands, the way can become obviously clear for their next step, domination of the United States...."[14]

Henceforth, Axis men-of-war would enter waters considered vital to

America's defense "at their peril." Under such circumstances, Roosevelt said, U.S. ships were under orders to shoot, even if not shot at first—but he called this *defensive* shooting. Only after "months and months of constant thought and anxiety and prayer," FDR piously declaimed in his conclusion, neither "hurriedly nor lightly" had he reached this decision. This high-seas encounter became known as Roosevelt's "shoot on sight" speech, despite his limp disclaimer, and was a major step toward full-blown war with Germany.

Two days later, the president ordered the U.S. Atlantic Fleet to escort British convoys in which there were no U.S. merchantmen. At the same time, Roosevelt followed through on Churchill's request for transports to deliver British soldiers to the Middle East. These included twelve passenger liners and twenty cargo vessels, manned by American crews. Fifty U.S. oil tankers had already been clandestinely transferred to Britain which had led to a gasoline shortage on the East Coast. Neither those in the Congress nor the American people were aware of these presidential actions.[15]

Earlier, on June 20, *U-203* had attempted to attack the U.S. battleship *Texas* in the mid-Atlantic. However, the submarine, unnoticed by the battleship or its escorts, was unable to get into position to fire its torpedoes. The U-boat commander's hostile intent brought an instant reproof from Hitler. According to noted historian John Terraine, "the reason why Hitler became so agitated ... was that he was about to commit the greatest blunder of his life on 22 June: the attack on the Soviet Union, Operation BARBAROSSA. This was a date in history whose full significance is immeasurable. It was the second turning point of the Second World War, creating an entirely new context for all that followed, an endless and mounting drain on Germany's resources which would ultimately consume them all, and with them the Third Reich and its Führer."[16]

On October 17, the destroyer USS *Kearny*, coming to the assistance of a 50-ship eastbound convoy under attack by a submarine wolf-pack was hit by a single torpedo. The explosion wounded twenty-four American sailors and blew eleven more over the side. With a big gash in her starboard side, the warship managed to limp back to Iceland on her own power. The missing sailors were the first to lose their lives on an American ship prior to Pearl Harbor. This battle was not a chance encounter like that of the *Greer*. The *Kearny* was part of a division of four U.S. destroyers based in Iceland that had hurriedly left port and steamed some 400 miles at flank speed to engage German U-boats already involved in a battle.

Ten days later, the always-agile Roosevelt played the "U.S. defense zone" card, saying in a speech that the *Kearny* had been safely within the U.S.-defined "security zone" when she was torpedoed. He claimed that

"...the shooting has started and history has recorded who fired the first shot."[17] While he seemingly had his radio audience on the edge of their chairs for more details, he immediately switched to a new subject, pointing out, preposterously, that he had just learned of a German scheme to abolish all religions throughout the world—"if Hitler wins." He also said he had a map that proved that Germany planned to conquer Latin America and divide it into five vassal countries and he would bring the map to his next press conference. At his next press conference, he failed to produce the map, saying it contained classified material. By his perfunctory coverage of this second confrontation, however, those of his inner circle sensed that Roosevelt had other fish to fry—in another ocean.

The third U.S. destroyer/*Kriegsmarine* submarine confrontation took place two weeks later, when the four-stacker *Reuben James* was torpedoed and sunk some 600 miles west of Ireland, inside FDR's enlarged security zone. The torpedo's explosion ignited the ship's forward magazine, blowing off the bow as far back as the No. 3 stack. The *James* remained afloat for only about five minutes, taking with her more than 100 of her crew. The *James* had been part of a five-destroyer group escorting a large convoy carrying Lend-Lease supplies to England. It was just before the sun rose, a favorite time for attacking U-boats[18], and the convoy and its escorts had not yet begun their daytime zigzagging. The *James* was struck with the torpedo just as she had changed course to follow-up on a radar contact. According to two U.S. historians, "in this instance, the Germans undoubtedly had international law on their side, or whatever remained that was being honored by the combatants.... Roosevelt might invoke freedom of the seas until red in the face, but that concept never gave wartime immunity to the escorts of convoys or to their charges, whether armed or not, whether belligerent or not."[19] The *James* bore the dubious distinction of being the only U.S. man-of-war sunk by the German navy during America's self-proclaimed "neutrality."

The day before the *Reuben James* was sunk, the armed oil tanker USS *Salinas* in a westbound convoy from Iceland was hit with two torpedoes. Her stern gun had opened fire on the fast-diving U-boat as escorting U.S. destroyers charged around the area, dropping depth charges where the submarine had last been seen. No wreckage surfaced and no tell-tale oil bubbled up to indicate a damaged submarine. The *Salinas* crew was intact and the holed ship managed to limp into Newfoundland for refitting. The *Salinas* incident was the fourth "undeclared" battle in the Atlantic between German U-boats and U.S. Navy ships. This incident got little attention at the time and practically none later on. For example, in his war-declaration speech on December 11, 1941, Hitler included the *Greer* and *Kearny* among his grievances against the United States, but overlooked the *Reuben James* and *Salinas*.

Historian Charles A. Beard, a truculent critic of FDR and his policies, wrote cogently that "the electric words 'America has been attacked,' instead of setting off the real war in the Atlantic, fizzled out in an anticlimax. If President Roosevelt had actually been seeking war in the Atlantic by exploiting German 'attacks,' he had apparently exhausted the possibilities of that expedient by November 1, 1941."[20] Roosevelt and his inner circle of advisers—Stimson, Knox, Morgenthau, and Ickes, "the belligerent old men in his cabinet"[21]—would turn to "the back door" to get their hands on Hitler and his Third Reich.

2

FDR's Personal Fifty-Destroyers-for-Bases Deal

> "We shall never surrender, and even if, which I do not for a moment believe, this island or a large part of it were subjugated and starving, then our Empire beyond the seas, armed and guarded by the British Fleet, would carry on the struggle, until, in God's good time, the New World, with all its power and might, steps forth to the rescue and liberation of the Old."
>
> Winston Churchill to the
House of Commons, June 4, 1940[1]

> "...you know well that the worth of every destroyer you can spare to us is measured in rubies."
>
> Winston Churchill to Franklin D.
Roosevelt, August 15, 1940[2]

> "I thought they were the worst destroyers I had ever seen, poor seaboats with appalling armament and accommodation. The price paid for them was scandalous."
>
> Admiral of the Fleet [Royal Navy] Lord Tovey[3]

All prior acts of American non-neutrality — and there were numerous instances of the clandestine supply of weapons to Great Britain[4] — paled into insignificance beside the "destroyers-for-bases" deal which was concluded on September 2, 1940 in an exchange of notes between Washington and London; FDR purposefully resorted to an "executive agreement" which bypassed the Congress. The U.S. agreed to transfer fifty Great-War-vintage destroyers to the Royal Navy as soon as they could be taken out of "mothballs"— none had been to sea for twenty years. In exchange, the U.S. would get ninety-nine-year leases for eight naval and air bases sites scattered from Newfoundland south to British Guiana: Antigua, Argentia, Bermuda, British Guiana, Jamaica, Newfoundland, St. Lucia, and Trinidad.

The destroyers were from a fleet of over one hundred that were moored at U.S. Navy bases along the east coast. As part of the agreement, U.S. Navy yards gave the four-stackers superficial refits and sent them up the East Coast to Halifax, Nova Scotia, where they would be recommissioned as Royal Navy men-of-war. To give the ships some identity the British classified them as *Town*-class destroyers, their new names coming from towns in England, Canada, and the United States.

Further refitting was done in Halifax, such as installation of radar and asdic[5], as the Royal Navy called their sonar gear for detecting and tracking submerged U-boats, addition of modern anti-aircraft guns, and up-to-date communications systems. They were painted, provisioned, and made ready for the Atlantic crossing. In theory, the reconditioned ships could then join the Royal Navy months before British new construction caught up with the demand.

The transaction was in clear violation of international law. Article 6 of Convention XIII of the Hague Conference of 1907 was straightforward: "The supply in any manner, directly or indirectly, by a neutral Power to a belligerent Power of war-ships, ammunition, or war materiel of any kind whatever, is forbidden."[6]

Domestic law was another "paper" impediment to the deal. In 1917 Congress had passed a statute making it unlawful for a neutral United States to transfer any "vessel of war" that had been "built, armed, or equipped" for that nation. Two months before the trade, however, a law was enacted that gave the president a loop hole. It declared that a warship could be transferred to a belligerent if the Chief of Naval Operations certified that the vessel "was not essential to the defense of the United States."[7] CNO Stark, who had not forgotten who had promoted him to his exalted position in the Navy, needed little arm-twisting to testify that the old four-stackers were not essential to the nation's defense.

The idea had been Winston Churchill's—and he first broached the subject to FDR as early as mid-May 1940, in his first message to the president, five days after becoming prime minister. It was the day after the Wehrmacht had crumpled French defenses near Sedan. Churchill wrote that "immediate needs are, first of all, the loan of forty or fifty of your older destroyers to bridge the gap between what we have now and the large new construction we put in hand at the beginning of the war."[8] He signed it "Former Naval Person," calculating that might strike a respondent chord in FDR, who was also a former naval person, as Assistant Secretary of the Navy in the Wilson administration. Churchill renewed his request on June 11 as the French army was disintegrating and the day after Italy declared war on France. Again on July 31, after France had surrendered, the prime minister appealed to Roosevelt, this time for "50 or 60 of your *oldest* destroyers," using as his rationale the ploy that Hitler was planning a cross-channel invasion of Britain and that these ships were vital for its defense. In his prose, Churchill was a master, mixing wonderful adjectives with a pinch of hyperbole: "Latterly the air attacks on our shipping has become injurious.... Destroyers are frightfully vulnerable to air-bombing, and yet they must be held in the air-bombing area to prevent sea-borne invasion.... Mr. President, with great respect, I must tell you that in the long history of the world this is a thing to do *now*" (italics in original).[9]

In between, the normally reticent King George VI got into the act. On June 26, he sent a personal letter to the president:

> The spirit here is magnificent, and the people of these islands, strongly reinforced by the Dominion contingents, are inspired by the thought that it is their own soil which they now have to defend against the invader. Their resolution and their confidence are supreme. As you know, we are in urgent need of some of your older destroyers to tide us over the next few months. I well understand your difficulties, and I am certain that you will do your best to procure them for us before it is too late. Now that we have been deprived of the assistance of the French Fleet — to put the least unfavourable interpretation on the present position — the need is becoming greater every day if we are to carry on our solitary fight for freedom to a successful conclusion.[10]

Churchill was never hesitant — when negotiations with Roosevelt stalled — to use the British Fleet as a bargaining chip. Or was it blackmail? On August 15, he telegraphed FDR, first stating that he was sure the president would "send us everything you can...," then flashing a little hyperbole: "you know well that the worth of every destroyer you can spare to us is measured in rubies." Then the prime minister got to the nub of his wire. "As regards an assurance about the British Fleet, I am, of course, ready to reiterate to you what I told Parliament on June 4. We intend to fight this out here to the end, and none of us would ever buy peace by surrendering or scuttling the Fleet."[11]

Earlier, on August 7, in a cable to Lord Lothian, British ambassador to Washington, Churchill showed his true colors. "It would obviously be impossible for us to make or agree to any declaration about the future disposition of the British Fleet. I have repeatedly warned you ... and the President of the dangers United States would run if Great Britain were successfully invaded.... I am very glad to find that these dangers are regarded as serious, and you should in no wise minimize them. *We have no intention of relieving United States from any well-grounded anxieties on this point*" (emphasis added).[12]

At his press conference on the 16th, Roosevelt tipped his hand, but only partly: "The United States Government is holding conversations with the Government of the British Empire with regard to acquisition of naval and air bases for the defense of the Western Hemisphere and especially the

Panama Canal." He stated that the U.S. would give something in return, but that he did not know what this would be. "He emphasized more than once that the negotiations ... were in no way connected with the question of destroyers." He repeated: "Destroyers were not involved in the prospective arrangements."[13]

The prime minister was playing for stakes far greater than the acquisition of a tiny fleet of decrepit destroyers. In his cables he introduced a new word to FDR — nonbelligerence — rather than neutrality. He was working to involve United States as an active belligerent in England's war with Germany, increment by increment. The fifty-destroyers deal tied the United States to Great Britain's war far more securely than any previews action heretofore.

On August 1, 1940, the *New York Times* showed its readers where it stood on the issue: four-square behind the transfer. It published a 3,800-word missive in the "letters to the editor" column titled "No Legal Bar Seen to Transfer of Destroyers." For those readers who were intimidated by the three full columns running down the page and continuing on the next, the subhead summarized the editorial's contents: "Ample Authority for Sale of Over-Age Naval Vessels to Great Britain Exists in Present Laws, According to Opinion by Leading Lawyers." The letter concluded that there was "no reason for us to put a strained or unnecessary interpretation on our own statutes contrary to our own national interests.... When vital interests of the United States are at stake, when the sentiment of the country is clear, the government should not hesitate to exercise powers under existing law. To seek an unnecessary reaffirmation of these powers from the Congress now would be to run a serious danger of delay and by delay possibly to endanger the vital interests of the people of the country in keeping war from our own shores." The warmonger Harold L. Ickes, Secretary of the Interior, insisted that the destroyers deal be consummated "by hook or crook."[14]

The fundamental approach of the Roosevelt Administration was now becoming clear. The interventionists defined the Axis powers as "outlaws," acting in concert. Further, it was British sea power that was serving as an essential element of the defense of America and the Western Hemisphere, especially in view of supposed Nazi infiltration of Latin America. Just as noninterventionists had long concluded that U.S. security was by no means linked indelibly to the survival of the British Empire, there was little proof that Germany posed an active military threat to the United States. But the Roosevelt steamroller was seemingly unstoppable. Respected *New York Times* military analyst Hanson Baldwin wrote sagely on September 8, 1940: "A new chapter of world history was written last week.... The destroyers steaming toward Halifax were not only symbols of an ever-closer Anglo-American *rapprochement*, but in the opinion of some observers, sealed what in effect was an unofficial alliance between the English-speaking nations and brought the United States far closer than ever before to entry into the war."

Three days after the deal was consummated, on September 5, an ebullient Churchill blithely told the House of Commons that "only very ignorant persons would suggest that the transfer of American destroyers to the British flag constitutes the slightest violation of international law, or affects in the smallest degree the non-belligerency of the United States. I have no doubt," he concluded, "that Herr Hitler will not like this transference of destroyers and I have no doubt that he will pay the United States out, if he ever gets the chance."[15] In one of his numerous postwar reminiscences published in his equally numerous book-length treatises on World War II, Churchill acknowledged that the transfer of U.S. destroyers to England "was a decidedly unneutral act by the United States" and Hitler would have been "justified" in declaring war. He wrote that the deal drew the U.S. "definitely nearer to us and to the war and it was the first of a long succession of increasingly unneutral acts in the Atlantic" that propelled America closer to the war in Europe.[16]

Two weeks before the signings, Roosevelt had written — hyperbolically, indeed — to Senator David I. Walsh, chairman of the Senate Committee on Naval Affairs, that the upcoming exchange would be "the finest thing for the nation that has been done in your lifetime and mine."[17]

Germany chose not to lodge an official protest with Washington after the transaction had been made public. Even during his later war declaration speech, Hitler did not select the destroyers-for-bases agreement for special condemnation. But later in the month, on September 27, came the announcement that Germany, Italy, and Japan had formed the Tripartite Alliance, a ten-year military and economic agreement that was generally understood to have been a response to the destroyers deal.

While Churchill had likened the value of the U.S. destroyers "to rubies," which are actually more expensive than diamonds, there was much restoration work to be done in Halifax to make them sea-worthy, not to mention war-worthy. Leaks and corrosion of piping systems bedeviled the repair crews and electrical systems typically required total overhaul. Many of the new crews, about 125 per ship, were landlubbers and some of them, like the displaced Frenchmen and Norwegians, were unable to read the English-language instruction manuals. "Overcoming such drawbacks, about forty of the fifty vessels managed to cross the ocean between September 1940, when the destroyers-bases deal was concluded, and the end of the year."[18]

How well did the reconditioned ships perform under the Union Jack? American historians Thomas A. Bailey and Paul B. Ryan gave a patriotic and enthusiastic thumbs-up. "Despite their handicaps, these outmoded craft ultimately saw plenty of action. They sank or participated in the sinking of an impressive number of U-boats ... they were especially useful in protecting convoys of Allied merchantmen across the North Atlantic.... At one time during the furious Battle of the Atlantic in 1941 they made up between one-fourth and one-fifth of the escorting warships."[19]

The British who sailed in the U.S. destroyers were less kind, if more forthright. They were not unwilling to "look into the horse's mouth" and did not like what they saw. "Their crews hated them. They were narrow ships which rolled viciously; their propeller shafts stuck out several feet beyond the stern and they were difficult to handle. They had a huge turning-circle which was not of much help when attacking a U-boat. They were certainly unsuited to Atlantic weather."[20] Admiral of the Fleet Sir Philip Vian gave another interpretation: "A contemporary naval opinion ... would be that although the U.S. vessels were tactically of the lowest order ... their mere presence thrashing about in the water around the convoy afforded some sort of deterrent against the U-boat...."[21]

One of the American destroyers became temporarily famous — the renamed HMS *Campbeltown*, originally the USS *Buchanan*. In the blackness before dawn on March 28, 1942, she crept quietly into the harbor of Saint-Nazaire on the French coast, then accelerated to flank speed and drove her bow into the main lock gate of the only drydock on the Atlantic large enough to handle the German battleship *Tirpitz*. After opening her sea cocks, the destroyer's crew of Commandos quickly scrambled down nets into the darkness and confusion, leaving the *Campbeltown* to sink, bow down, impaled in the lock gate — with five tons of explosives with time-delay fuses in bow compartments. The next morning, the ship blew up, smashing the dry dock and the unlucky German naval officers inspecting her. One disgruntled Royal Navy captain later suggested that such an ignominious end was "the best thing that could have happened to the Town-Class destroyers."[22]

By 1943, the old four-stackers were showing their age. For example, when HMS *Burnham* was dry docked for inspection, "her engineer officer walked along the bottom plates of the hull testing the rivets with a hammer. To his horror one rivet after another fell out in a shower of rust,"[23] and thirteen of those had been allocated for duty as aircraft target ships. In April 1944, the Royal Canadian Navy which had been lent six of the destroyers tried to return them to the U.S. Navy for scrapping. The RCN was told to handle its own disposal problems, "thank you." By war's end, every one of the few surviving destroyers had been sent to the scrap yards.

Just as the British had headaches with their side of the deal, so too did the Americans with their leases. In fact, all FDR had accomplished was permission from Great Britain to look for sites for future U.S. bases. There were still many details to be worked out between the two governments—and with the inhabitants of the proposed military facilities. The two locations that proved to be of most significance for the U.S. Navy in its coming "declared" war with Germany were Bermuda in the Atlantic and Argentia in Newfoundland. Bermuda was then as it is today a popular tourist resort and its residents were understandably reluctant to welcome disorderly U.S. servicemen overrunning their quiet streets and pink-sand beaches; it took some haggling to get the Bermudians finally to accept an American presence that was in the best interests of their country. Argentia, more than Bermuda, later proved to be extremely valuable for naval and air patrols protecting convoys eastbound across the Atlantic.

3

Lend-Lease:
To the Brink of War

> "More than any other single event prior to the actual declaration of war against Germany, the Lend-Lease Act signaled that participation."[1]
>
> "Put bluntly, the Lend-Lease Act was a virtual declaration of war on the dictators, conspicuously Hitler. It was an unprecedented and all-embracing commitment by one ["neutral"] nation to provide unlimited arms and other essentials of war to those countries that were resisting aggression, notably Great Britain."[2]
>
> Lend-Lease "was a delegation of power, in the great tradition, to the one man to whom power must always be given in a national emergency — the President."[3]
>
> Winston Churchill described Lend-Lease to Parliament as "the most unsordid act in the history of any nation."[4]

Prime Minister Winston Churchill later called it one of the most important letters[5] he ever wrote, and he gave it special treatment. Flamboyantly, he had it delivered to his fellow naval person on December 9, 1940, in a Royal Air Force seaplane which touched down alongside the USS *Tuscaloosa*, cruising in the Caribbean with FDR and Harry Hopkins. Churchill later claimed that Hopkins told him that Roosevelt had "read and re-read this letter as he sat alone in his deck-chair and that for two days he did not seem to have reached any conclusion. He was plunged in intense thought and brooded silently."[6]

Churchill began his 4,000-word letter by discreetly binding the cause of Great Britain with that of the United States: "...I submit with very great respect for your good and friendly consideration that there is a solid identity of interest between the British Empire and the United States...." He then softly threatened that a British defeat would mean the Royal Navy would become part of the *Kriegsmarine*, with obvious consequences for the security of the United States: "Only thus can those bastions of sea power, upon which the control of the Atlantic and the Indian Oceans depends, *be preserved in faithful and friendly hands*" (emphasis added). The prime minister was not merely looking for aid, he was seeking "supreme and decisive help to what is … the common cause."[7]

Then came his laundry-list of demands and recommendations; Churchill was not bashful. The primary need was to limit merchant shipping losses on the Atlantic approaches to England. To accomplish this, the "gift or loan" of more destroyers was "indispensable." To help Britain patrol the sea lanes, bases on the southern and western shores of Eire were required, "the good offices of the United States and the whole influence of its Government continuously exerted" for negotiation of such bases. Furthermore, the United States must build "not less than three million tons of additional merchant shipbuilding capacity." Additionally, "…could not United States naval forces extend their sea control over the American side of the Atlantic…?" Such a move, according to Churchill, "would not jeopardize control over the Pacific."[8]

"The Republic" must help Britain expand its domestic warplane manufacturing facilities by increasing delivery of American machine tools. Britain also needed many more military aircraft from the United States, Churchill wrote, particularly heavy bombers. He already had an inkling of the heavy losses these bombers would sustain, and suggested they be produced at the rate of 2,000 per month for England alone. Military equipment was needed to equip the entire British army "as already planned" and to equip another ten British divisions in time for "the campaign of 1942."

American production of small arms, artillery, and tanks should also be expanded "to the utmost" because it would later become necessary for the U.S. to arm other countries "trying to regain their freedom."[9]

The prime minister saved for last "the question of finance." He wrote: "The moment approaches when we shall no longer be able to pay cash for shipping and other supplies." Then, tortuously: "While we will do out utmost and shrink from no proper sacrifice to make payments across the exchange, I believe that you will agree that it would be wrong in principle and mutually disadvantageous in effect if, at the height of this struggle, Great Britain were to be divested of all saleable assets so that after victory was won with our blood, civilization saved, and time gained for the United States to be fully armed against all eventualities, we should stand stripped to the bone. Such a course would not be in the moral or economic interests of either of our countries."[10]

Churchill closed with a flourish: "If, as I believe, you are convinced, Mr. President, that the defeat of the Nazi and Fascist tyranny is a matter of high consequence to the people of the United States and to the Western

Hemisphere, you will regard this letter not as an appeal for aid, but as a statement of the minimum action necessary to the achievement of our common purpose."[11]

It took eight days for Roosevelt to absorb the prime minister's multifaceted message and to engage his speech writers and advisers in developing the catchy words and phrases that would help him sell the program to a mostly isolationist citizenry. At a press conference on December 17 FDR revealed the outlines of a new plan "he was considering" to aid Great Britain in its fight with Nazi Germany. He said that the legislation he would ask the Congress for would not repeal either the Neutrality or the Johnson Acts.[12] He declared that Britain was fighting the fight of all democracies, particularly America's. The president said the best defense of Great Britain was the best defense of the United States and that he was trying to do away with the "silly-fool dollar sign." FDR included his soon-to-become-famous parable about his neighbor's fire and his garden hose: "Suppose my neighbor's house catches fire and I have a length of garden hose four or five hundred feet away. If he can take my garden hose and connect it up with his hydrant, I may help him to put out the fire. Now what do I do? I don't say to him before: 'Neighbor, my garden hose cost me fifteen dollars; you have to pay me fifteen dollars for it.' No! What is the transaction that goes on? I don't want fifteen dollars—I want my garden hose back after the fire is over."[13] Although the allegory was aimed at simpletons, it remains a symbol in the annals of FDR's carefully crafted propaganda aimed at Americans. When a newsman asked the president whether the proposed scheme would bring America "more into the war than we are," FDR unhesitatingly shot back: "No, not a bit." Roosevelt's press conference had followed Treasury Secretary Henry Morgenthau, Jr.'s testimony earlier that day before a House Appropriations subcommittee that British Treasury officials could not place further orders in the United States unless financial aid were forthcoming.

The president followed up with more details in a fireside chat on December 29, when he presented his case to the American people for massive aid to Britain. First, he tied the fate of England to that of the United States. "Does any one believe seriously," he asked, "that we need fear attack while a free Britain remains our most powerful naval neighbor in the Atlantic?" If Britain should go down, he said, all nations in the Americas would be living at the point of a gun —"a gun loaded with explosive bullets, economic as well as military." He took up the issue of a "negotiated peace," pointing out that the contention that the Axis powers had no desire to attack the Western Hemisphere was the same "dangerous wishful thinking which has destroyed the powers of resistance of so many conquered people." Dramatically: "We must be the great arsenal of democracy. For us this is an emergency as serious as war itself. We must apply ourselves to our task with the same resolution, the same sense of urgency, the same spirit of patriotism and sacrifice as we would show were we at war."[14]

FDR was a man with a mission and he kept pounding away. His next opportunity to sell his ideas to the electorate came on January 6, in his message to the new 77th Congress on the State of the Union. His speechwriters, apparently harried by the necessity to produce three long speeches in three weeks, carelessly included phrases and sentences that appeared in FDR's two most recent speeches. To frighten his listeners, Roosevelt resorted to an audacious lie: "…today we have planes that could fly from the British Isles to New England and back without refueling." He also invoked the Royal Navy as America's principal defender for what seemed like the thousandth time. "There is much loose talk of our immunity from immediate and direct invasion from across the seas. Obviously, as long as the British Navy retains its power, no such danger exists." Roosevelt then defined a new national policy that, read by a critic in the cold light of objectivity 60 years later, comes across as meandering blather. The highlight of the speech was his declaration of "Four Freedoms"—"freedom of speech and expression"; "freedom of every person to worship God in his own way, everywhere in the world"; "freedom from want"; and "freedom from fear."[15]

Four days later, the Lend-Lease Bill was introduced to the Congress—patriotically labeled House Resolution 1776 and disingenuously titled "An Act Further to Promote the Defense of the United States." How would anyone find fault with an Act so defined? The original proposal gave the president essentially illimitable power to transfer weapons—and anything else he deemed necessary—to any nation he considered an ally. The response in the Congress and in the nation was immediate—loud and acerbic. Would not this bill, if it became law, give Roosevelt virtual dictatorial powers? Many Americans simply did not trust "perfidious Albion" and were convinced the British could come up with cash for American weapons, but were holding back. Others viewed Lend-Lease as a give-away to a country that hadn't paid its Great War bills. More importantly, H.R. 1776 seemed to open the path to certain war with Germany. The anti–Roosevelt newspapers nationwide seethed with fury at what they saw was FDR's duplicity. Concerned mothers marched on Washington and knelt on the steps of the Capitol, chanting "Kill Bill 1776, Not Our Sons." Pacifist organizations had a fat target to train their invective on: Veterans of Future Wars cynically prodded the president to name an unknown soldier, "so we'll know who he is before he gets killed."[16]

William Allen White, the head of the Committee to Defend America by Aiding the Allies, the leading interventionist organization, opposed the bill and was convinced it would lead to war. Thomas E. Dewey, running for governor of New York and FDR's likely opponent in the next presidential race, declared that Lend-Lease would "abolish the Congress for all practical purposes." The dean of Senate Republicans, Arthur Vandenberg of Michigan, recorded in his diary: "Should the U.S. become wrecked as a nation, you can put your finger on this precise moment as the time when the crime was committed." Renowned historian Charles A. Beard damned H.R. 1776 as a bill "for waging undeclared war." The president of the University of Chicago opined that "the American people are about to commit suicide."[17]

Charles A. Lindbergh was a leading witness in opposition to H.R. 1776 and his two appearances before the Congress drew large and vocal crowds (Chapter 4). During his testimony before the House Committee on January 24, 1941, he told the Congressmen that any negotiated peace to end the war as soon as possible would be preferable to prolonging the conflict. A prosecution of the war to a conclusive victory by either side could only result in "such a prostration of Europe as the world has never seen." He was asked which side he hoped would win the war in Europe. Lindbergh's answer was a curt "neither." Goaded by antagonistic questioning, he stuck to his basic view that Germany would remain the dominant power in Europe, and that America had to cooperate with any country that controlled Europe. He consistently denied that he hoped for a German victory. The duty of the United States, according to Lindbergh, was "not to cry down talk of peace," but to get its public in a state of open-mindedness about peace at once. A bright, confident witness, Lindbergh more than held his own, and Lend-Lease supporters in the House were happy to have him out of their spotlight.[18]

His testimony before the Senate Foreign Relations Committee was less confrontational, and the Senators, mainly Alben Barkley and Tom Connally, "seemed primarily interested in getting Lindbergh to state his views as clearly and unequivocally as possible. Only Senator Claude Pepper actually attempted directly to attack Lindbergh's testimony.... He repeatedly got Lindbergh to oppose flatly any sort of aid to Britain."[19]

The chief defender of the Lend-Lease Act was venerable war hawk and current Secretary of War Henry L. Stimson. In testimony before the House Foreign Affairs Committee a week before Lindbergh testified, he earnestly told the Congressmen that he was convinced that it was a sound general principle to trust the president. "My opinion is this: I have been impressed always with the tremendously sobering influence that the terrific responsibility of the Presidency will impose upon any man, and particularly in foreign relations.... That has applied to all of the gentlemen whom ... I have had the opportunity of observing closely....[20] I feel that there is no one else, no other possible person in any official position who can be trusted to make conservatively and cautiously such a tremendous decision as the decisions which would have to be made in a great emergency involving a possible war...."[21]

His testimony before the Senate Foreign Relations Committee was more of the same. "We are really seeking to purchase her [Great Britain's] aid in our defense. We are buying our own security while we prepare.... We are buying the protection which is accorded us by the continuance of the British sea power in the North Atlantic while our own main fleet is busy protecting us in the Pacific.... In our own interest — and purely in our own interest — it is good national policy to preserve today a hard-fighting Britain...."[22] Stimson neglected to say that British sea power in the Atlantic was hardly defending the United States; it was bitterly fighting a losing battle with the *Kriegsmarine*'s U-boats that were sinking British merchantmen far faster than British shipyards could replace them; even more important were the precious American cargos that were being sent to the bottom.

While the bill was being vigorously debated in the Congress, Winston Churchill cunningly swung his not-inconsiderable weight behind the legislation. In a radio broadcast in England on February 9, 1941— aimed at American citizens— he was at his alliterative best and that was excellent, indeed! He memorably invoked the almighty as extra insurance: "Here is the answer I give President Roosevelt: Put your confidence in us. Give us your faith and your blessing, and, under Providence, all will be well. We shall not fail or falter; and we shall not weaken or tire. Neither the sudden shock of battle, nor the long-drawn trials of vigilance and exertion will wear us down. Give us the tools, we will finish the job."[23]

The power of a strong-willed incumbent American president scarcely knows any bounds, as the history of the balance of the twentieth century and the beginning of the twenty-first would prove repeatedly — and the Congress passed the Lend-Lease bill 260 to 165 in the House and on March 11 in the Senate by 60 to 31, when it became law. Opponents of the bill managed to attach two minor amendments: its powers were limited to two years, and, more importantly, convoying the weapons was Britain's responsibility. The help of American warships was expressly forbidden. At a press conference following his signing of H.R. 1776 into law, Roosevelt deceitfully told newsmen he had never considered using U.S. Navy escorts for such duty. That could lead to shooting, the glib Roosevelt told his smiling audience of reporters and "shooting comes awfully close to war, doesn't it? That is the last thing we have in mind."[24]

Like the destroyers-for-bases deal, Lend-Lease was a clear-cut violation of international law. Preposterously, it was defended by interventionist attorneys in the United States as "restoring respect for international law by assuming the responsibilities of a good citizen in the community of nations."[25]

The passage of Lend-Lease was a watershed for the president. All of his subsequent actions showed that he viewed the United States as a belligerent from this date. But his numerous campaign promises—and especially the unambiguous pledge in the Democratic Party's platform for the 1940 election not to send America's sons into foreign wars—temporarily hamstrung him.

To illustrate the depth of Roosevelt's Machiavellianism, Harry Hopkins, envoy *sans portfolio* to Britain's prime minister, eleven days earlier in England, told Churchill matter-of-factly: "The president is determined that we shall win the war together. Make no mistake about it. He has sent me to tell you that at all costs and by all means he will carry you through, no matter what happens to him — there is nothing he will not do so far as he has human power."[26]

Churchill later wrote that once Lend-Lease had been signed into law "it transformed immediately the whole position.... There was no provision for repayment. There was not even to be a formal account kept in dollars or sterling. What we had was lent or leased to us because our continued resistance to the Hitler tyranny was deemed to be of vital interest to the great Republic ... the defence of the United States and not dollars was henceforth to determine where American weapons were to go."[27]

German propagandists made the most of what they considered the small margins of victory for Roosevelt by pointing out that the vote in both Houses "indicated clearly that there can be no question of public opinion being unanimous on problems of foreign policy.... The President has thus not achieved his often stated aim: a foreign policy enjoying the unanimous support of the nation ... despite the terror and intimidation [to influence the Congressional vote] employed by the American government, the bulk of the American people remain calm and do not approve the bellicose policy of their President...."[28]

American aid to Great Britain—first the fifty-destroyers-deal and then Lend-Lease—convinced the German Naval High Command (OKM) that it was time to employ "the sharpest use of every available weapon in order to finally shatter British resistance and compel them to sue for peace."[29] Grossadmiral Erich Raeder categorically labeled U.S. Lend-Lease "an entry into the war without the politico-military complications of an official declaration" and he wondered if "the political leadership of the Reich ought not to adopt at least diplomatic counter-measures." He concluded that supplies from the United States must be stopped and England be forced to surrender "with all speed."[30]

Earlier in January, the president had decided it was time to abolish the last restrictions imposed by the 1935 Neutrality Act on U.S. aid to Hitler's enemies. Faced with concerted opposition by Congress, he cannily decided to proceed by easily-digested stages. On October 9, he asked the House to repeal Section VI, which prohibited the arming of U.S. merchantmen; eight days later, the House voted to comply with the president's request. The Administration next recommended that the Senate Foreign Affairs Committee discuss repeal of Section VI and Sections II and III. On October 25, the Committee so voted. It was now up to the Senate. The vote, after partisan wrangling, went FDR's way, but only by a tiny majority. The House of Representatives also voted for repeal of the three most important sections of the Act; its vote was also close. Nevertheless, FDR was now free to send not only U.S. destroyers into the Atlantic to serve as escorts to the convoys bringing needed supplies to the British but armed American merchant ships with American crews as well.

From 1941 to 1945, about $50 billion in aid to 38 different countries was supplied. Most went to England, some $30 billion, with most of the remainder going to the Soviet Union, China, and France. The program was ended in August 1945 by President Harry S. Truman, an action resented in particular by Russian leaders, who were convinced the abrupt cutoff in aid was a political act intended to gain diplomatic concessions. While Lend-Lease was certainly indispensable to the military efforts of Great Britain, there is some dispute over its contribution to the Soviet war effort. The bulk of Lend-Lease aid arrived in Russia after 1942; by then the Wehrmacht had been stopped and ferocious Soviet counter-attacks had begun to drive German troops out of Russia.

4

Charles A. Lindbergh and the America First Committee

"If I should die tomorrow, I want you to know this. I am absolutely convinced that Lindbergh is a Nazi."[1]
                              Franklin D. Roosevelt to Henry
                              Morgenthau, Jr., May 20, 1940

"It is not only my own experience and judgment, but I do not know a single man who has known Roosevelt, friend or enemy, who trusts what he says from one week to the next. And the President has the reputation, even among his friends, for being a vindictive man."[2]
                            Charles A. Lindbergh, December 22, 1941.

"Imagine, in just fifteen years he had gone from Jesus to Judas!"[3]
                              Sister-in-law Constance regarding
                              Charles Lindbergh's reputation.

Polls consistently showed, right up to December 7, that isolationism was the majority view in the country. A Gallup Poll taken in early September, 1941 showed that 88 percent of Americans agreed with the views of the isolationist bloc.[4]

    Charles A. Lindbergh was certainly no Nazi, as Franklin Roosevelt was "absolutely convinced" he was, and as many Americans, Jews in particular, still believe more than sixty years later. But whether he was an anti–Semite, an even more unsavory slur, is less clear. Some of his closest associates were indeed "dues paying" anti–Semites and in some of his speeches in 1941 and amongst his meticulous journal entries, he betrayed a too-general denunciation of Jews. What is certain is that he was the most articulate voice in America in 1940 and 1941 trying to forestall Roosevelt's drive toward war. FDR would use all the powers of a popular incumbent president in an effort to destroy him.
    The wheels of his strut-braced, high-wing Ryan monoplane *Spirit of*

4—Charles A. Lindbergh and the America First Committee

St. Louis N-X-2115 had no sooner touched down on the sod at Paris' Le Bourget airport on May 21, 1927 than its 25-year-old pilot was catapulted from obscurity into instant worldwide acclamation. As he recalled, "I had no way of knowing that tens of thousands of men and women were breaking down fences and flooding past guards. I had barely cut the engine switch when the first people reached my cockpit. Within seconds my open windows were blocked with faces. My name was called out over and over again, in accents strange to my ears—on this side of my plane—on that side—in front—in the distance."[6] Charles A. Lindbergh had just been the first person to fly nonstop across the Atlantic Ocean.[7]

The frantic adulation in France would be repeated wherever he went. He received congratulatory messages from thirty-one countries around the world and medals and honors from their kings, presidents, and prime ministers. However, nothing equaled New York City's hysterical acclaim. His parade up Broadway on June 13 was cheered by over four million spectators who rained on his head an estimated eighteen hundred tons of tickertape. Whether Lindbergh liked it or not, he had become a celebrity.

He came to despise crowds, and "hated the mass society that gave birth to them ... he also hated the press, which acted as their midwife." To Lindbergh, "the masses, and by extension the democratic system, represented a descent into mediocrity, a universe ... whose only standard and measure of achievement was the ability to entertain, titillate, gratify low and trivial desires."[8]

Then on March 1, 1932, Lindbergh was hurled again into the world's limelight when his infant son, Charles, Jr., was kidnapped from the Lindberghs' new home in Hopewell, New Jersey. "Within twenty-four hours of the baby's disappearance, it was estimated that one hundred thousand peace officers and cooperating citizens were involved in the nationwide dragnet." That did not include the Boy Scouts of America, whose Chief Scout Executive ordered his entire membership, past and present—over 900,000 boys and young men—"to be alert and watchful ... in seeking clues or information as to the Lindbergh baby."[9] Official reaction to the kidnapping was also extraordinary. Every branch of government was involved in what was called the greatest manhunt in the nation's history. The media had a field day: radio broadcasts were interrupted with the latest bulletins from Hopewell and newspapers shoved stories on the repeal of Prohibition to inside pages to bring readers even more interesting news on the front pages. Congress responded to the crime by passing legislation that made kidnapping, if it involved two or more states, a federal offense punishable by death. It became known as the Lindbergh Law.

The child's decomposed body was finally found three months later in the woods some two miles from Hopewell. After positive identification by the infant's nursemaid and the pediatrician who had examined baby Charles shortly before the kidnapping, the baby's remains were autopsied as required by state law. The cause of death was found to be "a fractured skull due to external violence," likely caused when the kidnapper's homemade ladder broke and he dropped the baby. To forestall what he knew would be a carnival sideshow at a gravesite, Lindbergh insisted his son's remains be cremated. Compounding Lindbergh's suffering, and ratcheting up his loathing of the press, was the breaking in of the morgue by a news photographer to snap a picture of his dead son, "copies of which were being peddled for five dollars each."[10]

Baby Charles' death resulted in a sympathetic response in the United States and around the world that some said had not been equaled since Lincoln's assassination. Over 100,000 letters and telegrams poured into Hopewell. Official condolences arrived from "President and Mrs. Hoover, the Prince of Wales, General and Mrs. Chiang Kai-shek, Mexican President Ortiz Rubio, and Benito Mussolini." Incredibly, a Canadian women was moved enough to offer the Lindbergh's her one-year-old son for adoption, who, she wrote, "resembles the lost little angel almost 100%."[11]

Charles and his wife Anne were not yet out of the woods. On January 3, 1935, nearly three years after the kidnapping, the trial of suspect Bruno Richard Hauptmann began. If the hunt for the killer had been the biggest ever and the compassionate response to the baby's death had also been monumental, the trial in tiny Flemington, New Jersey, would be even more Brobdingnagian. The nation's leading radio commentators were there and famous lawyers helped to provide "color" for their broadcasts. Newspapers from across the country sent teams of their best reporters to cover every angle of the story. Also, seen around town were well-known authors seeking insights for their post-trial books that were sure to be best-sellers. Gawking crowds of ordinary citizens flooded the streets around the courthouse, jostling with each other to get a better look at the celebrities and the witnesses — particularly the Lindberghs. Many called the six-week tribunal the "trial of the century," others "a three-ring circus." Both were right.

Anne Lindbergh was the first Lindbergh called by the state. While her testimony was not critical, the prosecutor knew well that merely her presence would have a compelling influence on the jurors. The trial was an ordeal for her and she returned only once, to accompany her mother who had been called to testify about one of the family's servants. Her husband, on the other hand, appeared in court every day whether he was testifying or not. The evidence he presented was sharp, unambiguous, and damning. The most important testimony he gave was about the night he heard a voice shouting "Hey, doctor," inside a Bronx cemetery after he had delivered fifty-thousand-dollars ransom as demanded for the return of his son. The prosecutor asked him if he had heard the same voice since. "Yes, I have," Lindbergh answered crisply. "Whose voice was it, Colonel, that you heard calling "Hey, doctor?" Lindbergh turned his head slowly and looked directly at Bruno Hauptmann. "It was Hauptmann's voice," he said convincingly.[12] This brief exchange between prosecutor and witness, it was generally agreed, was pivotal in convicting Hauptmann. For the rest of his life, on the few occasions he talked privately about the trial, Lindbergh never showed doubt about his incriminating testimony.[13]

On the morning when the jury was scheduled to announce its decision an estimated seven thousand people stood around the courthouse. They shouted "kill Hauptmann" over and over in cadence, figuring they might influence the jury. The jury had already decided. It had responded to the foreman's question of guilt or innocence: the defendant was found "guilty of murder in the first degree."[14]

After the trial, the Lindberghs tried again to find peace in the United States, to be left alone by the media, to get the blinding glare of the spotlight out of their eyes. Husband and wife were fed up with guards at their gate, obscene newspaper headlines, even Anne's dominant and omnipresent mother. Only by going far away for a long time, they reluctantly agreed, could they lead a normal life. On December 22, 1935, the Lindberghs with son Jon secretly boarded a U.S. passenger-freighter, destination Liverpool, England. The press learned of their departure only when they were far into the Atlantic.

They spent three years in Europe, in England and France, in self-imposed exile. While there, Charles Lindbergh had an opportunity to firm up his views about America's relations with the European powers. The family would not return until war was imminent and Lindbergh patriotically felt that his place was in the United States.

Charles Lindbergh had first crossed swords with FDR in February 1934 when he wired the president a caustic message regarding FDR's cancellation of air-mail contracts with the country's three leading airlines. Instead the president had ordered the Army Air Corps to carry the mails. Postmaster General James Farley defended the president's action, claiming that the airlines, which held a virtual airmail monopoly, had been overcharging the government. Lindbergh, a former mail flyer himself, accused the president of acting hastily and "risking the destruction of the finest commercial airlines in the world" by cutting off their much-needed subsidies.[15] Further, he warned that the Army Air Corps' pilots were not trained for the kind of flying they would be called on to do: at night, in all kinds of weather, around-the-clock. FDR was subjecting them to unjustified risk, he said.

The nation's weather was unusually severe in February and March of that year and Lindbergh's ominous prediction was promptly borne out. "For the Air Corps planes flying the mails through snow storms and freezing rains it was an unprecedented disaster. Within days after the operation began five pilots had been killed and many others badly injured."[16] Even with improving weather Army planes crashed, especially at night; by early April twelve pilots had been killed. The press enthusiastically picked up the story and played up the president's disastrous decision.

FDR, looking for a way to squirm out, had his Secretary of War, George H. Dern, formally invite Lindbergh, a colonel in the Air Force Reserve, to sit on a committee that would review training of Air Corps pilots. But Lindbergh had the bit in his teeth and stubbornly refused to back down. He sent another stiff telegram to his commander-in-chief, on March 14, 1934, like the first, an "open" letter. In it, he sternly lectured the president: "I believe that the use of the Army Air Corps to carry the air mail was unwarranted and contrary to American principles. This action was unjust to the airlines whose contracts were cancelled without trial. It was unfair to the personnel of the Army Air Corps, who had neither equipment designed for the purpose nor adequate time for training in a new field." He declared that he could not serve "on a committee whose function it is to assist in following out an executive order to the army to take over the commercial air mail system of the United States."[17] Lindbergh had publicly jousted with the most important figure in the United States, forcing him to retreat and to restore mail delivery to the private sector. This was the first confrontation between the two proud men. Roosevelt was not a good loser — and he had an excellent memory!

While in Europe, Lindbergh followed air-power developments closely and was particularly intrigued by German accomplishments in military aviation. Neither he nor his wife had ever visited Germany, so when Major Truman Smith, U.S. Military Attaché in Berlin, invited him "in the name of General Göring and the German Air Ministry" to inspect German civil and military air facilities, Lindbergh was more than pleased to accept. He and his wife flew in their own plane into Berlin on July 22, 1936, and spent the next eleven days in Germany as the house guests of the Smiths. Lindbergh met the top Luftwaffe officials: Hermann Göring; General Erhard Milch, State Secretary for Air; and Colonel Ernst Udet, Technical Chief; as well as Hans Dieckhoff, German Ambassador to the United States. He was chaperoned by Göring himself, given tours of the Heinkel and Junkers manufacturing plants. He learned about the secret new Messerschmitt Bf-109, which would become the Luftwaffe's principal fighter plane in World War II. At the end of the month, Göring arranged a formal luncheon at his official residence on the *Wilhelmstrasse* in honor of his guest and on August 1, the Lindberghs attended the opening ceremonies of the 1936 Olympic games in Berlin as Göring's guests.[18]

This first visit was a stimulating experience for Lindbergh: he found Germany "in many ways the most interesting nation in the world today." While he had not been introduced to Hitler, he nevertheless concluded that "he is undoubtedly a great man, and I believe he has done much for the German people. He is a fanatic in many ways, and anyone can see there is a certain amount of fanaticism in Germany today." Lindbergh also left "with a feeling of great admiration" for ordinary Germans and their clean and orderly society.[19] He retained this latter view, despite being rigidly escorted by high-level Nazis everywhere he went.

In October 1937, the Lindberghs returned to Germany for a second visit. The Lilienthal Aeronautical Society, with prompting by Major Smith, invited Lindbergh to its annual meeting in Munich. During their two-week stay, Lindbergh visited the Focke-Wulf and Henschel aircraft factories and the Daimler-Benz aircraft-engine plant. He followed up his earlier visit to the Messerschmitt factory, and this time he was allowed to inspect the Bf-109 more closely.

Before the Lindberghs flew back to England on October 25, Charles helped Smith write a formal "General Estimate" of the Luftwaffe for analysis by the Army Air Corps back in the United States. Highlights of the report, mostly authored by Lindbergh, were that Germany had "outdistanced France" in nearly all military fields. As for Great Britain, its aircraft engines were superior to Germany's, but Germany was "rapidly closing the gap." However, the report failed to point out that the Luftwaffe was not a strategic air force, with heavy bombers intended to strike factories and cities behind the lines, like those in U.S. and British inventories. Rather, the Luftwaffe focused on tactical bombers, like the Junkers Ju-87 *Stuka* dive bomber, which was designed to support troops on the ground. Reviewing the report's findings after the end of the war, Smith nevertheless thought that the conclusions reached had stood up "extremely well."[20]

The following year, invitations to the Lindberghs from the Lilienthal Society, from the German Air Ministry, from America's new ambassador to Berlin, Hugh R. Wilson, and again from Major Smith, brought the couple back to Germany, this time for nineteen days, October 11 to 29, 1938. It would be their last visit to the Third Reich. Lindbergh was permitted to inspect the new Junkers Ju-88 twin-engine bomber and to fly the Messerschmitt Bf-109. His comments after his exhilarating solo flight were that he knew "of no other pursuit plane which combines simplicity of construction with such excellent performance characteristics."[21]

Then came Ambassador Wilson's now-famous stag dinner on October 18 at the American Embassy in Berlin honoring famous-flyer Charles A. Lindbergh. Wilson anticipated that his dinner, along with Lindbergh's appearance, might help build improve his relations with Göring. It was a noteworthy gathering of important diplomatic figures and luminaries in the aeronautical field. Chief among the Germans, in addition to Air Marshal Göring were Generals Milch and Udet and Doctors Ernst Heinkel and Willi Messerschmitt.[22] Göring and his aides fashionably arrived last. Wilson introduced the German to his guests and Göring shook hands with each in turn. When he reached Lindbergh, Göring slipped into his hand a small red box. Speaking in German, Göring, "in the name of the Führer," was awarding Lindbergh the *Verdienstkreuz Deutscher Adler*—Service Cross of the Order of German Eagle with Star—for his services to aviation and particularly for his trans-Atlantic flight, which, notably, Germany had never acknowledged. Lindbergh accepted the medal, all the guests applauded, and everyone sat down to dinner.[23]

At the time, neither Lindbergh nor Smith had been upset by the presentation of the medal. On their return to the Smith apartment, however, when the wives learned about the medal, both immediately anticipated its consequences. Anne Lindbergh quietly labeled it "the Albatross." Mrs. Smith told her husband that the medal would "surely do Lindbergh much harm."[24] Both women would be right.

Regarding the return of the medal, which would shortly be demanded by his detractors, Lindbergh wrote sensibly three years later, when the controversy had assumed an overarching significance in the United States: "It seems to me that the returning of decorations which were given in times of peace, and as a gesture of friendship, can have no constructive effect.... Even if war develops between us, I can see no gain in indulging in a spitting contest before than war begins."[25]

A month after Wilson's dinner Interior Secretary Harold L. Ickes began malicious attacks on Lindbergh. At a Zionist meeting, Ickes berated Lindbergh for accepting "a decoration at the hands of a brutal dictator who with that same hand is robbing and torturing thousands of fellow human beings." Ickes had found a chink in Lindbergh's tough mantle and with Roosevelt's approbation he exploited it at every opportunity.

During the late 1930s, even before the war began in Europe, America was divided between the interventionists, those who were supporters of England and France in their growing confrontation with Germany, — and the noninterventionists or isolationists, those who were opposed to their

4—Charles A. Lindbergh and the America First Committee

country's participation in a European war for any reason, real or contrived. Most Americans, by a large margin, were in the latter group. In early April 1939, for example, just as German military forces overran Norway and Denmark, a Gallup poll "showed three percent of the American people in favor of entering the war and ninety-seven percent in favor of keeping out.... Over the years the percentage was reduced from ninety-seven to approximately eight-five percent and remained the same right up to the attack on Pearl Harbor."[26]

The interventionists believed it was necessary to assure an Allied victory over the Axis powers, even if it meant the United States would end up a belligerent herself. To justify these beliefs, they raised the specter of a triumphant Germany as a threat to American security, ending in trans-Atlantic invasion. On the other hand, the isolationists cared little about Britain and "her war" with Germany and Italy, but cared greatly about the U.S. sending an expeditionary force to Europe "to rake British coals out of the fire" a second time. They also insisted that a Nazi invasion of the United States was preposterous propaganda originating in the White House.

Within the interventionist camp there were two different views on how to secure a British victory. The Roosevelt administration's public statements that supported "all-out aid short of war" fit the thinking of one sub-group. In May 1940, a Committee to Defend America by Aiding the Allies was formed to champion this viewpoint. While there was no official connection between this committee and the president, in fact it served as a shadow public relations agency for FDR. Those who believed that "all-out aid short of war" was insufficient to enable England to defeat Germany and Italy felt strongly that it would be necessary for America to intervene as a full-fledged belligerent. In April 1941, the Fight for Freedom Committee was formed to lobby for this radical wing. Interventionists held that American security and welfare were at stake and that Britain must win to prevent Germany from attacking the United States—that England (and her Royal Navy) represented the first line of defense of the United States. A negotiated peace between Germany and England was unacceptable; Hitler could not be trusted, according to their lights, and such a peace would only be a short-lived pause in hostilities.

The makeup of the noninterventionists was far more diverse and attracted bedfellows from across a far wider spectrum of political thought. There were pro–Nazi German-American Bund members and the blatantly anti–Semitic members of Father Coughlin's Christian Front and William Dudley Pelley's Silver Shirts. There were pacifist organizations such as the National Council for the Prevention of War and the Keep America Out of War Congress. Unaffiliated liberals who were opposed to the direction Roosevelt's war juggernaut was taking the United States wanted no part of war, fearing loss of hard-fought social gains; there were also still unsolved domestic economic and social problems, and they wanted the nation to concentrate on those issues. Conservatives feared that U.S. intervention might upset the nation's capitalistic system and would almost certainly bring more of the detested New Deal legislation. Such left-of-center stalwarts as publisher Oswald Garrison Villard, Socialist Norman Thomas, and well-respected revisionist historians Charles Austin Beard and Harry Elmer Barnes well remembered the broken promises of the Great War and were skeptical of FDR's new ones. Parents of teen-age sons who would almost certainly be called into the service and possibly maimed or killed if America went to war were avid noninterventionists. Americans in general distrusted the Europeans, the British in particular; they too were noninterventionists. Finally, plain-vanilla Roosevelt-haters who considered him devious and worse — and they were legion — identified intervention with FDR and the Democratic Party and were steadfastly opposed to both. American Communists were isolationists until June 22, 1941 when the Germans attacked the Soviet Union; from then on, they were staunch interventionists.

As war clouds gathered, the noninterventionists organized lobbying organizations of their own to further their agendas and to counter those of the opposition. The National Committee to Keep America out of Foreign Wars was headed by Hamilton Fish, Representative from New York, and Avery Brundage, well known for his work in the Olympics, chaired the Citizen's Keep America Out of War Committee. These were followed by Islands for War Debts Committee, the War Debts Committee and the Make Europe Pay War Debts Committee, their titles clearly spelling out their agendas.

On October 21, 1940, some fifty representatives of these and other antiwar groups gathered in Washington to amalgamate these organizations with similar programs into a single bloc that would be more effective in advancing the cause of nonintervention. Out of this meeting came the No Foreign Wars Committee, headed by Verne Marshall, editor of the Cedar Rapids (Iowa) Gazette. After announcing his new anti-war organization, he said that in opposing America's involvement in the present war, his committee would seek to counteract the "propaganda" of the Committee to Defend America by Aiding the Allies. That committee, Marshall stated, had developed "the same public psychology as that which was carefully created during the war period preceding our declaration of hostilities in April 1917.... Let no man accuse us of the No Foreign Wars Committee of being appeasers, fifth columnists, pro–Nazi, pro–British, pro–Fascist...." He said that arguments that Hitler would attack the United States if he conquered Britain were "purely poppycock."[27] The No Foreign Wars Committee had a brief career. Marshall's heavy-handed public-relations methods made little headway and both members and financial backers dropped away. Charles Lindbergh, the Committee's principal spokesman, tactfully resigned before it went belly up.

A far more promising group took its place as the national voice for Americans opposed to intervention in the war in Europe. It was the America First Committee (originally called the Committee to Defend America First) founded by anti-war students at Yale University. The students, encouraged by like-thinking professors at the Ivy League school, banded together under the leadership of twenty-four-year-old Douglas Stuart, Jr., heir to the Quaker Oats fortune and a third-year law student. They organized the Connecticut chapter of what became the most influential noninterventionist organization in the country; at the height of its appeal, it numbered 800,000 members with chapters coast to coast.

The Yalies had a simple platform: "1. The United States must build an impregnable defense for America. 2. No foreign power, nor group of powers, can successfully attack a prepared America. 3. American democracy can be preserved only by keeping out of the European war. 4. Aid short of war weakens national defense at home and threatens to involve America in war abroad."[28] Those words could have been written by Lindbergh. America First also had an impressive governing body, including New Dealers Hugh Johnson, who had headed the NRA, and prominent economist Stuart Chase; anti–Administration writer John T. Flynn; even Great War "Ace" Eddie Rickenbacker, then president of Eastern Airlines.[29] The wealthy Chicagoans William H. Regnery and Clay Judson also signed on, both becoming members of the National Committee chiefly involved in fund-raising. Also recruited were Henry Ford and Avery Brundage as well as Senators Burton K. Wheeler of Montana and Gerald P. Nye of North Dakota, who had headed the well-known Senate "Munitions Hearings" (Appendix F). The avowed isolationist General Robert E. Wood, Chairman of Sears, Roebuck and Company became chairman. Wood was certain that America had nothing to fear from Hitler. He claimed he had studied *Mein Kampf* and had concluded that the way to tame a rebel was to make him rich, and then he becomes conservative and settles down. Wood had no inkling, of course, that Hitler was already rich, based on royalties from huge sales of *Mein Kampf*!

America First got off to a flying start. Chapters quickly sprouted all over the country and membership soared (Appendix G). The savvy Ivy Leaguers used every "artifice of propaganda" to advance their cause: "speeches, public meetings, radio, newspaper editorials, posters, cartoons, magazines, pamphlets, books, advertisements, slogans, buttons, demonstrations, picket lines, street-corner agitators."³⁰ They blanketed the country with isolationist arguments to counter Franklin Roosevelt's flood of interventionist government propaganda. America First had a list of credible grievances against the British, some of which were the same as those of anti-war groups prior to America's entry into the Great War more than 20 years before. Great Britain was not fighting to preserve democracy (or even to defend America with her fleet); she was at war to keep her colonial empire intact; Germany's resurgent economy was a threat to traditional English markets and had to be put down; Europe's wars were not America's wars and the United States could not be the world's policeman. More importantly, the noninterventionists were certain that Britain could not defeat Germany without the full military participation of America, regardless of how much military aid the U.S. supplied. That meant a huge army and navy, cultivation of a giant armaments industry, involuntary conscription, and increased taxes. For seers, it also meant the birth of a new and ominous warfare state, changing America permanently.

On September 15, 1939, Lindbergh delivered his first radio address to the nation, covered nationally by the three major networks. He was speaking as private citizen, not as a spokesman for any organization. Before he went on the air, he was told by his good friend Truman Smith, by then a lieutenant colonel, that the Administration was "very much worried" about his active opposition to Roosevelt's foreign-policy initiatives. If he decided not to speak, Smith told him, a new cabinet position would be created for him, Secretary of Air. The message had worked its way through Secretary of War Harry Hines Woodring, Army Air Corps General Henry H. "Hap" Arnold and then to Smith. "Smith said he asked Arnold if he [Arnold] thought for a minute that I would accept. Arnold replied, 'Of course not.'"

Lindbergh's focus in this first address was an appeal for America to remain isolationist. He said: "If we enter fighting for democracy abroad, we may end up losing it at home." He invoked George Washington's warning against "entangling alliances" and stated that America "must be as impersonal as a surgeon with his knife" and not allow personal feelings to obscure the issue, "to affect our children's lives." He pointed out that "we will be deluged with propaganda, both foreign and domestic — some obvious, some insidious. Much of our news is already colored." The *New York Times* noted that the address was Lindbergh's first formal speech since August 28, 1931 when he talked to Japanese dignitaries in Tokyo, and that he was following in the footsteps of his father, the late Charles A., Sr., Representative from Minnesota, "and one of the few to vote against the entry of the United States into the World War in 1917."³¹

Lindbergh's diary entry recorded that the newspaper editorials he read about his radio talk were about ninety percent favorable. He mentioned that of the fifty letters he opened of the hundreds he received, about ninety-five percent were also favorable. There were also critics, one of whom was the popular syndicated columnist Dorothy Thompson. To come up with the right descriptive noun, she apparently looked in her dictionary of synonyms, rejecting his address as the rantings of a "somber cretin," a man "without human feeling." She also suggested that Lindbergh "has a notion to be the American Führer." Thompson had found a convenient whipping-boy, vigorously flogging him in three more columns in 1939, six in 1940, and four in 1941. Like the president, she believed Charles Lindbergh was a Nazi.[32]

A month later, in another speech to a nationwide radio audience which he titled "Neutrality and War," Lindbergh presented a four-point program for American neutrality: an embargo on "offensive" weapons and munitions; unrestricted sale by the United States of purely "defensive" armament; prohibition of American shipping from belligerent countries of Europe and their danger zones; and refusal of credit to all warring nations or their agents. Lindbergh emphasized that the war was not a struggle for democracy; it was over the balance of power in Europe.

As the elections neared, Lindbergh again took to the airwaves. In a speech that the *New York Times* headlined "Lindbergh Assails Present Leaders," he called for the election of "leaders whose promises we can trust, who know where they are taking us, and tell us where we are going. Lindbergh mentioned neither President Roosevelt nor Republican candidate Wendell L. Willkie by name, but urged voters, regardless of party, to support men who "believe sincerely in national defense, but wholly oppose involvement in foreign wars." The *Times* noted that while Lindbergh had used no names, his speech was a definite call for the election of Mr. Willkie.[33]

Douglas Stuart had been in touch with Lindbergh in November 1939 after his first anti-war address to the nation and when America First invited him to speak at Yale University at the end of October 1940, he accepted. In great Woolsey Hall on the Yale campus in New Haven, Connecticut, before some 3,000 students and faculty, Lindbergh presented his anti-war message for the "generation which is taking over the problems of life during the greatest period of mutation that man has ever known." Lindbergh expecting to be booed and hissed as he went along, but instead his audience sat spellbound, then erupted in a mammoth standing ovation as he finished.[34] Emotionally effected, Charles Lindbergh decided then and there that he must continue to speak out publicly and that he would do so under the banner of America First. He quickly became the organization's champion and the standard-bearer of isolationism. He delivered thirteen nationally broadcast addresses in the next year to overflow crowds, challenging the president, literally for the soul of America.

In the meantime, he would be called to testify on the Lend-Lease bill (Chapter 3) before both the House Committee on Foreign Affairs and the Senate Foreign Relations Committee. Lindbergh's appearances before the Congress drew large, vocal and generally supportive crowds. A highlight of his testimony before the Senate Committee followed Senator Claude Pepper's first question, which was an attempt to put Lindbergh's comments in an historical context: "Colonel, when did you first go to Europe?" "Nineteen twenty-seven, sir," he replied, which brought the house down in a prolonged demonstration of laughter and applause. Nonplussed, Pepper then made it clear to his fellow Senators and the overflow gallery that he intended to show that Lindbergh was pro–German. "Many people are puzzled," Pepper said to Lindbergh, "by the absence of any indication on your part of any moral indignation at what they consider outrageous wrongs which have been perpetrated and are being perpetrated by the German government."[35] That was a tough question for Lindbergh, and he evaded the answer, asserting blandly that the United States should not be the world's policeman.

With Ickes and others regularly attacking Lindbergh, Roosevelt generally remained above the fray. But when the right occasion arose he took advantage of the opportunity to strike out at his antagonist. On April 25, 1941, at a press conference, a well-prompted reporter asked why the Army had not asked Colonel Lindbergh to enter active duty. Roosevelt, awaiting the question, was well prepared. He first entertained the reporters with another one of his personal interpretations of American history, this time about Clement L. Vallandigham, the leader of the Copperheads, the Yankees who were sympathetic to the Confederate cause. "Well, Vallandigham, as you know, was an appeaser. He wanted to make peace from 1863 on because the North 'couldn't win.'" Then back-tracking to America's War for Independence: "...there was a place called Valley Forge and there were an awful lot of appeasers that pleaded with Washington to quit...." Was the president still talking about Lindbergh? "Yes," smiled Roosevelt, to laughter.[36]

The next day after he read the papers, Lindbergh saw no humor in Roosevelt's history lesson and considered his comments more than just a political attack; they were connected to his commission in the U.S. Army Air Corps. "As it is," he wrote in his diary, "a point of honor is at stake, and it may be necessary to tender my resignation. But I don't like to resign, for my commission in the Air Corps has always meant a great deal to me, and I would prefer to hold it."[37] On April 27, Lindbergh made his decision:

4—Charles A. Lindbergh and the America First Committee 51

"Have decided to resign.... I feel it is the only honorable course to take.... And if I take this insult from Roosevelt, more, and worse, will probably be forthcoming."[38]

Harold Ickes was also getting under Lindbergh's skin with his cutting harangues. Finally, in July, after Ickes referred to him as a "Knight of the German Eagle" for accepting his *Verdienstkreuz* from Göring, Lindbergh was provoked enough to defend himself. He wrote the president on July 16 in another open letter, stating that he had accepted the decoration "in the American Embassy, in the presence of your Ambassador "and he was there "to assist in creating a better relationship" between the two governments. Lindbergh concluded by asking for an apology from his cabinet appointee. Roosevelt never publicly responded and Ickes neither replied nor ever apologized.[39]

Lindbergh's first address as a member of America First was on April 17, 1941; it was a proselytizing message, highlighting his personal views and those of the Committee's: "Some of us, including myself, believe that the sending of arms to Europe was a mistake — that it has weakened our position in America, that it has added to the bloodshed in European countries, and that it has not changed the trend of the war. Other members of this committee have supported aid to Britain, trusting in the promises of our President and our congress that such aid would actually be 'short of war.' The America First Committee is open to any patriotic American citizen who opposes intervention, regardless of what his attitude on aid to Britain has been."[40] The *New York Times*, while it disagreed editorially with Lindbergh and America First, nevertheless gave front-page news coverage to his talks and included full transcripts of every speech Lindbergh delivered.

In subsequent addresses, Lindbergh continued to focus on favorite isolationist topics and slashed away at FDR's foreign-policy initiatives that were inexorably drawing the United States into the European war. One of the biggest problems the American Firsters faced was the necessity for assuming negative postures in opposing the Administration's actions. The Committee opposed the transfer of destroyers, it opposed Lend-Lease, it opposed convoys with U.S. Navy escorts, it opposed sending conscripts outside of the Western Hemisphere; it opposed FDR's provocative "shoot-on-sight" strategy; it opposed repeal of the key provisions of the Neutrality Act.

Then, on September 11, Lindbergh delivered what would prove to be his most memorable address at a rally in Des Moines, Iowa (Appendix I). Its focus was on none of the above. He charged that that "the three most important groups which have been pressing this country toward war are the British, the Jewish and the Roosevelt Administration." He declared that these groups and other "war agitators" had organized a step-by-step campaign to put America into the conflict. "Only the creation of sufficient 'incidents' remains; and you see the first of these already taking place...." If it were not for England's hope, Lindbergh declared, "that she can make the United States 'financially and militarily' responsible for the war, England would have negotiated a peace in Europe many months ago and be better off for doing so."

If Lindbergh had stopped there and moved on to other issues, the public's reaction would have been severe enough. But Lindbergh's candor — or was it his anti–Semitism? — pushed him into deeper waters.

He said he understood why American Jews desired the overthrow of the Nazi regime: "No person with a sense of the dignity of mankind can condone the persecution of the Jewish race in Germany." Instead of agitating for war, however, he advised "they should be opposing it in every possible way, for they will be among the first to feel its consequences. Their greatest danger to this country," he said of the Jews, "lies in their large ownership and influence in our motion pictures, our press, our radio, and our government." He concluded sagely that Roosevelt had won a third term on the basis of the international situation and that the "power of the Roosevelt Administration depends upon the maintenance of a wartime emergency."[42]

Lindbergh had purposefully taken on American Jewry. As might be imagined an avalanche of vituperative criticism descended on his head. To nearly every Jew in America overnight he had become *persona non grata* for as long as he lived — and for many decades beyond. The America First Committee managed to roll with the punch and it suffered no obvious membership loss, indicating perhaps that there were a lot of Jew-haters in America at the time.

These are Lindbergh's own impressions of his Des Moines speech that he chose to insert in his *Journal*: "It seemed that over eighty percent of the crowd was with us by the time I finished.... When I mentioned the three major groups agitating for war — the British, the Jewish, and the Roosevelt Administration — the entire audience seemed to stand and cheer. At that moment whatever opposition existed was completely drowned out by our support."[43]

Was Charles Lindbergh an anti–Semite? In William Jovanovich's introduction to Lindbergh's Wartime Journals[44] he noted that the "entries were printed exactly as written, except in the cases of certain personal references to living people, repetitions or material deemed 'not important enough to warrant adding to the length of the work as a whole.' That was, for the most part, true. But there were exceptions, several omissions in the published texts that were substantive in nature ... the bulk of these omissions centered on one subject, the Jews. None of the cuts contains any overt deni-

4—Charles A. Lindbergh and the America First Committee

grations of Jews.... But in so writing about a single tribe, he was segregating them in his mind from the rest of the nation; and to that extent he was, like many of his countrymen, anti–Semitic."

The following passage is from Lindbergh's journal entry of April 10, 1939 aboard the *Aquitania*, on his way back to the United States. *It was never published*, and one can guess why! After some rough weather that kept most of the passengers in their cabins: "The steward tells me that most of the Jewish passengers are sick. Imagine the United States taking these Jews in addition to those we already have. There are too many in places like New York already. A few Jews add strength and character to a country, but too many create chaos. And we are getting too many. The present immigration will have its reaction."[45]

One should also be judged by his or her bedfellows. On August 23, 1941, Lindbergh had dinner with Fulton Lewis, Jr., a nationally syndicated conservative news commentator, and William R. Castle, a former ambassador to Japan and Undersecretary of State. The three agreed that there was an imminent need for action should war start in Europe. They were also in accord on another subject. Lindbergh summed up its details in his *Journal*: "We are disturbed about the effect of the Jewish influence in our press, radio, and motion pictures.... Lewis told us of one instance where the Jewish advertising firms threatened to remove all their advertising from the Mutual system if a certain feature were permitted to go on the air. The threat was powerful enough to have the feature removed. I do not blame the Jews so much for their attitude, although I think it unwise from their own standpoint."[46]

Another of his good friends was Henry Ford, perhaps the best known Jew-hater in America; Chevrolets rather than Fords were the cars of choice for many Jews for that reason. During the early 1920s his newspaper, the *Dearborn Independent*, was used as a platform for his anti–Semitic rantings. Ford also published the notoriously anti–Semitic *Protocols of the Elders of Zion*. Charles Lindbergh had no supporter more zealous than Father Charles Edward Coughlin, an open anti–Semite with an enthusiastic following on the radio and through his weekly tabloid *Social Justice*. He ran Lindbergh's picture on the front page to help get his own message across.[47]

Following the Japanese attack on Pearl Harbor, America First ceased all noninterventionist activity and national headquarters released a statement urging its members to give their support to the nation's war effort and the president until the conflict with Japan was won. The America First Committee had obviously failed in its efforts to keep the United States out of war. It was unable to defeat a single Administration foreign policy initiative that came up for a vote in Congress. Sixty years later it remains conventional wisdom for many American seniors to condemn the isolationists of 1940–1941 as wrong-headed and America First as an inconsequential splinter-group consisting of rabid pro–Germans and anti–Semites. Another interpretation suggests, rather, that most Americans in 1941, as polls consistently showed, were opposed to U.S. entry into the war in Europe; thus America First and Charles A. Lindbergh represented a majority viewpoint.

5

FDR's Expendable "Three Small Vessels"

> As for water for his big crew, Slocum smiled sarcastically: "You have a set of international signal flags, don't you? If you run short of water, simply ask a passing Jap for some."[1]
>
> ... it was clear even to one far removed from top level planning that the mission was likely to be one way. If I managed to survive it would be by swimming....[2]

President directs that the following be done as soon as possible and within two days if possible after receipt of this dispatch. Charter three small vessels to form a quote defensive information patrol unquote. Minimum requirements to establish identity as a United States man of war are command by a naval officer and to mount a small gun and one machine gun would suffice. Filipino crews may be employed with minimum number of naval ratings to accomplish purpose which is to observe and report by radio Japanese movements in West China Sea and Gulf of Siam. One vessel to be stationed between Hainan and Hue and one vessel off Point de Camau. Use of Isabel authorized by President as one of these three but no other naval vessels. Report measures taken to carry out president's views. At same time inform me as to what reconnaissance measures are being regularly performed by sea by both army and navy whether by air surface vessels or submarines and your opinion as to the effectiveness of these latter measures.

This Top Secret directive was sent by CNO Stark to Admiral Thomas C. Hart, Commander of the Asiatic Fleet in Manila. It was dated December 1, 1941, and had originated in the Oval Office, from the Commander-in-Chief himself. Hart and his staff were puzzled; the fleet's reconnaissance aircraft were already covering the areas delineated. Aerial surveillance was a more effective and less confrontational method of surveillance than stationing vulnerable picket ships close inshore. Not incidentally, from Hart's perspective, the new orders ran counter to other recent directives that called for U.S. forces to avoid provocative moves. What was most astonishing to Hart, however, was the president's direction of what, at least on the surface, was a minor tactical operation. Were the three little ships being sent on a one-way mission? Perhaps to instigate war?

The answer to both these questions can only be affirmative. Roosevelt was playing for extremely high stakes. He was hoping for a Japanese "first strike"—as he had sought unsuccessfully in the Atlantic from Germany—so he could declare war with a unified electorate behind him. The lives of a couple of dozen U.S. and Filipino sailors and the destruction of their inconsequential ships apparently meant nothing to the president. When he sent the directive to Admiral Thomas Hart, Roosevelt *knew a Japanese six-carrier task force was bearing down on Pearl Harbor* (Chapter 6). For any number of reasons, the Japanese fleet might turn back before launching their aircraft; these suicide missions were "insurance" for a ruthless president.

December 1 had started off as a busy day in and around the White House. The president had just returned to Washington and met with Secretary of State Cordell Hull and Admiral Stark, who were scheduled to testify before a Congressional Committee later that day. Harry Hopkins then was driven in from Bethesda Naval Hospital[3] for a luncheon conference with FDR. Some important decision was about to be reached. "This important decision required such secrecy that Mr. Roosevelt dared not use the telephone to consult the "crafty" Mr. Hopkins … it can almost surely be conjectured that the problem discussed at the White House that noon was how to get America to enter the war if only Thailand, or only Singapore, should be attacked by Japan. And it can further be conjectured that the method finally devised was to create an 'incident' in which Japan would commit the first overt act by firing on the American flag and simultaneously sinking one or more American warships."[4] There was no time to resurrect FDR's "pop-up cruisers" ruse; FDR had to settle for a quick-reaction plan. Roosevelt's "three small vessels" stratagem was created that very afternoon.

In the Philippines there were three ships readily available for their unusual missions. Hart had one ready to sail immediately, the *Isabel*, which was specifically mentioned in the message, and was already a commissioned U.S. Navy vessel. The message also stated in rather oblique language that the other two vessels to be selected were not to be already-commissioned U.S. Navy vessels. There was no time for Hart to dither if FDR's deadline was to be met.

The *Isabel* was Admiral Hart's "holiday" flagship, a still-handsome 245-foot-long, 900-ton "miniature destroyer" that had been converted from a yacht to a man-of-war of sorts during the Great War. Then she had mounted a pair of torpedo tubes and four small three-inch guns. The torpedo tubes and depth-charge racks were long since gone, and age had reduced her original top speed of twenty-six knots to about half of that. The *Isabel*'s hull was white and her single deckhouse and twin stacks off-white. But her striking silhouette and neat paint job belied her true condition; *Isabel* was simply worn out and "although rating a Lieutenant Commander skipper, officers of that rank did not consider her a command worth seeking. One nominee had confirmed this view by taking a preliminary inspection walk, then proceeding to his cabin, where he shot himself."[5]

On December 3, Hart briefed its current skipper, Lieutenant John Walker Payne, Jr., on his ship's unusual mission. Payne later wrote: "Utmost secrecy was to be observed, actual orders were to be given verbally, memorized and recited to the Admiral. No one was to know the actual mission of the *Isabel* except the Admiral and myself until we were at sea, then the executive officer was to be taken into confidence. A fake operational dispatch ... was transmitted, ordering *Isabel* to search from Manila, west to the vicinity of the Indo-China coast for a lost PBY plane."

He was ordered to clear from the ship "all removable topside weights including motor boats and gangway; ... one additional pulling lifeboat and additional life rafts were taken on board." Additional orders were "to fight the ship as necessary and to destroy it rather than let it fall into enemy hands."[6] This last order probably brought a wry smile to Payne's face: in any sort of "fight," the *Isabel*'s pea-shooter armament and lack of above-decks armor would mean almost instant destruction.

The *Isabel* cleared Manila Bay's minefield on the morning of December 3 on its way to Camranh Bay. On that day, Admiral Hart's aerial reconnaissance revealed some fifty Japanese ships, including cruisers and destroyers, riding at anchor inside the bay. Two mornings later, there was a little excitement aboard the *Isabel*: a snooping Japanese Navy plane circled overhead at low altitude, apparently taking pictures. Throughout the day, the plane continued to reappear. By nightfall, just as the Indo-China coast was becoming visible to the crew, the *Isabel* received a message to return to Manila, an order Lieutenant Payne was pleased to comply with. The next day, a twin-engine Japanese bomber shadowed the *Isabel* for several hours before turning west and disappearing. Early on December 8 (Philippines time) the tiny warship entered Manila Bay, just hours after Japanese bombs and torpedoes had struck targets in Pearl Harbor. It had been "a near thing" for ship and crew. When Admiral Hart next met Lieutenant Payne, he greeted him: "Well! I didn't expect to see *you* again."[7]

If the *Isabel* scarcely resembled a man-of-war, the 47-ton schooner *Lanakai*[7] was not exactly a "ship" in Navy parlance. She was, in fact, a two-masted "windjammer," 83 feet long to the tip of her elongated bowsprit, and by no means pristine. In November 1941, Admiral Hart had sent the cruisers and most of the destroyers of his tiny Asiatic Fleet to Java to join up with the Dutch fleet. Eight of these warships were subsequently sunk in surface actions with Japanese ships. He kept twenty submarines, a single sub-tender, and his PBY reconnaissance planes. For safety Hart ordered his submarines to spend daylight hours fully submerged on the bottom of Manila Bay, exposing only their periscopes.[8]

The *Lanakai* had been used recently in sightseeing and inter-island commerce by her private owner. She had a checkered early career and had been in the U.S. Navy before as USS *Hermes.* Her most exciting days, however, were played out before Hollywood cameras for the 1937 cinematic blockbuster, *Hurricane*, starring a sarong-attired Dorothy Lamour.

Hart negotiated a charter for the *Lanakai* for "one dollar a year for the duration" from her patriotic owner, which included a crew of five civilian Filipinos as part of the package. A small three-pound cannon dating from the Spanish War was scrounged up in Cavite Navy Yard and mounted on her after deckhouse; that was the biggest gun that could be fired safely, the yard experts estimated, without wrecking the 27-year-old wooden-hulled ship. Two .30-caliber Lewis machine guns from the Great War were mounted forward, exceeding by one permanently mounted gun the minimum requirements for a U.S. Navy warship.

On December 4, U.S. Navy Lieutenant Kemp Tolley, who had just arrived in Manila, was summoned to report to the operations officer of the U.S. Asiatic Fleet, Commander H. B. Slocum, who proceeded to give Tolley the oddest order he had ever heard, and would likely ever hear! He was to take immediate command of an armed schooner, commission her in the U.S. Navy, and ready her for sea.

A day later, the first entry in the informal log of USS *Lanakai* recorded the ship's commissioning: "The Navy Yard band played the national anthem, the commission pennant was hoisted, then "God Bless America" was played to wind up the ceremony."[9] On December 7 (December 6 Washington time), the *Lanakai* was provisioned for sea, armed, fully crewed and ready to depart.

Tolley got his sailing orders from Commander Slocum. "Here are your orders," he said to the lieutenant, handing him a small envelope. "Open this only when you clear Manila Bay. I can tell you that you are headed for the coast of Indo-China. If you are queried by a Japanese man-of-war, explain you are looking for a downed U.S. Navy patrol plane." Tolley had two important concerns: a cantankerous radio transmitter and a limited supply of fresh water. The *Lanakai* had been built for a small crew, who had preferred beer to slake their thirst; as a commissioned U.S. Navy ship she carried nineteen sailors. The issues were no problems to Slocum. "You can work on the radio enroute. You have a radioman first class assigned." As for water for his big crew, Slocum smiled sarcastically: "You have a set of international signal flags, don't you? If you run short of water, simply ask a passing Jap for some."[10]

On the last day of peace, although no one on board the *Lanakai* knew it, Tolley inserted these remarkable entries into his log:

"At 1410 Navy Yard tug came alongside and took ship in tow to clear mooring.

"At 1415 Got underway in accordance with CinCAF confidential dispatch orders.

"At 1420 *Hoisted jib staysail and forestaysail*" (emphasis added).

By 4:45 P.M. the *Lanakai* had sailed approximately fifteen miles to an anchorage close to Corregidor Island at the mouth of Manila Bay. There had been no hurry to exit Manila Bay, since traversing the minefield guarding its entrance at night was prohibited.

"At about 3:30 A.M., a radioman nudged me awake with a message," wrote Tolley, "ORANGE WAR PLAN IN EFFECT. RETURN TO CAVITE." A graduate of Annapolis, he was familiar with Plan Orange, the secret U.S. plan for fighting the Japanese in the Pacific. Tolley then wrote into his log that he went topside to collect his thoughts in the cool night air. Why had the president deployed a seven-knot ship with no radio worth mentioning on a reconnaissance into hostile waters? Such a voyage might have made sense in the eighteenth or nineteenth centuries. In 1941, the U.S. Navy had airplanes that could scout the China Sea in one-twentieth of the time and at virtually no risk. Was the *Lanakai* supposed to provide the first shot FDR thought he needed to persuade Congress to declare war? Had the president stipulated that the *Lanakai* be staffed with a mostly Filipino crew because he wanted their deaths by Japanese gunfire to bring the Philippines into the war on the American side? Most disturbing of all, had the Commander-in-Chief sent Lieutenant Tolley and his crew on a suicide mission?[11]

Postwar, Tolley set out to prove that, in fact, he and his crew had been sent on a one-way mission. At first, Hart had refused to talk about the issue, he wrote. But when Tolley retired as a Rear Admiral years later, an older and more compassionate Hart was much more forthcoming. "Do you think we were set up to bait an incident," Tolley asked. "Yes, I think you were bait," was Hart's rejoinder.[12]

6

Pearl Harbor: FDR's Monstrous Conspiracy

"To be a 'revisionist' these days [1995] means that one believes Roosevelt deliberately exposed our fleet at Pearl Harbor to "lure the Japanese to attack," had full knowledge of the approach of the six-carrier task force across the north Pacific for that purpose, and refrained from alerting our forces in Hawaii in order that Japan's 'first blow' would be so devastating that it would coalesce our entire national political spectrum into support for entry into the war."[1]

"Japan has never harmed us. Japan is not threatening us. Japan has treated us better than any other world power in the matter of paying debts, courtesy to our visitors and residents, and never attempting to meddle in our affairs. Japan is the only world power that has paid back all sums borrowed without delay or default on a single penny. If we are going to answer this fair treatment of us by enmity, no incentive is left for any country to treat us as well in the future."[2]

"How could a nation rich in resources and land, and free from fear of attack, understand the position of a tiny, crowded island empire with almost no natural resources, which was constantly in danger of attack from a ruthless neighbor, the Soviet Union. America herself had, moreover, contributed to the atmosphere of hate and distrust by excluding the Japanese from immigration and, in effect, flaunting a racial and color prejudice that justifiably infuriated the proud Nipponese."[3]

"Pearl Harbor was not an accident, a mere failure of American intelligence, or a brilliant Japanese military coup. It was the result of a carefully orchestrated design, initiated at the highest levels of our government. According to a key memorandum, eight steps were taken to make sure we would enter the war by this means. Pearl Harbor was the only way, leading officials felt, to galvanize the reluctant American public into action."[4]

"It was God's mercy that Admiral Kimmel didn't have warning that the Japanese were about to attack Pearl Harbor.... If we had been warned, our fleet would have gone out to sea, and ... all our ships would have been destroyed one by one in deep water.... We

6—Pearl Harbor

would have lost the entire Pacific Fleet and eighteen to nineteen thousand men, instead of the ships and 3,300 men we did lose."[5]
Admiral Chester Nimitz

"When President Roosevelt told the Americans in the 1940 election that "I shall say again and again and again: your boys are not going to be sent into any foreign wars' he had already committed the United States to a huge program of military aid to Britain, and had drawn up the Rainbow contingency plans for a simultaneous war with Germany and Japan, and was soon to slap on Japan the embargoes which some people still believe pushed the Japanese into their attack on Pearl Harbor."[6]
The Economist (London)

"If you insist on my going ahead, I can promise to give them hell for a year or a year and a half, but can guarantee nothing as to what will happen after that."[7]
Admiral Isoroku Yamamoto to Prime Minister Fumimaro Konoye, September 1940, regarding the Imperial Navy's prospects if Japan went to war with the United States.

The idea that there was American foreknowledge of the Japanese air assault on Pearl Harbor is difficult for those who cling to the conventional wisdom of a "sneak-attack" to accept. They base their views on two allegations that propaganda has chiseled in granite in the United States: that U.S. cryptographers had failed to break JN-25, the Japanese naval code, prior to December 7; and that American intelligence could not know where and when the attack would take place because the attacking Japanese carrier force was steaming under radio silence. *Both allegations are patently false.* Not only had American cryptographers broken the Japanese naval code, so had the British, Dutch, and Nationalist Chinese. Their radio intercept stations were reading the messages between the task force and Imperial Japanese Navy Headquarters. *Some in Washington knew the Japanese First Air Fleet was steaming to Pearl Harbor— but the Navy and Army commanders in Hawaii were purposely kept in the dark.*

Further compounding the conspiracy, as much irrefutable evidence now makes clear, FDR and his small cabal of military and civilian advisers applied an economic stranglehold around Japan, forcing them to attack. Beforehand, a barrage of government lies and hyperbole demonized the Japanese as aggressors threatening American security, conditioning the American public to war.

On the night of February 8, 1904, four Japanese torpedo boats made a surprise attack on the Russian fleet at Port Arthur. The tiny ships sank two Russian battleships and disabled two more, while escaping undamaged. Earlier that evening, a Japanese cruiser squadron convoyed troop transports to the Korean city of Chemulpo (Inchon), where they landed 3,000 infantrymen who moved inland to capture Seoul. The next morning, the commander of the cruisers sent a message to the Russians, declaring that a state of war existed between the two countries. The Russo-Japanese War had begun. It climaxed with the Battle of Tsushima at the end of May 1905, during which the Japanese destroyed an entire Russian fleet. "Although Russian armored ships outnumbered the Japanese by fourteen to twelve, every major Russian vessel was sunk or captured, and, on the Japanese side, not a ship was lost or crippled. The Russians lost 4,830 men, Japan only 117."[8] This great Japanese victory was far more lopsided than the Spanish-American war triumphs of Admiral George Dewey at Manila Bay and Admiral William T. Sampson at Santiago Bay, and U.S. Navy war planners took notice.

These planners had also taken notice eight years earlier, when a resolution proposed in the Congress to annex Hawaii brought a formal Japanese protest that Hawaiian independence was "essential to the good understanding of the Powers that have interests in the Pacific." Japan followed up by sending a cruiser to Hawaii to back up her note, but elected not to inflame relations and withdrew the warship after a brief stay.[9]

In 1909, Homer Lea wrote *The Valor of Ignorance*, a "creative" history that purported to reveal Japanese plans to attack the United States, encouraging the "yellow peril" advocates. Lea projected that the Japanese would overrun the Philippines and capture Hawaii. Japan would then send a 100,000-man army to land on the west coast of the United States. "In three months' time," he assured his readers, "Japanese forces would control California, Oregon, Washington, and Alaska, and there would be no way of shaking off the yellow horde until the American people came to their senses, recognized that their experiment with democracy had been folly, and established a monarchy."[10] Despite its serious shortcomings, Lea's book became required reading for U.S. Army and Navy planners. It was translated into Japanese as *The War Between Japan and America* and sold "a remarkable 40,000 copies."[11]

In 1918, Lenin, acting as an all-knowing seer, prophesized accurately that America and Japan, while allies at that time, were certain to become enemies: "The economic development of these countries ... has stored up a great mass of inflammable material which renders inevitable a desperate conflict between these two powers for mastery of the Pacific Ocean and its shores."[12]

In 1925, Hector C. Bywater, a British journalist with an exceptional understanding of naval warfare, published a novel, *The Great Pacific War: A History of the American-Japanese Campaign of 1931–1933*, that graphically portrayed a surprise attack on the U.S. Pacific Fleet in Pearl Harbor. Simultaneously, the Japanese launched amphibious assaults on Guam and the Philippines; both had been acquired by the United States at the end of the Spanish-American War. Bywater had figured out the size and shape of a likely future war between Japan and the United States and, remarkably, his projections proved accurate sixteen years later.

The *New York Times* gave the review of the book the front page of its September *Book Review* section: IF WAR COMES IN THE PACIFIC—*An Imagined Conflict Between the Navies of Japan and the United States*. *Times* book reviewer Nicholas Roosevelt concluded his analysis by suggesting "that the intemperance of our Congress and people on the one hand and the discipline of the Japanese on the other hand might some day bring about an incident which might lead to war. If such an unhappy day ever arrives, those who have read Mr. Bywater's fantasy will realize that we will be embarking upon the most futile contest that the world has ever witnessed."[13] Captain Isoroku Yamamoto was then in Washington as naval attaché[14] and he presumably read both the review and Bywater's book. For naval officers on both sides of the Pacific, *The Great Pacific War* was mandatory reading.

In 1991 came another installment of the background to the Japanese attack on Pearl Harbor: *Visions of Infamy: The Untold Story of How Journalist Hector C. Bywater Devised the Plans that Led to Pearl Harbor*. In this book, its author, William H. Honan, worked diligently to convince his readers that Yamamoto had copied Bywater's ideas for Operation Z,[15] and that the U.S. Navy in turn followed Bywater's scheme of amphibious island-hopping across the Central Pacific to close in on the Japanese home islands. In 1925 such consecutive amphibious landings were radical ideas.[16]

Following the Joint Army/Navy Exercise held in February 1932 in the waters off Pearl Harbor, U.S. war planners took a Japanese surprise attack much more seriously. Admiral H. E. Yarnell, in an unorthodox move, had left his slower battleships and cruisers behind in California as he ran his two aircraft carriers, *Saratoga* and *Lexington*, and their escort destroyers at flank speed to strike Pearl earlier than its defenders expected. He compounded the surprise by launching his attacking aircraft in the dark before dawn and on a Sunday. Yarnell caught most of the defenders' planes on the ground and quickly gained air supremacy.[17]

In 1938, Vice Admiral Ernest J. King conducted another simulated air attack on Pearl Harbor originating from North Pacific waters. Admiral Alan Kirk, head of the Office of Naval Information in 1941, described King's practice attack this way: "His tactics were exactly those employed by the Japanese on the 7th of December, except King's attack (by the Black Fleet, the Japanese) was later in the day not early morning. By golly, he took his carriers north of Oahu, launched his airplanes in bad weather ... and appeared over the Blue Fleet (USA) to the startling consternation of everyone concerned."[18]

On October 7, 1940, 42-year-old Lt. Commander Arthur H. McCollum, head of the Far East desk of the Office of Naval Intelligence, completed a secret U.S. foreign policy initiative that called for goading Japan into an overt act of war against an isolationist United States. Would an America at war with Japan trigger the declarations of war from Germany and Italy which his commander-in-chief sought? McCollum thought so.

McCollum was an old Japanese hand. He had been born in Nagasaki, had learned Japanese before learning English, and thoroughly understood the many nuances of Japanese culture. Following the death of his father, his family returned to the U.S. After graduating from the U.S. Naval Academy Ensign McCollum was posted to the American embassy in Tokyo as a naval attaché where, among other ceremonial activities, he taught the young Prince Hirohito the latest American dance steps. In 1928, the Navy ordered McCollum to return to Tokyo as a language instructor at the combat intelligence center for the Pacific Fleet, one of America's most important cryptographic facilities.

McCollum's eight-action memorandum,[19] as it came to be called, was intended to incite a Japanese attack not only on the principal U.S. holdings in the Pacific (Hawaii and the Philippines), but also against the British (Singapore and Malaya) and Dutch (Dutch East Indies) colonial assets in the region. Japan's loudly proclaimed Greater East Asia Co-Prosperity Sphere, while intended principally to give Japan access to the region's resources and at the same time reduce the economic influences of the three imperialist nations, also was also a bona fide Asia-for-the-Asians policy.[20]

McCollum prefaced his list by reciting the fashionable old axiom: "The one danger to our position lies in the possible early defeat of the British Empire with the British Fleet falling intact into the hands of the Axis powers. The possibility of such an event occurring would be materially lessened were we actually allied in war with the British.... To sum up: the threat to our security in the Atlantic remains small so long as the British Fleet remains dominant in that ocean and friendly to the United States."[21] Items A, B, and C were covert but D, E, F, G, and H quickly became obvious to the Japanese as soon as they were implemented.

    A. Make an arrangement with Britain for the use of British bases in the Pacific, particularly Singapore.
    B. Make an arrangement with Holland for the use of base facilities and acquisition of supplies in the Dutch East Indies [now Indonesia].
    C. Give all possible aid to the Chinese government of Chiang Kai-shek.

D. Send a division of long-range heavy cruisers to the Orient, Philippines, or Singapore.

E. Send two divisions of submarines to the Orient.

F. Keep the main strength of the US Fleet, now in the Pacific, in the vicinity of the Hawaiian Islands.

G. Insist that the Dutch refuse to grant Japanese demands for undue economic concessions, particularly oil.

H. Completely embargo all trade with Japan, in collaboration with a similar embargo imposed by the British Empire.[22]

Before any of McCollum's recommendations were executed, the president took the United States four giant steps closer to war: he sent the first peacetime Draft Act to Congress; he called up the National Guard to active duty; he traded fifty old U.S. destroyers for leases of bases on British territory (Chapter 2), and he signed legislation creating a two-ocean navy.

If McCollum's plan was to succeed — and give Franklin Roosevelt the war he wanted — Japan must be viewed by the American people as the undoubted aggressor and must commit the first overt act. An open-sea engagement between the Pacific Fleet and elements of the Imperial Japanese Navy would not serve Washington's short term needs, regardless of the outcome. Japan could claim that its right to sail the open seas had been abridged by American men-of-war if Admiral Kimmel attacked first. Roosevelt's wild scheme for a blockade of Japan had been summarily rejected by his admirals, and his "pop-up cruisers" ploy had not worked. There had to be a better way.

Around 9 P.M. (11 A.M. in Hawaii) on December 7, 1941, Winston Churchill was having dinner in London with two guests, Averell Harriman, FDR's special envoy, and John Winant, U.S. Ambassador to Britain. Churchill's butler reportedly broke into the room suddenly and excitedly announced that he had just heard over the radio that Japan had attacked Pearl Harbor. Churchill quickly rose to his feet saying, "We shall declare war on Japan," and immediately went to his office and asked for a call to be put through to Roosevelt. Winant was surprised that Churchill accepted such momentous news so readily, simply on what his butler had told him, without even bothering to contact either Downing Street or the Foreign Office. When Churchill returned, Winant asked: "Don't you think you'd better get confirmation first? You can't declare war on a radio announcement." Churchill shrugged off the suggestion.[23] Was that because he had already known what had happened?

Forty years later in a discussion with the historian John Toland, General Albert C. Wedemeyer was able to confirm the advanced knowledge of the Dutch concerning the Japanese attack. During a meeting in 1943, Vice Admiral Conrad E. L. Helfrich of the Royal Netherlands Navy had wondered aloud to Wedemeyer why the United States had been surprised at Pearl Harbor. Helfrich declared that his government had broken the code and knew when and where the Japanese were to strike their first blow against America. Wedemeyer recalled that Helfrich had been surprised that we did not know this—"and when I explained that I doubted seriously that this information was known in Washington prior to Pearl Harbor attack, Helfrich was skeptical because it was his clear recollection that his government had notified my government."[24]

These retrospectives accounted for two of the three nations involved in the purposeful economic boycott of Japan that drove the Nipponese to open hostilities. What about the third, the United States?

When Woodrow Wilson appointed Franklin Roosevelt assistant secretary of the Navy in 1913, he arrived in Washington at a time of rising tension between Japan and the United States. Six years earlier, President Theodore Roosevelt had kindled Japanese animosity by severely restricting Japanese immigration. In 1913, this policy was expanded by California legislation forbidding the sale or long-term lease of land to Japanese residents, including citizens. The Japanese government protested this overt racial discrimination. The jingoistic press quickly picked up the controversy and expanded it into an imminent threat of war. Secretary of State William Jennings Bryan refused to be stampeded, however, despite an attempt by a joint Army-Navy board to force mobilization of U.S. forces in the Pacific. Wilson sensibly disallowed such saber-rattling and forbade the board to meet again without his permission.[25]

A group of naval officers then took the lead in anti–Japanese confrontation and found an ally in Assistant Secretary of the Navy Roosevelt. He and his wife Eleanor were Delanos, and his grandfather, Warren Delano, had made his fortune in the "China Trade," a euphemism for opium smuggling. During World War II, columnist Westbrook Pegler accused FDR of hypocrisy for accusing others of benefiting from ill-gotten gains while ignoring the shady practices of his own grandfather, "whose riches derived from the degradation and wretchedness of the Chinese people.... Certainly with their special interest in the family history [the President and Mrs. Roosevelt] must have come upon the evidence long ago that they were living richly on the profits of a slave traffic as horrible and degrading as prostitution."[26]

It was a simple matter for the officers to draw Roosevelt onto their side. The young secretary was a disciple of U.S. Admiral Alfred Thayer Mahan, the loud voice of naval imperialism, and from him "not only received guidance in the use of the navy as an instrument of diplomacy, but also confirmation of his belief that Japan was one of America's major enemies."[27]

In the 1920s, out of public office, Roosevelt temporarily moderated his views on Japan. In 1923 he wrote a letter to the Baltimore *Sun*: "Japan and the United States have not a single valid reason, and won't have as far as we can look ahead, for fighting each other." That same year, writing privately, he said that to build new fortifications and large navies "will do harm not only to the governments immediately concerned, but to the general future peace of the world."[28]

By the time he took office as president in 1933, Roosevelt had reverted to his old Japan-baiting persona, launching the largest naval building program in U.S. history, obviously directed at Japan. As president-elect, he had announced that he supported nonrecognition of the Japanese puppet state of Manchukuo. He then picked as his Secretary of the Navy the aggressive navalist Claude A. Swanson, who at his first press conference declared his top priority was the expansion of the U.S. fleet as rapidly as possible to the upper limits of the London Treaty.

What were the underlying causes of Franklin Roosevelt's antipathy towards Japan? One historian has written critically that his "personal attitude toward Japan had no realistic basis in historical or economic knowledge. It was purely sentimental and mystical, founded primarily on the fact that some of his ancestors had made money trading with China and also on the fantastic stories about aggressive Japanese programs for the future which had been told to him by a 'Japanese schoolboy' who had been a fellow student at Harvard shortly after the turn of the century." As for Secretary of State Cordell Hull, he "was equally innocent of the history of the Far East — indeed, of most history of any kind — and his hostile attitude toward Japan was framed against the background of his pharisaical international idealism which bore little or no relationship to the actual history of public affairs and the relations between nations."[29]

America had been snooping on Japanese government radio wavelengths since the immediate post–Great War years. All nations, of course, eavesdrop on the encoded governmental and military radio communications of all other nations, allies or prospective enemies, in peace and imminent war, and work continuously to break newly introduced codes. During wartime, the stakes can be enormously high; knowing beforehand the enemy's order of battle, for example, can spell victory even for an outnumbered and outgunned army.[30]

By 1941, there were twenty-two U.S. radio intercepting stations in the Pacific, operating twenty-four hours a day, seven days a week. There were also four cryptographic stations that decoded the Japanese messages from the intercept stations; two of these were in Oahu — Station H and Station HYPO. One, Station CAST was on Corregidor Island outside Manila Bay in the Philippines; and the last, Station SAIL was near Seattle, Washington. These stations, staffed by the best of the Navy's cryptographers, tracked every diplomatic move of the Japanese government.[31]

The principal Japanese code system was known as *Purple* and transmitted messages involving the most sensitive diplomatic dispatches to and from the Japanese Foreign Ministry and its overseas ambassadors. In Berlin, Japanese ambassador Baron Hiroshi Oshima often met with Hitler and his lieutenants to discuss secret German strategy; Oshima, in turn, transmitted Hitler's secrets to Tokyo in *Purple*. FDR, for example, learned about Germany's plans for attacking the Soviet Union by means of a *Purple* intercept on June 14, 1941.[32]

"The most explosive controversy involving America's foreknowledge of Japan's attack on Pearl Harbor," Robert Stinnett has written, "involved the *Kaigun Ango* [Navy Code], a complex matrix of twenty-nine separate codes. To assemble and dispatch the First Air Fleet to Hawaii by radio, the Japanese Navy used four of these separate codes. By the fall of 1941, U.S. cryptographers had solved all four — as had the British, the Dutch, and Nationalist Chinese. "A sixty-year cover-up has hidden American and Allied success in obtaining the solutions of the *Kaigun Ango* prior to Pearl Harbor. American naval officers hid key code documents from congressional investigators. Naval intelligence records, deceptively altered, were placed in the US Navy's cryptology files to hide the cryptographic success."[33]

One of the two principal myths regarding the Pearl Harbor attack was that the Japanese task force heading to Hawaii was operating under radio silence. In fact, even before they had arrived at their assembly area, several ships transmitted movement messages that were readable by U.S. naval cryptographers in Washington. These movement signals "are substantiated by intercept records of Station H. None of the movement reports were shown to the 1945–1946 congressional investigation or to the one in 1995 [Senator Strom Thurmond's one-day hearing]."[34] Instead, Navy witnesses lied to the investigators, saying that radio intelligence had "lost" the First Air Fleet because of radio silence. The conspiracy was spread wide: Commander Edwin T. Layton, head of intelligence for Kimmel, smoothly stated in his congressional testimony that in the twenty-five days before the attack, "neither the Japanese carriers nor the carrier commanders were ever addressed or heard on Nippon radio frequencies."[35] His testimony was a blatant cover-up. The radio intercept reports had been logged in, but Layton chose not to pass along this vital information to his commander!

Navy radio monitoring stations other than Layton's Station H had intercepted the transmissions: Corregidor, Guam, Hawaii, and Dutch Harbor, Alaska. British cryptographers at Singapore and the Dutch in Java also recorded the same broadcasts. Vice Admiral Nagumo, aboard his flagship *Akagi*, "continually broke radio silence" as did Vice Admiral Gunichi Mikawa, commander of the battleships and cruisers, and Captain Kiichi Haegawa.[36] According to Stinnett, Americans never learned of the existence of these records—"all were excluded from the many investigations [ten] that took place from 1941 to 1946 and the congressional probe of 1995." The damning evidence he used as conclusive proof are two radio dispatches sent by Yamamoto to the First Air Fleet on November 25 while the thirty-one warships were still swinging at their anchors at Hitokappu Bay ... awaiting instructions to steam to Hawaii.

Japan's preparations for war took an ominous turn in July 1941. That was the month Roosevelt put into place the last of McCollum's action items, Action H — a strangling embargo that was intended to provoke strong counterstrokes by Japan. Intercepts of *Purple* code transmissions throughout the summer revealed Japan's reaction to FDR's tightening of the economic screws: 500,000 Japanese citizens were inducted into the armed services; Japanese merchant ships from all over the world were recalled to home waters; and Japanese warships and air squadrons were withdrawn from China. War clouds were gathering.

By October, Japanese fleet movements pointed to the imminence of an act of war. Corroborating evidence regarding Japanese plans for aggressive action came from Ambassador Joseph Grew in Tokyo, who had an informant inside the Imperial Palace. Grew reportedly had learned that on November 5, with Emperor Hirohito present, an Imperial Conference decided on war and Japan's military was given the go-ahead for the conquest of Southeast Asia. Specifically, Admiral Yamamoto was charged with smashing the Pacific Fleet in Pearl Harbor, thus clearing the way for the amphibious invasions of the Malay Peninsula, the capture of Singapore, the attack on the Philippines, and the capture of Guam, Wake and Midway Islands.

The Japanese, nevertheless, still sought a diplomatic solution and were working to negotiate a settlement in Washington up to the last day of peace. But FDR did not want an accommodation. He wanted a war.

At the end of November, Stark ordered Admiral Kimmel to deliver pursuit planes to Wake and Midway Islands, using the Pacific Fleet's two aircraft carriers. Stark rarely did anything on his own; he was FDR's mouthpiece, if not his sycophant. *The order to get the U.S. carriers out of Pearl Harbor and out of harm's way was almost certainly Franklin Roosevelt's.*

Early on the morning of November 28, the carrier USS *Enterprise*, under command of Rear Admiral William F. "Bull" Halsey, with its deck cargo of twelve Grumman F4F *Wildcats*, cleared the entrance to the harbor and its protecting minefield. Designated as Task Force 8 and escorted by eleven of the fleet's newest destroyers and cruisers, it set a course for Wake Island. Wake had become a vital stopover for B-17 bombers on their way from California to reinforce the Philippines, and the F4Fs were intended to strengthen the defenses of the tiny bastion. On December 5, USS *Lexington* as flagship of Task Force 12, commanded by Rear Admiral John H. Newton, departed Pearl for Midway Island with reinforcements of eighteen *Wildcats* tied down to its deck; it, too, was escorted by a screen of late-model warships.

The last intercept of a message from Yamamoto to the First Air Fleet was on December 2. It read: "Climb Niitakyama[37] 1208, repeat 1208." According to the historian James Rusbridger: "It hardly needed a code breaking genius to deduce that this was the date of the opening attack." This was the only radio message giving the date of the attack; previously, it had been mentioned only as Y-Day in the operational orders given to the First Air Fleet in Hitokappu Bay before it got underway.[38] Hitokappu Bay was an inlet on Etorofu Island in the Kurile Islands group, the rendezvous for the assembly of the 31 ships that formed the First Air Fleet: six aircraft carriers, two fast battleships, two heavy cruisers, one light cruiser, eleven destroyers, three type "I" submarines, and a supply train of six oil tankers.

Earlier, on November 25, a message from Yamamoto to his fleet was decrypted: "The task force will move out of Hitokappu Wan [Bay] on the morning of 26 November and advance to the standing-by position on the afternoon of 4 December and complete refueling."[39] For the first time, the decrypts showed the outline of the Task Force's mission. It was steaming out of the Kuriles to begin a long voyage that required refueling at sea in eight days. Its destination, while not stated, nevertheless could be deduced. The distances between Hitokappu Bay and the four likely targets were: Manila — 2,257 nautical miles; Java — 3,060 nautical miles; Pearl Harbor — 3,150 nautical miles; Singapore — 3,394 nautical miles.

Japanese aircraft carriers could steam at up to 34 knots for launching and recovering aircraft; to conserve fuel they normally cruised at about half that speed, covering about 400 nautical miles per 24-hour day. While the First Air Fleet might be heading south, possibly to link up with a landing force, it might also be shaping a course due east toward Pearl Harbor. Wake Island and Guam were unlikely targets because their military importance did not justify such a large battle fleet. Thus for those who could read the Japanese naval code, JN-25, the intercept messages told a straightforward story: a powerful Japanese fleet was at sea, almost certainly intending to commence hostilities, and one of its likely targets was Pearl Harbor.

While Admiral Isoruku Yamamoto had planned Operation Z meticulously, and the commander of every ship in the battle fleet had a 50-page set of operational orders, three instructions were missing: the date the fleet would assemble and depart Hitokappu Bay; the date for at-sea refueling; and the date of the attack itself.[40] The last two instructions could not be passed on until the diplomatic negotiations in Washington had been concluded one way or the other — war or (temporary) peace. They had to be transmitted by radio — and they were. This irrefutable fact in itself demolishes the fable of radio silence.

However, as late as 1979 the U.S. government continued to support the fiction of the First Air Fleet's radio silence and the supposed inability of the U.S. Navy to decode its messages. President Jimmy Carter authorized the National Security Agency that year to declassify a stack of Japanese intercepts. However, before they were sent to the National Archives, where they would be available to the public, all references to JN-25, were deleted. Furthermore, not a single decrypt was released *that had been read before December 7* [emphasis added], giving the undeniable impression that no Japanese naval messages had been decrypted before the attack. Stinnett insists that records of Station H indicate without doubt that Yamamoto sent thirteen radio messages between November 24 and 26. "All thirteen are missing," according to him, "from the intercept file of Japanese naval messages released to the National Archives by President Jimmy Carter in 1979."[41]

After Japan surrendered in August 1945, the Navy erected a tough roadblock for researchers. TOP SECRET was stamped on all the documents even remotely related to code breaking, and they were stored in safes. This meant, in particular, that the radio intercepts and subsequent decryption of Japanese messages during the critical eleven days between the *Kido Butai*'s departure from Hitokappu Bay on November 27 and its launching of aircraft on December 7 were effectively excluded from all of the ten Pearl Harbor investigations.

On December 7, 1941, in Hawaii, sitting on the ground, tightly bunched, were some 400 U.S. Army Air Forces, Navy, and Marine aircraft. Orders from Washington to General Walter C. Short had focused on the danger of sabotage which would coincide with a Japanese attack; guarding closely clustered planes was easier than if they were spread out. Fifty-eight of the USAAF's total of 230 aircraft were bombers, although thirty-three were obsolete Douglas B-18s. There were twelve modern B-17 *Flying Fortresses* and thirteen up-to-date Douglas A-20 *Havoc* twin-engine attack bombers. It would soon be learned that the B-17s, with their vaunted Norden bombsight's for high-altitude "precision" bombing, were totally useless against maneuvering ships and not much better against small stationary targets.[42]

Defending the skies over Pearl Harbor was an assortment of single-place pursuit planes, of both modern and obsolete designs, hangared at Hickam Field close to the naval base and at other fields nearby. The largest group of about 100 were nominally state-of-the-art Curtiss P-40 *Warhawks*, with speeds over 300 mph, but not particularly nimble. Forty were second-tier Curtiss P-36 *Hawks*, lacking in speed, altitude performance, and firepower. Finally, there were fourteen diminutive Boeing P-26s, the company's first monoplane design, with fixed landing gear and braced wings. In 1934, when the P-26s were introduced, they were considered "hot ships"; in 1941, they were hardly suited for combat. The balance were observation and utility aircraft whose performance was second to their reliability.

The most important U.S. Navy planes based in Hawaii were the Consolidated PBY *Catalinas*, big, slow twin-engine flying boats wonderfully suited to their mission of long-range reconnaissance. There were sixty-nine *Catalinas*, based at Kaneohe Naval Air Station on the east coast of Oahu. Also based at Kaneohe were a collection of forty utility and scout-observation planes, plus a fleet aircraft pool averaging twenty replacement carrier-based fighters and dive bombers.

Marine Air Group Two, based at Ewa Field, consisted of twenty-nine Douglas SBD *Dauntless* and Chance Vought SB2U *Vindicator* scout bombers, a fighter squadron of eleven Grumman F4F *Wildcats*, and a utility squadron consisting of eight aircraft. The *Dauntlesses* and the *Vindicators* were sound, workhorse airplanes, but easy prey for Japan's *Zeros*. The F4F *Wildcats* were also no match for the faster, more maneuverable *Zeros* and were replaced in 1943 by the more powerful F6F *Hellcats* which fought on equal terms with the *Zeros*. Another excellent fighter was the big and powerful gull-winged Chance Vought F4U *Corsair*, which came later to the Pacific and which was a favorite of the Marine Corps. There were also the fighter, bomber, and torpedo planes that were assigned to the *Lexington* and *Enterprise* carriers, both of which were based at Pearl Harbor. The third carrier assigned to the Pacific Fleet was the USS *Saratoga;* on December 7 it was in San Diego, undergoing routine maintenance.

In contrast to the mix of modern and obsolete U.S. aircraft, the Japanese First Air Fleet boasted 427 late-model aircraft aboard six fleet aircraft carriers plus catapult-launched floatplanes from their battleships and cruisers for reconnaissance. The carrier air groups consisted of 144 Nakajima B5N torpedo planes, 138 Aichi D3A dive bombers, and 138 Mitsubishi A6M Type 0 fighters, flown by the most experienced aviators in any navy.

The B5N *Kate* was the Japanese Navy's standard torpedo plane, having entered service in 1937. Armed with the world's best aerial torpedoes[43] it was a lethal threat to any ship afloat, and could also serve as a high-level bomber. The D3A *Val* was a sound, if slow, dive bomber with excellent stability, equivalent in most respects to the U.S. Navy's *Dauntless*. Its spatted, non-retractable landing gear belied its overall capabilities. The cream of the Japanese Imperial Navy's aircraft was the outstanding A6M *Zero* air-superiority fighter. Until its non-sealing fuel tanks proved obsolete in 1944, its exceptional speed, maneuverability, and range made it the most fearsome fighter in the Pacific.[44]

Launching point for the Pearl Harbor attackers was 200 miles north of Oahu. The pilots and aircrew were roused out of their bunks at 3:30 A.M., December 7, Hawaiian time; in Washington it was 9 A.M. The fourteenth part of the message directed to Japanese ambassador Nomura, containing Japan's final response to Cordell Hull's ultimatum,[45] had already reached Washington and been decoded. It read: "The Japanese government regrets to have to notify hereby the American government that in view of the attitude of the American government it cannot but consider that it is impossible to reach an agreement through further negotiation." That was about as unambiguous a declaration of war as could be couched in diplomatic argot. Another message accompanied it, instructing the Japanese Embassy to submit the entire fourteen-part reply to the State Department at exactly 1 P.M. that afternoon. No tea leaves were needed here either: Japan would strike at 1 P.M. Washington time.

The evening before, the cunning president had covered himself by sending an unprecedented last-minute cable to Emperor Hirohito. He appealed to the Emperor "for the sake of humanity ... to give thought in this definite emergency to the ways of dispelling the dark clouds ... to restore traditional amity and prevent further death and destruction in the world."[46] *It was a bluff.* The president received no reply, nor had he expected one.

At 5:30 A.M., while it was still dark, the heavy cruisers *Tone* and *Chikuma* catapulted off seaplanes to reconnoiter Pearl Harbor to ensure the Pacific Fleet was in the harbor. After a tense half-hour, without waiting for a confirmation, Vice Admiral Nagumo ordered the commanders of the six carriers to turn into the wind, make flank speed, and launch their aircraft. The engines of the planes on the flight decks had already been warmed up and they took off immediately: forty-three *Zeros* first, then 100 *Val* bombers for both high-level and dive bombing, and finally forty *Kate* torpedo planes. This launch sequence was mandated by the takeoff distance required for each plane; the lightest fighters, in forward positions, were flown off first; the last to go were the heavy torpedo-carrying planes whose pilots had the luxury of almost the entire flight deck for acceleration and safe liftoff. Only one plane was lost on takeoff. It took just forty-five minutes for the well-trained and enthusiastic ground crews to bring the second wave of planes up from the hangar decks, warm up their engines, and launch them: fifty-four high-level bombers and seventy-eight dive bombers.

By 7:00 A.M., as the sun was coming up, this great armada of 315 silver airplanes with black wings and red-circle insignia was spread across the clear skies in loose formation at four levels: torpedo bombers at 9,000 feet; high-level bombers at 10,000 feet; dive bombers at 11,000 feet; and at 14,000 feet, the *Zeros,* their pilots continuously swiveling their heads watching for signs of defending aircraft above and below, left and right.[47] There would be none.

On Hawaii, ground-to-air radar was a recent addition to the islands' defenses. The mobile station that searched the northern skies was located at the northernmost tip of Oahu on top of Opana Mountain, giving it unobstructed coverage of the northern quadrant, the most likely direction of an attack. It was normally in operation from 4 A.M. to 7:00 A.M., with a two-man crew. That fateful Sunday morning, the truck was late to take the two operators, Specialist Third-Class Joseph L. Lockhard and Private George E. Elliott, back to their barracks for breakfast, giving the men extra time to familiarize themselves with the new system. At 7:02, 140 miles out, Elliott picked up on the scope what appeared to be a large group of aircraft approaching from the northwest. Unsure of himself, he asked his partner to check it out. Lockhard concurred: it was "something completely out of the ordinary; probably more than 50"; the biggest flight he had ever picked up.[48]

From this point the fate of 2,326 people, the men-of-war of the Pacific Fleet and the Army's air fleet hinged on the judgment and decisions of three men — and on the inadequacies of military protocol.

Lockhard argued they should close down the station and get breakfast. Elliott, "hanging in," telephoned the Information Center on a direct line to report what he had observed. There was no answer. Elliott then used a portable cranked phone and reached the switchboard operator, who told him nobody was around. By this time, Elliott was not taking "no" for an answer and insisted the operator try to find somebody to help.

Lieutenant Kermit A. Tyler was still at the Information Center, the only officer on duty there, because at 7 A.M. all personnel except the switchboard operator and himself had left for breakfast. Tyler had no particular assignment, and later told investigators that he didn't know why he was there at all, as there was nothing for him to do "but twiddle his thumbs." The switchboard operator quickly located Tyler and he called back. Lockhard took the call and quickly summarized what was going on. Tyler was tired; he was on his second tour of duty. He had been told that a flight of twelve B-17s were due in from the mainland that morning. Assuming that the "large group" was, in fact, the B-17s, he told Lockhard to "forget it" and to shut down the station. Lockhard backed off; he had received an order from an officer and he had learned that third-class specialists do not go over officers' heads. Mesmerized by what they were seeing on the scope, the two enlisted men continued to watch the big air fleet as it headed into Oahu, losing the image behind the mountains 20 miles distant. They shut down the radar at 7:45 A.M. and trudged down the mountain to find their truck.

At 7:50 A.M. Commander Mitsuo Fuchida in the lead aircraft of the first wave radioed the flagship carrier *Akagi* the soon-to-be-infamous "Tora, Tora, Tora [Tiger, Tiger, Tiger]" code word that Pearl Harbor was undefended, surprise was complete, and the attack had begun precisely according to plan. Eighteen ships were sunk or seriously damaged, including eight battleships. All but the *Arizona*[49] and *Oklahoma*, among the battleships, were later repaired and saw action as island-bombardment vessels. A total of 188 planes were destroyed on the ground, 96 Army and 92 Navy. Of the 2,403 military personnel killed in the attack, 2,008 were Navy (nearly half killed on the *Arizona*), 218 Army, 109 Marines, and 698 civilians (most killed by "friendly fire").

Chiuchu Nagumo's fateful decision not to refuel and rearm his mostly intact air fleet[50] and immediately fly them off on a third and perhaps fourth wave attack on remaining targets in Pearl Harbor has been called by some observers Japan's second biggest strategic mistake after her first, which was to go to war with America. These "remaining targets," left intact, would prove to be of enormous significance in Pacific battles yet to come. There were three: the easily identified cluster of above-ground oil storage tanks at the corner of the Southeast Loch[51]; the submarine base with five submarines tied to shore bollards; and the port installations, including repair yards. Destruction of the oil-tank farms would have prevented U.S. carrier task forces from operating in the western Pacific for months to come. Sinking the submarines and more importantly razing their sophisticated support facilities would have put a severe crimp in the Navy's projected submarine blockade of the Japanese home islands.

There were two more targets that Nagumo let slip through his fingers: the two U.S. carriers in the vicinity that could have been located and picked off one at a time, along with their escorts. Early Sunday, Task Force 8 — *Enterprise*, three cruisers, and nine destroyers — was about 500 miles west of Hawaii, headed back to Pearl Harbor, having flown off its F4F fighters to Wake Island. In a high-seas battle, the First Air Fleet held all the aces: in addition to far greater numbers of aircraft, their *Zeros* would have overwhelmed the Navy's inferior *Wildcats*; their torpedo planes carried superior torpedoes; some of their 30 submarines would also have joined the battle. Moreover, the Japanese carriers had a one- or two-knot speed advantage over both the *Enterprise* and *Lexington,* allowing them the choice of avoiding or forcing action in the heat of combat.

Japan had committed the first overt act — and Franklin Roosevelt had his war. The "bait" this time had not been the little *Isabel* nor even the wooden schooner *Lanakai* with their tiny crews, nor the modern cruisers sent into the Bungo Straits. It was the U.S. Pacific Fleet. And the Japanese air strike would be acknowledged to be the greatest military and naval disaster in American history.

The next day, FDR delivered a speech before a joint session of the Congress asking for a resolution declaring that a state of war existed between the United States and Japan. He began his speech with words that all American schoolchildren remember. "Yesterday, December 7, 1941, a date that will live in *infamy*, the United States of America was suddenly and deliberately attacked...." Calling for a declaration of war, Roosevelt described the Japanese strike an "unprovoked and *dastardly* attack." One might wonder how many Americans knew then — and know today — what "infamy" meant and just what kind of attack a "dastardly" one was.

At the same time, Stimson spoke for his fellow cabinet members, observing that the Japanese "have solved the whole thing by attacking us directly in Hawaii." His initial reaction was "relief that the indecision was over and that a crisis had come in a way which unites all our people.... I feel that this country united has practically nothing to fear while the apathy and divisions stirred up by unpatriotic men have been hitherto very discouraging." Later he told his military aide, Major Eugene Harrison, that FDR could "never have gotten the country to war without Pearl Harbor."[52]

Two weeks previously, on November 25, Stimson had made an entry into his diary that is powerful evidence that Roosevelt and his closest advisers deliberately planned to provoke the Japanese into attacking Pearl Harbor. He described a noon meeting of the "war cabinet" which, besides Roosevelt and Stimson, consisted of Hull, Knox, Marshall, and Stark. "There the President ... brought up the event that we were likely to be attacked perhaps [as soon as] next Monday ... and the question was how we should *maneuver them into the position of firing the first shot* without allowing too much danger to ourselves. It was a difficult proposition" (emphasis added).[53]

In a 52-page chapter in his book entitled "Maneuvering the Japanese into Firing the First Shot,"[54] noted revisionist Charles A. Beard later inferred that the administration had purposely manipulated the Japanese into shooting first, but as a cautious historian could not say so explicitly. Beard also noted the findings of the Joint Congressional Committee: "In their Conclusions, the majority denied that 'the President, the Secretary of State, the

Secretary of War, or the Secretary of the Navy tricked, provoked, incited, cajoled, or coerced Japan into attacking this Nation in order that a declaration of war might be more easily obtained from the Congress.... They refrained from using in this sentence the word 'maneuvered.'"[55]

> No American will think it wrong of me if I proclaim that to have the United States on our side was to be the greatest joy.... England would live; Britain would live; the Commonwealth of Nations and the Empire would live. How long the war would last or in what fashion it would end no man could tell, nor did I at this moment care. Once again in our long island history we would emerge ... safe and victorious. We should not be wiped out.... Being saturated and satiated with emotion and sensation, I went to bed and slept the sleep of the saved and thankful.

So wrote the immutable warrior Winston Churchill on December 7, who had toiled so diligently to bring America into the war.[56] The next day at a war cabinet meeting, a minister suggested to him that Great Britain should continue its amiable approach to the United States. Churchill's response: "Oh, that is the way we talked to her while we were wooing her; now that she is in the harem, we talk to her quite differently."[57]

Two days after the Pearl Harbor attack, FDR delivered a radio address that is scarcely remembered, almost certainly for good cause. In it, he accused Hitler of a string of disreputable schemes that had influenced the Japanese to attack America. The speech was a skein of bold lies and vulgar exaggerations of historical fact, transparently intended to bait the Führer into declaring war. "We know that Germany and Japan are conducting their military and naval operations with a joint plan." "Germany and Italy consider themselves at war with the United States without even bothering about a formal declaration." Then came a wholly fabricated tale of intrigue: "Your government knows Germany has been telling Japan that if Japan would attack the United States, Japan would share the spoils when peace came. She was promised by Germany if she came in she would receive the control of the whole of the Pacific area and that means not only the Far East but all of the islands of the Pacific and also a stranglehold on the west coast of North and Central and South America."[58]

The facts were quite the opposite. Germany and Japan never had a common naval plan, the Germans being as shocked as nearly every American by the attack. Japan had never been interested in attacking the west coasts of North, Central, or South America; her goal was a new order in the Far East as defined by the Greater East Asian Co-Prosperity Sphere.

Foreign Minister Joachim von Ribbentrop was an early morning visitor to Hitler's Berlin headquarters that same day. He brought the news that General Hiroshi Oshima, Japanese ambassador to the Third Reich, was demanding an immediate declaration of war against the United States. Ribbentrop told the Führer that he did not believe that Germany was bound to do so, since the Triparte Pact obligated such action only in the event of a direct attack on Japan. Hitler's response was that he could not accept this loophole: "If we don't stand on the side of Japan, the pact is politically dead," Hitler responded. "But that is not the main reason. The chief reason is that the United States already is shooting at our ships. They have been a forceful factor in this war and through their actions have already created a situation of war."[59]

There were other arguments for Hitler's precipitate action: his move would be a useful propaganda tool for Goebbels, since a new, powerful ally would be a morale builder after the recent defeats of the Wehrmacht by the Soviet Union; and Japanese help would offset any disadvantages brought about by America's entry into the war. Furthermore, he could turn loose Admiral Doenitz's U-boat fleet off the east coast of the United States.

Ribbentrop, however, considered Hitler's fateful decision a gigantic mistake. He knew that it had solved one of Roosevelt's main domestic problems. The president would not have to issue a declaration of war on Germany, and generate a flood of opposition from the many Americans who had been opposed to U.S. entry into the war. Perhaps even more important, American's unity — gained by the attack on Pearl Harbor — would be solidified. Most historians would later agree with Ribbentrop, that next to Hitler's invasion of the Soviet Union, his unilateral declaration of war against the United States had been his greatest blunder.

On December 11, Hitler addressed an expectant Reichstag, declaring that Roosevelt was as "mad' as Woodrow Wilson. "First he incites war, then falsifies the causes, then odiously wraps himself in a cloak of Christian hypocrisy and slowly but surely leads mankind to war, not without calling God to witness the honesty of his attack.... I have therefore arranged for passports to be handed to the American *chargé d'affaires* today...." Wild cheering interrupted his speech. Hitler waited for quiet before he concluded — Germany was "at war with the United States, as from today."[60] Franklin Roosevelt finally had his war with Germany!

In the United States, the clean-up of incriminating evidence also began on December 11. Rear Admiral Leigh Noyes, the Navy's Director of Communications, told a gathering of his staff that day it was necessary to destroy "all notes or anything in writing" pertaining to the attack. Noyes' curt declaration had instituted the 54-year censorship strategy that relegated to Navy vaults all pre-Pearl Harbor diplomatic and military intercepts and directives. But Noyes had violated Navy protocol when he carelessly used the word "destroy." Memoranda written by Navy personnel in Navy offices relating to naval matters belong to the people of the United States; they cannot be destroyed except by authority of Congress.[61] Fleet Admiral Ernest King threatened not only loss of Navy and veteran's benefits to any intercept operator or cryptographer who disclosed that the U.S. had broken the Japanese naval code—but imprisonment as well. General George C. Marshall ordered his staff to put a lid on the affair, telling a group of his aides that "this goes to the grave with us."[62]

Franklin Roosevelt also had some cleaning up to do himself. Following America's entry into the war, a chorus of Congressional leaders from both parties loudly raised the question why the great naval base in the Pacific had been so unprepared. There were calls for a high-level investigation. The influential Senator Arthur Vandenberg, a Michigan Republican, recommended to the president that a special bipartisan Congressional Committee be convened to uncover the facts.

FDR, anxious to begin the massive cover-up required to hide his complicity, preempted the Congressional uproar. On December 8 he sent Navy Secretary Frank Knox to Pearl Harbor to assess damages and fix responsibilities—and to prepare a report "for his eyes only." Knox acknowledged that one of his objectives was to head off the "prospect of a nasty congressional investigation."[63] He was back in the United States three days later and the following day delivered his twenty-nine page report to FDR. This one-man investigation was the first of ten inquiries stretching as far into the future as 1995.[64] Knox's personal report was not what the president was looking for, but it made no difference: he had no intention of releasing it to the public.[65] While it did not make Admiral Kimmel and General Short obvious scapegoats to ease FDR and members of his administration out of the limelight, Knox did conclude that both commanders "would have to go." Roosevelt moved as swiftly as Knox. The next morning, the president called a meeting and ordered Stimson and Knox to hold press conferences that day and to cover "only the parts listed on a piece of paper he handed to Knox.... It was to be admitted that neither military nor naval forces had been prepared for the air attack, but that, once engaged, the defense was heroic."[66]

To the anxiously waiting newsmen in his office that afternoon, Knox related a graphic tale of gallantry under fire that he had cut out of whole cloth. He acknowledged what everyone already knew, that the Army and Navy had not been on the alert. This fact alone, he said, called for a formal investigation which would be empanelled immediately by the president. Knox then read off FDR's purposefully abbreviated list of ships lost: the battleship *Arizona*, the target hulk *Utah*, three destroyers, and an old minelayer. It hadn't been such a disaster after all for the Pacific Fleet—and the nation gave a collective sigh of relief.

Roosevelt was as good as Knox's word and that afternoon empowered Stimson and Knox to recommend two Army and two Navy members for his *own* board of inquiry, adroitly heading off the Congress for the time being. Above all, FDR was concerned about his own complicity in the attack and wanted no embarrassing facts disclosed. The next day, Roosevelt informed both Cabinet officers that he accepted their recommendations and told them he was appointing Supreme Court Associate Justice Owen J. Roberts to head the panel. Roberts had been a strong supporter of the pro-interventionist Committee to Aid America by Aiding the Allies and his newly acquired black robes, in the eyes of most Americans, distinguished him as a man of impeccable integrity. The Roberts Commission, as it was called, first met on December 17 and delivered its final report of 13,000 pages to the president on January 24, 1942. Predictably, the report scapegoated Admiral Kimmel and General Short: the attack was successful due to their errors of judgment and both were charged with dereliction of duty. The report nevertheless spread the blame broadly, concluding that the success of the attack "resulted largely from a sense of security due to the opinion prevalent in diplomatic, military, and naval circles, and in the public press, that any immediate attack by Japan would be in the Far East."[67]

Vice Admiral James O. Richardson, former Commander of the Pacific Fleet, who had been relieved of his command by the president because of his insistence that the fleet be based on the West Coast rather than at its vulnerable anchorage in Hawaii, begged to demur with the findings. It was an opportunity for him to strike at least a glancing retaliatory blow at FDR and he pulled out all the stops. "It is the most unfair, unjust and deceptively dishonest document ever printed by the Government Printing Office. I cannot conceive of honorable men serving on the commission without greatest regret and deepest feeling of shame."[68] Richardson went on, getting close to the truth: "...when the President realized the extent of the damage done by the attack ... he lost his nerve and his head, ordering the convening of the Roberts Commission, *believing that he could protect his own position by focusing public attention on Pearl Harbor*" (emphasis added).[69] Admiral William Standley, the highest ranking officer on the commission, later called Roberts' performance during the investigation "as crooked as a snake."[70]

Indicative of Justice Roberts' veracity was his dinner at the home of fellow Supreme Court Justice Felix Frankfurter on January 20, 1942. Stimson was also a guest. By any measure of jurisprudence, such a meeting was highly irregular. Stimson candidly recorded that the three of them "sat up until twelve o'clock talking over with Roberts the view he had formed on the general situation in Hawaii as distinguished from his decision which is not ready for announcement."[71] That midnight rendezvous was kept secret. It did not become public knowledge until Stimson's book, *On Active Service in Peace and War,* was published seven years later, when it no longer mattered.

Subsequently, there were eight more formal investigations of the Pearl Harbor attack by the Army and the Navy and by the Congress, the last in 1995, the most thorough being the Joint Congressional Investigation that began hearings on November 15, 1945, and lasted six months. The committee consisted of six Democrats and four Republicans. The principal surviving participants were called to give evidence. Henry Stimson, who had much to tell, had a heart attack the day it was announced that he would be summoned as a witness. Written questions were given to him; he answered only those he chose. Stimson recovered his health shortly after the hearings closed.

When the hearings got underway, involved Americans anticipated that they would learn details of the breaking of the Japanese code prior to the attack. They were wrong. While "witnesses introduced intercepts into evidence and read decrypted messages ... none of the details involving the interception, decoding, or dissemination of the pre-Pearl Harbor *naval messages* saw the light of day" (emphasis added). Only diplomatic messages from the *Purple* code were released. "It was a total sham."[72]

As might be anticipated, the committee's Democratic majority carried out its whitewashing mission by concluding that there was no evidence that the president or his administration had provoked the attack or knew it was coming. They attributed the disaster to the failure of both Hawaiian commanders to either conduct air reconnaissance or to maintain a high state of readiness. By contrast, the minority report of two Republican members of the committee censured the president for not taking "quick and instant executive action on Saturday night, December 6 and Sunday morning." They concluded that in addition to the two Pearl Harbor commanders, Stimson, Marshall, Knox and Stark were guilty of improperly discharging their duties.[73]

The Democrats on the panel had an overall strategy to protect their leader: they buried incriminating facts under a massive weight of testimony and evidence. There were eleven volumes of evidence; ten volumes of exhibits; seventeen volumes of hearings of the earlier investigations; one volume of the findings and opinions of the Roberts Commission, the Army Pearl Harbor Board, the Naval Court of Inquiry, and the Hewitt Inquiry. Lastly there was one volume covering the Report of the Joint Committee and the Minority Views of Senators Homer Ferguson and Owen Brewster. It was a massive, daunting cache of unorganized data that few would choose to unravel.

The administration rewarded loyalty and paid off those who, during the various hearings, testified in its behalf during the hearings, hid behind secrecy, or simply "failed to remember." General Marshall was made a permanent five-star general and was later moved up to the cabinet; committee chairman Senator Alben Barkley became vice president; Colonel W. Bedell Smith was made a three-star general and later appointed ambassador to the Soviet Union; Senator Scott Lucas became senate majority leader; majority member John W. Murphy and associate general counsel Samuel H. Kaufman got lifetime Federal judgeships.[74]

Historian John Toland has thoroughly studied the Pacific war in his three books: *But Not in Shame: The Six Months After Pearl Harbor*, 1961; *The Rising Sun: The Decline and Fall of the Japanese Empire, 1936–1945*, 1970; and *Infamy: Pearl Harbor and Its Aftermath*, 1982. He concluded his analyses in *Infamy* of the immediate events prior to the attack by focusing on what he called "an extraordinary train of happenings" in Washington on Sunday morning, December 7, that "only make sense if it was a charade, and Roosevelt and the inner circle had known about the attack."[75]

At 10 A.M., the president's naval aide delivered to him the just-decoded and translated Japanese response to Hull's ultimatum, including the 14th part. Roosevelt, still in bed, remarked, "It looks like the Japanese are going to break off negotiations." According to his aide, FDR didn't seem "perturbed." Amazingly, Roosevelt then calmly went about his Sunday morning routine, which included a visit to Admiral Ross McIntire's on-premises office for treatment of his sinus condition.[76]

Slightly earlier, there were several curious events. Stimson had forgone his regular Sunday morning horseback ride with his aide, Major Harrison, and arrived at his office about 9:30. Stark was already in his office and had finished reading the 14-part message. General Marshall's office had received not only the 14-part message, but a second one instructing Ambassador Nomura to deliver the entire message to Hull at 1 P.M. At about 10:45, rejecting the idea from his subordinates that he personally alert the Philippine and Hawaiian commands, Stark phoned the president instead. Told that Roosevelt was busy, Stark hung up — and did nothing!

The normally punctual Chief of Staff George Marshall finally arrived at his office just before 11. After reading the decoded messages, he immediately filed a warning message of his own to the Hawaiian and Philippine commands, but it took almost another hour — until about 11:45 — before the message was sent on its way. The fastest way was by telephone with a scrambler, but he chose not to use the phone; he later defended this decision by saying he feared an eavesdropper might also have a descrambler. Instead, the momentous warning was sent by Western Union. It arrived in Hawaii after the Japanese planes had returned to their carriers.

Pearl Harbor continues to be a symbol of Japanese perfidy and despite the passage of more than six decades, the nature of the aerial assault, a "sneak attack," still resonates powerfully in the nation's psyche. The plethora of books on World War II — "the good war" conducted by "the greatest generation" — continue to belch forth tired old clichés of good versus evil. And television, where nearly all Americans get nearly all their information, routinely and ignorantly stamps Pearl Harbor in unmistakable patriotic colors. Uncle Sam is portrayed as a manly boxer who had gone down for a nine-count after a sneaky rabbit punch, but pushes himself up, shakes off the cobwebs, and then heroically wins with a knock-out.

What about Franklin D. Roosevelt's complicity? Could the commander-in-chief of America's Army and the Navy he was purported to love have been the architect and engineer of the disaster at Pearl Harbor and thus of America's involvement in World War II? The evidence of his guilt appears overwhelming. As a young boy: "His special love was for boats.... He was fond of pictures and accounts of vessels, particularly war vessels. His mother tells how he listened with awe to conversations of naval men when he was a youth on visits to England."[77] As an adult, he retained his earlier fascination with men-of-war: "He is above all a lover of naval arms. He is one of those men whose mind and imagination are fascinated by battleships and guns. He is also one — as frequently happens in these lovers of arms— who is disposed to be somewhat truculent in his notion of the uses of these arms."[78]

Like Americans in general, the president believed that Japanese sailors and their ships were third-rate. Pearl Harbor, in his view, could absorb a "hit" from the Japanese and shrug it off. His apparent shock when he learned of the attack was not because of the attack *per se*, but because of the extent of the destruction wrought. The penny toys sold in Woolworth with "made in Japan" labels were considered representative of that country's laggard technology and manufacturing capability. One fable making the rounds of official Washington in 1941 was that Japanese warships with their tall, pagoda-like superstructures would capsize during sharp maneuvers. The Japanese air force, too, was considered inferior, their planes no match for the Americans'; they were supposedly copiers, hence their planes, ships, and guns would always be obsolete. Moreover, Japanese pilots were alleged to be unable to see in the dark and, like all their race, had genetic defects in the inner ear affecting their balance and their capabilities as airmen.

Toland has concluded that it was a war that "need never have been fought." After so many years, his counterfactual scenario rings true: "Imagine if there had been no war in the East. There would have been no Hiroshima and perhaps no threat of nuclear warfare. Nor would it have been necessary for America to have fought a grueling, unpopular war in Korea and a far more tragic one in Vietnam...."[79]

On May 25, 1999 the Senate voted 52 to 47 to clear the names of Husband E. Kimmel and Walter C. Short. "There is no longer any reason to perpetuate the cruel myth that Kimmel and Short were singularly responsible for the disaster at Pearl Harbor," said Senator William V. Roth, Jr., Republican of Delaware, "who has led the struggle to clear the names of the two officers and restore their wartime ranks."[80]

7

FDR's Tomfoolery: Unconditional Surrender

"*Gagged by this idiotic slogan, the Western Allies could offer no terms, however severe. Conversely, their enemy could ask for none, however submissive. So it came about that, like Samson, Hitler was left to pull the edifice of Europe down upon himself, his people and their enemies.*"[1]

"*World historical tomfoolery of the first order.*"
Josef Goebbels, Nazi Minister of
Public Enlightenment and Propaganda,[2]
referring to FDR's unconditional surrender edict

"*It is difficult to recognize a single desirable war or peace objective that was advanced by the Casablanca slogan.*"[3]

"*Unwilling to endure a larger-scale Okinawa, the American generals made plans to clear the caves and tunnels [of Kyushu] with chemical weapons — something that has gone nearly unreported for half a century.*"[4]

"*Based on a detailed investigation of all the facts, and supported by the testimony of the surviving Japanese leaders involved, it is the Survey's opinion that certainly prior to 31st December, 1945, and in all probability prior to 1st November, 1945, Japan would have surrendered even if the atomic bomb had not been dropped, even if Russia had not entered the war, and even if no invasion had been planned or contemplated.*"[5]

"*At the very moment the United States was destroying the apparatus of censorship and repression of the Japanese imperial state, dismantling the giant zaibatsu firms that it pinpointed as the economic roots of fascism, and proclaiming its commitment to democratic and constitutional rule, the occupation authorities, under the direction of General Douglas MacArthur, implemented secret mechanisms of censorship. U.S. censors set out to mold Japanese public opinion, to shield the United States from public criticism, and to preserve a U.S. monopoly on information pertaining to the effects of the atomic bomb on its victims.*"[6]

> "Unconditional surrender prolonged the war by nearly two years; led to colossal and needless losses in lives, money, property, historic monuments, and art treasures; helped to put Russia in a dominant position in the Old World; disrupted the economic life of Central Europe; and cost the United States in excess of twenty-five billion dollars in the effort to restore the damaged areas."[7]

On January 9, 1943, President Roosevelt and an entourage of Army, Navy, and Air Force commanders boarded a train in Washington to take them to Florida, where they transferred to planes for a long flight to Casablanca, Morocco, in North Africa. The trip was Top Secret. Waiting for them there was Prime Minister Winston Churchill with an even larger contingent of British military policy-makers. The Conference was code-named SYMBOL. There Roosevelt concocted a controversial slogan — unconditional surrender — that lengthened the war, needlessly killed tens of thousands of soldiers, sailors, and airmen on both sides, and resulted in the destruction of some of the greatest cities of the world, along with their civilian populations.

The two leaders and their advisors wrangled for two weeks over such weighty issues as the priorities of the war in Europe versus the war in the Pacific; how to defeat the German U-boat threat in the Atlantic; ways and means of expanding the strategic air war over Germany; how to resolve the conflict between rival Free French generals Charles de Gaulle and Henri Giraud, both of whom had been invited to the sessions; and the coordination of joint operations in the Mediterranean area. The most contentious subject of all dealt with the planned U.S./British amphibious landings on the coasts of Hitler's *Festung Europa*, the second front Josef Stalin had been demanding for months.

U.S. Army Chief of Staff General George C. Marshall had been so angered by the British rejection of the American proposal for an invasion of France across the English Channel later in 1943, he had threatened to shift U.S. forces in England to the Pacific. He, like all his fellow officers, looked upon the Mediterranean area as a sideshow that would drain troops and equipment from the principal effort, which was the amphibious landings in France. Hard-bitten Admiral Ernest King, the navy chief, also a supporter of an early cross-Channel invasion, was even more antagonistic toward the British, especially after they told him that green U.S. troops in training in the UK were far from ready to confront the Wehrmacht.[8] Among the lower ranks, there was general hostility toward the manipulative way Churchill had sweet-talked Roosevelt into another year of joint warfare in the Mediterranean, a region of little strategic important to the United States, but of immense significance to the crumbling British Empire. Through the

Mediterranean ran the Empire's lifeline, the short sea route to the Dominions east of the Suez Canal and to the Persian Gulf's oilfields.

Nevertheless, there was grudging agreement on three fundamental concepts: the European axis of Germany and Italy was the Allies' most dangerous foe and must be defeated first; the U-boat war in the Atlantic was the most important immediate battlefield and the shortage of convoy escort ships and merchantmen were critical needs; and some sort of second front would have to be opened in 1943 to show "good faith" to the Soviets who were desperately battling the Wehrmacht. This second front would be a joint Anglo-American invasion of the big Italian island of Sicily off the toe of the peninsula. Plans for this operation were roughed out by the British, code-named HUSKY, and a D-day set for July 25 during "the favorable July moon" since the amphibious landings would be at night. As a sop to the Americans, the British agreed to name General Dwight D. Eisenhower supreme commander with British General Harold Alexander his deputy.

While the Sicilian operation was envisioned as an end in itself by the Americans, and not as a stepping-stone for the invasion of Italy proper, Winston Churchill thought otherwise, and was quietly looking ahead. A prompt HUSKY success, in the prime minister's view, would lead inexorably to an attack on what he called the "soft underbelly" of the Axis. During the Great War, as First Lord of the Admiralty Churchill had supervised the 1915 British assault on Gallipoli, an earlier "soft underbelly." Gallipoli had been a disastrous failure: "With the possible exception of the Crimean War, the Gallipoli expedition was the most poorly mounted and ineptly controlled operation in modern British military history."[9] Churchill's second "underbelly" "proved to be boned with the Apennines, plated with the hard scales of Kesselring's armor, and shadowed by the wings of the Luftwaffe."[10] It would not be a second Gallipoli, but came very close!

At the conclusion of the conference at noon on January 24, reporters and photographers, who had been purposely flown in from Algiers, finally had an opportunity to hear from, photograph, and question the two leaders on the results of the historic meeting. A jauntily attired and broadly smiling FDR had been wheeled out earlier, and seated next to Churchill in front of the newsmen, many of whom sprawled informally on the grass. Standing behind were the senior commanders of both nations. The president announced first that the United States and Great Britain had reached total accord on the future conduct of the war and that any disagreements had been ironed out to everyone's satisfaction. That was a brazen lie. While the two leaders themselves apparently had argued amiably, their staffs had been at loggerheads on most of the issues. In fact, much of the conference had been devoted to the resolution of the disagreements. Concessions and compromise had been the order of the day. Indeed, the negotiations at Casablanca were the most contentious ever to occur between the Western Allies.

After answering the correspondents' questions, Roosevelt loosed his bolt from the blue. Almost offhandedly, he announced that he and the prime minister "were determined to accept nothing less than the unconditional surrender of Germany, Japan, and Italy." That, he explained, did not imply the destruction of the people of those nations but rather the destruction of their "philosophies of fear and hate." Reportedly, Churchill agreed by audibly muttering "hear, hear!"[11] The just-concluded conference, Roosevelt went on enthusiastically, should be called "the unconditional surrender meeting," neglecting to tell his attentive audience that during the two weeks' of meetings, not once had he brought the subject up for discussion.

British Air Marshal Sir John Slessor who was at the conference, wrote after the war that he did not recall a discussion of unconditional surrender at any of the sessions, and "as far as I remember the use of the words in the President's address to the Press Conference ... made no particular impact on our minds at the time.... It is difficult to believe that any subsequent explanations putting its meaning in a less unpalatable form, had any effect in countering its value to Goebbels in stiffening German resistance — to which was added ... the preposterous Morgenthau plan for the deindustrialization of Germany."[12] But FDR in his conniving style, chose to present it to the world as an agreed-upon *fait accompli,* which it was not. The communiqué of the meeting did not mention unconditional surrender.[13]

Lord Hankey, who was also part of the British delegation in Casablanca, was more critical. He wrote in 1950 that "the communiqué itself was a bit thin — not very substantial pablum for press-men who had come so far and were in a state of high expectancy. The work of the Conference had been of major military importance ... and not much could be said about the plans to the press even 'off the record.' Unconditional Surrender, therefore, provided a useful make-weight to the colourless communiqué. Yet — what a lot of trouble, and how many human lives, how much destruction and what misery would have been saved ... if it had never been accepted as a worthy war aim."[14] Hankey also did some homework when he got back to England: "English history appears to record no case of a demand for 'Unconditional Surrender' before 1943!" He examined fifteen major wars since the end of the sixteenth century "to support this statement. Nearly all our major wars in Europe involved continental nations as well ... and, in accordance with the usual practice these wars were brought to an end by the conclusion of a Peace Treaty."[15] Hankey then reviewed the impact of Roosevelt's edict on Germany and Japan, writing that "it was not surprising that the Germans held out to the last possible moment. They intended to hold out longer still behind the mountain barriers of Bavaria, Austria, and North Italy ... the object of this desperate expedient was to try and secure better terms than Unconditional Surrender ... Fortunately the General [Eisenhower] foiled this plan but the episode shows the desperation to which the phrase had driven our principal enemy." As for Japan, she held out "with equal, if not greater tenacity.... In these circumstances, to secure Unconditional Surrender without excessive prolongation of the war" the allies decided at Potsdam to use the atomic bomb.[16]

In an effusive mood, FDR then proceeded to give his attentive audience an erroneous American history lesson. He described Confederate General Robert E. Lee's conference with Union General Ulysses S. "Unconditional Surrender" Grant at Appomattox Court House in 1865. According to FDR, Grant kept insisting on unconditional surrender of Lee's army while Lee beseeched him for rations for his starving troops. Finally Lee accepted Grant's surrender terms. Grant then sent Union army rations through the lines and magnanimously allowed Confederate officers to keep their horses for plowing. In fact, Grant had come by his nickname three years earlier when he had laid siege to Fort Donelson. When the Confederate commander sought to negotiate a withdrawal, Grant refused, insisting his terms were unconditional surrender, demands that were not unusual for a military commander besieging a fortress or a city. This inaccurate history lesson, which no one in the press corps dared correct, was repeated by FDR whenever he could button-hole any unsuspecting listener and "demonstrated the dangers of a gentleman's C, FDR's usual grade at Harvard."[17]

U.S. military officers who posed with their British counterparts during the picture-taking ceremonies were vehement in their criticisms of the president's words, but later and out of earshot of the commander-in-chief. General Eisenhower, for example, considered that unconditional surrender would achieve nothing but lost American lives. In February 1945 he gave his homespun views on the military impact of FDR's credo: "If you were given two choices—one to mount the scaffold and the other to charge twenty bayonets, you might as well charge twenty bayonets."[18]

General Albert C. Wedemeyer, who had spent two years in Berlin at the German War College in the 1930s and knew many of the Wehrmacht's generals personally, was an even more intense critic. He felt strongly that the new slogan would "unquestionably compel the Germans to fight to the very last." Then, presciently: "This worried me, for I was confidant that there were many people in Germany—more than we were permitted to realize because of anti–German as distinct from anti–Nazi propaganda—who wanted to get rid of Hitler. Our demand for unconditional surrender would only weld all of the Germans together." To buttress his point, Wedemeyer quoted Sun-Tzu, the ancient Chinese strategist: "Soldiers when in desperate straits lose the sense of fear. If there is no place of refuge, they will stand firm."[19] He concluded that a combination of errors in strategic planning by the Allies and unconditional surrender "certainly lengthened the war by a full year."[20]

General Ira Eaker, commander of the USAAF's Eighth Air Force, was also standing in the back row during the post-conference photo session. He had flown into Casablanca to fend off the Royal Air Force in its on-going attempts to coerce the Americans into discarding their hallowed daylight "precision bombing" doctrine and join the British in their indiscriminate nighttime bombardment of German cities. He recalled that when he returned to England to tell his staff about unconditional surrender, they all mocked the term, agreeing that once announced to the Germans, they would fight to the bitter end. "There wasn't a man who was actually fighting the war who I ever met who didn't think this was about as stupid an operation as you could find."[21]

In Berlin, Josef Goebbels was delighted when he learned of Roosevelt's pronouncement; it was splendid grist for his propaganda mill. He told his staff: "I should never have been able to think up so rousing a slogan. If our Western enemies tell us, we won't deal with you, our only aim is to destroy you ... how can any German, whether he likes it or not, do anything but fight on with all his strength?"[22] While it is difficult to assess the overall impact of Goebbels' propaganda efforts in sustaining the morale of German civilians, he undoubtedly helped convince the population to continue what they were doing so well: digging themselves out of the wreckage of their homes from the incessant Allied bombing raids and at the same time skillfully performing their jobs without respite. In 1944, when Hitler named him Reich Plenipotentiary for a Total War Deployment, the versatile Goebbels showed his mettle as a hands-on leader. "This remarkable man was the dynamo in a National Socialist machine that was beginning to show signs of collapse: visiting bombed-out areas, spurring the *Gauleiters* on to more effective forms of local relief, introducing at long last a sixty-hour working week, rounding up idlers and making them help with the clearing of rubble, the building of new shelters ... and exhorting and bullying the public in dozens of speeches and articles."[23] As late as 1944, German production had been reduced only by 14 percent and armaments by less than 7 percent.[24]

Elsewhere in the German capital, Admiral Wilhelm Canaris, the head of the Abwehr, remarked cogently to one of his deputies: "...the students of history will not need to trouble their heads after this war, as they did after the last, to determine who was guilty of starting it. The case is, however, different when we consider guilt for prolonging the war. I believe that the other side have now disarmed us of the last weapon with which we could have ended it. Unconditional surrender, no, our generals will not swallow that. Now I cannot see any solution."[25]

FDR later, defensively, claimed that the unconditional surrender term had just "popped into his mind." He recalled that he had been busy rounding up all those he wanted to attend the news conference and as a result was less than fully prepared. That was deceitful nonsense. The lap notes that he had dictated beforehand contained essentially identical phrases about the new policy. Buttressing this interpretation, Harry Hopkins wrote in his description of the conference that the president consulted notes as he talked. Photographs show him holding his lap notes. Among the notes: "The President and the Prime Minister, after a complete survey of the world war situation, are more than ever determined that peace can come to the world only by a total elimination of German and Japanese war power. This involves the simple formula of placing the objective of the war in terms of an unconditional surrender by Germany, Italy and Japan."[26] Unconditional surrender would turn out to be anything but a simple formula and these "two words were to hang like a putrefying albatross around the necks of America and Britain,"[27] in the portentous view of a noted chronicler of the war.

Roosevelt had confided to his son Elliott, who was with him in Casablanca, that as a bonus, unconditional surrender would certainly appeal to Marshal Stalin, that "Uncle Joe might have made it up himself." To the contrary, Stalin's coldly rejected it; unlike FDR and Churchill, he was unwilling to increase the burden on his troops by strengthening German resistance. Until the last months of the war, when Stalin relented and allowed the phrase to be included in the Yalta Declaration, his generals refused to abide by the slogan.

In propaganda messages to the German people, he was careful to reassure them that victory by the Red Army would not mean their destruction. For example after the great Soviet triumph at Stalingrad, one month after Casablanca, Stalin declared: "Occasionally the foreign press engages in prattle to the effect that the Red Army's aim is to exterminate the German people.... This is a stupid lie and a senseless slander against the Red Army.... It would be ridiculous to identify Hitler's clique with the German people and the German state. History shows that Hitlers come and go, but the German people and the German state remains."[28] Stalin successfully enlisted many of these high-ranking prisoners-of-war in a National Committee of Free Germans to address radio appeals to their former *Kamerads* to end the war. Thus, while FDR was blindly insisting that "the United Nations would never negotiate an armistice with the Nazi Government, the German High

Command, or any other group or individual in Germany," Stalin was pursuing the sensible policy of trying to divide the German people from their Nazi rulers—and, more importantly, separating German soldiers from their government.

In a hate-mongering speech before the House of Commons on September 21, 1943, Churchill picked up the thread of unconditional surrender. At first charging that Prussia was the source of "the pestilence" and that "Nazi tyranny and Prussian militarism are the two main elements in German life which must be absolutely destroyed," Churchill accused the German people of "twice within our lifetime, and three times counting that of our fathers, of plunging the world into their wars of expansion and aggression. They combine in the most deadly manner the qualities of the warrior and the slave. They do not value freedom themselves, and the spectacle of it in others is hateful to them."[29] This was no-holds-barred wartime propaganda and absurd to boot: that an inherently warlike Prusso-German spirit—a genetic trait, perhaps, from Churchill's bigoted perspective?—was responsible for starting the two previous European wars (the Franco-Prussian war of 1870–1871 and the Great War of 1914–1918) as well as the current conflict.[30] Like FDR's defiant Casablanca pronouncement, the prime minister's speech demanded that only one war aim was acceptable to the Allies: total defeat of the enemy.

The U.S. State Department under Cordell Hull had always been treated cavalierly by Franklin Roosevelt. He rarely consulted Hull and minimized his role in important foreign policy negotiations. The State Department was Roosevelt's, not his Secretary of State's. Hull first learned about FDR's pronouncement of unconditional surrender from the newspapers and was aghast. But there was little he could do about it. In his *Memoirs* he gave two rational reasons for his opposition to unconditional surrender. Blandly, he wrote "that it might prolong the war by solidifying Axis resistance into one of desperation.... The second reason was that the principle logically required the victor nations to be ready to take over every phase of the national and local Governments of the conquered countries, and to operate all governmental activities and properties. We and our Allies were in no way prepared to undertake this vast obligation."[31]

The first application of the Casablanca formula was Italy's signing of an armistice with the Allies in September 1943. It proved to be a confused business. A far more messy operation would follow on its heels as the Allies moved up the peninsula. Napoleon had described Italy as a boot. "You must, like Hannibal, enter it from the top." The Allies came in through the toe.

Earlier in the summer, the Allies had invaded and occupied Sicily. The Germans under the leadership of Field Marshal Albert Kesselring, a Luftwaffe officer who was comfortable as a ground-war tactician, skillfully withdrew his entire army and its 10,000 wheeled vehicles across the Straits of Messina, the three-and-a-half-mile wide waterway between the island and the toe of Italy. "In a foretaste of what was to come in Italy [for the invading Allied armies], clever use of the mountainous terrain enabled some 60,000 German troops to hold off 450,000 Allied soldiers for thirty-eight days."[32] Remnants of the Italian army also made good their retreat back to the mainland.

Before pursuing Kesselring's forces and the Italian army across the Straits, the Allies paused for three weeks to reorganize and refit. In the meantime, they mounted a propaganda offensive to soften up the Italian army, and to destroy civilian confidence in Benito Mussolini's tottering government. In radio addresses, Roosevelt and Churchill declared sternly that Italy's only hope of survival lay in "honorable capitulation to the overwhelming power of the military forces of the United Nations." The wording of the ultimatum was a round-about way of saying that Italy would not have to surrender unconditionally, at the same time revealing Churchill's growing disenchantment with the Casablanca formula.

Earlier in July, the Fascist Grand Council deposed and imprisoned Mussolini, and named Marshal Pietro Badoglio prime minister. Badoglio, 72, had a long and distinguished military and diplomatic career. He had been Chief of the General Staff at the end of the Great War, governor of Libya, and commander of the Italian forces that invaded Ethiopia. He was opposed to Italy's entry into World War II on the side of Germany, and had resigned in protest.

Two days later, Eisenhower broadcast a second radio appeal to the Italian people, this time offering them a chance to surrender if they stopped supporting the Germans and returned all Allied prisoners-of-war. He did not mention unconditional surrender. The next day, stubbornly, Roosevelt went on the air to muddy the waters and undo whatever good Eisenhower might have done. He declared that Allied surrender terms for Italy remained the same as those for Germany and Japan: unconditional surrender. Hopes for an orderly surrender with little bloodshed had vanished.

On September 3, the new Badoglio government signed a secret armistice with the Allies. Its terms were straightforward: immediate cessation of hostilities, return of all prisoners-of-war, transfer of all Italian aircraft and shipping, and the demobilization and disarmament of the country. There was still no reference to unconditional surrender. Secretary of State Hull wrote later that it was rather, "a negotiated surrender, and the terms of the armistice was agreed to in discussions in Lisbon, Portugal, between representatives of the Anglo-American Combined Chiefs of Staff and Marshall Badoglio."[33] By then, Kesselring had declared martial law and was going full bore to defend Italy. He moved heavy concentrations of elite Wehrmacht troops onto the peninsula and put his best engineering battalions to work with the Todt Organization, the builders of the impregnable U-boat pens in France, to construct stout defensive lines integrated with the natural barriers of the Apennines. This mountain range, with one peak as high as 9,500 feet, runs south from the area of Genoa to the foot of the boot.

Then on September 20, the Allies presented a revised version of the armistice agreement to Badoglio titled "The Unconditional Surrender of Italy." It stunned the new premier, who protested that his plenipotentiary had never signed an agreement with those words, which he insisted were humiliating to Italians. He felt strongly that the Allies had deceived him. The words stayed in to the immediate detriment of the Allies. Whatever initial enthusiasm had been generated at the signing of the armistice disappeared, playing into the hands of the German defenders. Kesselring disarmed the Italian troops, making them into bona fide neutrals, and sent them home as civilians.

The end of 1943 brought eventual defeat to Germany a certainty for those in position to know the facts and who chose to discard their rose-colored glasses. USAAF P-51 *Mustang* fighters, with their new Packard-built *Merlin* engines, were escorting bombers in deep penetrations of Germany all the way to the targets and back, returning air superiority to the Allies. Around-the-clock bombing of German cities had become a reality. In the Atlantic, U-boats were harried from the air by long-range B-24s and depth-charged to destruction by growing swarms of U.S. and Royal Navy destroyers. The Mediterranean was again open to Allied shipping. The Wehrmacht during the year had lost over one million men, dead or taken prisoner. Military and civilian wounded overflowed German hospitals. The killing went on.

Instead of reaching Rome in a few weeks as had been initially projected, the Allies were forced to fight for every foot of Italy, in the mud and then the freezing cold of winter against the Germans who held the high ground. While the Allies had far more armored vehicles and artillery, the battlefield was effectively leveled by the mountainous terrain and the cruel weather, with heavy rain day after day. The almost continuous battles were close-quarter combat, fought with grenades and bayonets, harking back to the slaughter in the trenches of the Great War. Hitler had demanded that the Gustav Line, the name given to the cross-peninsula defensive redoubts, be constructed to "fortress strength." The meticulously planned and constructed defensive system, employed interlaced trenches, concrete bunkers, interconnected minefields, and barbed wire that took advantage of the terrain. Concealed sniper locations guarded approaches and camouflaged self-propelled guns and dug-in tanks were emplaced on the high ground. The accurate, fast-firing 88 mm cannon seemed to be everywhere, and was the best artillery piece of the war, with its flat trajectory and unmistakable *whoomp*. Every small village became a well-defended strongpoint that took its toll in U.S. and British casualties. The Germans seemingly booby-trapped everything in the path of the attackers, from downed trees that had to be cleared, to battle-damaged Wehrmacht vehicles that beckoned to souvenir-hunting GIs.

The anchor to the line was the Casino Massif, atop which sat the medieval abbey. The battle to capture Cassino was later called the "bitterest and bloodiest of the Western Allies' struggles against the Wehrmacht on any front of the Second World War." In January, Hitler sent a rousing directive to Kesselring's troops: "All officers and men ... must be penetrated by a fanatical will to end this battle victoriously, and never to relax until the last enemy soldier had been destroyed." Reflecting the Casablanca edict: "The battle must be fought in a spirit of holy hatred for an enemy who is *conducting a pitiless war of extermination against the German people*" (emphasis added).[34]

The Allied landings at Anzio at the end of January were confined to a narrow beachhead for four months before breakout, a zone that became an infamous killing field. Rome was 30 miles to the north and was declared an "open city" by Albert Kesselring, rightfully concerned about the Eternal City's treasures. U.S. Army jeeps entered Rome unopposed on June 4. General Mark Clark's Fifth Army had spent 275 days fighting its way there since landing at Salerno in early September. Enroute the Fifth Army had suffered 125,000 casualties, with 12,000 GIs killed and a sobering casualty rate of 41 percent.[35] Airpower "was applied in its crudest form as a great, blunt, inaccurate and invariably counter-productive instrument of war largely waged against civilians." Over 8,000 USAAF aircraft were lost between September 1943 and May 1945 in Italy[36] about the same number of heavy bombers, their fighter escorts, and fighter-bombers as were shot down over Germany in only a slightly longer period.

It had been a war of attrition and left Italy devastated. British General J. F. C. Fuller treated the Italian campaign contemptuously: "This foolishness [unconditional surrender] ... trapped the British and American forces into tactically the most absurd and strategically the most senseless campaign of the whole war. Unconditional surrender transformed the [Churchill's] "soft underbelly" into a crocodile's back; prolonged the war; wrecked Italy; and wasted thousands of American and British lives.... It was the first taste of the bitter fruit of unconditional surrender."[37]

Had the Allied armies in Italy contributed proportionately to their losses to the eventual defeat of Germany? The traditional positive argument is that the Allies had successfully tied down Wehrmacht divisions which might have been otherwise deployed in France to counter the invading troops coming ashore in Normandy on June 6. Another objective was the building of airfields in Italy for the bombing of Germany by the newly constituted Fifteenth Air Force. That mission had been accomplished, too. On November 1, General Jimmy Doolittle of Tokyo bombing fame took command of the Fifteenth. By then nearly 50 airfields had been completed, many with paved or steel-plank runways, some over a mile long to handle take-offs of heavily loaded B-17s and B-24s. Six months later, Doolittle's Fifteenth had an operational strength of 1,200 heavy bombers.[38]

At the end of July 1944, Allied forces broke through German defenses at Avranches. There was an open plain ahead and Paris was within easy reach. Field Marshal Guenther von Kluge, removed from command, killed himself, leaving behind a stern letter to his Führer. "Make up your mind to end the war. The German people have borne such untold suffering that it is time to put an end to this frightfulness. There must be ways to attain this end, and above all, to prevent the Reich from falling under the Bolshevist heel."[39] Other German generals also used the Avranches breakout as cause for despair. Adolf Hitler, the acknowledged dictator of Germany, did not budge; neither would Franklin Roosevelt, the freely elected sole decision-maker of America! The killing and destruction continued apace.

In late 1944, the Allies' unconditional surrender formula coupled with threats to the very structure of Germany by the Morgenthau Plan (Appendix L) ensured that the Germans would fight ferociously, if not to the last man, as the Japanese with their Bushido Code were doing on Pacific islands. In November, the Wehrmacht decisively defeated U.S. forces driving toward the Rhine River. On December 21, German troops, clad in white to blend in with the snow-covered terrain, stunned complacent American commanders by smashing through the Ardennes forest with 250,000 men and 1,000 tanks, in a bold attempt to recapture Antwerp and cut off Allied supplies. What became known as the Battle of the Bulge would be the costliest engagement of the war for the American army, resulting in a staggering 80,000 casualties. "Ringing well as a slogan of unlimited defiance, it [unconditional surrender] yet closed the door upon any negotiated peace; hence it induced in all German minds the despairing fury of the cornered rat."[40] Historian Fuller suggested that "in a sane war" such a military catastrophe "would have brought hostilities to an immediate end; but because of unconditional surrender the war was far from being sane."[41]

And the slaughter went on, well beyond the point at which Germany was a defeated nation. The German generals knew when the war was lost, as they would acknowledge in postwar interrogations. Had Roosevelt been willing to compromise his *Diktat*, peace might have concluded much earlier, with enormous savings in lives. But the commander-in-chief of U.S. military forces remained obdurate.

On August 5, following the Normandy amphibious landings, Allied Supreme Headquarters reported that total Allied casualties from June 1 to July 20 were 115,665. America's share of the carnage included 11,026 killed, 52,669 wounded and 5,832 missing.[42]

Postwar, ex-generals of the Third Reich willingly shared their views of the significance of the Allied edict of unconditional surrender on the duration and intensity of the war. British historian Basil H. Liddell Hart interviewed many of them and found agreement "on the futility of having pursued the war beyond the summer of 1944, and certainly beyond the failure of the Ardennes offensive."[43] "All to whom I talked dwelt on the effect of the Allies' 'unconditional surrender' policy in prolonging the war. They told me that but for this they and their troops ... would have been ready to surrender sooner, separately or collectively. But the Allied propaganda never said anything positive about the peace conditions in the way of encouraging them to give up the struggle. Its silence on the subject was so marked that it tended to confirm what Nazi propaganda told them as to the dire fate in store for them if they surrendered."[44]

Liddell Hart himself felt that unconditional surrender was an "expensive" phrase that "sounded so simple and neat" yet "proved a source of worse complications than it was intended to avoid." He believed that it prolonged the war "far beyond its likely end," just as the generals he interviewed told him, and realigned the European balance of power with Russia on top. Field Marshal Albert Kesselring remarked that he had been too busy with his operations on the Italian front to have been able to discuss the Casablanca pronouncement with his fellow officers at the time, but he believed the demand would prolong the war. His view on what would have "constituted a reasonable settlement included the end of the Nazi government, restoration of prewar boundaries, and German payment of reparations to restore war damage and to help revive the European economy."[45] Remarkably, these terms nearly matched those of *Die Schwarze Kapelle* (Chapter 8). Field Marshal Erich von Manstein said that the Allied demand "naturally lengthened the war. This was the surest means to weld the Germans to the Hitler regime." General Hasso von Manteuffel considered it a major mistake on the part of the Allies, "a boomerang which resulted in sacrifices of life ... which were entirely unnecessary because Germany had conclusively lost the war with the breakthrough at Avaranches in July 1944." He related that frontline soldiers had "only begun to fight after they learned of the demand for unconditional surrender."[46]

Field Marshal Erwin Rommel's detailed reaction to unconditional surrender can only be guessed at, since he died before the end of the war, but from his notes of a meeting with Hitler in May 1943 it appears that he knew the war was lost. Rommel had outlined a gloomy scenario to the Führer. "Hitler listened to it all with downcast eyes," Rommel wrote. "Suddenly he looked up and said he, too, was aware that there was very little chance of winning the war. But the West would conclude no peace with him.... He had never wanted war with the West. But now the West would have their war — have it to the end.[47] Just before he took a poison pill to avoid Gestapo torture for his ties to Schwarze Kapelle, which were tenuous at best, he told his young son: "The enemy in the east is so terrible that every other consideration has to give way before it."[48]

Panzer General Heinz Guderian was perhaps the most outspoken in his personal denunciation of FDR and FDR's policy. He maintained that condescending United States policy toward the Soviets was ruinous. Roosevelt underestimated and misunderstood Stalin and Bolshevism. Russia was not "another form of democracy" as the Americans originally believed, but a total dictatorship, according to Guderian. "Not to have realized this was the greatest mistake of Roosevelt." After the Casablanca conference, he stated, the Germans knew they could expect no generosity from the Western Allies. He described Roosevelt as "the gravedigger not only of Germany but also of Europe."[49]

Grand Admiral Karl Doenitz, commander of the *Kriegsmarine*'s submarine fleet, who was named "president of the Reich" and his legal successor by Hitler on April 30 just before Hitler's suicide in May 1945, wrote in his *Memoirs* that by the summer of 1943 he had considered Germany's military situation hopeless. He kept his pessimism to himself, he wrote: "My conviction that the attitude adopted by our opponents precluded the possibility of any peace by negotiation...."[50] Later on, after the Teheran Conference, Doenitz declared that "in the event of our submitting we should have no rights whatever, but would be wholly at the mercy of our enemies...." As to what that meant, "some idea can be gathered from Stalin's demand at the Teheran Conference for four million Germans to serve as forced labor in the USSR.[51] Grossadmiral Erich Raeder, in his retrospective, stated that what he knew of the aims of the "Beck-Goerdeler" group, a.k.a. Die Schwarze Kapelle, to replace a bad government, was meritorious but unworkable because of Allied insistence on unconditional surrender.[52]

In June 1944, Pope Pius XII cautioned FDR through Myron Taylor, his Vatican envoy, "that the temple of peace would stand and endure only if established on the foundation of Christian charity, not alloyed with vindictive passion or any elements of hatred." He told Taylor that he deemed the demand for unconditional surrender to be "incompatible with Christian doctrine."[53]

At a press conference in Hawaii on July 29, 1944, a reporter asked FDR if unconditional surrender also applied to Japan in the Pacific. Roosevelt, without hesitation, answered in the affirmative and then proceeded to chastise those who were critical of his policy. In the last year of the war in the Pacific, according to the postwar United States Strategic Bombing Survey, among the urban populations of Japan, belief in eventual victory had declined precipitously, from nearly unanimous to less than fifty percent.[54] In this same period, a factional struggle had begun among the Emperor's chief advisers. The two most influential were the military and the naval, the military insisting on fighting the war to the bitter end and the naval inclined toward a negotiated settlement. With the loss of Saipan in July 1944, the naval clique forced the retirement of General Hideki Tojo, premier and leader of the recalcitrants. His successor was General Koiso, who was replaced by General Teiichi Suzuki after the Americans landed on Okinawa on April 1, 1945. Suzuki planned to end the war. He believed the way to do this was to ask the Soviet Union, not yet in the war, to intercede as a neutral mediator.[55] "This clutching at a straw must have made clear to the Western Allies the catastrophic position Japan had reached, if only because the price Russia would demand for mediation could not possibly be less than the abandonment of all her conquests.... Nothing short of this would have satisfied the Russians, who had not forgotten the events of 1904–1905."[56]

In Washington on June 18, Stimson and his Assistant Secretary, John J. McCloy, were preparing for an important meeting with the Joint Chiefs and the president to decide whether to tighten an already choking blockade and bomb even Japan's smaller cities into rubble — or whether to land troops on the main islands. McCloy was opposed to both plans. He and former ambassador Joseph C. Grew, who had been discussing the issue for some weeks, agreed that Japan should be offered an honorable surrender. At the meeting, in addition to Stimson and McCloy, were President Harry Truman, his chief of Staff, Admiral William D. Leahy, and two of the Joint Chiefs—King and Marshall. Air Force General Arnold, recovering from a heart attack, was represented by Lt. General Ira C. Eaker. The president went around the table asking for opinions. Marshall insisted it was necessary to invade; while losses would be heavy, air power alone would not do the job. Eaker confirmed Marshall's judgment, stating that bombing had not been able to defeat the Germans. Admiral King nodded his assent, as did Stimson. The president turned to Leahy. Candid as always, he forcefully denounced FDR's Casablanca edict. "I do not agree with those who say that unless we obtain the unconditional surrender of the Japanese that we will have lost the war. I feel no menace from Japan in the foreseeable future, even if we are unsuccessful in forcing unconditional surrender. What I do fear is that our insistence on unconditional surrender will only result in making the Japanese more desperate and increase our casualty lists. I don't think this is at all necessary."[57] But Leahy was a minority of one and he was overridden six to one.

The Japanese named the defense of their home islands *ketsu-go*, or decisive operation. "Its aim, the strategists revealed to American interrogators after the war, was not to achieve total victory, but to inflict heavy casualties on the invaders.... Eventually, it was hoped, the Americans would mitigate their demand that Japan surrender unconditionally."[58] Far more than with Germany or Italy, unconditional surrender to the proud Japanese struck at the epicenter of their culture and civilization. On July 13, a message was intercepted from Foreign Minister Shigenori Togo to Ambassador Naotake Sato in Moscow requesting Sato to give the following message to Molotov: "His Majesty the Emperor, mindful of the fact that the present war daily brings greater evil and sacrifice upon the peoples of all belligerent powers, desires from his heart that it may be quickly terminated. But so long as England and the United States insist upon unconditional surrender the Japanese Empire has no alternative but to fight on with all its strength for the honor and the existence of the motherland."[59] The next day another message was intercepted from Togo to Sato that noted that "unconditional surrender is the only obstacle to peace."[60] In fact, unconditional surrender would continue as the only barrier to peace between the United States and Japan *even beyond* the nuclear destruction of Hiroshima and Nagasaki.

An ominous sidebar to the scheduled invasion of the main islands of Japan were U.S. plans for a gigantic preemptive poison gas attack to accompany the invasion.[61] Army planners had selected fifty urban targets that were "especially suitable for gas attacks," including the great cities of Tokyo, Osaka, Yokohama, Kobe, and Kyoto. The first assault, on the southernmost Japanese home island of Kyushu, was code-named Operation OLYMPIC, and was set for November 1, 1945. The gas attack would be launched fifteen days before the amphibious landings. B-29s from bases in the Marianas and new ones on nearby Okinawa plus navy fighter-bombers from aircraft carriers would drench targets in early morning raids with an estimated 54,000 tons of phosgene gas, mustard gas, and hydrogen cyanide. It was estimated that the gas attacks "might easily kill five million people and injure many more." On June 18, 1945, President Truman met with his chief military and civilian advisers to discuss the gas attacks. "Apparently the ... plan was approved at that conference." Three days later orders were given to step up production of a variety of poison gases to provide stockpiles in the massive quantities required.[62]

Until this first planned use of poison gas, it had been the long-established policy that chemical and biological agents would never be used by American forces except in retaliation for a chemical-biological attack (Appendix K). This policy was based on a 1943 speech by President Roosevelt in which he declared "categorically that we shall under no circumstances resort to the use of such weapons unless they are first used by our enemies." By then Franklin Roosevelt was dead. Even if he had still been alive, pressure from his generals and admirals likely would have gotten him to change his mind, for FDR had always shown he was willing to sacrifice principals for political gain; his creative propagandists could have come up with one convincing pretext or another to justify gas use. Further, Germany had surrendered, and Japan's chemical warfare capabilities, whatever they might have been, had been materially reduced by heavy B-29 bombing. Without threat of retaliation, the use of gas had become irresistible. Chemical warfare tests showed that certain poison gases were ideal against tunneled-in defenders; these gases, when pumped into cave openings as liquids, would pool, then quickly evaporate and expand to achieve concentrations sufficient to kill even soldiers with masks.[63]

Following the nuclear destruction of Nagasaki on August 9, Japanese leaders struggled over the issue of accepting the Potsdam Declaration (Appendix M) and surrendering unconditionally. The Soviet Union had declared war on Japan on August 8; as promised, three months after Germany's surrender, Red Army troops were storming through Manchuria and Korea. Okinawa had fallen. The U.S. Navy blockade of the home islands was impenetrable. A captured B-29 pilot reportedly had told the Japanese that a third nuclear bomb would be dropped on August 12. How many more would the Americans rain down on Japanese cities?

Finally, Emperor Hirohito intervened and through Prime Minister Kantaro Suzuki announced that Japan would accede to the demands of the Potsdam Declaration but with one condition, that the Emperor would remain as a sovereign ruler. This was not the "unconditional surrender" that had been the ongoing impediment to peace negotiations since the amphibious landings on Italy. Secretary of State James Byrnes, who had replaced the ailing Cordell Hull, stubbornly insisted that the American electorate would harshly repudiate the president if he accepted the offer. But other key advisers, namely Stimson,[64] newly appointed Secretary of the Navy James Forrestal, and Leahy, prevailed on President Harry Truman to end the war.

Overruling his chief cabinet officer, Truman directed Byrnes to issue a formal statement accepting the Japanese offer of peace. Byrnes was intransigent to the last, adding an addendum that required Hirohito to sign the surrender papers, which he did not do. On August 15, the Japanese government accepted the Potsdam Declaration and the war was over.

What stubbornly remain are two contentious questions: was it necessary for the United States to have dropped two nuclear weapons on Japan and why a cloak of secrecy thrown over the devastation to the two cities and their populations? In 1952, Truman and Eisenhower planned a joint statement describing the enormous destructive power of the new generation of thermonuclear bombs and the dangers of an arms race—"but the idea was abandoned for fear that this might incite panic.... What has been lost sight of is the role Hiroshima concealment has played in encouraging subsequent American cover-ups.... Surely Hiroshima was the mother of all cover-ups ... creating patterns of concealment that have been applied to all of American life that followed. Secrecy has been linked with national security—and vice versa—ever since."[65]

8

FDR Ignores Die Schwarze Kapelle

"...Roosevelt and his planners still preferred to employ American might. And here lay ... the tragedy of the war, for the entire military, industrial and intellectual might of the Anglo-Saxon world was being committed to end a government and an ideology when a single pistol shot might have achieved just that."[1]

"D-Day was one of the greatest political blunders of all time. If Great Britain and the United States had uttered a single word publicly of encouragement to the conspirators then Montgomery and Eisenhower would have walked ashore, and Rommel would have been there to salute them.... Only fools could have failed to perceive that the real enemy was Russia and that one day the western powers would need a strong and democratic Germany to act as a counterweight to Bolshevism."[2]

"The American attitude toward the conspiracy had set fast, and it would not change. The Third Reich was to be destroyed by a direct confrontation in battle; there was no room for political settlements of any sort."[3]

"Stories of a resistance movement did not fit into the concept of unconditional surrender. My belief that President Roosevelt was determined to establish the guilt of the entire German people, and not only the Nazi regime, for bringing on World War II had already received confirmation in the summer of 1942."[4]

"I swear by God this holy oath that I will render unconditional obedience to the Führer of the German Reich and people, Supreme Commander of the German Armed Force, Adolf Hitler, and that as a brave soldier I will be prepared at all times to give my life for this oath."[5]
  Oath of Allegiance by the German Officer Corps.

One of the principal myths that flourished during World War II and persisted well beyond the end of it, due to the Roosevelt administration's dedicated cover-up and ceaseless anti–German propaganda, was that no significant internal opposition to Adolf Hitler ever existed. "And the way in which the inescapable evidence of a counter-movement leading up to the attempt on Hitler's life was interpreted was in exact conformity with these views. Opposition only began, it was believed, when, confronted with defeat, the 'Prussian generals' attempted to save their own lives—and preserve the General Staff for a third world war."[6]

Had the war in Europe ended in January 1945, following the Wehrmacht's abortive Ardennes offensive, 222,360 fewer U.S. casualties would have resulted. Had it ended in July 1944, following the Allied breakout at Avranches, there would have been 582,586 fewer U.S. casualties; in January 1944, 700,749 fewer casualties; in July 1943, 740,000 fewer U.S. casualties; and in January 1943 after the German defeat at Stalingrad, when many of Germany's leading generals concluded that the war was irrevocably lost, over 760,000.[7]

July 20, 1944, was a hot summer's day in Rastenburg, East Prussia, where Hitler kept his headquarters, Wolfschanze (Wolf's Lair). Colonel Claus von Stauffenberg had taken a morning courier flight from Berlin to meet with Adolf Hitler to report on the progress of the recent formation of two new divisions from older home-guard reservists (Landwehr). These new divisions were being staffed with younger and more experienced officers in an attempt to stall the advance of the Red Army into Poland and East Prussia. Hitler had ordered the reorganization earlier in the month and was anxious to learn its status. Stauffenberg was planning not only to brief his Führer but to assassinate him.

When Stauffenberg arrived at the Wolfschanze he was surprised to learn that his meeting, instead of being held in Hitler's underground reinforced-concrete bunker, had been moved above ground to a small hut of wood-plank construction with a bulletproof outer layer. All the windows were open. Those two factors would sharply reduce the effectiveness of his explosives.

His first job was to arm his two bombs, inert lumps of plastic explosives, two kilograms (2.2 pounds) each. It was ticklish work even for someone with two eyes and ten fingers. Stauffenberg had neither: he had one eye, one arm, and only three fingers on his remaining left hand. Two years before, his staff car had been strafed by an Allied fighter plane in North Africa and he had been grievously wounded. Wehrmacht doctors patched him up the best they could and after rehabilitation released him for active duty. He had regained his strength and even learned how to put on his uniform with three fingers. He also resumed his role as one of the ringleaders of Die Schwarze Kapelle, the name the Gestapo assigned to this secret anti–Nazi organization.

An ingenious part of his apparatus was the noiseless time-delay fuse,[8] a cylindrical assembly much like a fat pencil. It used a thin-wall metal tube filled with cotton wadding, through which ran a thin wire that held back a spring. When the wire was severed, the spring was released and a pointed-nose firing pin would travel forward to strike and ignite the detonator, in turn exploding the bomb. A highly corrosive acid was enclosed in a separate glass capsule abutting the cotton-filled tube. When the fuse was crushed, the acid capsule broke, saturating the cotton with acid and burning through the retaining wire. The diameter of the retaining wire determined the approximate time delay.

Stauffenberg had selected 30-minute-delay fuses which he calculated would give him sufficient time to place his bomb-filled briefcase close to Hitler, deliver his brief status report, then leave promptly. If he was delayed, he planned to leave the room, excusing himself to use the washroom. That apparently would not have been a problem; in those conferences, Stauffenberg knew that officers were always coming and going.

Just before he went into the briefing hut, Stauffenberg carefully removed the fuses from the priming charges and crushed them with a pair of pliers specially adapted for his three-fingered hand. Pieces of the unusual tool were discovered later in the wreckage of the briefing hut, certain evidence that one-handed Stuffenberg had been the assassin. Then he looked through a tiny inspection port to determine that the spring with the striker was still compressed, removed a safety pin, and gently re-inserted the fuses into the primer charges. He silently marked the time. Because the weather was warm, the chemical reaction would be speeded up. A 30-minute time delay could become 20 minutes, and Stauffenberg knew it.

For some reason, unexplained to this day, he took only one armed bomb into the conference room. "No one knows for certain why Stauffenberg did not place the second bomb in his briefcase alongside the one whose timer had already been activated, *since the explosion of one would surely have set off the other as well*, whether armed or not" (emphasis added).[9] It was a momentous mistake that changed history.

The conference room had a large, heavy-legged rectangular table in the middle. General Wilhelm Keitel introduced Stauffenberg to Hitler who shook hands with him. General Walter Warlimont remembered the scene: "The classic image of the warrior through all of history. I barely knew him, but as he stood there, one eye covered by a black patch, a maimed arm in an empty uniform sleeve, standing tall and straight, looking directly at Hitler ... he was ... a proud figure, the very image of the General Staff officer—the German General Staff Officer—of that time."[10] Stauffenberg was then helped to a seat next to Hitler.

Stauffenberg put his briefcase on the floor and pushed it under the table as close to Hitler's legs as he could before it bumped into one of the table's thick supports. After a few minutes, he decided not to wait for Hitler to beckon to him for his briefing, and he left the room quickly. Stauffenberg did not know that after he left, Hitler had gotten up from the table to address a large wall-mounted map some distance from the table.

Stauffenberg was on his way, together with his adjutant, to pick up their car when they heard a powerful explosion from the direction of the briefing hut. The time of the explosion coincided closely to the pre-set fuse setting. One of Stauffenberg's co-conspirators testified later that he and Stauffenberg had observed a person covered with the Führer's cloak being carried out of the demolished hut and presumed it was Hitler. "Stauffenberg was certainly convinced of it."[11] The two then drove to the airfield and boarded their Heinkel He-111 for the return flight to Berlin.

Of the twenty-four people in the conference room when the bomb went off, four died of their wounds. Hitler had been only slightly bruised, although his trousers were in tatters. He had burns on both thighs, the hair on his legs was singed, and both of his eardrums were pierced. "The experts were later unanimous that in a true bunker the amount of explosives brought into the conference room by Stauffenberg would have killed everybody...."[12]

That night, Stauffenberg and three fellow conspirators were rounded up. Following an impromptu court martial, they were condemned to death. The four were led into a courtyard, placed one after the other in front of a sand pile alongside the building, and shot by a firing squad of ten noncommissioned officers of the Guard Battalion. Just before he was shot, Stauffenberg shouted: "Long live holy Germany!"[13] The bodies were buried with their uniforms and decorations in a cemetery in Schoneberg. The next day, Heinrich Himmler ordered the bodies exhumed and cremated. Their ashes were then scattered.

The same night, Hitler addressed his nation by radio. He had not done so for several months, for he had no good news to report from the military fronts: the Allies had landed in Normandy the month before, Rome had been liberated, and the Red Army had just recaptured Minsk. "I am addressing you for two reasons," he declared. "First, so that you shall hear my voice and know that I personally am unhurt and well; and second, so that you shall hear the details about a crime that has no equal in German history." Hitler then described the crime. "An extremely small clique of ambitious, unscrupulous, and at the same time foolish, criminally stupid officers hatched a plot to remove me and, together with me, virtually to exterminate the staff of the German High Command. The bomb that was placed by Colonel Count von Stauffenberg exploded two meters away from me on my right side. It wounded very seriously a number of my dear collaborators. One of them has died. I personally am entirely unhurt apart from negligible grazes, bruises or burns." As for retribution, the criminal elements "will now be exterminated mercilessly ... we will settle accounts in such a manner as we National Socialists are wont." The Führer concluded that the outcome of the plot was "a clear sign of Providence that I am to carry on with my work."[14]

The next day Hitler briefed the heads of the newly appointed board of inquiry, which soon numbered four hundred people, and set guidelines for the judicial proceedings. He again denounced the conspirators: "The basest creatures that ever wore the soldier's tunic ... This time I will fix them. There will be no honorable bullet for these criminals, they will hang like common traitors. We will have a court of honor to expel them from the service; then they can be tried as civilians.... The sentences will be carried out within two hours. They must hang at once, without any show of mercy."[15]

Following the failure of the July 20 plot, all significant internal resistance to Hitler and his regime ended. The known military conspirators were made to stand before judges of the People's Court "clutching at their trousers, in crumpled and dirty civilian clothes, deprived of their belts, braces, ties, even their false teeth, lest they try by suicide to thwart the executioner." Nearly all were sentenced to death by hanging; in the case of German officers, the sentence was the ultimate disgrace. The hangings went quickly. A hemp loop was placed around the victim's neck, he was lifted off the ground by the executioners, an upper loop of the rope was hung on a large hook similar to a butcher's meat-hook, and the condemned man was dropped.[16] Wives and children were also taken into custody, the women to await death by malnutrition, the children parceled out to *SS* families and given new names.

In the weeks following, a tidal wave of arrests swept over Germany, engulfing not only the men who were connected with the revolutionary attempt — but also hundreds whom the Gestapo considered might be dangerous in the future. Authoritative estimates hold that upwards of 7,000 people were arrested. Of these, some were arbitrarily executed, either by firing squad or hanging. Others, those who were thought to be helpful in identifying their compatriots, were gruesomely tortured to extract information, and then hanged, sometimes with narrow-gauge wire which slowly strangled the victims. Others were indicted and then tried by the People's Courts before being executed. After the war, German documents revealed that 4,980 people were executed in Germany in the weeks following the assassination attempt.[17]

The next morning Washington buzzed with the news from Germany. Asked by reporters whether he knew anything about the coup, FDR denied any foreknowledge of the incident and simply reaffirmed the Allied insistence on unconditional surrender. More than that he would not say. It was then and would remain so into the immediate postwar years, official U.S. policy—originating in the White House—to deny the existence of an anti–Nazi resistance movement inside Germany. Not only was the German resistance ignored, the U.S. actively worked to censor information from any source dealing with the subject. Churchill, too, dismissed the anti–Hitler plot out-of-hand. He suggested in his remarks to the House of Commons that high-ranking Nazis were murdering each other, and what else could one expect from a criminal regime? After the war Churchill admitted that he had been "misled" about the nature and size of those involved in the conspiracy. In the Soviet Union there was no comment from any important political figures, but on July 23 a press spokesman caustically announced that the fate of Germany would be decided on the field of battle. "Hitlerite Germany will be driven to her knees not by insurgent officers, but by ourselves and our Allies.... Our troops move faster than the consciences of the Fritzies."[18]

Two weeks later, Hitler declared to a gathering of party leaders that since July 20 he had "gained a confidence" he had never had before and said that he would now be able to "carry on the struggle" better than anyone else who might lead the German people. He pledged a fight to the finish: ""I believe that I am necessary to the nation, that it needs a man who will under no circumstances capitulate."[19]

The great *New York Times*, never a "court newspaper," but during Roosevelt's wartime years sometimes acting like one and nearly always a staunch supporter of FDR's often-misguided foreign policy initiatives, also had its say. On August 9, with two weeks to contemplate its response, weighed in with a long lead editorial, HITLER HANGS HIS GENERALS. It credited the German officers' corps with a tradition "based on the fundamental military virtues of discipline, honor and patriotism.... And because as a body, and according to its lights, it held these virtues high, it was able to command the respect of the German people, including those who opposed it. But Nazism had changed all that ... the details of the plot suggest more the atmosphere of a gangster's lurid underworld than the normal atmosphere one would expect within an officers' corps and a civilized Government." In fact, the plotters had attempted the assassination of "the head of the German state and Commander in Chief of its army by means of a bomb, the typical weapon of the underworld." The editorial added an interesting twist—that one of the reasons propaganda minister Goebbels revealed details of the plot, including the "show trials" of the conspirators, was to establish a second "stab-in-the-back" legend to absolve the ruling regime from responsibility. "After the last war it was the generals who accused the home front ... of stabbing the army in the back and losing the war. Now the Nazis are using the same trick against the generals to save themselves."

Newsman Louis P. Lochner, former head of the Berlin office of the Associated Press, experienced first-hand Roosevelt's pigheaded attitude concerning the German underground. In November 1941, Lochner had been invited to sit in on a meeting of the Schwarze Kapelle. There he met the group's leaders, learned about their ideals and goals, and was impressed by their sensible views. They asked him to talk to FDR and find out what kind of anti–Nazi government would be acceptable to the United States. As an incentive they gave him the radio code of two groups opposed to Hitler so that Roosevelt could be in touch with them directly.[20] When Lochner returned to America in June 1942, he attempted, unsuccessfully, to get a hearing through the president's appointments secretary. Finally he resorted to a personal note revealing the existence of the codes and emphasizing they were for Roosevelt alone. There was no immediate reply but after several days he was told that the subject was "most embarrassing" and requesting him to attend to other matters. What Lochner didn't know then, but would learn later, was that Roosevelt's refusal to see him was official U.S. policy in keeping with unconditional surrender—formulated "not only to withhold encouragement to German resisters but to avoid any important contact. Recognition of the existence of any anti–Hitler movement within Germany was forbidden."[21]

Two years later, Lochner experienced first hand Roosevelt's censorship policies while in Paris. He had learned that a group of anti–Nazi Germans living in Paris actively maintained contact with their fellow conspirators in Germany, and that there was a constant coming and going of agents. Lochner considered it a fine news story and wrote it up. When he tried to wire it to the United States, his report was censored, in total. He met with the chief censor at SHAEF, wondering how his article was considered a violation of U.S. or Allied security. He was told there was a special regulation—"a personal one from the president of the United States in his capacity as Commander-in-Chief, forbidding mention of any German resistance movement."[22]

Roosevelt's policy of enforced silence was effective, if the paucity of references to the anti–Nazi movement in the memoirs of U.S. diplomats and military figures is a sufficient measure. After the war, radio stations in the American Zone of Occupation inside Germany were prohibited from mentioning that there ever was a Schwarze Kapelle or even hinting that on July

20, 1944 a bomb had been placed close to Hitler's feet by a patriotic German officer.

There had been earlier attempts on Hitler's life. In 1929, a disgruntled SS guard planted a remote-controlled bomb under the speaker's podium before a speech in the *Sportspalast* in Munich. The bomber apparently had an urge to go to the toilet and by a curious happenstance, someone had locked him in the men's room and he was unable to set off the bomb.[23] Another assassination plot in Munich took place ten years later in the *Burgerbraukeller*, a huge beer hall. The would-be assassin, a Communist sympathizer, would later claim his goal was peace. He skillfully rigged a time bomb inside a pillar at the back of the speakers' platform, set to go off in the middle of Hitler's speech. Hitler did not begin his speech on time, and was repeatedly interrupted by wild cheering. Normally, Hitler remained on the podium greeting well-wishers, but not that night. He rushed out of the building and into a waiting car. Hitler was some miles away heading to the railroad station. when the powerful bomb exploded, killing seven and wounding sixty-three, including the father of Eva Braun, who later was Hitler's mistress and then his bride.[24]

Further plots on Hitler's life would come later when the Führer's armies began to experience reversals. It was understood by all the conspirators that the German General Staff would never participate in a plot to overthrow the Führer while he was victorious. Only when the Wehrmacht suffered a major defeat would the fighting generals support a conspiracy.

Adolf Hitler was a difficult target. He was protected by a personal bodyguard of forty specially trained and dedicated SS officers in "*Leibstandarte Adolf Hitler.*" It was estimated that upwards of 100,000 agents of various internal security organizations were continuously at work to uncover exactly what the Schwarze Kapelle was up to— the overthrow of the Nazi regime.[25]

Hitler's cars were big Mercedes-Benzes, including a huge 7.7 liter Model W150, his favorite. Each had bulletproof glass and reinforced bodywork, including armor in the doors and underside to protect against bombs embedded in the road. When he traveled by car, Hitler always was in a convoy of similar automobiles to confuse possible assassins.

He had two Focke-Wulf Fw-200 *Condors*[26] for his personal use, large, four-engine, long-range transports, with wingspans the same as Boeing *Flying Fortresses*. Both were specially armored and reconfigured with a reinforced bulkhead separating Hitler's personal space from that of the other passengers and supposedly fitted with an automatically deployed parachute in the unlikely event the plane was attacked in the air. His *Condor* was always escorted by a group of Messerschmitt Bf-109 fighter planes piloted by the Luftwaffe's best.

While Hitler preferred to travel long distances by plane, he also had a special "Führer train" at his beck and call. It consisted of eleven coaches, with a saloon, dining car, and conference car — plus a coach for his bodyguards and one for the press that always accompanied him. That train, too, was specially armored and protected its passengers with bulletproof glass.

"His greatest security measure, however, turned out to be his own temperament. He instinctively liked to keep people guessing about what he would do, and to catch them wrong-footed.... He always made his mind up about when and how to travel at the last moment, and he would frequently decide not to go at all ... curiously it was not until very late in the war that attendees at meetings had to leave their pistols outside and briefcases were searched."[27]

Allen Welsh Dulles was not new to espionage. During the Great War he had worked in Switzerland as an intelligence gatherer for the U.S. Foreign Service. Then, as later, he was convinced that an Anglo-American-German tripartite alliance would be a certain guarantee of peace. Between the wars, he had mingled with top German industrialists and bankers through the good offices of Sullivan & Cromwell, the prestigious New York City law firm for which he worked. When Hitler declared war against America, Dulles joined William Donovan's OSS. He arrived in Berne, Switzerland in December 1942, his "first and most important task to find out what was going on in Germany.... Washington wanted to know who in Germany were really opposed to the Hitler regime and whether they were actively at work to overthrow it."[28] According to another source, the Western allies already "had a very clear picture of what was happening in wartime Germany ... even before Allen Welsh Dulles took control of the OSS...."[29]

But did Washington, i.e. Franklin Roosevelt, want honest answers to those two questions? Dulles's own recounting of his wartime experiences and those from other credible sources clearly indicate that not only had the president personally shut himself off from this knowledge, but he mandated a government cover-up that extended into the postwar years. He refused to respond to Dulles's continuing entreaties to open up a dialog with members of the German underground seeking an early end to the butchery. The reason for Roosevelt's head-in-the-sand attitude has intimately related to his unconditional surrender edict. An armistice would mean "conditions," and FDR could accept none.

German historian Peter Hoffmann put FDR's intransigence in a more charitable light. "Viewed from Washington, the United States was not merely fighting the Nazi regime but a people permeated by an illiberal inhuman ideology who had learnt nothing from a fearful defeat in another similarly imperialist war. In face of Hitler's claim to total power, a total victory must be won."³⁰ Additionally, the United States could give no assurances to the conspirators without consulting her allies. If Stalin learned that the Americans were "dealing with Nazis," he would feel free to do the same and perhaps conclude a separate peace with Hitler, always a concern of the two western Allies.

Dulles, before it became clear to him that his primary mission was effectively a charade, yearned to explore the idea of U.S. collaboration with key members of the Schwarze Kapelle. He complained to Washington that he did not understand what U.S. policy was in that regard, and what support, if any, the United States could give to the resistance movement. In April 1944, one group of the conspirators asked Dulles for guarantees that if they would overthrow Hitler, Britain and America would negotiate a peace with the new government, after which the German army would fully engage the Soviets. Dulles responded to the peace feeler by reporting to Washington that the Germans were anxious to prevent Central Europe from becoming ideologically and politically under the control of Russia.

Dulles later quoted a diary entry in 1945 of one of the plotters, General Albrecht von Kessel, that "some of the conspirators were convinced the unconditional surrender formula jeopardized and possibly destroyed six years of work by the anti–Nazi opposition" and "made it most difficult to drive a wedge between Hitler and the German people." Kessel then vilified the vagueness of unconditional surrender: "A fort can surrender and its defenders are taken prisoner until the end of the war. Was this, then, to be the fate of the whole German people — to be prisoners for a limited period of time, or possibly to be permanently enslaved.... If unconditional surrender did not mean slavery why weren't the German people enlightened?"³¹

Initially Dulles loyally supported FDR's doctrine of unconditional surrender as sound psychological warfare. As the war progressed, however, he became discouraged by the impact of the unbending policy on the German resistance which offered the conspirators no reason to risk their lives at the brutal hands of the Gestapo. Dulles soon understood why the anti–Nazi opposition inside Germany "never attained anything like the form or scope of the resistance in other Hitler-dominated countries." Other underground organizations received large-scale support: "arms and supplies were smuggled to them, they maintained organized liaison with foreign powers or their own governments in exile, which could ... help them organize, inform them, instruct them, render them financial aid ... and give them the hope and moral support that kept alive their faith in ultimate deliverance." Dulles could offer them nothing. "The axman's shadow was omnipresent ... no one came forward from the highest places to challenge the wisdom of that messianic proclamation of vengeance, unconditional surrender."³²

By February 1943 the question of Fahneneid—assassination—no longer troubled the plotters. That was the month Field Marshal Friedrich von Paulus surrendered his great Sixth Army at Stalingrad, including 24 generals, 2,000 officers, and nearly 100,000 ragged and wounded Feldgrau. This pivotal battle had already claimed some 175,000 Wehrmacht casualties and was considered the worst military defeat in German history.[33] In Berlin, Goebbels proclaimed three days of mourning in honor of those who fell at Stalingrad. During the period all places of entertainment, including theaters and movie houses, were closed. Total war was coming to Germany.

The Night of the Long Knives in June 1934, in which Hitler ordered the murder without trial of "a hundred men, perhaps two hundred—the exact number will never be known"[34] to consolidate his power, was the first overt indicator of the fundamental criminality of Hitler and his regime. But it was the momentous Führer conference of principal military officers on November 5, 1937 that energized the Schwarze Kapelle on its path to treason.[35]

Hitler began talking at 4 P.M. and immediately swore those in attendance to secrecy. He requested "in the interest of a long-term German policy, that his exposition be regarded, in the event of his death, as his last will and testament." Germany's future depended on acquiring adequate Lebensraum and her first objective must be to secure her eastern and southern flanks, he declared. That meant the annexation of Czechoslovakia, Austria and Poland, either by diplomacy or force. Italy would not object to the elimination of the Czechs but he said he was unable to estimate what her attitude would be regarding Austria. Poland, he said, with Russia at her rear, would have little inclination to go to war with Germany. When Hitler felt the Wehrmacht was ready, he would then invade Russia with a blitzkrieg.

It was getting dark by the time Hitler finished. The lecture had been an impressive example of his oratorical skills. Hitler rarely glanced at his notes, reeling off facts and figures "in a startling display of photographic memory, a gift reportedly shared by Caesar, Napoleon and Lenin."[36] The meeting finally was adjourned at 8:15 P.M.

Hitler's remarks met with mixed reactions from his audience, most of the attendees skeptical of what they had just heard. Not so Foreign Minister Konstantin von Neurath, who took the Führer at his word. When he got back to his office, he was so agitated that he suffered a mild heart attack. Two days later, driven by his principles, he ignored his oath of secrecy and met with Generals Ludwig Beck and Werner von Fritsch to discuss ways and means to get Hitler to abandon his war plans. Fritsch, it was agreed, would emphasize to Hitler the military dangers of a continental war, and Neurath would argue the political pitfalls. In the event, neither man succeeded. As for Beck, he had no intention of trying to talk Hitler out of his plans; rather, he would work secretly to unseat him and, if necessary, to assassinate him.

The German resistance movement, from its beginnings after Hitler became chancellor in 1933, was convinced that Hitler's removal from power was vital if the organization was to succeed. The civilian group, headed by Carl Goerdler, preferred that Hitler should be taken prisoner. Their views were that if he was killed, a dangerous legend might be created that, if Hitler had lived, all might have gone well for the nation. A living Hitler put on trial before the world would expose him and his system.

The military conspirators, headed by Colonel General Ludwig Beck, reached a different conclusion. They knew it would be extraordinarily difficult to take Hitler alive. They understood better the views of German soldiers and they knew personally what their oath of allegiance to Hitler meant to them and also recognized that a considerable fraction of the German people were still mesmerized by Hitler. The generals wanted to break this spell at one stroke, immediately freeing German soldiers of their oath of allegiance to Hitler. The conspirators agreed to kill Adolf Hitler.

While every German military officer had sworn fealty to his Führer, some were willing to break their oath for a "higher duty." Chief of Staff General Franz Halder, on the brink of joining the conspiracy, explained his dilemma during his postwar interrogation at Nuremberg. "I am the last masculine member of a family who for 300 years were soldiers. What the duty of a soldier is I know. I know, too, that in the dictionary of a German soldier the terms 'treason' and 'plot against the state' do not exist. I was in the awful dilemma of one who had the duty of a soldier and also a duty which I considered higher. Innumerable of my old comrades were in the same dilemma. I chose the solution for the duties I esteem higher."[37]

The conspirators conceived a plan to assassinate Hitler, *Operation Flash*, as well as a scheme to seize power after the assassination, *Case Valkyrie*. General Henning von Tresckow, Field Marshal Guenther von Kluge's chief of staff, was selected to direct the operation. The plan was to lure Hitler to a meeting at Kluge's headquarters at Smolensk on the Russian front, then plant a time-bomb on his *Condor* that would explode in mid-air on the return flight. The semblance of an accident was considered more acceptable to the German population than outright murder.

Tresckow and one of his junior officers, Fabian von Schlabrendorff, put the bomb together, forming the plastic explosives in a shape and size that was similar to two bottles of Cointreau, the schnapps sold in square bottles. The wrapping allowed the chemical time fuse to be triggered from the outside without disturbing the package. (It was the same type of fuse used by Stauffenberg sixteen months later.) Schlabrendorff was at the airport just before Hitler's *Condor* took off. Moments before he gave the package to a colonel in the Führer's party who had agreed to deliver it to a friend at Wolfschanze, Schlabrendorff pressed down hard on the wrapping, crushing the fuse and triggering the bomb. Hitler boarded the plane and it took off. The bomb was expected to detonate somewhere over Minsk, but several hours passed without news of a mid-air accident. Word finally came through that Hitler had arrived without incident in Rastenburg. What had gone wrong? Schlabrendorff had to retrieve the bomb before it exploded or was discovered. He managed to recover it intact and carefully disassembled the bomb; to his dismay, while the firing pin had been released, the detonator was a dud.

Undeterred, the conspirators tried again a week later, this one a suicide mission. It, too, failed. Four more attempts were made on Hitler's life between September 1943 and February 1944. These also were abortive. Were the Gods on the Führer's side?

Finally would come Colonel Claus von Stauffenberg's brave assassination attempt, and, while he, too, would be unsuccessful, the explosion in Wolfschanze electrified the world.

Those who were trying to kill Hitler and overthrow the Nazi regime were neither gangsters nor ordinary murderers, nor were they the "criminal clique" of "limited numbers but important in influence" that Hitler called them in his radio address to the German people. Nor was it a spontaneous coup attempt by disgruntled military officers. The plotters were part of a large, secret group called Die Schwarze Kapelle (The Black Orchestra) by the Gestapo. High-ranking German officers, including many Wehrmacht generals, and important civilians had been working together to overthrow the Nazi government since Hitler had become Reich Chancellor in 1933. By 1940, the Schwarze Kapelle had become a basic, if covert part of the German military-political scene. The Schwarze Kapelle had "cells" in "every important command center in the German army, as well as adherents at all the major intelligence, signals, operations and supply centers, in the military governments of the occupied territories, and in all German Wehrkreise or 'military districts' into which the Reich had been divided for the purposes of administration, mobilization and industry."[38]

Colonel General Ludwig Beck, Chief of the General Staff, was the nominal head of Die Schwarze Kapelle and had been a consistent foe of National Socialism. He had warned Hitler before the war that his aggressive tactics meant a conflict with all of Europe and eventually with the United States—a war which Germany could not win. When the Führer abrogated the Munich Pact in 1939 and marched on Czechoslovakia, Beck resigned in protest. Beck had felt that he owed his country a greater duty than blindly following a leader who to him was bent on its destruction. Beck stayed in the Army, temporarily taking over command of the German First Army. But Hitler was concerned with such a dedicated foe in a position of power, and he forced Beck into retirement. As an unemployed general, Beck could then apply his talents full-time to leading the conspirators.

In the spring of 1944, just prior to D-day, Beck attempted to establish contact with the Allied government. Beck's purpose was to find out the terms by which the Allies would be prepared to conclude peace with a Germany minus Hitler and the Nazi regime. This was an important issue, since it had been difficult to recruit new adherents without being able to discuss what lay in store for Germany after Hitler was unseated. Beck sent several messages to Allen Dulles on the subject and they were duly passed on to Washington. Like all of Dulles' messages to Washington concerning the Schwarze Kapelle, Beck's appeals were never acknowledged.

Later on that summer, Beck insisted that the plot to kill Hitler must move forward despite the Allied insistence on unconditional surrender, saying that "crime after crime and murder after murder have multiplied in the name of the German people, and that it is a moral duty to put a halt with all available means to these crimes committed in the usurped name of our people."[39]

As Beck was the military leader, Carl-Friedrich Goerdeler headed the civilians within Schwarze Kapelle. He had been deputy mayor of Konigsberg (now Kalingrad in Russia), and then mayor of Leipzig in 1930. He was at first a loyal supporter of Hitler but had never joined the Nazi Party and gradually saw Hitler's policies for what they were. The Nazi anti–Semitic laws had been abhorrent to him from the start and as mayor he had resisted pressure from local Nazis seeking to remove a statue of Jewish composer Felix Mendelssohn that stood outside the *Gewandhaus* Concert Hall. In 1936 he traveled to Scandinavia to lecture on economic issues. When he returned to Leipzig he found that his Nazi deputy had ordered the statue taken down. He insisted that it be replaced or he would resign. Despite Goerdeler's popularity as mayor, his resignation was accepted.[40]

He was immediately offered a new job as an economic adviser by the well-known liberal industrialist — and foe of Hitler — Robert Bosch. Friedrich Krupp of the mighty Ruhr steel- and arms-making dynasty, an early supporter of Hitler, by 1936 also had become disenchanted; he, too, quietly helped finance Goerdeler. More importantly, these two men gave Goerdeler the "cover" he needed to fight Hitler's regime. His contacts extended practically to all non-Communist groups in the conspiracy. In 1937, while in the United States, he left with one of his friends a "political testament" which showed he was aware of the direction toward which the German people were drifting. At the same time, back in Germany, he strove to convince the generals of the dangers of Hitler's misguided policies.[41] Goerdeler was kept under observation by the Gestapo but had enough powerful protectors to keep them at bay until the very end.[42] Beck and Goerdeler formed the core of a network of people in the Army, the Church, the Abwehr, the Foreign Office, the conservative opposition, and even the Berlin police force.

The surviving generals interviewed in the immediate postwar years agreed that in the spring of 1944 many sought an armistice with the two western powers. They were certain that by summer Allied forces would be landing in France, and they wanted to avoid the enormous casualties that would result. The generals also indicated that German forces would continue to fight the Soviet Union if an armistice so stipulated. Germany, they insisted, "would be willing to pay reparations for war damages, surrender all territory gained by conquest, disarm, and accept the trial of alleged war criminals under accepted principles of existent international law."[43] But Franklin Roosevelt, blinded by his intense hatred of Germany and Germans, and transfixed by his own Casablanca declaration, elected to fight it out to the bitter end. Censorship made certain that the American people never learned there were any "good Germans" remaining in Germany to negotiate with and government propaganda convinced most of them that the German people were intrinsically warlike, even genetically evil, and they therefore deserved severe punishment.

Furthermore, on the Allied side, "it was an almost universally accepted view ... that there was not and never had been a German opposition to Hitler worth speaking of ... it was only when the 'Prussian generals' were faced with defeat that that they started a movement to save their skins and to preserve the General Staff for World War III."[44] Even after the Schwarze Kapelle delivered a dossier that revealed the secret Nazi missile development program at Peenemunde, as an indicator of good faith, the Allies continued to ignore the motives behind it, despite their willingness to take advantage of the treason by bombing the facility. Remarkably, following the assassination attempt on July 20, "British radio began regularly broadcasting the names of people alleged to have a hand in the coup." Allied leaflets were circulated "heaping scorn on the conspirators, just as the Nazis' propaganda was doing."[45]

And like faulty U.S. intelligence concerning Hitler's "butter as well as guns" policy,[46] American diplomats and military leaders acted as if they never knew that the Nazi party was a minority party. In fact, before the Nazis took power in January 1933, the Nazi Party never polled more than thirty-seven percent of the vote. Even after the burning of the Reichstag and the rigged elections of March 1933, those voting for the Nazis totaled only forty-four percent of the electorate.[47]

As the war was winding down, Allied propagandists joined with their Nazi contemporaries in belittling the conspirators and questioning their motives. In the House of Commons on August 2, 1944, Churchill declared that "the highest personalities in the German Reich are murdering one another, or trying to, while the avenging armies of the Allies close upon the doomed and ever-narrowing circle of their power." The happenings of July 20 were simply a manifestation of "internal disease."[48] In the United States, total silence! In the early postwar period, U.S. government censorship clamped down on publication of articles and books that shed light on the German resistance. Further, in American prisoner-of-war and internment camps, German military officers who had been part of the conspiracy were confined indiscriminately along with SS officers and other dyed-in-the-wool Nazis.

Panzer General Guderian wrote in his postwar retrospective that he had known nothing of the July 20 plot on Hitler's life and had talked to nobody about it. He asked, rhetorically, "what were the actual results of the attempt made to assassinate Hitler...? The man who was to be killed was in fact slightly wounded. His physical condition, not of the best beforehand, was further weakened. His spiritual equipoise was destroyed forever. All the forces of evil that had lurked within him were aroused and came into their own. He recognized no limits any more."[49] Guderian also commented that "as far as foreign policy was concerned the conditions necessary for success of the undertaking did not exist"[50] and that "the links between the leaders of the conspiracy and important figures in the enemy countries were very slender." As far as those who suffered "a bitter death, only a small proportion were actively involved in the conspiracy. The great majority merely knew something about it and out of loyalty to their friends kept silent...." Guderian posed the inevitable question: "what would have happened had the assassination succeeded? Only one fact seems beyond dispute: at that time the great proportion of the German people still believed in Adolf Hitler and would have been convinced that with his death the assassin had removed the only man who might still have been able to bring the war to a favourable conclusion." Guderian concluded: "It also seems unlikely that our enemies would have treated us any better in consequence than they actually did after the collapse."[51]

There is no unanimity among the views of the many German historians who have probed the motives of the resistance movement. Hans Rothfels, whose investigations were the first to be translated into English, concluded that the German conspirators were possessed with: "Stronger impulses of a purely human character ... which could claim universal validity.... They were much more than merely the opposite poles to Hitler and his baneful system."[52] Theodore S. Hamerow asked: "Were the men who tried to overthrow Hitler in the summer of 1944 motivated primarily by a concern for the welfare of Germany or some broader moral principle above national interest? Or were they selfishly seeking to overthrow the existing Nazi government to gain personal ascendancy in a new one? Or were they hoping to salvage their own self-respect as it became evident that Germany was certainly losing the war?"[53]

Another interpretation came from Joachim Fest. By the summer of 1944, he wrote, the conspirators' "sole remaining ambition ... was to save as much of Germany's 'substance' as possible from the impending catastrophe."[54] Evidence later proved how well founded their motives were. One study showed: "that while slightly more than 2.8 million German soldiers and civilians died during the nearly five years between the beginning of the war on September 1, 1939 and the attempt to assassinate Hitler on June 20, 1944, 4.8 million died during the nine and a half months before the war ended in May 1945. These figures appear even more shocking if we calculate how many were killed on average every day during those two periods. Before the attempted coup 1,588 Germans were killed daily; after it 16,641 perished, even though the war had obviously been lost."[55]

9

Treasury Secretary Henry Morgenthau Jr.'s Scorched-Earth Plan

"One would search the records of previous settlements after wars among European powers without finding anything remotely comparable with the Morgenthau Plan, the deliberate stunting of a nation's economic recovery …"[1]

"Just strip it. I don't care what happens to the population. I would take every mine, every mill and factory and wreck it…. Steel, coal, everything. Just close it down…. Make the Ruhr look like some of the silver mines in Nevada."[2]

       Henry Morgenthau, Jr. to his staff, 1944.

"We have got to be tough with Germany and I mean the German people not just the Nazis. We either have to castrate the German people or you have to treat them in such a manner so they can't go on reproducing…."[3]

       Franklin D. Roosevelt to Henry Morgenthau, Jr., August 19, 1944.

Henry Morgenthau, Jr. was a "nut" and a "blockhead," and "didn't know shit from apple butter."[4]

       Harry S. Truman, privately, to his cronies, 1954.

By mid-summer 1944 American forces had broken through German defenses at Avaranches and General Patton's Third Army was poised to strike east. On the Italian front Rome had been liberated by Allied forces and the Americans were about to capture Florence. The Red Army had begun its massive offensive against German forces in the Ukraine. French troops were about to enter Paris, and the British army would occupy Brussels early in September. German U-boats in the Atlantic had finally been defeated and the Reich was being bombed into rubble, day and night, by thousand-plane USAAF and RAF raids. The Allies were confronted with the urgent necessity to plan for peace with Germany. The most controversial scheme was the Morgenthau Plan which called for the "pastoralization" of Germany.

Henry Morgenthau, Jr., Secretary of the Treasury, wrote in his diary that on August 6, 1944, aboard an airplane to Europe, one of his assistants had given him a copy of a draft of the War Department's proposed plan for administering postwar Germany. To pass the time on the droning sixteen-hour flight, he recalled that he had "settled back to read it, first with interest, then with misgivings, finally with sharp disagreement."[5] Morgenthau had his own firm ideas on how Germans should be treated and they differed widely from the War Department's.

His mission ostensibly was to study the financial situation in Europe and to blueprint the currency that would be used by Allied occupying forces in postwar Germany. He insisted years later that his only purpose in making the trip was to study currency issues. That was not quite the whole truth. In fact, he had other motives. Morgenthau had also made arrangements to tour the battlefronts, talk with GIs, including his son, Henry III, and see for himself what had been accomplished in the two months since the D-Day landings in Normandy. At the top of his agenda, however, were appointments with important U.S. military officers, for he was intent on lobbying for a program of venomous retribution against Germany and the Germans, an area far removed from his sphere of accountably. He was eager to play a major role in shaping the European peace, particularly with regard to Germany. He had the ear of the president, and he was never reluctant to invoke his close ties with FDR to ride roughshod over the sensibilities and responsibilities of others in the administration. Needless to say, for those reasons, he had no friends among his associates in the cabinet. Morgenthau was an obsessive Germanophobe like his father (Appendix D) and what came to be called the Morgenthau Plan (Appendix L) was his personal vendetta.

Henry Morgenthau, Jr.'s ties to Franklin D. Roosevelt ran deep and long. In 1915, Morgenthau had bought a tract of land in Duchess County, New York, close to FDR's estate in Hyde Park. He named it Fishkill Farms, and planned to operate a dairy farm and an apple orchard. Over the years, he conscientiously postured himself as a successful "gentleman farmer" and an agricultural expert (on apples) to boot. He was neither. But he always insisted that his farm should appear to visitors to be a serious, profitable enterprise, rather than the hobby it started out as and the political ends it would eventually serve, and he purposely gave it the run-down appearance of a working farm with unpainted barns and sheds. "In fact the farm sustained huge losses most of the time, but its fabled success was accepted by almost everyone."[6]

Henry Morgenthau III wrote that he never learned how or when his father met Roosevelt, but he gives evidence that during the Great War FDR, then the Assistant Secretary of the Navy, had asked for Henry, Jr.'s help on a political matter. In 1920, Roosevelt was the Democratic Party's vice presidential nominee as James M. Cox's running mate and Henry, Jr. was given his first political assignment. The Cox-Roosevelt ticket was soundly trounced in the election by Warren Harding and the Republicans.

The following August, infantile paralysis crippled Roosevelt, temporarily forcing him out of the political arena. He spent more time in Hyde Park, bringing him into closer contact with Morgenthau. In 1928, when FDR ran for governor of New York, Morgenthau threw himself into his successful campaign as FDR's "advance man," seeing valuable dividends down the road. FDR won a second term in 1930 by an overwhelming majority and overnight became the Democratic Party's presidential front-runner.

When Roosevelt was elected president in 1932, Morgenthau expected to be named Secretary of Agriculture, but farm leaders from the Midwest and South opposed the idea of a Jew in the Cabinet. Instead, he got a lesser post, chairman of the Farm Credit Administration. A year later, good fortune fell Morgenthau's way. FDR's first Treasury Secretary, William Woodin, died suddenly and there was a vacancy to be filled. No shrinking violet, Morgenthau went directly to the president to petition for the job. Because of his loyalty, which Roosevelt valued above all else, FDR appointed Morgenthau to the more prestigious post despite his lack of experience in financial matters. *Fortune* questioned the appointment of the "son of a Jewish philanthropist" who had "spent most of his life farming." And a big Republican contributor suggested testily that FDR had managed to appoint "the only Jew in the world who doesn't know a thing about money."[7]

Morgenthau's first meeting, the next day, was lunch with General Dwight D. Eisenhower in his mess tent in Portsmouth. He was anxious to find out how Eisenhower planned to treat Germans when he arrived in Germany. A Treasury aide recalled that Eisenhower said that "he was going to treat them rough," and then, turning grim, Eisenhower emphasized that the Germans deserved to be punished and that "the ringleaders and the *SS* troops should be given the death penalty without question." As for ordinary Germans, they were guilty of supporting the Nazi regime and should be treated harshly as well. "I certainly see no point in bolstering their economy or taking any other steps to help them." This was music to Morgenthau's ears. Eisenhower's concluding remarks, however, did not sit too well with the Treasury Secretary: "I emphatically repudiated one suggestion [of Morgenthau's] I heard that the Ruhr mines should be flooded. This seemed silly and criminal to me."[8]

Eisenhower went into further detail in his own recollection of the meeting: "...following upon the conclusion of hostilities, there must be no room for doubt as to won the war. Germany must be occupied. More than this, the German people must not be allowed to escape a sense of guilt, of complicity in the tragedy that has engulfed the world. Prominent Nazis, along with certain industrialists, must be tried and punished. Membership in the Gestapo and in the SS should be taken as prima facie evidence of guilt. The General Staff must be broken up, all its archives confiscated, and members suspected of complicity in starting the war or in any war crime should be tried. The German nation should be responsible for reparations to such countries as Belgium, Holland, France, Luxemburg, Norway, and Russia. The war-making power of the country should be eliminated. Possibly this could be done by strict controls on industries using heavy fabricating machinery or by the mere expedient of preventing any manufacture of airplanes. The Germans should be permitted and required to make their own living, and should not be supported by America. Therefore choking off natural resources would be folly."[9] Eisenhower then stated that "these views" were presented to everyone who queried him on the subject, then and later, and were given to President Harry S. Truman and new Secretary of State James Byrnes for their summit meeting in Potsdam in July 1945.

David Eisenhower wrote years later that his grandfather's brief luncheon meeting with Morgenthau was destined to be a "source of recurring rumors" about his role in formulating a "hard-peace occupation policy in postwar Germany." According to his grandson, Eisenhower's brief involvement with Morgenthau, as superficial as it was, haunted his postwar career in politics, first surfacing in the 1948 primaries, and again in the 1952 presidential campaign.[10]

After returning from Europe, Morgenthau had a meeting with the president to discuss what he had learned in Europe about the postwar treatment of Germany and Germans. The often-ambivalent Roosevelt appeared to agree with him as he outlined his vindictive postwar plans to convert the most powerful industrial state in Europe into a farming nation. Roosevelt, too, was intent on punishing Germany and the Germans.

On August 26, in a memorandum to War Secretary Stimson, the president showed where he stood on the issue, criticizing a to-be-published *Handbook for Military Government in Germany* that had been drawn up as a guide to the military for their occupation of Germany: "This so-called *Handbook* is pretty bad.... It gives me the impression that Germany is to be restored just as much as the Netherlands or Belgium, and the people of Germany brought back as quickly as possible to their prewar state.... I do not want them to starve to death, but ... if they need food to keep body and soul together ... they should be fed three times a day from Army soup kitchens.... They will remember that experience all their lives."[11]

Convinced he had the president behind him, Morgenthau appointed an internal Treasury Department team headed by Assistant Secretary Harry Dexter White, to draft a preliminary plan "with strict attention to the Secretary's specific instructions," namely that it be severe. He demanded that the plan convert the Ruhr into a huge ghost town. If the region were "stripped of its machinery" and its mines "flooded, dynamited, wrecked," he pointed out, Germany would be "impotent to wage more wars." When White sensibly cautioned that shutting down the Ruhr would impoverish millions of German workers and seriously impact the rest of Europe which would depend on the coal and steel from that region for the rebuilding of devastated areas, Morgenthau was not to be budged: "I am for destroying it first and we will worry about the population second.... I am not going to budge an inch.[12] Furthermore, it was insufficient, in Morgenthau's view, to merely capture or execute Hitler and his aides, nor even just to free the nations that Germany had occupied. He felt strongly that the German people had to be re-educated, starting with the children.

To draw all his aides to his side, Morgenthau introduced an additional argument: "The Ruhr is the place that closed down the steel mills in Birmingham, the coal mines in England, that caused the misery and the low standards of living in England.... It is the competition.... Now, as soon as you start arguing with me, and I begin to give way ... they will do just what they do in the hills of Pennsylvania—they will mine bootleg coal.... A fellow will have a coal mine in his basement, and those fellows are so clever and such devils that before you know it they have got a marching army. Sure is a terrific problem. Let the Germans solve it. Why the hell should I worry about what happens to their people? ... I can be overruled by the president, but nobody else is going to overrule me."[13]

White had one last suggestion intended to moderate Morgenthau's extreme views. He recommended that the Ruhr be permitted to mine coal in order to alleviate the severe coal shortage that Britain and all of Western Europe would certainly face at the end of the war. Morgenthau remained implacable: "To answer as to letting them produce coal, that doesn't answer what I have in mind.... I am not going to give in while I have got breath."[14] This last statement apparently was sufficient to end disagreement within the Treasury Department, and the indiscriminant gutting of the Ruhr became the sine qua non for Morgenthau's postwar plan for Germany.

Stimson, upon returning to Washington at the end of July from a fact-finding mission to the Normandy battlefield, learned that the administration was deeply involved in the development of a policy for the postwar treatment of Germany and Germans. He also learned that Morgenthau was in the van of discussions on the subject, a cause for concern for Stimson who knew the treasury secretary's predilections.

There were then two distinct views in Washington regarding how a defeated Germany should be treated: "doves," who favored a firm but discriminating hand that would result in the rebuilding of Germany as a flourishing, peaceful good-neighbor in middle Europe, perhaps, and "hawks," who advocated a victor's malevolent peace that would crush Germany for years if not decades to come. Stimson was a student of John Maynard Keynes, whose famous post–Great War book, *The Economic Consequences of the Peace,* had convinced him that the fundamental basis of enduring peace must be economic stability.[15]

Intent on forestalling Morgenthau, Stimson met with the president and suggested he appoint a Cabinet Committee to thrash out the different views. Roosevelt agreed and named five to the new committee: Stimson and Morgenthau along with Cordell Hull and Frank Knox. Roosevelt soon added his close confidant Harry Hopkins to the group.

The night before the first meeting of the new Cabinet Committee, Stimson dined at Morgenthau's home with White and Assistant War Secretary John J. McLoy. Stimson recorded in his diary that the dinner conversation had been pleasant but that Morgenthau, "a Jew," was "not unnaturally, very bitter ... and would plunge out for a treatment of Germany which I feel sure would be unwise." Morgenthau had been infuriated when Stimson remarked: "I think we can't solve the German problem except through Christianity and kindness."[17]

The first meeting of the Cabinet Committee, Stimson recalled, confirmed his worst fears. Hull had teamed with Morgenthau and both proposed the destruction of the industries of the vast Ruhr-Saar region to turn it into agricultural land — regardless of that area's importance to Germany and to the well-being of nearly all of Europe. Harry Hopkins went along with their folly by insisting that Germany be further prohibited from manufacturing steel in the same zone, a prohibition which Stimson felt "would pretty well sabotage everything else." Stimson found himself a minority of one. He recorded in his diary: "In all my four years that I have been here I have not had such a difficult and unpleasant meeting ... we were irreconcilably divided." He made a record of his own views "for history — to show future generations that not every high official under Roosevelt had run 'amuck at this vital period.'"[18]

Later that day he sent a long memorandum to the president with copies to his three active colleagues on the committee.[19] It stated frankly his strong opposition to the proposed obliteration of German industry, in particular of the Saar and Ruhr regions: "I cannot conceive of such a proposition being possible or effective and I can see enormous general evils coming from an attempt to so treat it." He followed with a brief history lecture for his four readers: "During the past eighty years of European history this portion of Germany was one of the most important sources of the raw materials [coal and iron ore for steel and bauxite for aluminum] upon which the industrial and economic livelihood of Europe was based. Upon the production which came from the raw materials of this region those years, the commerce of Europe was very largely predicated. Upon that production Germany became the largest source of supply to no less than ten European countries, viz: Russia, Norway, Sweden, Denmark, Holland, Switzerland, Italy, Austria-Hungary, Rumania, and Bulgaria; and the second largest source of supply to Great Britain, Belgium, and France. By the same commerce, which in large part arose from this production, Germany also became the best buyer or customer of Russia, Norway, Holland, Belgium, Switzerland, Italy, and Austria-Hungary; and the second-best customer of Great Britain, Sweden, and Denmark." Like every good history professor, Stimson brought his readers into the present: "I cannot treat as realistic the suggestion that such an area in the present economic condition of the world can be turned into a nonproductive 'ghost territory' when it has become the center of one of the most industrialized continents in the world, populated by peoples of energy, vigor, and progressiveness."[20]

Stimson might also have mentioned that in the late 1800s and into the turn of the next century, during the great railroad-building boom in Canada and the United States, both countries were major importers of products from Krupp, Germany's giant steelmaker. Krupp's proprietary crucible steel-making process for seamless railway wheels was superior to everything on the market. For example, the Canadian Pacific Railway advertised to its passengers that Krupp steel "tires" were used exclusively throughout the C.P.R. systems for their safety. In the United States, nine major railroads were also equipping their cars with Krupp wheels and were also using Krupp rails. In 1880, for example, E. H. Harriman had placed a single order for 25,000 tons of eighty-pound rails for the Southern Pacific, a year's supply.[21]

Henry L. Stimson was a self-assured figure in the cabinet, fifteen years Roosevelt's senior, a long-time Republican whom FDR had chosen because of his extensive experience in military and foreign affairs. The president understood the political price he would pay if his war secretary ever resigned, which gave Stimson plenty of clout in bureaucratic in-fighting.

At the next day's meeting, September 6, Stimson recorded in his diary that FDR no longer appeared ready to accept Morgenthau's key premise, that the Ruhr's mines and factories should be demolished. Stimson's long memorandum apparently had struck pay dirt. But Roosevelt nevertheless continued to be ambivalent, arguing "that Great Britain was going to be in sore straits after the war and ... that the products of the Ruhr might be used to furnish raw material for the British steel industry."[22] Stimson also noted that the attitude of Hull had moderated. Morgenthau had brought along his unchanged first proposal and refused to compromise. The discussions were stalemated.

Pugnacious Henry Morgenthau, Jr. was not about to accept defeat or even to have his program watered down, and he requested another joint hearing with the president. The next meeting was set for September 9, giving sufficient time for both cabinet officers to have their staffs do additional research and to polish final drafts of their memoranda.

Morgenthau's revised paper was formally titled "Program to Prevent Germany from Starting a World War III" (Appendix L), certainly a loaded and leading title, and was essentially a rebuttal of Stimson's memorandum of three days earlier. Henceforth it would come to be known as the Morgenthau Plan. It stated categorically that it was a delusion that Europe needed a Germany with strong industries, but it was a fact that the mines and factories of the Ruhr had in the past been overly aggressive competitors of Great Britain in particular. Copies had also been prepared for the upcoming two-power conference in Quebec the following week. It contained suggestive sections that would appeal to the British; one was titled "How British Industry Would Benefit by Proposed Program."[23]

Stimson's counter-memorandum again repeated his strong opposition to Morgenthau's idiotic policy for Germany's Ruhr. Such a policy, he stated firmly, would lead to another European war, not peace; it would generate sympathy worldwide; and most importantly, it would destroy resources that would be needed desperately for the postwar rebuilding of Germany and other devastated areas of Europe. When Stimson later had time to study Morgenthau's well-crafted paper, he considered it the same cheap wine, but in a new bottle. Irritably, he penned in the margins: "Childish folly! ... A beautiful Nazi program! ... This is to laugh!" Next to the section on how the Morgenthau Plan would benefit British trade, he wrote: "Bribe to U.K."[24]

It represented a remarkable retreat from the Atlantic Charter (Appendix H) solemnly signed by Roosevelt and Churchill three years earlier. That document had proclaimed that the United States and the United Kingdom would "endeavor ... to further the enjoyment by all States, great or small, victor or vanquished, of access, on equal terms, to the trade and to the raw materials of the world which are needed for their economic prosperity."

There matters stood when Quebec Conference I — OCTAGON — convened on September 11. It was there, on the 13th, after being invited by FDR to join the conference, that Morgenthau officially unveiled his postwar scorched-earth policy for postwar Germany.[25] Morgenthau recalled that he had barely begun his presentation to Roosevelt and Churchill "before low mutters and baleful looks indicated that the Prime Minister was not the most enthusiastic member of my audience.... He growled angrily that the proposals were unnatural, un–Christian and unnecessary," and even rejected the supposedly positive economic consequences of the plan, of Britain taking over German markets. Churchill "turned loose on me the full flood of his rhetoric, sarcasm and violence." He looked on the Treasury Plan, he said, as equivalent to "chaining him to a dead German." Churchill declared vehemently that while he was all for disarming Germany, "we ought not prevent her from living decently" and the German people must not be allowed to starve.[26]

The next morning Churchill presented a radical new face, to the surprise of Morgenthau. The previous evening's acrimonious condemnation of his plan had been replaced by the prime minister's smiling support. Had it been Lord Cherwell who had twisted Churchill's arm overnight? Cherwell, a professor of Physics at Oxford University and a Germanophobe scarcely less extreme than Morgenthau, was then one of Churchill's most influential confidants. Had the prime minister been influenced by Morgenthau's ploy that if Germany would be left without industries, Great Britain would be able to take over her former markets in the postwar world? Or had Morgenthau quietly blackmailed Churchill and Great Britain with his $6 billion Lend-Lease Phase II program? That financial-aid package was intended to support nearly bankrupt Great Britain from the end of the war in Europe until the end of the war with Japan. From the British standpoint, acquiescence to Morgenthau's plan, no matter how ill-conceived and constructed, was a small price to pay for the British Empire's solvency. On September 15, 1944, Churchill took it upon himself to dictate the final memorandum, 226 words long. Churchill's language included reference to Germany's conversion "into a country primarily agricultural and pastoral in its character," but it did not state that all German mines were to be destroyed and the country's factories razed or carted away, as Morgenthau had hoped for. The president accepted the Churchill memo, signing it "O.K. F.D.R." Churchill added his initials and the date: "W.S.C. 15 9."[27]

Back in Washington after the conference, Morgenthau could scarcely contain himself over what he considered "his Quebec triumph." He told his staff that the conference had been the high point of his entire career in government and that he had gotten more personal satisfaction out of his forty-eight hours in Canada than with anything else he had ever been connected with.

Stimson and Hull did not see it Morgenthau's way when they learned of the events that had taken place in Canada in their absence. Stimson considered Cherwell "an old fool ... who had loudly proclaimed that we could never cross the Channel and ... the robots [V-1s and V-2s] could never do any damage. He is a pseudo scientist ... for whose attainments nobody has much respect." Stimson was equally antagonistic toward Morgenthau, feeling that the "Carthaginian attitude of the Treasury" was in the saddle. "It is Semitism gone wild for vengeance," he later wrote, "and, if it is ultimately carried out (I cannot believe that it will be), it as sure as fate will lay the seeds for another war in the next generation."[28]

While the delighted Morgenthau may well have thought his plan "signed, sealed, and delivered," in fact the Secretary of War had one remaining arrow in his quiver. He sent FDR a third memorandum on the subject on September 17 which — patronizingly — "was designed to appeal to FDR, the hasty signer of ill-considered memoranda, to Franklin D. Roosevelt, the farsighted and greatly humanitarian president of the United States."[29] Five days later, Stimson learned that FDR had read the memorandum and wanted to talk to him about it. When Stimson had lunch with the president later in the week, he flattered FDR by commenting that his leadership in the war had been on a "high moral plane" and he "must not poison it with hatred or vengeance." Morgenthau was the wrong man to launch such a campaign against Germany, Stimson told him, and such actions by a man of his ethnicity would be misinterpreted.

The president insisted to Stimson that he had no desire to turn Germany into an agrarian nation and had not approved anything like that; he had merely wished to save some of the Ruhr's business for Great Britain, which was bankrupt. "Mr. President, please don't say that abroad until you have refreshed your memory with this paper," Stimson declared, pulling out a copy of the Roosevelt-Churchill memo with the initials "O.K. F.D.R." FDR did not get flustered easily, but Stimson recalled that the Quebec document with his initials "staggered" him. The president told Stimson he had not the faintest recollection of the document nor his signing it.[30] Was this "memory loss" a sign of the deepening illness that was affecting his cognitive capabilities, or another example of his routine deceitfulness?

Cordell Hull also refused to allow the issue to lie quietly. He, too, visited the president and recalled in his diary that he had spoken "bluntly." "I said ... that Morgenthau's plan was out of all reason, and that no experts, no appropriate officials of our Government ... and no other Governments had anything to do with its preparation." Furthermore, Morgenthau's plan "would wipe out everything in Germany except land ... only sixty percent of the German population could support themselves on German land, and the other forty percent would die."³¹ Hull concluded his stern peroration that once Morgenthau's proposals were picked up by the press, and the president was connected to them, he would be seriously wounded politically. FDR was then quietly planning his run for a fateful fourth term. Roosevelt said little, but did reply that "he had not actually committed himself to Morgenthau's proposals. In fact, he did not seem to realize the devastating nature of the memorandum of September 15 to which he had put his 'O.K. F.D.R.'"³²

As soon as the story leaked, the nation's press, generally hostile to Morgenthau, eagerly played up the divisions within the cabinet as well as the obvious flaws in the punitive program. In the view of many the Morgenthau Plan represented Jewish retribution for Hitler's treatment of Germany's Jews. Arthur Krock, influential columnist for the *New York Times*, wrote two articles in late September bearing on the inflammatory issue. On September 22 — "Why Secretary Morgenthau Went to Quebec"— he wondered why the Secretary of the Treasury and not the Secretary of State had been at the Quebec meeting. "Does this mean that Mr. Morgenthau has become the President's adviser on foreign affairs instead of Mr. Hull?" he asked rhetorically.

On the following day the *Wall Street Journal,* on page one, broke open the story of Morgenthau's controversial plan: "Treasury Plan Calls for Dismemberment, Ban on Most Heavy Industry." The article called the scheme "Carthaginian" which was the same word privately used by Stimson, suggesting, perhaps, that the leak had originated in the War Department. A day later, other newspapers revealed that the plan had split the Cabinet Committee. The *Washington Post* called the Morgenthau Plan "senseless," and stated that if the Germans suspected that total destruction of their society lay ahead, "they will fight on." It was just six weeks before what was expected to be a tight presidential election and Americans were being told of a schism within the president's cabinet.

By September 29, Krock was in a position to head a column titled "A Good Example of the Value of Publicity" and point to FDR's abandonment of Morgenthau's postwar plan for Germany — and that "arrangements for postwar Germany are again being handled in an orderly manner: the State Department dominant in the political sector, the War Department in the military, and the Treasury confining itself to its proper concerns instead of trying to take over the whole problem." He wrote that the upsurge in critical commentary throughout the United States was based on the use by Josef Goebbels and his propaganda apparatus of an Allied program to convert Germany into an agricultural nation. "It was clear that Dr. Goebbels would ask why Germans should not die to the last man to resist a conquest after which (he would say) no German could hope to enjoy even the driest fruits of incessant labor." In the same *New York Times* article, Krock wrote that FDR "did not favor" the Plan and "never did."

Under fire from many directions, FDR tried to distance himself from the Morgenthau Plan which had so quickly turned sour. He went so far as to send a memorandum on October 20 to Hull, writing lamely that he "disliked making detailed plans for a country which we do not yet occupy." In England at the same time, Churchill, under heavy pressure from his own cabinet, also disowned his involvement and approval of the plan he had personally dictated.

Capping the avalanche of domestic criticism was Governor Thomas E. Dewey's campaign speech the night before the 1944 election in which he lambasted the president's support of the Morgenthau Plan. He charged that it had been equivalent to ten fresh German divisions in France and encouraged the Germans to fight to the last man. Dewey also attacked the fundamental premises of the Morgenthau Plan as unworkable. Earlier, on October 18 in the heat of the presidential campaign, Dewey had exploited the disarray in FDR's cabinet in a radio speech. He pointed out, mockingly, that when FDR went to Quebec he took [invited] Morgenthau, "whose qualifications as an expert on military and international affairs are still a closely guarded military secret" instead of the veteran Stimson.[33] A week later Joseph Kennedy, who was jealous of Morgenthau because he coveted his Cabinet post, publicly insisted on knowing why Morgenthau had been allowed to go to Quebec. It was "sheer madness," and the interference of a "proved incompetent," he wrote.[34]

Josef Goebbels' propaganda ministry had a field day, jubilantly blaring that the Morgenthau Plan intended to convert Germany into a huge potato patch and was clear proof that the United States was out to destroy Germany. While Goebbels did not greet the announcement of the Morgenthau Plan in quite the same way as *New York Times* columnist Krock had suggested, his propaganda rebuttal was thorough. He ran bold headlines in the party's newspaper and elsewhere: "Morgenthau Surpasses Clemenceau; Forty Million Germans Too Many; Roosevelt and Churchill Accept the Jewish Murder Plan at Quebec," backing up his headlines with supporting quotes from U.S. and British newspapers. Goebbels also referenced a chauvinist article from the London *Spectator* that outrageously declared it was "only right that Germany should be crippled for all time, even if this would require that German women and children starve."[35] At that time, the U.S. Army was fighting ferocious German resistance to capture Aachen, their first major city inside Germany. Goebbels exhorted that city's citizens that "every house should resemble a fortress" to avoid the horrible fate of the Morgenthau Plan. In October 1944, Goebbels broadcast: "It is a matter of complete indifference whether, in the course of executing their plans of destruction, the Americans wish to destroy our tools, machinery and factories, or whether the Bolsheviks want to take them, along with our workers, to Siberia. From neither enemy can we expect any mercy or protection whatsoever if we deliver ourselves up to them."[36]

There are some indications that Churchill was concerned that Roosevelt might use the Morgenthau Plan as a substitute for future Lend-Lease aid to England in light of plans to destroy German industry and create new markets for Britain. In fact, he had threatened to "do business largely within the Empire" in postwar Europe if America backed out on Lend-Lease.[37]

Roosevelt never formally repudiated the Morgenthau Plan. But enormous damage had been done; the price in desperate resistance by the Wehrmacht would be reflected in the continuing high Allied casualties in the last months of the war. In the postwar United States Zone of Occupation in Germany some vestiges of the Morgenthau Plan survived in Joint Chiefs of Staff Memorandum 1067. But Henry Morgenthau, Jr.'s goal of converting the Germany he so detested into an industry-less country had been sensibly abandoned.

Immediately after FDR's ill-fated fourth-term victory Cordell Hull, fed up and ill, retired. Hull had always been aggravated by Morgenthau's meddling into foreign policy areas but had been particularly incensed by his latest incursions. His wife told a friend that the conflict with Morgenthau over his plan had affected both his health and morale. After years of Roosevelt's calculated ill-treatment she said, "the Morgenthau business was the final blow."[38] In private conversations, Roosevelt had always belittled Hull. He considered the former senator from Tennessee not particularly bright, and even went so far in private conversations as to cruelly mimic his lisp. FDR had appointed Hull to conciliate the southern wing of the Democratic Party but he rarely was interested in Hull's advice. FDR preferred to be his own secretary of state, like many presidents before and after him.

With the death of his all-powerful champion on April 12, 1945, Henry Morgenthau, Jr. overnight found himself a beached whale. Not only was his cherished plan for postwar Germany a goner but his days as an influential cabinet officer were numbered. During the years he had been a principal advisor to the president and a powerful wheeler-dealer in the administration, Harry Truman was an inconspicuous senator from Missouri known principally for his ties to the corrupt Pendergast political machine. So on April 14, 1945, when Morgenthau walked into the Oval Office to greet the new president and wish him well, he arrogantly presumed the inexperienced Truman would look to him for counsel. In this snap judgment Morgenthau was dead wrong. Truman, like so many in Washington who had come into contact, even superficially, with the imperious treasury secretary, knew him as a toady who had never hesitated to flaunt his close ties to FDR and to impose his will into political areas beyond his domain. Besides, the new president understandably wanted his own advisors.

On the day after FDR's interment in Hyde Park, Truman addressed a joint session of the Congress and restated one of FDR's principal war policies: that unconditional surrender remained a keystone. But Truman was privately cynical of the former president's wartime leadership and while writing his memoirs in 1954, expressed his view that "it probably would have been better had there been no policy of unconditional surrender." Without Roosevelt's edict, Truman argued in retrospect, the Germans might have surrendered when they felt the war was lost — after Stalingrad and the D-Day landings. "This would have saved lives and allowed a much easier recovery for all of Europe and especially Germany." He also told his aides that he had never been in favor of "that crazy Morgenthau Plan."[39]

Truman's opportunity to get rid of Morgenthau arose on July 5, 1945, when a petulant Morgenthau told Truman that unless he was invited to the Potsdam conference, he would resign. That dovetailed with Truman's thinking and he told Morgenthau that he had been in the process of appointing a new treasury secretary. Morgenthau replied that if Truman had doubts about his staying, he wanted to resign immediately. The two agreed that Morgenthau would stay until after the Potsdam Conference when he could announce his resignation.

In 1954, Truman privately boasted about this confrontation with Morgenthau in which he bested him, putting his own spin on the events. When plans were being made for the Potsdam conference, Truman recalled: "Morgenthau came to see me and said 'he had to go along.' I told him, 'I don't need you and it's not your business...' He said, 'If I can't go to Potsdam, what's going to happen to the Morgenthau Plan?' I said they could throw it out the window. He said he would quit. 'All right,' I said, 'I accept your resignation right now.'"[40]

No longer a president's advisor, the still-feisty Morgenthau published a book in 1945, *Germany Is Our Problem*, filled with his warped and prejudiced views. He wrote cynically that as early as August 1944, "fanatical young corporals ... are weeping as bitterly as Hitler did in 1918. Soon, like him they will be dreaming of another chance at world conquest and reminding each other in beer halls and shabby eating places how narrowly they missed success this time."[41]

According to Morgenthau, Germany's industrial leaders did not wait for final defeat in World War II before beginning mobilization for World War III. He insisted that this view was not a guess: "It is a proved and documented fact." The supposedly unassailable "fact" was actually based on an obscure report that Morgenthau claimed was given to the U.S. Army by an anonymous Frenchman "for whose reliability military intelligence can vouch." One of the documents in the report discussed a meeting in August 1944 attended by representatives of leading German industrial firms with business interests in France. Also present were engineers from manufacturing plants as well as officials of Germany's armaments and naval ministries. The presiding official, a Dr. Scheid, director of Hecho and a high-ranking Nazi, told the group that German industrialists must be aware that the war could not be won and that they "must take steps in preparation for a postwar commercial campaign."[42]

Morgenthau continued with his nonsense-filled tale of German intrigue, discussing details of a program to organize an underground Nazi movement after defeat. Each of Germany's big factories would create separate research bureaus, "hidden in the cities or camouflaged in villages near water-power sites under the guise of studying hydroelectric resources. All plans, drawings and documents needed to continue research into new weapons of war were to be turned over to the bureaus...." Finally, because it was understood that many Nazi leaders would be tried and executed as war criminals, it was the job of the industrialists to "find safe places in the research bureaus" for less conspicuous Nazis, according to Morgenthau.[43]

Morgenthau showed his deeply etched hatred of Germans and Germany throughout his angry book as the following crude passage illustrates: "In discussions of what to do with Germany, she has been compared to a mental patient, a problem child, a whole zoo of animals ranging from snakes to apes, a case of retarded development...."[44]

Until he died in 1967, Henry Morgenthau, Jr., stubbornly stuck by his conviction that his plan for postwar Germany had been the right one. His biographer, Yale historian John Morton Blum, who produced a comprehensive three-volume work based on Morgenthau's diaries, argued that the plan had been flawed. Morgenthau, still confrontational in his declining years, figuratively slapped Blum on the wrist: "You're too young to know whether the Morgenthau Plan was a mistake," he told Blum. "And I'll bet you — though I won't be around to collect — that you're going to have to fight Germany again before you die."[45]

10
Roosevelt: Feeble and Dying

> "It is, of course, easy to say that Roosevelt, broken on the wheel of service, was with tremendous courage giving the last ounce of his waning strength in the service of his country. But, after all, his country in that critical moment of history was entitled to something more in a leader than the last ineffectual ounces of his strength."[1]

> "The health of the chief executive is his own private business."[2]
> Dr. Ross T. McIntire, White House Physician

> "...the President's medical files had been in the care of his personal physician, the late Admiral Ross McIntire. They had been kept in a safe at the Bethesda Naval Hospital. The combination to this safe had been known to but two people: the hospital's Commander and Admiral McIntire. Shortly after the President's death, the records were found to have 'disappeared.' What happened to them no one knows to this day."[3]

Among all of Franklin Roosevelt's lies and cover-ups during his twelve-and-a-half years in office, his concealment of his failing health during his last sixteen months in office stands out as uniquely perfidious. He was dying of cardiovascular disease and he knew it, yet he had the audacity to run for a fourth term. It was a selfish decision by a man with few scruples, and the United States paid dearly for his arrogance. His private physician conspired with FDR to keep his irreversible illness a secret from the American people.

Roosevelt is easy to fault in his last year in office. In the summer of 1944, he spent five weeks to and from Hawaii on trains and ships, for a *two-and-a-half–hour* meeting with his Pacific commanders. The only justification for this length journey was Roosevelt's health; he had desperately needed a long vacation at that time, but the American people were not told this. In Hawaii, the persuasive General Douglas MacArthur bent the feeble Roosevelt like a willow reed into permitting MacArthur's militarily wasteful agenda to stand. FDR let Henry Morgenthau, Jr., bamboozle him into supporting Morgenthau's vengeful and unworkable scheme to turn industrial Germany into farmland (Appendix L). He chose to disregard pleas from American Jewry to order the bombing of the German death camps. FDR played no noticeable role in the selection of Harry S. Truman as his running mate and gave every indication of apathy. That same summer, he sided with Chiang Kai-shek in his confrontation with General Joseph W. Stilwell. He compliantly replaced Stilwell even though Chiang was more interested in fighting the Communists than the Japanese. Of more significance for the future was the president's refusal to diplomatically engage Ho Chi Minh, allowing the French to regain their dominance in Indochina, and leading to America's ten-year war in Vietnam.

In September he signed a nuclear-sharing agreement with Churchill in Hyde Park, telling neither the State Department nor Truman anything about it. In January 1945 he left for the Yalta Conference, ignoring his new vice president; on his return, he told Truman nothing about the discussions or the agreements. More significantly, in the last months of his life, FDR did not "make the slightest attempt to inform Truman about the complicated workings of the American government, the vast array of cabinet departments and independent agencies that had grown by leaps and bounds during the New Deal and war years, over which the president presided in very personal ways."[4]

On April 12, 1945, FDR died of a massive stroke, his sudden death a shock to nearly every American. But not to all! It was not unexpected by the few visitors allowed to meet with him in his last months, and who were stunned by obvious signs of his rapid physical decline. It was not unexpected to those diplomats with whom he mingled in Yalta in February who observed not only his parchment-like pallor, sunken cheeks, and tremulous fingers, but also his precarious cognitive capabilities. It was not unexpected to his Secret Service detail, who closely attended him whenever he left the White House, which was increasingly rare, and were bound by oath to keep silent. And not to his attending cardiologist, Dr. Howard Bruenn, and not even to his conniving personal physician, Dr. Ross T. McIntire.

One of the perquisites that comes with the office of President of the United States is the service of a full-time personal physician. The only restriction on the selection is that he (or she) must come from the medical corps of the Armed Services. Roosevelt recalled meeting Dr. McIntire, then a Navy Commander, several years before becoming president. Admiral Cary T. Grayson, former personal physician to Woodrow Wilson (Appendix E), had introduced him to McIntire. Later, as president, Roosevelt selected McIntire to be his personal physician. McIntire was an "eye, ear, nose, and throat" specialist, which likely contributed to his selection because FDR suffered from recurrent sinus infections and other upper respiratory problems. Like Woodrow Wilson did with Grayson, FDR formed an easy-going relationship with the informal McIntire, promoting him to an Admiral and also naming him chief of the navy's Bureau of Medicine and Surgery.

McIntire was a physician of only modest skills, even in his own specialty. Robert H. Ferrell wrote gently that he "was the protégé of an individual [Cary Grayson] whose medical knowledge had not been celebrated."[5] Dr. Bert E. Park, who analyzed FDR illnesses and published a book on his findings in 1980, was sterner; it was a case of "one incompetent physician recommending another." Dr. Joel E. Boone had been Herbert Hoover's personal physician and had been passed over in favor of McIntire. Boone recalled that whenever he went into Grayson's office, the admiral's desk was covered with unopened medical journals.[6] In fact, Grayson had spent the last eighteen months of Wilson's tenure in office as far more a public relations executive than a doctor. He was involved nearly full-time in a joint cover-up of the president's crippling stroke with Wilson's wife and his press secretary (Appendix E).

Author Hugh Gregory Gallagher, a polio victim himself, has also lambasted Ross McIntire as a physician of questionable ability. Through the years, "the only doctoring McIntire ever did for his eminent patient consisted of dosing him on a daily basis with nose drops and sinus sprays, irrigating his sinuses with saltwater douches, and experimenting with one of the more extreme treatments of the day: cauterization of the sinus tissues by means of red-hot wire loops stuck up the nose ... the years of dosing with drops brought the president only marginal relief, while as the same time it served to increase his already elevated blood pressure."[7]

McIntire like Grayson was also entangled in a corrupt relationship with his president. As early as 1937, there was a hint of the cover-up to come of Franklin Roosevelt's illness. Postmaster General James Farley wrote in his autobiography: "The President's condition so concerned me that I had a long talk ... with Admiral Cary T. Grayson ... about Roosevelt's health.... I told him that while I had a great deal of respect for ... Ross T. McIntire, I thought it highly essential that some prominent physician be called in to go over the President thoroughly. Grayson said it was important not only to get a good doctor, but *one who would not talk*..." (emphasis added).[8] Eight years later, following FDR's fourth-term inaugural, Farley in a phone conversation with Secretary of State Cordell Hull opined that Roosevelt "was a sick man ... and should not be called upon to make decisions affecting this country and the world."[9]

Amazingly, McIntire's care of the president was redolent of the country doctor of bygone years. He appeared at the White House every day before 9 A.M. and went straight to FDR's bedroom, where Roosevelt typically spent most of the morning in bed, reading newspapers and conducting informal presidential business. Sometimes he even held mini-conferences propped up in bed. The morning visit was part of McIntire's daily "look-see" regimen, as he referred to it. He was there to observe, and "produced neither thermometer nor stethoscope, nor looked at the presidential tongue nor felt of the pulse and rarely asked a question." He sat beside the bed and observed his patient's color, listened to his speech, and checked on the tilt of his chin, the higher the better, apparently, and watched how "he tackled his orange juice, cereal and eggs."[10] McIntire claimed that this procedure told him all he needed to know. Promptly at five-thirty each day, he was back at the White House for a second "look-see."

Beginning in December 1943, when the president returned from the Teheran Conference, his declining vitality became an issue in the White House. His daughter, Anna Boettiger, who by then was living with her husband in the White House watching over her father's condition, insisted to a reluctant McIntire that he find out why.[11] It was agreed that the president should have a comprehensive physical examination.

An understandable question immediately arises: why his daughter and not his wife? What about Eleanor Roosevelt during her husband's last months? Why wasn't she in the White House helping oversee Franklin's medical treatment? The answer is simple. The two had long ago agreed to lead separate lives and Eleanor rarely saw Franklin, and then only when it was politically expedient to be seen together. Divorce was out of question, the principal reason being his mother, the former Sara Delano, who as a devout Episcopalian was against divorce. Sara was a strong-willed woman and in addition she controlled the family purse strings. Dr. Howard Bruenn, who became FDR's cardiologist and was thus in a position to know, later recalled that Eleanor paid no attention to him and that "in the worsening of her husband's illness she had much to answer for."[12]

Roosevelt was rolled into an examination room at Bethesda Naval Hospital for a head-to-toe, two-day physical on March 28, 1944.[13] That first morning, he preliminary results of the examination shocked all the attending physicians. As FDR was lifted onto the table, he was short of breath. His blood pressure was dangerously high, and fluoroscopy and X-rays of his chest showed an enlargement of the heart. "Furthermore, a review of McIntire's records (which Bruenn noted he had some difficulty in obtaining from McIntire) reflected the presence of this condition as early as 1941, even though no acknowledgement of it [or treatment] had been made."[14] Further testing also revealed obvious signs of congestive heart failure.

"At the end of the examination Bruenn completed his diagnosis: hypertension, hypertensive heart disease, cardiac failure (left ventricular) and–the sole instance in which Admiral McIntire had been correct — acute bronchitis."[15] Dr. Park, corroborating Bruenn's diagnoses, wrote that "these clinical findings in relation to Roosevelt's leadership capacity are immediately obvious to any physician remotely familiar with the effects of diastolic hypertension, anemia, COPD (chronic obstructive pulmonary disease), and CHF (congestive heart failure) on the neurological system, and hence on *cognitive and emotional function*" (emphasis added).[16]

Years later, during a personal interview, Bruenn told Ferrell that the president's condition was "God-awful."[17] Bruenn's recommendations had been what was "standard treatment of the period for heart disease: immediate bed rest for several weeks, digitalization, a light diet, sedation as needed for sleep, and codeine for the cough."[18] McIntire instead told FDR to get more rest and prescribed only a codeine cough syrup. One is left to wonder why McIntire had not insisted that Roosevelt give up his heavy smoking from the first day the doctor took on FDR as his patient.

Following his check-up of the president, Lt. Commander Howard Bruenn was invited to join the full-time medical staff in the White House. Bruenn's first step was a demand for a drastic reduction in the number of the president's daily appointments. McIntire went along with the recommendation, if reluctantly, for the notes entered into the presidential appointments calendar in March and April of 1944 show a steady reduction in the number of visitors until the pages became blank. At a press conference seven days later, McIntire disingenuously told reporters that the president's health was "satisfactory.... When we got through, we decided that for a man of 62-plus we had very little to argue about...."[19]

McIntire's motives for such obvious deceit can only be guessed at. Was it misplaced loyalty to the president — and to hell with the nation? Was there some measure of professional jealousy, as indicated by his reluctance to call in cardiac specialists who would show up McIntire's superficial medical capabilities? There was, of course, Roosevelt's fourth term to be considered. Certainly Roosevelt would not have stood a chance at reelection if Americans knew the truth about his health. Had Roosevelt simply told McIntire to "lay off?"

Or had Roosevelt early on made a secret pact with McIntire that, above all else, demanded that he conceal details of the president's health, that he be continually reported to the press in "excellent health for a man of his age?" In the author's view, this last scenario best fits the characters of the two men. Franklin Roosevelt was adept at slippery diplomacy, as earlier chapters in this book clearly show — and he never let scruples get in his way. As for Dr. Ross McIntire, the fact that he later selected the seedy George Creel to write his autobiography give hints to his credibility.

There were three successful conspiracy models for McIntire to emulate. Twenty-five years before, Grayson, together with Wilson's wife, Edith, and his press secretary, Joseph Tumulty, had engineered an air-tight cover-up of the incapacitating stroke that left Wilson a cripple for the last 18 months of his presidency. McIntire obviously knew all about that chicanery. In 1893, President Grover Cleveland underwent clandestine cancer surgery aboard a yacht in Long Island Sound; it had been covered up for 20 years (Appendix A and Appendix E).

Currently, McIntire had Franklin Roosevelt's remarkably successful concealment of the massive disability resulting from his polio to guide him. FDR was a paraplegic, unable to stand without braces nor walk, even a few steps, without being supported. The American public had only a vague idea that the president was lame, for the true extent of his paralysis was carefully hidden. When Roosevelt left the well-ordered confines of the White House, his staff of specially trained Secret Service handlers followed specific rules. He was never to be observed being lifted, especially in the presence of newsmen and photographers. When it was necessary to move him in or out of a car, this was done preferably in a garage or behind a screen. Roosevelt had perfected a special method for moving from wheelchair to car when he couldn't be hidden. One of his Secret Service agents described it: "He would turn his back to the car and allow an agent to lift him from his wheelchair to a standing position. He would reach backward and grab the car door with both hands and then he'd actually surge out of your arms first to the jump seat, then to the rear one. He did this with such speed and grace that literally thousands who saw him at ball games, rallies and inaugurations never suspected his condition."[20]

He was never to be seen by the public in a wheelchair and no photographs of FDR in a wheelchair were ever published. In fact, there are only two such photographs in existence. Either he was propped up to appear as if he were standing on his own, with his hidden steel leg braces latched (painted black on the bottom to blend in with his dark trousers and black shoes) or leaning on a sturdy podium bolted to the floor if he was giving a speech. When he moved about in public, he always grabbed with his powerful hands the arm of an experienced and trusted aide — often one of his strong sons. It was acceptable to show FDR seated, but not his chair being carried with him in it. An important injunction was that under no circumstances were photographs to be taken showing FDR appearing to be crippled. The press photographers understood that there were to be no "candid" shots, only posed shots of a smiling, upbeat FDR, typically with his long cigarette holder at a jaunty angle. Roosevelt was most comfortable, as was his Secret Service detail, when he was seated in the back seat of an open car.

For this cover-up to be successful, the press was expected to cooperate — and they did. In 1936, for example, at the Democratic National Convention, when Roosevelt fell off a ramp leading to the rostrum, the press obediently stayed quiet: there were no photographs, no mocking cartoons, and not even a brief reference to the incident's occurrence.

It was the Secret Service's job to ensure complete accessibility for Roosevelt in his wheelchair, which required construction of ramps wherever he went. "These were not merely simple ramps ... upon occasion the Secret Service would actually raise the entire level of a street to the level of the building entrance by means of temporary but extensive wooden trestles and scaffolding.... This allowed the president to appear to 'walk' seemingly naturally from his car into a building."[21] "Image control" extended to the more elaborate cover-ups of his infirmity used at formal occasions in the presidential mansion. For example, White House gardeners would sometimes erect a wall of foliage at the far end of the reception hall. A special seat, like a bicycle saddle, would be concealed among the foliage; sitting on the hidden seat, the president would appear to all the guests to be standing erect.

FDR had been able to hide his paralyzed legs but it was much more difficult to conceal his wasted face — the parchment-colored skin, the dark bags under his eyes, the hollow cheeks, the overall sallow look of a tired old man, a man that few would elect to be president of the United States if he were observed close-up.

From March 28, 1944, Roosevelt apparently knew exactly what was ailing him, if he had not suspected before. It was not bronchitis and influenza, as McIntire had reported. He had been wheeled into a suite at Bethesda Hospital with a sign over its entrance: Electrocardiograph Department. Soon after, Bruenn began appearing at the White House in McIntire's stead, ministering to him morning and evening. Bruenn was a heart specialist and FDR realized he was a cardiac case.

From that time on, FDR drastically and willingly changed his lifestyle. If he realized his illness was irreversible, he nevertheless tried to keep his head above water as long as he could. That meant curtailing his hours of work and expanding his hours of relaxation. In the first five months of 1944, for example, Roosevelt absented himself from the White House for a total of nine weeks. Even that figure is misleading; throughout March, FDR was so sick that he rarely got out of bed. On April 8, FDR left the White House for *Hobcaw*, Bernard Baruch's 23,000-acre estate in sunny, warm South Carolina. He did not return to the White House until May 10, after a month spent resting, sleeping late, and "fishing," which consisted mostly of snoozing in a chair in the sun. It had been hoped that, away from the pressures of his office for an extended period, FDR would have recovered as he had in the past. He did not that time, nor ever again. Five doctors were called in to examine him. Caretaker McIntire saw to it that their reports were never made public, nor did he ever report the president's blood pressure readings at the time. According to him, Roosevelt had recovered from infections of the sinus and chest and that he was "well and active."

Despite McIntire's disarming summary for public consumption, Bruenn knew better. He set up a strict regimen for the president—which tells the whole and accurate story. "He was to have breakfast from 8:30 to 9:00; office hours from 11:00 to 1:00; from 1:00 to 2:00 luncheon, but *no business guests*; 3:00 to 5:00 office hours; then 45 minutes massage and ultra-violet rays and rest *lying down* until 7:30; 7:30 to 8:00, dinner in quarters, no night work and sleep for 10 hours" (emphasis added).[22] This schedule translated into a *four-hour workday*—not simply for a convalescent period, but for the remainder of Roosevelt's life. The American public never knew this.

Roosevelt confided in no one that he planned to run for a fourth term, but later admitted to his son, James, that the reason he had run again for the presidency was to "maintain a continuity of command in a time of continuing crisis.... The people elected me their leader and I can't quit in the middle of the war." At the Democratic Convention in July 1944, the president's health was an important topic of conversation, if only behind FDR's back. He had lost a lot of weight and his clothes hung on his body adding to his general appearance of an exhausted old man. "Roosevelt's gauntness was not unusual for persons with severe heart problems. Doctors would term this condition "cardiac cachenia."[23] McIntire stated preposterously in his book that "every possible checkup proved him organically sound," and that FDR could be expected to "stand up under the strain of four more years."[24]

Following his nomination for a fourth term, and of Harry S. Truman as his running mate, FDR was off on a political junket to Honolulu, to meet with his Army and Navy commanders, crossing the continent in six leisurely days aboard his private luxury train, following by a relaxing voyage aboard a comfortable U.S. Navy man-of-war. Historian Flynn wrote that on the outbound leg of his journey the president "made one slip." He was photographed delivering his acceptance speech in an ordinary room at a Marine base.[25] The news photograph, without the normal intervention of FDR's handlers, shocked the nation; it revealed, for the first time, his haggard, emaciated face. In addition, the news shot showed part of the white uniform of a naval officer standing in the background. Who was he and why was he in the picture? The Washington correspondent of the Chicago *Tribune* wanted answers. He went to the Associated Press and got a copy of the original photograph before it had been cropped to fit the newspapers' format and took the shot to the Navy Department for identification. The man in the white uniform was a Navy physician, Lt. Commander Howard Bruenn, a noted Boston cardiac specialist in civilian life who had been specifically recruited to watch over the health of the man another doctor, Ross McIntire, had unceasingly proclaimed had just a lingering cold. Bruenn would remain close to FDR's side until he died.[26]

After the election, Roosevelt treated Harry S. Truman cavalierly, failing "to inform his successor of anything, military, diplomatic, or administrative, save one casual admission about the atomic bomb.... He told him nothing about the agreement with Churchill over nuclear-sharing concluded at Hyde Park on September 18, 1944; in fact, he did not even inform the State Department. When he returned from Yalta he did not discuss with Truman anything that had taken place there." Equally important, the imperious president never sat down with his vice president to discuss the "mechanism of the American government, the responsibility for which Truman inherited just before the country underwent a complicated conversion from a wartime to a peacetime economy and when he was dealing with an increasingly hostile Soviet Union."[27] The nation deserved better.

Roosevelt then managed to squeeze in a month's relaxation in Warm Springs, Georgia. He interspersed these long vacations with three-day workweeks in Washington. He typically left Thursday evenings to spend four days at Hyde Park or at his new get-away, *Shangri-La*.[28] All of this time, he studiously avoided the public when he could; with few exceptions, the appearances he made were carefully choreographed and crowds were kept at long range so they could not see his wizened countenance.

Who was there to tell the American people they had a dying president who was behind his desk only three or four hours a day, only three days a week, with months off in between? It would not be Stephen Early, the president's press spokesman. It was the reporters' responsibility, those on the White House beat. Where were they all this time? There was an important story to tell the American people. But the press had been conditioned to treat the crippled president with kid gloves since 1933, and although there had been rumors of his prolonged absences, not a single newsman followed up. So much for an independent press to serve the information needs of a democracy!

As part of the tightly orchestrated cover-up, dating prior to March 1944, Roosevelt traveled incognito during his visits to Bethesda for his sinus problems. These clandestine appointments involved using different aliases, so that there were no records of a Franklin D. Roosevelt ever having been treated there. Navy personnel encountering him in the halls must have recognized the man in the wheelchair or gurney as their president. But these were military personnel and could be commanded to shut up, which they did.

An interesting example of the depths which Roosevelt's Secret Service contingent would plumb to hide his infirmities occurred during the final days of the 1944 presidential campaign. The contest between FDR and New York Governor Thomas E. Dewey remained close and uneasy Democrats warned that their standard bearer must appear before a large public gathering, the bigger the better, to put the health issue to rest once and for all. FDR was scheduled to give a speech in New York City on October 21. What better opportunity than for him to tour the city—all five boroughs—in a motorcade to give his followers a chance to cheer him?

Roosevelt arrived in the city in a cold and windy rainstorm. It was decided the rotten weather was, in fact, a fine opportunity to prove his detractors wrong, that he was willing and more than able to serve four more years. He rode in an open car for nearly five hours, the rain pouring down on his fedora while crowds of New Yorkers lining the streets urged him on. He wore long-johns, wrapped himself in a fur robe under his Navy cape, and kept his feet and legs warm with an electric heater.

> Neither the press nor the public knew that at points along the parade route the Secret Service had commandeered garage space. As the presidential cavalcade passed the garage, the President's car was turned out of the parade into the warmth of the heated building. Secret Service agents quickly lifted the president from the car and stretched him out full length on blankets laid on the floor. They removed his clothes down to the skin. He was toweled dry and given a rubdown. He was redressed in dry clothes, brandy was poured down his throat, and he was lifted back into the car. The pit stop was quickly done, and the President was soon back in the cavalcade.[29]

In the weeks after his fourth-term victory and before his inauguration on January 21, 1945, Roosevelt was forced to come out of hiding from behind the barricades of the White House and meet with his cabinet and other administration officers to discuss plans for the coming four years. People saw him up close who had not seen him for months—and their reactions ranged from disbelief to horror to grief. Robert Sherwood, who had last seen him in September, remarked that he was "unprepared for the almost ravaged appearance of his face." Winston Churchill's physician, Lord Moran, who had observed FDR in September when the two world leaders met in Quebec, was more descriptive: "You could have put your fist between his neck and his collar."[30] The author John Gunther, who sat across a desk from Roosevelt just before the inauguration, wrote that he had been terrified when he saw his face. "I felt certain that he was going to die. All the light had gone out underneath the skin. It was like a parchment shade on a bulb that had been dimmed."[31]

Two days after his inauguration and a perfunctory inaugural address of four-and-a-half minutes, the shortest on record, FDR boarded the heavy cruiser USS *Quincy* in Norfolk, Virginia. He was heading to Yalta in the Crimea for a meeting with Churchill and Stalin and would be out of sight of American reporters, photographers, and the American people for over a month.

Much has been written about Franklin Roosevelt's inept diplomacy at the Yalta Conference, ARGONAUT, in February 1945 and that he "gave away the farm" to a stronger negotiator, Josef Stalin. The Soviet leader held much stronger cards and Roosevelt, even with his cognitive abilities diminished, knew that. The Red Army already occupied two-thirds of Poland, much of Eastern Europe and was driving resolutely toward the German border. To a far greater extent than either Roosevelt or Churchill, Stalin was willing to absorb high casualties to occupy land. The Soviet Premier was not about to negotiate away what his nation's youth had paid for in blood. Furthermore, Russia had a million soldiers who could support the United States in its war with Japan, and Roosevelt knew that, too. Yalta effectively recognized the realities of Soviet hegemony in Eastern Europe and set the stage for what later became the cold war.

Robert E. Sherwood has acknowledged the controversy that surrounded the Yalta Conference. He wrote: "Yalta has been blamed for many of the ills with which the world was afflicted in the years following the total defeat of Nazi Germany and Japan. The belief has grown that Roosevelt made various "surrenders" to the Russians ... and the more kindly critics attribute these to the fact that he was a dying man."[32] Sherwood, who was not at Yalta, nevertheless concluded that "Roosevelt appears to have been in full possession of all his faculties."[33] FDR's Chief of Staff, Fleet Admiral Leahy, who was in Yalta, loyally gave an even more glowing report: "It was my feeling that Roosevelt had conducted the Crimean Conference with great skill and that his personality had dominated the discussions."[34]

Other more objective observers, who were at Yalta, tell a different story. Lord Moran wrote in his diary: "To a doctor's eye, the President appears a very sick man. He has all the symptoms of hardening of the arteries of the brain in an advanced stage, so that I give him only a few months to live. But men shut their eyes when they do not want to see, and the Americans cannot bring themselves to believe that he is finished. His daughter thinks he is not really ill, and his doctor [McIntire] backs her up"[35] Churchill's interpreter, A. H. Birse, thought FDR looked "worn out. The former self-confidence and firmness of tone, so evident at Teheran, seemed to have gone. His voice was that of a man weary in spirit ... he had become a shadow of his former self."[36] Another physician wrote retrospectively in his detailed clinical evaluation of Roosevelt's health that his decision-making capacity by the time of the Yalta Conference had been

> impaired by a combination of hypertension [high blood pressure], diffuse atherosclerosis [fatty deposit accumulations under the inner lining of the arterial wall, leading to strokes and heart attacks], chronic obstructive pulmonary disease, and congestive heart failure [cardiac output insufficient to meet the body's normal requirements for oxygen and nutrients]. He also suffered from transient episodes of clouding of consciousness, termed 'encephalopathy,' [a condition resulting from lack of oxygen to the brain] which intermittently and adversely affected his political skills.... Most patients with metabolic encephalopathy cannot concentrate well and suffer from brief periods of confusion, disorientation, and lethargy.[37]

At Yalta FDR's daily schedule was that of a man recuperating from a serious illness, not a fully engaged diplomat playing for high stakes. He slept late, remaining in his quarters until noon, generally unavailable to his advisers during that time. He met with his doctors and had a quiet lunch by himself. He then saw members of the U.S. delegation. Then it was back to bed for his afternoon nap mandated by Dr. Bruenn. At four Roosevelt would reconvene the summit, always in the Livadia Palace, the president's residence, so he did not have to undergo the stress of getting in and out of a car. The high-level meetings typically lasted three to four hours, after which there was a one-hour recess, during which the president would get a massage and rubdown. At dinner time, the three leaders would get together again to dine and informally discuss issues.

There are other signs that FDR was a doddering bargainer during the conference. When he first arrived in the Crimean resort, he immediately requested of his two fellow negotiators that the daily plenary sessions be limited to three hours, preferably in the late afternoon (after his mandatory nap). Stalin and Churchill readily agreed, FDR's sunken cheeks, hollow-eyed gray countenance, and quivering fingers being obvious indicators of his failing health. More importantly, Stalin did not want Roosevelt to die on his home turf. Presumably, the Russian leader breathed a quiet sigh of relief on February 12 when he bid goodbye to the president, sending him on his way with a less-than-vigorous handshake. Earlier, Marshal Stalin was reported to have said that had he known FDR was so sick, he would have been willing to move the conference to a more convenient location for the president.[38]

Anna Boettiger was with her father at Yalta and midway through the conference wrote a letter to her husband back in Washington that sheds much light on a darkened corner of FDR's last weeks: "...Ross and Bruenn are both worried because of the old 'ticker' trouble — which, of course, no one knows about but those two and me ... am using all the ingenuity and tact I can muster to try to separate the wheat from the chaff— to keep the unnecessary people out of OM's [the old man] room and to steer the necessary ones in at the best times.... I have found out through Bruenn (who won't let me tell Ross that I know) that this 'ticker' situation is far more serious than I ever knew. And the biggest difficulty in handling the situation here is that we can, of course, tell no one of the 'ticker' trouble. It's truly worrisome — and there's not a heluva lot anyone can do about it. (Better tear off and destroy this paragraph)."[39]

During the plenary sessions, Roosevelt's slow reactions and his inability to grasp ideas were apparent to those who were dealing with him; these were obvious markers of his advanced disease. Bruenn recalled that four days into the conference, when there had been heated discussions over the future of Poland, Roosevelt for the first time exhibited an irregular pulse, a danger sign. Bruenn restricted Roosevelt to bed all the next morning, on top of the afternoon nap earlier mandated. These required rest periods sharply limited the time FDR could spend in strategy sessions with his advisors before the plenary sessions with Stalin and Churchill. In retrospect, the question was not *if* FDR's debilitating condition contributed to the outcome of the conference — but *how much*.

Nonetheless, FDR managed to accomplish two of his goals: establishment of an international peace-keeping organization, the United Nations (Appendix J), and getting an agreement from the Soviets to enter the war with Japan. At the time, the atomic bomb was an unproven weapon, and plans were being finalized for U.S. amphibious assaults on the Japanese home islands. Russian help was looked upon as an important way to share the burden of the expected high casualties.[40]

In Washington on February 28, after FDR's return from Yalta, there was a press conference to put to rest "reports from Europe that the president had been ill." The *New York Times* reported to the contrary, that companions of the president on the 14,000-mile trip were "unanimous" in the view that FDR's health was excellent throughout. McIntire added that despite "long sessions of hard work" the president stood up well under the strain. Presidential assistant Jonathan Daniels said he had never seen him "looking better." One can ask: if the president was in such radiant health, why hadn't he been at the press conference?

If FDR's physical appearance had deteriorated so noticeably by the beginning of 1944, how far back was it apparent that his cognition had worsened as well due to his progressive disease? That is more difficult to determine. One example is Roosevelt's endorsement of the Morgenthau Plan (Chapter 9 and Appendix L) in September 1944, at the QUADRANT

Conference in Quebec. The harsh plan initially drew little support, and within a month was repudiated by nearly everyone. Why had FDR signed on to it in the first place? When War Secretary Stimson confronted him with his initials okaying the document, Roosevelt was surprised, or feigned surprise. FDR claimed he did not remember signing the important document.

Some historians posit that if Roosevelt had been a healthy man, the Honolulu Conference in July 1944 with General Douglas MacArthur and Admiral Chester M. Nimitz almost certainly would have gone differently — and the drive across the Pacific probably would have been far less costly in American lives. Nimitz's Navy strategy consisted of moving westward across the Pacific to the Japanese home islands by way of Formosa. MacArthur's Army plan, on the other hand, was to retake the Philippines, first the big island of Leyte then Luzon, then to island-hop to Okinawa, thence to Japan's home islands. Was it necessary to recapture the Philippines, which took so many U.S. lives?[41] Why not simply bypass the archipelago, marooning thousands of Japanese troops as had been done with the strong Japanese naval base at Truk? Driving MacArthur's decisions, however, were his giant ego, misplaced pride, and pecuniary stake in his strategy.

When he was "recalled" from Corregidor just before his army of Filipinos and Americans surrendered to the Japanese on Bataan in 1940, he had said melodramatically that he "would return"; he insisted in Honolulu he could not let down the Filipinos. He previously had a lucrative contract with the president of the Philippines, Manuel Quezon, as the self-proclaimed "field marshal" of the tiny Filipino army of 4,000. If his command was tiny, his salary and expenses of $33,000 per year were decidedly otherwise; he was the highest paid military officer in the world.[42] Without a physically strong president, there was no one to stand up to MacArthur's flamboyant demands.

Further, records that came to light ten years after MacArthur's death in 1964 reveal that he became much wealthier "when the Philippines were engulfed by the military disaster for which the general bore a large measure of responsibility." Among the private papers of Richard Sutherland, MacArthur's former chief of staff was a copy of "Executive Order No. 1 of the President of the Philippines." It had been executed on January 3, 1942, a week after Quezon and MacArthur had moved inside Corregidor, and endorsed the transfer of $640,000 from the Philippine Treasury to MacArthur and his closest aides "in recompense and reward, however inadequate, for distinguished service rendered between November 15, 1935 and December 30, 1941." MacArthur's share of the largesse was $500,000.[43]

After the president's death on April 12, 1945, Ross McIntire hurriedly engaged the first willing and supposedly able ghost-writer he could find to write his autobiography. The ghost was George Creel, a hack journalist with a long resume, and the book, *White House Physician*,[44] a grand apologia for Rear Admiral Ross T. McIntire's long stint as FDR's medical caregiver. Creel tried vainly to cover McIntire's muddy tracks. For example: "In writing of Teheran and Yalta, it has become the fixed habit of many editors and columnists to state without qualification that Franklin Roosevelt was a sick man, even a dying man in the last year of his life. I am adjudged as having deliberately deceived the people of the United States by the issuance of statements that the President was sound organically and in fairly good health."[45]

McIntire, of course, had his own disreputable actions to conceal. According to the historian Robert H. Ferrell, "the admiral was wary about telling him [Creel] anything. He virtually refused to go beyond his public statements." One letter to McIntire summed up their uncomfortable relationship: Creel asked for more information, "For God's sake." Then he added. "Do not fall down."[46]

As these two examples illustrate the book was also filled with nonsense, a specialty of writer George Creel. The president was a warship designer, according to McIntire: "Night after night I watched him working away on rough designs for giving ships greater defensive strength, and just as he first suggested cruisers of the *Guam* and *Alaska* class, so was the *Independence* type of airplane carrier his brain child."[47] And: "The President's seemingly inexhaustible energy had never ceased to amaze me...."[48]

John T. Flynn, no friend of the president, summarized Franklin Roosevelt's last months as president and his impact on the United States of America. He likened him to a chief of staff who would have been "summarily removed if he did not have the decency to resign. A department head in peacetime as feeble as Roosevelt would have been promptly relieved. Yet this America, so powerful ... so tremendous ... now, in the crucial moment of victory when she would capture or lose the fruits of the victory, put her fortunes into the hands of a drooping, jaded and haggard man, a mere shell, drifting wearily to the grave. But the American people did not know this."[49]

11

Was Adolf Hitler Planning to Attack the United States?

"Tons and tons — quite literally — of the German archives and of their top-secret plans, memoranda, and correspondence fell into the hands of the victors at the end of the war. These documents were winnowed and studied with care for months and months by dozens of investigators in a meticulous search for every shred of evidence which could be presented at the Nuremberg trial ... it transpired that nowhere in these papers was there to be found any evidence of any German plans to attack the United States."[1]

In 1939, when asked what goals Germany would pursue after defeating France and Great Britain, Josef Goebbels responded: "You must know whose turn it will then be — the United States."[2]

"On October 29, 1940 he [Hitler] informed his military leaders that he was most interested in the German plans to occupy the Atlantic islands 'with an eye to the future war with America.'"[3]

"War is the most natural, the most every-day matter. War is eternal, war is universal. War is life. Any struggle is war. War is the origin of all things."[4]

Adolf Hitler, 1933

"I have always said that if Great Britain were defeated in war I hoped we should find a Hitler to lead us back to our rightful position among the nations."[5]

Winston Churchill, November 7, 1939.

On the front page of the April 24, 1971, issue of the *New York Times* is a photograph of a stern-faced Kaiser Wilhelm II in fur-trimmed cape, Pickelhaube on his head. It was part of an article titled "A Footnote: Kaiser's Plan to Invade U. S." that outlined a formal German plan "to attack and invade the United States at least 14 years before the United States entered World War I, in 1917." According to Holger H. Herwig, who was the *Times*' source, the plan was called Operation Plan III which involved sending the German High Sea Fleet with troop ships into the Caribbean. From a base there, East Coast cities would be bombarded, then German troops would be landed on U.S. soil.

Herwig told the *Times* that his evidence was contained in 1,500 handwritten pages that he found in the German military archives at Freiburg. The invasion plans were clearly spelled out and, Herwig claimed, frequently were done in the handwriting of such German military leaders as Admiral Alfred von Tirpitz, Admiral Otto von Diederichs, Count Alfred von Schlieffen, and Major Erich Ludendorff. The German fleet would first coal in the mid-Atlantic Azores, then steam to Puerto Rico or the nearby island of Culebra to set up a base. New York City would then be shelled by the fleet's big guns and an amphibious landing of infantry and engineers made on sparsely populated western Long Island. The attacking forces would then split up, part going north along the coast to Boston and part heading south to Norfolk, Virginia. For the invasion to succeed, however, the war planners needed complete surprise. On that point, the plan was deemed unrealistic and abandoned, since how could a large invasion fleet steam 3,000 miles across the Atlantic Ocean without being detected?[6] More than "unrealistic," Operation Plan III was a hare-brained scheme that could scarcely have been successful. Its compilers, according to Historian Herwig's handwriting analyses, belied their reputations as Germany's foremost military planners.

Any analysis of Adolf Hitler's plan to attack the United States must begin with an understanding of German-American relations in three important historical eras: the period of colonial rivalry from 1889 to 1905, the Great War from 1914 to 1918; and the Nazi period from 1933 to 1941, when Germany declared war against the United States.

In the 1880s both countries were new entries in the imperialist race. Until then, the United States had focused its energies on westward expansion into former Spanish and British colonial regions, forcefully removing or killing the native Indian residents and stealing their land. Germany, under conservative Chancellor Otto von Bismarck, in the same period had begun to build a colonial empire. Taking advantage of Anglo-French rivalry at the time, the Reich acquired four African colonies — Togoland, the Cameroons, German Southwest Africa, and German East Africa — plus outposts in the Pacific: New Guinea, the Bismarck Archipelago, the North Solomon and the Marshall Islands. The United States made up for lost time with giant imperialist strides of its own at the end of the nineteenth century and into the twentieth: annexing Hawaii in 1898, Guam and Puerto Rico in 1899, Tutuila and Pago Pago in Samoa in 1900, the Philippines in 1902, and the Panama Canal Zone in 1904.

The first serious clash between the two colonial newcomers involved the far-away Samoan Islands, three tiny dots in the South Pacific east of Australia, which Henry Adams referred to as "wretched little lava heaps."[7] Germany, the United States, and Great Britain had all signed treaties with Samoan rulers for coaling stations. A civil war over who would rule the islands, the Malietoa or the Tupua tribes, complicated matters. The United States encouraged the Malietoas, while Germany backed the Tupuas. Incited by garish headlines in jingoistic newspapers across the country, Americans began to take notice. So, too, did the Congress. America's honor apparently was at stake, and alleged German provocations had to be answered with force.

President Benjamin Harrison, in March 1889, dispatched envoys to Samoa to investigate. They were instructed, in classic imperialist jargon: "…this government cannot accept even temporary subordination and must regard it as inconsistent with that international consideration and dignity to which the United States, by continental position and expanding interests must always be entitled."[8] In Germany the situation was calmer. To Bismarck, "the entire Samoan question smacked too much of the 'new world' of trade, commerce, and industry in which he felt ill at ease."[9] In March 1890, the Kaiser dropped his renowned "pilot," signaling a new era for Germany, which would henceforth pursue a track leading to *Weltmacht* (world power). This would necessarily collide with America's global aspirations—with grave consequences for both nations.

On May 1, 1898, Commodore George Dewey's Asiatic Fleet decisively defeated a decrepit Spanish fleet in Manila Bay in the Philippines at the start of the Spanish-American War and the U.S.-German competition heated up again. Vice Admiral Otto von Diederichs and his cruiser squadron, based in nearby Kiaochow, China, seized by Germany in 1897, was ordered to proceed to Manila Bay "to show the German flag." There, in mid-July, the two fleets came close to exchanging salvos. Petty incidents, such as *droit de visite* (inspection rights); failure of a German warship promptly to display her colors; and movement of German ships at night, ostensibly forcing Dewey to train spotlights on them, thereby showing his position to the Spanish on shore, were blown out of proportion to their significance. American newspapers inflamed the situation with provocative headlines calling for war and news stories filled with half-truths. The *Chicago Daily Tribune* headlined its October 5 issue: MAY HAVE WAR WITH GERMANY. CONFLICT WITH UNITED STATES IS THOUGHT IN BERLIN OFFICIAL CIRCLES TO BE NEAR.[10] On November 25, the *Washington Post* wrote: "We know … that in the German Government the United States has a sleepless and insatiable enemy." That naval confrontation has been described as "the single most destructive event in German-American relations prior to the first World War."[11]

11—Was Adolf Hitler Planning to Attack the United States?

John Hay, ambassador to the Court of St. James's in 1898 shared his Germanophobic views with the influential Senator Henry Cabot Lodge: "The Vaterland is all on fire with greed, and terror of us. They want the Philippines, the Carolines, the Samoas—they want to get into our markets and keep us out of theirs.... There is to the German mind, something monstrous in the thought that a war should take place anywhere and they not profit by it."[12]

In 1899, another civil war erupted in Samoa, this time pitting Germany against both Britain and the United States. However, Germany had a new foreign minister, Prince Bernard von Bulow, who saw no reason for a military confrontation. In the Reichstag, he acknowledged that the peoples of Europe would never sanction a war over "an island group ... of whose 30,000 inhabitants barely 500 were Europeans...."[13] But there was a tough-minded naval officer in the admiralty he had to contend with, Rear Admiral Alfred von Tirpitz. He was a student of America's Alfred T. Mahan, an enthusiastic supporter of German *Weltpolitik*, a clever manipulator of public opinion, and an astute war planner. Samoa was already of great strategic importance, he told von Bulow, as a way station on the route between Kiaochow to South America and would be a key part of the planned "German world cable."[14]

Nevertheless, Samoa II was also resolved without shooting. The peace settlement in the fall of 1899 yielded Germany the lion's share of the Samoan Islands, while the United States retained the biggest island in the group, Tutuila, with its excellent harbor at Pago Pago. Great Britain received the Tonga group, Savage Island, Lord Howe Island, and most of the German Solomon Islands.

As for the Philippine archipelago, America got it all and Germany got nothing, despite von Diederichs' interference in Manila Bay. President William McKinley allegedly had told a visiting missionary group, a year after he sent U.S. troops to "benevolently assimilate" the Filipinos in 1899, how he had arrived at his final decision to annex the islands: "I didn't want the Philippines, and when they came to us as a gift from the gods, I did not know what to do with them.... I walked the floor of the White House night after night until midnight; and I am not ashamed to tell you gentlemen, that I went down on my knees and prayed Almighty God for light and guidance ... that there was nothing left for us to do but to take them all, and to educate the Filipinos, and uplift and civilize and Christianize them, and by God's grace do the very best we could by them ... And then I went to bed and went to sleep and slept soundly."[15] When this supposed rationale for annexing the Philippines was made known in Berlin, it reinforced Kaiser Wilhelm's angry conviction that never again would his *Reichsmarine* be inferior to the U.S. Navy, as it had been in confrontations in Samoa and the Philippines. By 1917, at their next, more portentous showdown, the ratio of German to U.S. dreadnoughts would be 19:14 in favor of Germany. Had the Great War not upset the German Navy's big-warship construction schedule, the Reichsmarine by 1920 was expected to be able to take on the United States Navy and the Royal Navy in a colossal high-seas clash. That projected fleet included 38 battleships and 22 battle cruisers.

The revisionist historian Harry Elmer Barnes observed at the beginning of the Great War in August 1914: "We were made to feel that the Entente was fighting the cause of the small and weak nations against the ruthlessness of a great bully. We were inevitably led to believe that the war had been started through the deliberate determination of Germany to initiate her alleged long-cherished plan to dominate the planet, while the Entente had proposed diplomatic settlement from the beginning and had only taken up arms in self-defense with the utmost reluctance. This theory of the German provocation of the war and the German lust for world dominion was played up in the newspapers ... until the danger from Germany struck terror in the hearts of Americans.[16]

While President Woodrow Wilson publicly exhorted Americans to be neutral, in his private conversations he leaned from the start toward the Allied cause, abetted by his robustly pro–Allied aides, particularly his chief confidant Colonel Edward M. House, nearly all his cabinet, and every one of his ambassadors. The staunchest Anglophile of all was Walter Hines Page, Wilson's minister in London, who strove unceasingly, even conspiratorially, to draw America into the war on the Allied side.

The president was keenly sensitive to public opinion. He supposedly held at bay for as long as he could the growing outcry for war against Germany because he was uncertain the nation was ready. It was publication of the secret "Zimmermann Telegram" (Appendix B) in March 1917 and the resumption of unrestricted submarine warfare by Germany the previous month that probably pushed Wilson over the edge; the only certainty is that it was Woodrow Wilson who pushed America into the war.

On the night of May 31, 1916, a fleet of Reichsmarine men-of-war (twenty-two battleships, five battle cruisers, eleven light cruisers, and sixty-three destroyers) slipped their cables and sortied to attack Allied shipping in the North Sea. Their commanders were also hoping to meet the British Grand Fleet, decisively defeat it, and break the tightening British blockade. By mid-afternoon of the next day, an equally formidable Royal Navy force (twenty-eight battleships, nine battle cruisers, thirty-four light cruisers, and eighty destroyers) was heading its way. At four P.M., the first salvos from the big-gun battleships signaled the start of the engagement. The "first

11—Was Adolf Hitler Planning to Attack the United States? 155

round" would go to the Germans: two British battle cruisers sunk, the *Indefatigable* and *Queen Mary*. Two hours later, a "second round" would begin. The German battle cruiser *Lutzow* was disabled, but nevertheless managed to sink the battle cruiser *Invincible*. The battleship *Pommern* was the only capital ship lost on the German side before the fleets disengaged.[17] The final scorecard of losses: Royal Navy — three battle cruisers, three cruisers, eight destroyers, 6,097 sailors; Reichsmarine — one battleship, four cruisers, eight destroyers; 2,551 sailors.[18] It would be known as the Battle of Jutland, and would be the last time during the war that the Germans would risk another major naval battle.

In this war, there would be no confrontations between surface warships of the Reichsmarine and the U.S. Navy, only between American destroyers and German submarines in the Atlantic — and in earnest. Instead, American soldiers would brutally fight German soldiers in the trenches of France with rifles, bayonets, cannons, and poison gas.

For over three years the British Admiralty had been reluctant to introduce the convoy system in the Atlantic, and their warships remained detached from their merchantmen. But the ever-increasing toll of sinkings by U-boats finally forced a change. On May 24, 1917, the first convoy steamed east from Hampton Roads, Virginia; the only merchantman sunk was a straggler. Henceforth merchant ships and passenger liners would not sail unescorted. "Of the 1,100,000 American troops brought across the Atlantic in convoy between May 1917 and November 1918, only 637 were drowned as a result of German submarine sinking."[19] Further, Germany's hopes that their submarines would starve the British into surrendering had been dashed.

In June and July 1918, those U.S. soldiers who were already in action were giving a good account of themselves. In the fierce action at Belleau Wood at the end of June, more than half of the 10,000 Marines engaged were killed or wounded. The Germans gave their new foes high marks: "The moral effect of our fire-arms did not materially check the advance of the infantry," recorded a German officer in the heat of the battle ... the nerves of the Americans are still unshaken." A visiting historian seventy-six years later observed: "In the war cemetery at the edge of the wood are the graves of 2,288 American soldiers and the names of a further 1,060 who have no known graves. In another cemetery a few hundred yards away are 8,624 German graves."[20]

In October, General John J. Pershing was concerned that the Germans would start up the war again in the spring, if allowed the respite of an Armistice. But his appeal for unconditional surrender fell on deaf ears. Lloyd George and Clemenceau were confident of crushing Germany, even if its army did not surrender on the field of battle. Armistice talks would continue, but so would the killing. After the Armistice, Pershing was angry that the war had not continued until the Germans had thrown down their arms in the field. He remarked: "I suppose our campaigns are ended but what an enormous difference a few more days would have made.... Had they given us another week, we would have *taught* them."[21]

The destructiveness of the First World War, in terms of the numbers of soldiers killed, exceeded that of all other wars known to history. Germany lost 1,800,000; the United States 48,000. The Central Powers, the losers, lost 3,500,000 soldiers on the battlefield, the Allied Powers, the winners, lost 5,100,000. Astoundingly, on average there were more than 5,600 soldiers killed on each day of the war.[22]

Following the Armistice on "the 11th hour of the 11th day of the 11th month" in 1918 and the signing of the Versailles Treaty in Paris on June 28, 1919, both the United States and Germany withdrew from international politics—the United States voluntarily, Germany by the hated *Diktat* of the Paris treaty. The U.S. Congress had failed to ratify the Versailles Treaty[23] and America's main concern in Europe was reparations, leading to the Dawes Plan in 1924 and the Young Plan in 1930.

By the terms of the Versailles Treaty, Germany's military was severely restricted: the army to 100,000 troops, the navy to 15,000 men, and no air force. The Reich was forbidden to build tanks, heavy artillery, aircraft for military purposes, submarines, and warships displacing more than 10,000 tons. All of Germany's colonies, totaling some 1.2 million square miles in area, were divided up and parceled among the conquerors. Germany also lost territory in Europe, including Alsace-Lorraine and, for fifteen years, the coal-rich Saar basin to France. The lost regions dispossessed Germany of nearly half of her coal and more than 60 percent of her iron-ore deposits. The final indignation was the internationalizing of Germany's major waterways; the navy lost its control over the Kiel Canal, the critical link between the North Sea and the Baltic.

On June 4, 1940, following the ignominious retreat of the British Army across the English Channel, Prime Minister Winston Churchill addressed Parliament "in one of the most remarkable feats of propaganda ever performed by a head of state ... turned a disastrous defeat in France into an inspiring boost for British morale."[24] Eloquently, he closed with a dramatic passage aimed at influencing U.S. public opinion as much as that of the English. In sonorous tones he vowed that Great Britain would never surrender: "We shall defend our island, whatever the cost may be. We shall fight on the beaches, we shall fight on the landing-grounds, we shall fight in the fields and in the streets, we shall fight in the hills; we shall never sur-

11—Was Adolf Hitler Planning to Attack the United States? 157

render, and even if, which I do not for a moment believe, this island or a large part of it were subjugated and starving, then our Empire ... would carry on the struggle, until, in God's good time, the New World with all its power and might, steps forth to the rescue and liberation of the Old."[25] What American reading that marvelous paragraph would not have sympathized with the British cause?

However, there is ample evidence that Adolf Hitler purposely allowed the British to retreat across the English Channel. His "Führer order" of May 22 stopped the Wehrmacht's advance in its tracks for three days. "On wheeling north, Guderian's Panzer Corps headed for Calais while Reinhardt's swept west of Arras toward St. Omer and Dunkirk. On the 22nd Boulogne was isolated by Guderian's advance, and next day Calais. That same day Reinhardt reached the Aire-St. Omer Canal, less than twenty miles from Dunkirk—the only escape port left to the BEF. The German armoured forces were much nearer to it than the bulk of the BEF." At that moment, von Rundstedt told me [Liddell Hart], a sudden telephone call came from Colonel von Grieffenberg at OKH, saying that Kleist's forces were to hold on the line of the canal. It was the Führer's direct order. I questioned it in a message of protest, but received a curt telegraph in reply: "The armoured divisions are to remain at medium artillery range from Dunkirk [a distance of eight or nine miles]."[26]

General Kleist recalled that when he got the order it made no sense to him. "My armoured cars actually entered Hazebrouck, and cut along the British lines of retreat.... But then came a more emphatic order that I was to withdraw behind the canal. My tanks were kept halted there for three days."[27] Meanwhile the British forces streamed back towards Dunkirk, and formed a strong defensive position to cover their re-embarkation. The German tank commanders had to sit and watch the British slipping away under their very noses.

On May 24, two days after the Panzer divisions had been halted in full stride, Hitler met with von Rundstedt and his staff at their headquarters in Charlesville. According to General Blumentritt, "Hitler was in very good humour, admitting that the course of the campaign had been 'a decided miracle.' He would conclude a reasonable peace with France and then the way would be opened for a similar agreement with Britain."[28]

Hitler then apparently astonished his listeners by speaking with admiration of the British Empire, its strides in civilization, and of the necessity for its continued existence. He remarked that the creation of the Empire had been achieved by means that were often harsh, but "where there is planing there are shavings." He compared the British Empire with the Catholic Church, saying both were essential elements of stability in the world. He insisted that all he wanted from England was her acknowledgment of Germany's preeminent position on the continent. The return of Germany's lost colonies was desirable but not essential and he would even offer to support Britain with Wehrmacht troops if she should be involved in any international difficulties. He concluded by saying that his aim was to conclude a peace with England that she would regard as compatible with her honor. Von Rundstedt, who had always sought agreement with France and Britain, was satisfied. After Hitler was gone, von Rundstedt commented: "Well, if he wants nothing else, then we shall have peace at last."[29]

Later, Blumentritt's thoughts ran back to Hitler's comments. He felt that the three-day halt at Dunkirk that had been called by Hitler had been some sort of political scheme to make peace easier to reach. If the British Army had been captured at Dunkirk, Blumentritt mused, the British people might have felt a stain to their honor which must be avenged; by letting the Army escape, Hitler hoped to conciliate the British people. This conviction of Hitler's deeper motive was later confirmed by his procrastination over subsequent plans for the invasion of England; according to Blumentritt: "He showed little interest in the plans and made no effort to speed up the preparations."[30]

In *The Testament of Adolf Hitler*, Hitler briefly referred to the three-day halt in France: "Churchill was quite unable to appreciate the *sporting spirit* [emphasis added] of which I had given proof by refraining from creating an irreparable breech between the British and ourselves. We did, indeed, refrain from annihilating them at Dunkirk."[31]

As it turned out, the British, banking on America's almost-certain entry into the war, rejected all of Hitler's peace initiatives out of hand. Hitler's three-day gamble had not paid off. Instead, as General Heinz Guderian wrote in his memoirs, the Supreme Commander's intervention on May 24, for the left wing to stop on the river Aa, was "to have a most disastrous influence on the whole future course of the war."[32]

More than sixty years after the successful evacuation of the British Expeditionary Force from France, the British continue to resent any suggestion that Adolf Hitler may have purposely engineered the so-called "miracle" at Dunkirk immortalized by their own propaganda as a great victory. "To understand the significance of Hitler's probable political motive does, however, requires a readjustment of the British propaganda image of him as the raving dictator hell-bent on the destruction of Britain and her Empire."[33]

Was this attitude of Hitler toward England prompted only by the political idea, which he apparently had long entertained, of securing an alliance with her? Or was it inspired by a deeper feeling? Did his actions on May 22 suggest that Hitler, a complex individual, nurtured a mixed love-hate feeling toward England similar to that of Kaiser Wilhelm II's during the Great War? Indeed, Wilhelm II was Queen Victoria's favorite grandson.

Other indicators of Hitler's plans for the future was his disinterest in building a large surface navy or a strategic air force. Aircraft for his Luftwaffe were tactical weapons, such as the Junkers Ju-87 *Stuka* dive bomber, to support the Wehrmacht; when Hitler initially retaliated for the Royal Air Force's bombing of German cities, the principal high-level bomber in his inventory was the modest twin-engine Heinkel He-111, with a bomb load of 2-1/2 tons over a normal range of less than 900 miles. Emphasis was on the development of artillery and tanks — and submarines. In these areas, German arms were acknowledged as the best in the world. The Krupp 88 mm cannon, for example, was unmatched as an anti-aircraft weapon, as a stand-alone anti-tank gun, as the main cannon on Tiger and Panther tanks, and as deck-mounted cannons on U-boats. Although overwhelmed in the Atlantic by Allied anti-submarine forces, German U-boats were nevertheless superior to equivalent U.S. and British designs: they could submerge more quickly, could dive to greater depths, and from late 1943 on were fitted with *Schnorkels* to allow underwater operation of their diesel engines. Too late in the war and too few in numbers, the Luftwaffe's sensational Messerschmitt Me-262 *Swallow* twin-jet interceptor was considered the best of its type in World War II.

Hitler had been influenced by two Prussian military giants, Frederick the Great and Karl von Clausewitz, both of whose thinking was based on land armies. Clausewitz's book, *On War*, today is recognized internationally as perhaps the most influential work of military philosophy in the western world. There is no record of Hitler having read influential American navalist Alfred T. Mahan, whose book, *The Influence of Sea Power on World History*, was required reading for military officers elsewhere in the world.[34] As a result, neither he nor his advisers had any grasp of the strength of the "salt-water" powers.[35] "To them," according to his German-American advisor, Ernst F. S. Hanfstaengl, "International power politics were based on the limitations inherent in land warfare, and in my decade of struggle to influence the workings of Hitler's mind I never succeeded in bringing home the importance of America as an integral factor in European politics."[36]

Two among many unofficial overtures which Germany addressed to Great Britain in the prewar years indicate that Hitler's political ambitions were in the East, not in the West. In 1937, Hermann Göring, while entertaining the British ambassador to Germany, Sir Neville Henderson, at a stag hunt at his hunting lodge, suggested that there should be an agreement between Germany and England focusing on two clauses: Germany would recognize the supreme position of Great Britain in overseas affairs and would place all her resources at the disposal of the British Empire in case of need; in turn, Great Britain would recognize Germany's predominant continental position in Europe. At about the same time Joachim von Ribbentrop, then German ambassador to England, offered a virtually identical suggestion to Winston Churchill. Not yet prime minister, Churchill responded that the British government would not accept such terms. Ribbentrop said abruptly: "In that case war is inevitable."[37]

Further evidence of Hitler's disregard for America came on November 5, 1937, during the high-level meeting at which Hitler first outlined in details the steps by which he was determined to seize additional living space — Lebensraum — for Germany. The records of this momentous meeting do not indicate that the German dictator even considered the position or possible intervention of the United States. On May 23, 1939, when final plans to initiate hostilities against Poland were set, the role of the United States again appears to have been ignored. "Even when the Nazis weighed the possibilities of prolonged conflict, the records fail to mention the contingency that America might ally herself with the European democracies.... With an understandable faith in Germany's traditional military greatness ... the Führer ... did not appreciate the fact that American industry and troops actually turned the tide against Germany in 1918. This fatal misconception, in conjunction with the enhanced sense of invincibility which he acquired in the opening phase of the war, played a major part in Hitler's prompt and foolhardy declaration of war on the United States after Pearl Harbor."[38]

Despite Hitler's repeated disclaimers of any interest in acquiring territory or political power in the Western Hemisphere, others in his hierarchy spoke less circumspectly. On July 8, 1938, Hermann Göring, the proud head of the Luftwaffe, addressing German aircraft manufacturers, called on them for daring innovations. He suggested a rocket or long-range bomber which could reach New York with a five-ton payload. Such a weapon, the Reichsmarschal said, would please him and "would shut up those arrogant people over there."[39] The August 12, 1940, issue of *Facts in Review*, the principal German propaganda publication in the United States, published in English, quoted a less bellicose Göring: "There were no planes in Germany which, when loaded with bombs, could fly to America and return." He opined that "America simply cannot be invaded by air or sea. That is particularly true if her armaments and national defense are appropriate to or commensurate with the country's size, population, resources and industrial production, not to mention the spirit of the people.... If American defenses are what they should be, particularly if America's air force is properly developed, built up, organized and strategically based, *America can defy any group of powers. No one would be so idiotic as to attempt an invasion*" (emphasis added).[40] This statement by the Reichsmarschal must be taken with a grain of salt, however; he was talking directly to America's isolationists.

As the United States sharply increased aid to Britain with the passage of Lend-Lease in March 1941, Hitler and the leaders of his armed forces became increasingly aware of latent American power. Grossadmiral Erich Raeder impressed on Hitler the importance of capturing Gibraltar and Suez so as to close the Mediterranean to the Allies "before the U.S.A. steps in." Raeder also believed it might also be necessary to seize the Spanish and Portuguese islands in the Atlantic, the Canaries and the Azores, to forestall a British or American takeover. At a conference with his chief naval officers on November 14, 1940, Hitler had focused on the Atlantic islands, in particular the Azores, for another reason. The minutes of that meeting revealed his plan to bomb American cities: "The Führer believes that the Azores would afford him the only facility for attacking America, if she should enter the war, with a modern plane of the Messerschmitt type, which has a range of 12,000 kilometers [7,500 miles]. Thereby America would be forced to build up her own antiaircraft defense, which is still completely lacking, instead of assisting Britain."[41]

Again, on May 22, 1941, Hitler brought up the subject of the Azores during a meeting with his navy chiefs: "Führer seeks the occupation in order to deploy long-range bombers against the United States."[42] Ten days earlier, a Luftwaffe plan, "Tasks for Long-Range Planes,"[43] had been given to Göring for his review. A principal "task" was the bombing of U.S. industrial sites in Indiana and Tennessee. The plan specified either the Focke-Wulf Fw-200C, Heinkel He-177, or the new Messerschmitt Me-264 *Amerika-Bomber*, flying from Brest with 5.5 tons of bombs and refueling in the Azores on its return leg.

Later that summer, July 14, 1941, Hitler received the new Japanese ambassador, General Hiroshi Oshima. During the meeting, "Hitler gave the clearest definition to date of his ultimate plans concerning the United States. For one brief moment abandoning his original timetable, he urged that the two partners proceed against the United States across two oceans in his own lifetime.... Now was the time to strike."[44]

Hitler declared in his "victory" speech on July 19, 1940, after defeating the French and driving the British Army back cross the English Channel, that it had never been his intention to destroy the British Empire and made a public peace offer: "In this hour I feel it to be my duty before my conscience to appeal once more to reason and common sense in Great

Britain as much as elsewhere. I consider myself in a position to make this appeal, since I am not the vanquished, begging favors, but the victor, speaking in the name of reason. I can see no reason why this war must go on."[45] If Adolf Hitler saw no reason for the war to continue, the warrior Winston Churchill saw no reason for the war to stop! He wanted no part of a negotiated settlement and was working diligently to ease Franklin D. Roosevelt and America step-by-step into the conflict, thereby insuring a crushing victory for the British Empire. Hitler's conciliatory words were followed by private diplomatic overtures by Germany through Sweden, the United States and the Vatican, none of which bore fruit.

As the summer of 1942 passed, Hitler repeatedly criticized the "cowardly Americans," and by comparison applauded the courageous British. He exhibited at least a superficial knowledge of American history at the same time he gave it a fascinating interpretation when he commented: "If only Britain had supported the Southern States in the American Civil War! And what a tragedy that God allowed Germans to put Lincoln firmly in the saddle."[46]

Hermann Rauschning, a close confidant of Hitler, after the war wrote a detailed account of the many hours he had spent in Hitler's company. He recalled a conversation one evening in the early spring of 1933 that was "most revealing of Hitler's political opinions about America, and showed how far-reaching were his plans even then, and how mistaken was the belief that National Socialism had political aims only in the east and southeast of Europe." Hitler indicated a special interest in Brazil: "We shall create a new Germany there.... We shall find everything we need there."[47] Later that night Rauschning listened to a discussion that covered the outlines of the future German overseas Reich. He recalled that he was amazed to hear that the Führer was also planning to reach out to the Pacific. Hitler expressed an interest in reacquiring the former German island empire, taken from Germany in the Versailles Treaty, which would embrace the Dutch possessions and all of New Guinea. Hitler also commented that Japan must not be permitted to grow too big.[48] About the United States, Hitler had his preconceived views which no argument could budge, according to Rauschning. His firm opinion was that the United States would never participate in another European war. Further, he believed America, with her millions of unemployed, was on the brink of a revolution.

As early as 1925, when *Mein Kampf* was published, Hitler made his principal goals clear: rearmament in defiance of the hated Versailles Treaty; the abolition of democracy; territorial expansion to give Germany the Lebensraum of a great nation; racial "purity"; and the "elimination" of the "Jewish threat."[49] *Mein Kampf* was enormously successful; inside Germany,

11—Was Adolf Hitler Planning to Attack the United States?   163

a copy of the book was given to all newly married couples, and all Germans were expected to buy it and read it.

Rauschning wrote that in June 1933, he was present at a dinner-table conversation in Hitler's flat during which one of the guests suggested the value of friendly relations with the United States. Hitler's response was a tirade against America: "This is the last disgusting death-rattle of a corrupt and outworn system which is a blot on the history of this people. Since the Civil War, in which the Southern States were conquered, against all historical logic and sound sense, the Americans have been in a condition of political and popular decay. In that war, it was not the Southern States, but the American people themselves who were conquered. In the spurious blossoming of economic progress and power politics, America has ever since been drawn deeper into the mire of progressive destruction. A moneyed clique ... rules the country under the fiction of a democracy ... The beginnings of a great new social order based on the principle of slavery and inequality were destroyed by that war...."[50]

Hitler also showed his devious side by stating he was "willing to sign anything. I will do anything to facilitate the success of my policy. I am prepared to guarantee all frontiers and to make non-aggression pacts and friendly alliances with anybody. It would be sheer stupidity to refuse to make use of such measures merely because one might possibly be driven into a position where a solemn promise would have to be broken. There has never been a sworn treaty which has not sooner or later been broken or become untenable."[51] On the subject of Lebensraum, Hitler was adamant: "We need space to make us independent of every possible political grouping and alliance. In the east we must have mastery as far as the Caucasus and Iran. In the west, we need the French coast. We need Flanders and Holland. Above all we need Sweden. We must become a colonial power. We must become a sea power equal to that of Britain."[52]

One high-ranking German military officer who did take the United States into account was Colonel General Ludwig Beck, Chief of the Army General Staff. Beck was strongly opposed to Hitler's planned attack on Czechoslovakia. In 1938 he wrote several negative memoranda to Hitler which predicted disaster for Germany if she pursued what he called "National Socialist adventures."[53] His gloomy analyses assumed that a takeover of Czechoslovakia would involve not only England and France, but America as well. Furthermore, Beck doubted that Germany could sustain a prolonged war even if America remained only a supplier to her enemies— and told Hitler as much. These arguments fell on deaf ears: on August 10, at a meeting of his top generals, Hitler declared that regardless of "the defeatism of the General Staff, he would proceed with his plans. America was not mentioned and Beck's resignation followed a week later."[54] Beck then devoted his efforts to unseat — and kill, if necessary — his Führer, to whom he and all his fellow military conspirators had sworn allegiance (Chapter 8).

Through 1941, the United States was not regarded as a factor in German land strategy in Europe. One of Hitler's principal planners, Colonel Friedrich Hossbach, recalled that there was "not one word [spoken] of the real military and political situation and the position of the United States" in the important meetings with Hitler at which long-range plans were discussed.[55] Hitler himself had a general contempt for the prowess of American soldiers based on his Great War experiences. To him, U.S. intervention in 1917 had been "a farce." Current American rearmament programs were based on "lies pure and simple" and American production figures were "gigantic exaggerations."[56]

As Germany attempted to secure Hitler's *Fortress Europa*, it is understandable that he dismissed a successful invasion by the Allies as militarily untenable. He had assigned the defenses in France facing the English Channel, where the Allied amphibious forces had to land, to Field Marshal Erwin Rommel, one of World War II's most renowned military tacticians. In Hitler's view, without such an invasion there was no role for American forces in Europe.

The last four words of America's Rainbow Five plan provided an unambiguous declaration: "The Defeat of Germany" (in 1943). Rainbow Five had been mysteriously leaked to the press just days before the Japanese attack on Pearl Harbor. Did the Reichschancellor have a similar long-range plan and a timetable to invade, defeat and occupy the United States, as part of his "thousand-year Reich?" Or, being a military opportunist, had he relegated such an idea to a later time, after he had defeated Great Britain and Soviet Russia and consolidated his gains throughout Europe? Or was he awaiting terrible new weapons from his cadres of engineers and scientists with which to engage the Americans? Or, was Hitler's only concern the mastery of middle Europe for Nazi Germany and the defeat of hated Communism?

His own words (or the words of ghost-writers) in the form of speeches and books, and the testimony of contemporary witnesses shed light on his plans. From *Mein Kampf* (*My Struggle*) published in 1924, to *Zweites Buch* (*Second Book*) published in 1928 but not released, to *Hitler's Table Talk* (covering the period 1941–1945), to *The Testament of Adolf Hitler* (covering the period February–April 1945), Hitler's words cover a broad period in his growth and maturity: from Munich beer-hall rabble-rouser — to political head of one of the world's most powerful nations — to his last days in a Berlin bunker. Like the skilled politician he was—and almost certainly the most compelling political speaker of the twentieth century—Hitler tailored his spoken words to his audience. They ranged from giant, thundering audiences in the Nuremberg stadium—to small groups of generals standing with him around a map table—to a few dinner guests intent on hearing his ideas on many subjects. These documents clearly illustrate that Hitler was not the one-dimensional, stilted demagogue World War II Allied propaganda made him into.

In *Mein Kampf*, Hitler developed his fundamental racist theme that Germans were a superior people. They would hold on to their preeminence, he wrote, by three violent, aggressive actions. First, they would eliminate the alien Jewish population in their midst, the Untermenschen (subhumans). Second, by conquering lands in Eastern Europe they would assure themselves of adequate space—Lebensraum—on which to live and proliferate. Before this war could be launched, however, according to Hitler, France had to be dealt with, to eliminate a threat to its rear. Third, they would invade Soviet Russia and eliminate despised Communism, at the same time gaining adequate space. Throughout the 1920s, Hitler preached these principles over and over, in every city and hamlet where his dedicated helpers could round up an audience for his powerful presentations. In 1924, Hitler sent one of his itinerant fund raisers to Detroit, Michigan, to solicit the inveterate anti-Semite Henry Ford. Ford abstained—and Hitler remained aloof.

Hitler's *Second Book*, dictated by him in 1928 but not published then, was discovered in the archives of captured German documents in Alexandria, Virginia in 1958 by the historian Gerhard L. Weinberg, and finally published in English in 2003. It contains a number of references to the United States, none of which unambiguously pointed to a future war between the two countries. He was concerned that Europe was permitting its "best blood" to immigrate to America, with the likely result that European nations would ultimately be reduced to a continent of "degenerate, animalistic" pleasure seekers. Hitler concluded: "But it is thoughtless to believe that the conflict between Europe and America would always be of a peaceful economic nature...."[57] This book, too, like *Mein Kampf*, was written before he became chancellor and before Hitler could legitimately assess the political structure of postwar Europe and Germany's role in it.

What had drawn his attention to America? There is evidence that Hitler had begun cultivating an interest in industrial and economic development, particularly the automotive industry. Hitler had always been attracted to automobiles and he had been increasingly impressed by the great number of American cars on German roads. By the mid-1930s Hitler was personally involved in the development of the successful Volkswagen (people's car), designed by the legendary Ferdinand Porsche, and the equally significant Autobahn, which set the standard throughout the world for safe, high-speed, limited-access highways.

Weinberg makes a broad and credible leap from Hitler's fascination with cars to his belief in America as a threat to Germany's hegemony:

> Far from being the melting pot Americans imagined it to be, the United States was in fact a homogeneous country, a gathering in of the finest Nordic racial stock from each European country. This not only explained why Americans had made such good use of their living space; it also led [Hitler] to the conclusion that they were exceedingly dangerous people ... only a Eurasian empire under German domination could successfully cope with this menace. A third war was added to the original two.... One of the major tasks to be performed by the National Socialist movement, therefore, must be the preparation of Germany for this conflict.[58]

Weinberg has suggested that during the four-year period before he was elected chancellor Hitler was preoccupied by domestic issues, in particular the Young Plan[59] that involved the second renegotiation of Germany's Great War reparation payments. Then, in 1933, "the evidence indicates that the economic situation affected Hitler's thinking. The world depression was on everyone's mind.... It is clear ... that Hitler was tremendously impressed by the fact and impact of economic depression in the United States. This came to be one of his favorite topics and a major theme of National Socialist propaganda.... He saw the movie *The Grapes of Wrath* several times and assumed that it represented the whole United States for all time."[60]

What did Hitler know about the United States and its people? During his early years in Vienna and Munich, Hitler had been an omnivorous reader of newspapers and books, and he told a party comrade that even after he became chancellor he continued to read Karl May's novels of the early American West and American Indians.[61] While Hitler spoke no English and had no intercourse with Americans prior to 1933, he did have a close relationship with someone who knew the United States well, Ernst F. S. Hanfstaengl, a "Harvard-educated art dealer, historian, pianist, bon vivant and sometime court jester of the Hitler circle."[62] Hanfstaengl had close ties to America. He had been a guest of Theodore Roosevelt and in 1910 met New York State Senator Franklin D. Roosevelt. He remained in New York running his family's business during the Great War, returning to Germany in 1921.

In 1922, while living in Munich, Hanfstaengl for the first time heard Adolf Hitler speak. He had been told beforehand that Hitler was a "most remarkable fellow ... he has a most persuasive line about German honor and rights for the workers and a new society." The meeting was in a giant beer hall, with every seat taken. It was on November 22, and was Hitler's first public appearance since serving a short prison sentence for breaking up a meeting. Hanfstaengl recalled: "The atmosphere in the hall was electric.... In his heavy boots, dark suit and leather waistcoat, semi-stiff white collar and odd little moustache, he [Hitler] really did not look very impressive—like a waiter in a railway-station restaurant."[63]

Hanfstaengl sat close to the podium observing Hitler carefully, noting his arm and hand movements, which he—an accomplished pianist—likened to a skilled violinist. Hanfstaengl also studied the audience: "Where was the nondescript crowd I had seen only an hour before?.... Only a few yards away was a young woman, her eyes fastened on the speaker. Transfixed as though in some devotional ecstasy ... she was completely under the spell of Hitler's despotic faith in Germany's future greatness."

The finishing touch to his address was a mug of beer passed up to him from which he took a long draft. "It was hard to decide whether Hitler drank to give the malt-minded Munichers a chance to applaud, or whether they applauded to give him a chance to drink. It had been a masterly performance," and Hanfstaengl remembered that he had been "impressed beyond measure by Hitler.... He seemed to have no conception of the part America had played in winning the war and viewed European problems from a narrow, continental standpoint. Here, at least, I felt I could put him right."[64] Hanfstaengl decided that night he would join Hitler's entourage.

Diplomatic relations between Washington and Berlin during the period from 1933 to 1939, between Hitler's election as chancellor and Germany's attack on Poland to start World War II, had been significantly different than U.S. relations with other countries. It was not only the repressive character of the Third Reich that caused condemnation of the new regime; other autocratic governments had not met with the same level of hostility. What was unacceptable to many Americans was Germany's institutionalized anti-Semitism. The very word Nazi became a pejorative and moviegoers felt comfortable hissing *Movietone News* clips of Third Reich parades. The swastika was a despised symbol and Hitler's prominent moustache an object of derision and caricature.

The attitude of ordinary Germans toward the United States, by contrast, was ambivalent. On the one hand, the obvious wealth and material progress of America compelled their admiration. On the other, Germans tended to look down on the ethnic conglomeration and the democratic government of the United States. To the dogmatists of racial purity in the Third Reich, the mixture of races was an object of scorn. The 1929 stock market crash strengthened negative attitudes toward America; to many Germans, it confirmed their belief in the basic corruption of the nation's political and social system. Finally, the hostility with which Germans viewed the United States was attributed to its population of Jews, who, according to Nazi racial creed, occupied key positions in politics, finance, newspapers, and radio, which gave them power disproportional to their numbers. Anti-Semites in the United States have long assigned the same influences to American Jews who, they claim, rule Wall Street, publish the influential *New York Times*, and pull the strings behind the scenes in Hollywood.

FDR's contentious "quarantine-the-aggressor" speech of October 5, 1937 marked the end of what had been sensible, if frosty, diplomatic relations between the two countries. It also marked the beginning of America's prominence on the international scene. After whistle-stop campaign speeches across the western states, supporting his unprecedented run for a third term, the president stopped in Chicago to cut the ribbon on the new Outer Drive Bridge on Lake Michigan. It had just been completed by the Works Progress Administration (WPA), one of the New Deal's few success stories. FDR's address, instead of being a standard pipe-racks campaign speech covering domestic concerns, dealt with issues of war and peace, and was aimed boldly at Japan in its war with China as well as at Germany and Italy. The president likened the global situation to a disease: "It seems to be unfortunately true that the epidemic of world lawlessness is spreading. When an epidemic of physical disease starts to spread, the community approves and joins in a quarantine to protect the health of the community against the spread of disease."[65] FDR closed his address with words he would use often, with variations, in the coming months: "America hates war."

The *New York Times*'s editorial of October 6 commented that it was uncertain that the president was calling for concerted action against the "law-breakers" or that his speech was merely a "well-deserved rebuke" of those nations. "At least it can be said that an eloquent voice has expressed the deep moral indignation which is felt in this country against policies of ruthlessness and conquest."

The reactions in Tokyo, Berlin, and Rome were immediate and acerbic. The Japanese Foreign Office devoted a special press conference to comment on both the speech and the *Times* editorial. The press spokesman reminded his audience that Western powers, particularly the United States, were hypocritical, using "exclusion acts" that restricted the rights of Japanese to "life, liberty and the pursuit of happiness" and to the right of her people "to seek such opportunities elsewhere." In Germany, two leading Berlin newspapers, the *Berliner Tageblatt* and the *Berliner Lokal-Anzeiger,* deleted reports of FDR's address in afternoon editions after carrying them in the morning papers. The Italians were especially incensed at Roosevelt's statement that stressed the necessity of "drawing a sanitary cordon" around certain countries.

On November 7, 1938, diplomatic relations between the two countries took a further nosedive. A young Polish Jew, Herschel Grunspan, living in Paris, shot and mortally wounded Ernst vom Rath, the third secretary of the German embassy. Grunspan had sought revenge for the fate of his parents, who were among the 17,000 German Jews of Polish origin deported to Poland; when Poland refused to accept them, they were stranded, without shelter, in a "no man's land" between Poland and Germany. Germans lashed out viciously in retaliation. For two days, organized paramilitary groups as well as anti-Semitic ruffians ransacked and burned Jewish shops and synagogues while the police looked the other way. In business sections of German cities, the rampaging Nazis gleefully smashed storefronts, littering sidewalks with glass, giving a name to the pogrom — Kristallnacht. Dozens of Jews were randomly killed. As punishment for the damage, the Jews were assessed a collective fine of almost one billion marks. New decrees were passed which made life extremely difficult for the Jews. Hugh R. Wilson, U.S. ambassador to Berlin was recalled and Hans Dieckhoff, Germany's ambassador, left the United States. Neither would return to his overseas post.

In his public addresses prior to Germany's invasion of Poland on September 1, 1939, Hitler repeatedly denied in public that he had any intention of attacking the United States. For example, in a Reichstag speech in January 1939, he stated that an attack on the U.S. could be "disposed of with a mere laugh." After Germany invaded Poland, the climate had changed somewhat, certainly driven by vitriolic American political attacks on Hitler and his regime. Hitler's two-hour and seventeen-minute Reichstag speech in the Kroll Opera House in Berlin on October 29, 1939, personified the change. Two weeks earlier, Roosevelt had cabled Hitler and Mussolini an open letter for pledges that they would not preemptively attack thirty-one specifically named nations.[66] FDR asked for assurances of nonagression for "ten years at least — a quarter of a century, if we dare look that far ahead."[67] Historians Bailey and Ryan contended that FDR's appeal: "Read in the cold light of today [1979], seems not only ... sophomoric but naively presumptive. Hitler was most unlikely to honor the proposed pledge...."[68]

William L. Shirer, news correspondent at the time and later author of two well regarded books on the Third Reich, *The Rise and Fall of the Third Reich* and *Berlin Diary*, was in the visitor's gallery. He ranked the speech "as the greatest of all Hitler's oratorical efforts. Its appeal lay in its sophistry, sarcasm, and dramatic references to past injustices and present prejudices."[69]

First Hitler gave "an assurance regarding those territories which would after all give him [FDR] the most cause for apprehension, namely, the United States itself and the other States of the American continent. And I here solemnly declare that all the assertions which have been circulated in any way concerning an impending German attack or invasion on or in American territory are rank frauds and gross untruths, quite apart from the fact that such assertions, as far as the military possibilities are concerned, could have their origin only in a stupid imagination."

Then he proceeded item-by-item to mockingly dissect FDR's letter. He listed the questions that he found in Roosevelt's message and replied individually to each, introducing each reply with the same word, Antwort [answer]. He intoned the word in such a derisive way that every time he repeated it—and he repeated it thirty-one times—his deputies and those in the galleries roared with delight.[70] Hitler concluded his remarkable political polemic by suggesting that a wealthy United States was in a position to be concerned with the problems of the whole world; he was in a sphere much smaller, and his humbler concerns were thus limited only to his people.

Franklin Roosevelt was understandably ferocious at Hitler's searing denunciation, but chose not to respond. The most fervent isolationists, by contrast, reveled in Hitler's skillful humiliation of FDR and were delighted to have such an effective presentation of Germany's views. Senator Gerald Nye of North Dakota, a major noninterventionist, commented tersely, "He [FDR] asked for it."[71]

In June 1940, in a direct reply to an interview with Karl von Weigand, an American journalist, Hitler stated that the idea of a German invasion of America was "childish and grotesque." A year later he avowed to former Ambassador John Cudahy that rumors of a forthcoming invasion of America by Germany were ludicrous—and the warmongers in the United States knew it.[72]

During postwar testimony at the Nuremberg War Crimes Trial, Reichsmarshal Hermann Göring (sentenced to death by hanging but swallowed a poison pill to cheat the hangman) stated that "there was never any threat against the American continent." Foreign Minister Joachim von Ribbentrop (sentenced to death by hanging and hanged) told the jurors that Hitler "was unalterably opposed to war with America." Rudolph Hess (sentenced to life imprisonment and served his term) declared that "Germany had no designs on America. The so-called German peril was a ridiculous figure of the imagination. Hitler's interests were European."[73] While many of Hitler's statements, like Roosevelt's, were lies or hyperbole, these "gallows" statements at Nuremberg by his closest associates should be given credence.

11—Was Adolf Hitler Planning to Attack the United States?   171

In the days following his declaration of war against the United States on December 11, 1941, Hitler was pulled in opposite directions. On one hand he belittled U.S. military power and considered American GIs inept and even cowardly. On the other, he finally acknowledged that U.S. entry into the Great War in 1917 had decisively resolved that war. He knew, too, that Germany's unrestricted submarine warfare had given Woodrow Wilson the pretext he needed to bring America into the fight. This time around, Hitler would be more careful as reflected by Grossadmiral Raeder's directives to his U-boats in the Atlantic in 1940 and 1941 to avoid incidents that might provoke a U.S. declaration of war.

Historian Michael Gannon takes up the subject of Hitler's declaration of war against the U.S., suggesting these reasons, one or several: "perhaps for vengeance pure and simple against Roosevelt ... perhaps because ... war with the United States was inevitable anyway ... perhaps because he saw this action as necessary to get Japan totally committed against England; perhaps because he relished the prospect of huge U-boat successes against U.S. naval vessels and shipping; or perhaps because he agreed with his foreign minister, Ribbentrop that "a great power does not allow itself to be declared war on, it declares war itself."[74]

It is also logical that Hitler's views underwent a sea change, particularly as the war ground on and German casualties, military and civilian, mounted into the millions and German cities were razed to the ground. Certainly the indiscriminate bombing raids of German cities by the USAAF and the RAF hardened Hitler's hatred of the Americans and English. In the absence of heavy, four-engine bombers like the U.S. *Flying Fortresses* and *Liberators* and British *Lancasters* in his Luftwaffe, Hitler employed the V-1 and V-2 guided missiles[75] as his Vergeltungswaffe or revenge weapons.

Albert Speer, a close associate of Hitler and his personal architect, was one of the twenty-two top-Nazi defendants in the Nuremberg War Crimes Trial, and was sentenced to twenty years' imprisonment. His clandestine diary, written intermittently over that twenty-year period (and hidden in his shoes before he smuggled out pages), later published as *Spandau— The Secret Diaries* in 1976, included these musings (emphasis added):

March 29, 1947. "Suppose that in the autumn of 1942, Hitler ... had managed to build up a position extending from the Caspian Sea along the Volga to Stalingrad. It would have been protected on the south by the insurmountable massif of the Caucasus. Had he succeeded, *it would have meant a great step forward in his strategic concept of achieving domination of the world step by step.*"[76]

April 19, 1947. "In Hitler's march to the east, *the idea of world conquest was of course predominant.*"[77]

April 20, 1947. "Here I am, fifty-four years old, and you can see the condition I'm in. *But I'll have to lead the great clash with the USA. If only I have time enough, there would be nothing finer for me than to stand at the head of my people in that decisive struggle as well.*"⁷⁸

November 18, 1947. "I recall him ordering showings in the Chancellery of the films of burning London, of the sea of flames over Warsaw, of exploding convoys, and the rapture with which he watched those films. I never saw him so worked up as toward the end of the war, when in a kind of delirium he pictured ... *the destruction of New York in a hurricane of fire. He described the skyscrapers being turned into gigantic burning torches, collapsing upon one another....* Then ... *he declared that Saur must immediately carry out Messerschmitt's scheme for a four-engine long-range jet bomber. With such range we could repay America a thousand-fold for the destruction of our cities.*"⁷⁹

March 24, 1960. "*Hitler's Table Talk* does not give an altogether accurate picture of Hitler.... Hitler tended to falsify himself when he sat as the table in the Führer's Headquarters."⁸⁰

In his *Testament*, Hitler rarely discussed the United States but when he did his comments were scathing. He defended his disinterest in acquiring colonies, suggesting that Europe's policies of colonization had ended in failure. "I have not forgotten the one instance of apparent success ... and it is that monster which calls itself the United States.... And monster is the only possible name for it! At a time when the whole of Europe — their own mother — is fighting desperately to ward off the Bolshevist peril, the United States, guided by the Jew-ridden Roosevelt, can think of nothing better to do than to place their fabulous material resources at the disposal of these Asiatic barbarians, who are determined to strangle her."⁸¹

Hitler offered a novel reason for the eastward expansion of the German peoples: "The rigorous climate with which the East confronts them allows them to retain their qualities as hard and virile men.... Transplant a German to Kiev, and he remains a perfect German. But transplant him to Miami, and you make a degenerate of him — in other words, an American."⁸²

In four sentences, Hitler showed an insightful interpretation of Japan's attack on Pearl Harbor. "Japan's entry into the war caused us no misgivings, even though it was obvious that the Japanese had made a present of a cast-iron pretext to Roosevelt for bringing in the United States against us. But Roosevelt ... was already quite resolved to go to war and annihilate National Socialism, and he had no need of any pretexts. Such pretexts as were required to overcome the resistance of the isolationists he was quite capable of fabricating for himself. One more little swindle meant nothing to him."⁸³

11—Was Adolf Hitler Planning to Attack the United States? 173

H.R. Trevor-Roper, a distinguished British historian, presented a number of intriguing counterfactual issues in his Introduction to the *Testament*. "If Hitler did not admit error in making war on Europe, what about his attack on Russia? ... If only Hitler had been content with his gains ... if only he had stopped after the conquest of France ... he would then have made Germany undisputed master of Europe, reversed the verdict of 1918, restored the Bismarckian Reich, and done all this at trivial cost.... Even Britain would have had to come to terms ultimately with the new reality.... If only Britain had been sensible in 1940 or 1941, Hitler would have exclaimed what an idyllic peace would have been established ... Germany over France, England over Italy.... Germany would have settled down to digest Europe, to enjoy victory, to liquidate the Jews. Surely Britain ... would understand and sympathize with such moderate, reasonable ambitions." Trevor-Roper concluded that Adolf Hitler would not have then been satisfied with such "reasonable ambitions. Germany, secure in her rear, could then have thrown herself ... into her real task, the mission of Hitler's life, the *raison d'etre* of National Socialism — the destruction of Bolshevism."[84]

Another source of information that sheds further light on Hitler's thinking are his private, candid discussions during dinners at his residences. These discussions were recorded by various attendees over a four-year period, collected by Hermann Rauschning and published as *Hitler's Table Talk 1941–1944— His Private Conversations*. The following are examples which include references to the United States.

July 25, 1941. "England and America will one day have a war with one another, which will be waged with the greatest hatred imaginable. One of the two countries will have to disappear."[85]

January 5, 1942. Special guests: Dr. Todt, Sepp Dietricht, General Gause, Colonel Zeitzler. "I'll never believe that an American soldier can fight like a hero."[86]

January 7, 1942. "I don't see much future for the Americans. In my view, it's a decayed country. And they have their racial problem, and the problem of social inequalities. Those were what caused the downfall of Rome, and yet Rome was a solid edifice that stood for something. Moreover, the Romans were inspired by great ideas. Nothing of the sort in England today. As for the Americans, that kind of thing is non-existent. That's why, in spite of everything, I like an Englishman a thousand time better than an American.... Everything about the behaviour of American society reveals that it's half Judaised, and the other half negrified. How can one expect a State like that to hold together!"[87]

Night of January 17–18, 1942. "Recently one of our new Messerschmitts fell into enemy hands. They were dumbfounded. An American magazine wrote that the opinion was widespread that the Germans had only mediocre material, but that it was necessary to yield to the evidence that within three years, at least, the United States would not be able to produce an aircraft of that quality."[88]

January 26, 1942. "The Americans are admirable at mass-production, when it's a question of producing a single model repeated without variation in a great number of copies. That's lucky for us, for their tanks are proving unusable. We could wish them to build another 60,000 this year.... I'm convinced that when they come along with their twenty-eight-tonners and sixty-tonners, the smallest of our tanks will outclass them."[89]

February 2, 1942. "The great success of the Americans consists essentially in the fact that they produce quantitatively as much as we do with two-thirds less labor. We've always been hypnotized by the slogan: 'the craftsmanship of the German worker.' We tried to persuade ourselves that we could thus achieve an unsurpassable result. That's merely a bluff of which we ourselves are the victims. A gigantic modern press works with a precision that necessarily outclasses manual labor. American cars, for example, are made with the least possible use of human labor. The first German manufacture of the sort will be the Volkswagen. In this respect, we are far behind the Americans. Moreover, they build far more lightly than we do. A car of ours that weighs 1,800 kilos would weigh only 1,000 if made by the Americans.... In America, everything is machine-made, so that they can employ the most utter cretins in their factories."[90]

February 7, 1942. Special guests: Dr. Todt and Minister Speer. "The people in the United States who were originally responsible for the development of engineering were nearly all of German stock (from Swabia and Wurtemberg)."[91]

February 17, 1942. "I've just been reading a very fine article on Karl May. I found it delightful. It would be nice if his works were republished. I owe him my first notions of geography, and the fact that he opened my eyes on the world. I used to read him by candle-light, or by moonlight with the help of a huge magnifying-glass. The first thing I read of that kind was *The Last of the Mohicans.*"[92]

April 22, 1942. "It is reported that the Metropolitan Opera House in New York is to be closed; but the reasons given for its closing are certainly false. The Americans do not lack money; what they lack are the artists required to maintain the activities of the greatest of their lyrical theaters. One requires but little knowledge to know that the most famous operas are all of German, Italian or French origin, and that among the artists who perform them the Germans and the Italians are the most celebrated. Our newspapers must not miss this opportunity! Copious comment should be made on this illuminating pointer to the cultural standard of the United States."[93]

July 18, 1942. Hitler refers to an earlier meeting, prior to the outbreak of war, in which he and Lloyd George discussed Germany's *autobahnen*. "During our conversation that old fox Lloyd George asked me what thickness of concrete I proposed to use? The American motor highways have 5 or 6 centimeters of concrete, and Lloyd George could hardly believe me when I told him that ours would have from 25 to 30 centimeters."[94]

August 1, 1942. Special guest: Field Marshal Keitel. "Conversation turned to a book entitled *Juan in America*. In it the author paints a picture of the unbelievable conditions which reign in the intellectual and political circles of the United States, and of the astonishing credulity of the American citizen. He stated that this credulity was not an exclusively American characteristic, and that in Britain, too, the people swallowed everything they were told. According to the Americans themselves, America has the finest, biggest and most efficient of everything in the wide world; and when one then reads a book like this about them, one sees that they have the brains of a hen.... It is very difficult to argue with Americans. They immediately shout: 'Say, take a look at what our workers earn!' True, but let us take a look at the shady side as well.... At one time they had no less than 13 million unemployed.... I grant you than our standard of life is lower. But the German Reich has 270 opera houses.... They have clothes, food, cars and a badly constructed house — but with a refrigerator!"[95]

FDR initially was regarded as a moderate compared to two of his cabinet officers, Henry Morganthau, Jr. and Harold Ickes. Ambassador Hans Luther had noted as early as 1934 that Morgenthau's anti-German bias was "a deep revulsion, indeed hate for us." (Appendix D). Ickes' vitriolic anti-Nazi speeches and press conferences resulted in frequent protests to the State Department. Indeed, Ickes finally replaced New York City's Mayor Fiorello LaGuardia as the American *bete noir* of the German press. Hitler himself was reported to have been "exceedingly irritated" at Ickes' harangues and went so far as to mention him by name in a speech early in 1939."[96] Albert Speer wrote in his *Memoirs*: "Press reports were crucially important in forming his [Hitler's] opinions; they also had a great deal to do with his mood. Where specific foreign news items were concerned, he instantly formulated the official German position, usually highly aggressive."[97]

Much is contradictory in Adolf Hitler's thinking regarding an attack on the United States, whether before or during the war or in planning for an assault after his armies had overrun the Soviet Union. While it was feasible to shell East Coast cities from submarines during both wars, such actions would have been of negligible strategic value. During World War

II, the Germans could have done what the Japanese had begun, bombing cities and important industrial targets with seaplanes carried close to the coast by modifying existing submarines to become tiny aircraft carriers. The Luftwaffe was overseeing the development of the *Amerika-Bomber* and Hitler talked about capturing the Azores for an air base for such bombers.

But to *invade* and *conquer* the United States was a different story. There was little likelihood Hitler could have transported armies and their equipment and supplies across the Atlantic Ocean to successfully attack the United States. Nevertheless, America's propagandists during World War II focused on the homily "that if we don't fight them over there, we'll have to fight them over here."[98]

Epilogue

> "At this point in history [1948], the American Republic has arrived under the theory that the President of the United States possesses limitless authority to misrepresent and secretly to control foreign policy, foreign affairs, and the war power."[1]
>
> "You said we're headed to war in Iraq. I don't know why you say that. I'm the person who gets to decide, not you."[2]
> President George W. Bush to journalists, January 2, 2003
>
> "Patriotism is the last refuge of a scoundrel."[3]
> James Boswell, April 7, 1775

I have portrayed Franklin D. Roosevelt's wartime years in a harsh light. Some would ask: Don't you have anything good to say about the man? My answer: His courtiers, and they were numerous, have already done that, and a second generation of apologists continues to do so.

Why focus on his flaws? Call me an iconoclast. Indeed, FDR remains an icon to those American seniors who vividly remember his dynamic presidency during the dark days of the depression. The other side to Franklin Roosevelt needs telling.

He directed U.S. naval forces to commit acts of war while America was ostensibly at peace.

He bypassed the Congress in his calculated march to war, subverting the Constitution he had sworn four times to uphold.

Once America was fully engaged as a belligerent power, relentless wartime propaganda created a presidency far bigger than life, crediting him with a clairvoyance he never possessed, at the same time veiling FDR's flawed decision-making in a haze of obfuscation.

He took advantage of all of the enormous powers of a wartime president of the United States, a dictator by any definition.

He worked in secrecy, allowing few to know the details of his agreements with foreign governments.

He was immune to criticism. To second-guess the president's handling of the war was unpatriotic, a word as foul as it was heinous.

He lied to the American people continuously and, some would say, spectacularly.

He died a valiant casualty of the war, in the view of most Americans, as if he had been cut down on a landing beach in the Pacific. That, too, was a lie.

Appendix A
President Grover Cleveland's "Toothache," 1893

The full story of a secret and remarkable operation performed on President Grover Cleveland in which his entire upper jaw was removed and replaced with a vulcanized-rubber prosthesis was not revealed until twenty-four years had elapsed. Until then, the operation had been covered up, known only to the immediate family, important administration officials, and the medical team that performed the complicated surgery.

The operation took place soon after the start of Cleveland's second term, on July 1, 1893. As the *New York Times* reported on September 21, 1917, "...owing to the fact that Mr. Cleveland was then in the midst of his sound-money fight with Congress no detail was allowed to leak out concerning it. In spite of the fact that several newspapers printed article intimating the facts, they were denied in *toto*, and until today the country had not been aware that anything out of the ordinary happened to the President."

Dr. R. M. O' Reilly, then White House physician and later Surgeon General of the U.S. Army, discovered the first symptoms which led to the operation. The president had come to him to examine a slight "roughness" in his upper jaw. O'Reilly found a growth, about the size of a quarter. A biopsy was performed and the pathologist (who was kept in the dark as to the identity of the patient) reported the growth was malignant. The date was June 18, 1893.

O'Reilly recommended an immediate operation and July 1 was fixed as the date. Cleveland meanwhile rightfully feared the effect on the public that knowledge of his cancer would have. The presence of cancer then, far more than a hundred years later, was regarded as almost a certain death sentence. After a meeting with Colonel Daniel Scott Lamont, Secretary of War and a close friend of Cleveland's, it was decided to perform the surgery aboard the steam-yacht *Oneida*, owned by Elias Benedict, another friend. Performing the operation and letting the patient recuperate at sea, it was agreed, would assure optimum secrecy. Further, the *Oneida* was a ship the president frequently had sailed on, so if occupants of passing vessels noticed Cleveland relaxing in the sun no suspicions would be aroused.

On June 30, after calling a special session of Congress for August 7 — the session which repealed the silver clause of the Sherman Act — Cleveland left

Washington for New York City, where he went straight on board the *Oneida*, which was tied up at a pier on the East River. Waiting there for him were Commodore Benedict and Colonel Lamont and the surgical team: Doctors W. W. Keen, Joseph D. Bryant, E. G. Janeway, John F. Erdman, and Ferdinand Hasbrouck, a dental surgeon.

The president spent the night aboard ship. If he was spotted and newsmen learned his whereabouts, "the public was to be told the President was going to his summer home by sea. This would have held up: Cleveland was known to have logged upwards of fifty thousand miles as Benedict's guest."[1]

After breakfast the next morning, the lines were cast off and the *Oneida* chugged slowly down the river and into Long Island Sound. The patient was seated in a makeshift operating theater, and sedated with nitrous-oxide ("laughing gas," for a further half century the preferred anesthetic by many dentists). Keen described the surgery:

> The entire left upper jaw was removed from the first bicuspid tooth to just beyond the last molar, and nearly up to the middle line. The floor of the orbit — the cavity containing the eyeball — was not removed as it had not yet been attacked. A small portion of the soft palate was removed. This extensive operation was decided on because we found that the antrum — the large cavity in the upper jaw — was partly filled by a gelatinous mass, evidently a sarcoma. The entire operation was done within the mouth, without any external incision, by means of a cheek retractor, the most useful instrument I have ever seen for such an operation, which I had brought back from Paris in 1866. The retention of the floor of the orbit prevented any displacement of the eyeball. *This normal appearance of the eye, the normal voice, and especially the absence of any external scar greatly aided in keeping the operation a secret* [emphasis added].[2]

On July 5, the *Oneida* steamed north to Buzzards Bay, Massachusetts, the president's summer home, where he was able to walk to his house. On July 17, the same surgical team met Cleveland again aboard the *Oneida*, this time to remove all additional tissue around the wound that looked even slightly like an artificial jaw. With this in place, his speech was excellent, its quality remaining unaltered.

On September 18, on the anniversary of the laying of the cornerstone of the Capitol, the president put to rest the reports that he had been in ill health. The *New York Times* reported the next day the scene on the Capitol Plaza as Grover Cleveland addressed the throng: "They saw a man in the flush of vigorous health, clear eyed, strong, and comfortable to look at, and when he spoke his voice rang out over the crowd so that it could be heard by the furthermost listener. Even the people at the platform could hear him, although his words were spoken to the accompaniment of chimes at the top of the Library Building."

Many years later Keen disclosed that Cleveland himself, at the time, considered that "to keep the operation a profound secret was wise, and one might say imperative."[3] Cleveland's vice president, Adlai E. Stevenson, never learned of the operation.

Appendix B
The Zimmermann Telegram, January 17, 1917

The famous Zimmermann Telegram (from German Foreign Minister Arthur Zimmermann to Herr von Eckhardt, the German minister in Mexico) read: "We intend to begin unrestricted submarine warfare on the first of February. We shall endeavor in spite of this to keep the United States neutral. In the event of this not succeeding, we make Mexico a proposal of alliance on the following basis: make war together, make peace together, generous financial support, and an understanding on our part that Mexico is to reconquer the lost territories in Texas, New Mexico, and Arizona. The settlement in detail is left to you. You will inform the president [of Mexico] of the above most secretly as soon as the outbreak of war with the United States is certain and add the suggestion that he should, on his own initiative, invite Japan to immediate adherence and at the same time mediate between Japan and ourselves. Please call the president's attention to the fact that the unrestricted employment of our submarines now offers the prospect of compelling England to make peace within a few months. Acknowledge receipt."—Barbara W. Tuchman, *The Zimmermann Telegram* (New York: Viking Press, 1958), 146.

Appendix C

Woodrow Wilson's Fourteen Points, January 8, 1918

Delivered to the Congress

   I. Open covenants of peace, openly arrived at, after which there shall be no private international understandings of any kind but diplomacy shall proceed always frankly and in the public view.
  II. Absolute freedom of navigation upon the seas, outside territorial waters, alike in peace and in war, except as the seas may be closed in whole or in part by international action for the enforcement of international covenants.
 III. The removal, so far as possible, of all economic barriers and the establishment of an equality of trade conditions among all the nations consenting to the peace and associating themselves for its maintenance.
  IV. Adequate guarantees given and taken that national armaments will be reduced to the lowest point consistent with domestic safety.
   V. A free, open-minded, and absolutely impartial adjustment of all colonial claims, based upon a strict observance of the principle that in determining all such questions of sovereignty the interests of the populations concerned must have equal weight with the equitable claims of the government whose title is to be determined.
  VI. The evacuation of all Russian territory and such a settlement of all questions affecting Russia as will secure the best and freest cooperation of the other nations of the world in obtaining for her an unhampered and unembarrassed opportunity for the independent determination of her own political development and national policy and assure her of a sincere welcome into the society of free nations under institutions of her own choosing; and, more than a welcome, assistance also of every kind that she may need and may herself desire. The treatment accorded Russia by her sister nations in the months to come will be the acid test of their good will, of their comprehension of her needs as distinguished from their own interests, and of their intelligent and unselfish sympathy.
 VII. Belgium, the whole world will agree, must be evacuated and restored, without any attempt to limit the sovereignty which she enjoys in com-

mon with other free nations. No other single act as this will serve to restore confidence among the nations in the laws which they have themselves set and determined for the government of their relations with one another. Without this healing act the whole structure and validity of international law is forever impaired.

VIII. All French territory should be freed and the invaded portions restored, and the wrong done to France by Prussia in 1871 in the matter of Alsace-Lorraine, which has unsettled the peace of the world for nearly fifty years, should be righted, in order that peace may once more be made secure in the interest of all.

IX. A readjustment of the frontiers of Italy should be effected along clearly recognizable lines of nationality.

X. The people of Austria-Hungary, whose place among the nations we wish to see safeguarded and assured, should be accorded the freest opportunity of autonomous development.

XI. Rumania, Serbia, and Montenegro should be evacuated, occupied territories restored; Serbia accorded free and secure access to the sea; and the relations of the several Balkan states to one another determined by friendly counsel along historically established lines of allegiance and nationality; and international guarantees of the political and economic independence and territorial integrity of the several Balkan states should be entered into.

XII. The Turkish portions of the present Ottoman Empire should be assured a secure sovereignty, but the other nationalities which are now under Turkish rule should be assured an undoubted security of life and an absolutely unmolested opportunity of an autonomous development, and the Dardanelles should be permanently opened as a free passage to the ships and commerce of all nations under international guarantees.

XIII. An independent Polish state should be erected which should included the territories inhabited by indisputably Polish populations, which should be assured a free and secure access to the sea, and whole political and economic independence and territorial integrity should be guaranteed by international covenant.

XIV. A general association of nations must be formed under specific covenants for the purpose of affording mutual guarantees of political independence and territorial integrity to great and small states alike.

Appendix D
The Portentous Lie of Ambassador Henry Morgenthau, Sr., 1918

> *The Allied and Associated Governments affirm and Germany accepts the responsibilities of Germany and her allies for causing all the loss and damage to which the Allied and Associated Governments and their nationals have been subjected to as a consequence of the war imposed upon them by the aggression of German and her Allies.* — Article 231, Versailles Treaty, June 29, 1919

"This greatest of human tragedies was hatched by the Kaiser and his imperial crew at the Potsdam conference of July 5, 1914,"[1] wrote former U.S. Ambassador to Turkey Henry Morgenthau, Sr. and his collaborator Burton C. Hendrick in a book published a month before the Armistice was signed. The "tragedy" the two were referring to was the Great War — and the "Potsdam conference," the Kaiser's Crown Council of German military, business, and diplomatic leaders to plan "Germany's war" a month hence. It was a meeting that had never taken place!

The conspirators would prove to be successful beyond their most optimistic expectations. Hendrick was the first winner, reaping three Pulitzer Prizes over the next decade for his biographies. Morgenthau had to wait longer for a vicarious reward. It was not until 1933 that President Franklin Roosevelt appointed his son, Henry, Jr., to be Secretary of the Treasury, the post Henry, Sr. had coveted since he had entered politics.

If the carefully crafted deceit had served only its temporary wartime function as patriotic propaganda and at the same time been part of an image-building campaign for an ambitious politician, it could be dismissed as wartime exigency and routine public relations. The fiction, however, was neither short-lived nor inconsequential.

Secretary of State Robert Lansing, in Paris for the peace conference, was chairman of the "Commission on the Responsibility of the Authors of the War and on Enforcement of Penalties." He oversaw the preparation of a report which was the basis for the two most onerous clauses of the entire treaty, Articles 231 and 237. Lansing, whose hatred of Germany once the war had begun in Europe was matched only by his later detestation of Bolshevism, happily embraced Morgenthau's views of Germany's certain guilt for starting the war. Although he had read the apologias of all of the countries making up the Central Powers, Lansing gave most credence to the account of his fellow American.

Like many German Jews immigrating to America in the late 1800s, Morgenthau's family landed in New York City's Ellis Island in 1866 well-to-do. According to Henry, the eldest of nine children, his father had $30,000 in cash, a fortune at the time. Henry moved quickly through the city's public school system, attended the elite tuition-free College of the City of New York and then was accepted at Columbia University law school in 1875, being admitted to the Bar two years later at 21. He practiced law from 1879 to 1899, then went into real estate speculation. In 1905, he founded the Henry Morgenthau Company, catering to prosperous clients seeking to invest in land and rental properties.

He wrote that he entered politics "suddenly" in 1911 after a luncheon meeting with governor of New Jersey Woodrow Wilson. He was impressed with the governor's views and decided to hitch his wagon to Wilson's 1912 campaign for the presidency. He was more than an ordinary glad-hander and speaker during the campaign; the wealthy Morgenthau was also a major personal financial contributor to Wilson. In his memoirs, Morgenthau does not indicate when he first considered a cabinet post, preferably Secretary of the Treasury, as equitable payback, but by the successful end of the campaign that post had become a near-fixation.

A month after the inauguration, he was offered not a cabinet post but the ambassadorship to faraway Turkey. Turkey had a large Jewish population and Palestine was then being targeted by Zionists in America as the future home of Jews worldwide. A Jew as a U.S. representative in that part of the world could be helpful to "his people." Morgenthau at first rejected the idea of being a token Jew and declined the offer. But he became convinced that an ambassadorship to any country was better than no ambassadorship, and he grudgingly accepted. He arrived in Constantinople in November 1913.

Morgenthau proceeded diligently to handle the undemanding formal duties incumbent on a foreign envoy. He relished his exalted status as the representative of a powerful nation, and the trappings of the position fueled his mammoth ego. His son, Henry, Jr., was with him and Henry, Sr. proudly exposed him to many of the people with whom he worked.

When the war broke out in August 1914 and Turkey aligned with the Central Powers, Morgenthau's responsibilities quickly multiplied. The departing Allied envoys left their embassies and their nationals in his custody; at one point Morgenthau had eight national groups under his protection.

Morgenthau later wrote that by the end of 1915, he had begun to feel the strains of his added responsibilities, and that a vacation back home would do him good. It was a calculated subterfuge: Wilson's reelection campaign had begun to loom large. Morgenthau left Turkey in early February 1916 on an "official leave of absence" of 60 days, as he first characterized his departure. He landed in New

York in February to a well-orchestrated hero's welcome concocted by city politicians and business confederates anxious to share his limelight.

He gave American reporters at the dock a revised explanation why he had "temporarily" left his post in a time of crisis. It was so he could be with his family at the marriage of his son, Henry, Jr., he told them. Of course, he would return to Constantinople promptly; there should be no question of that! He told the reporters mawkishly that whenever he had felt weak in his distant outpost and sought renewed strength for the many tasks that beset him, he "would look up at the picture of Woodrow Wilson on one side of my desk and at the picture of Abraham Lincoln on the other."

The extravagant coverage of Morgenthau's return was only the start for the *Times*. In the weeks and months to come, the paper would loyally track and flamboyantly report nearly every activity of Morgenthau's. The *Times* created for Morgenthau the persona of a savvy diplomat who had courageously safeguarded the American flag in that hotbed of foreign intrigue, the Dardanelles—and a patriot with important messages to deliver to Americans.

There were three reasons for the *Times*' fervent embrace. Adolph S. Ochs, publisher of the influential paper, was also a Jew, and the anti–Semitism so rampant at the time drew Jews together clannishly. Morgenthau had also been Ochs' realtor in the transaction that acquired for the *Times* the Manhattan property that later became world famous as Times Square. More importantly, both were staunch Germanophobes. The two would work symbiotically to help push America into the Great War, to demand rigorous prosecution of the war once the nation became a belligerent, and to ensure as vindictive a peace treaty in Paris for the "Huns" as could be written by the victors.

Morgenthau was the more zealous anti–German; while many contemporary German-Americans maintained ties to relatives in Germany, Morgenthau had purposefully cut himself off from his forebears, cultivating a festering hatred of Germany and Germans. His attitudes are perhaps best reflected when he talked about the German ambassador in Constantinople, Baron Hans von Wangenheim: "Physically he was one of the most imposing persons I have ever known. When I was a boy in Germany the Fatherland was usually symbolized as a beautiful and powerful woman, a kind of dazzling Valkerie; when I think of modern Germany, however, the massive, burly figure of Wangenheim naturally presents itself to my mind ... there stands, I would say, not the Germany which I had known, but the Germany whose limitless ambitions had transformed the world into a new place of horror. And Wangenheim's every act and every word typified this new and dreadful portent among the nations."[2] His son, Henry, Jr., would also grow up detesting Germans and Germany.

At the end of April, Morgenthau officially tendered his resignation as American envoy to Turkey. The press announcement from Washington pointed out that the former ambassador would now be free to take an active part in the upcoming election campaign. Unencumbered, Morgenthau vigorously threw himself into Wilson's campaign for a second term. He wrote that he had found the Democratic Party in disarray and that party faithfuls were resigned to a

Republican victory and, grandiloquently, that the reelection of Wilson was necessary to America's safety and to the cause of humanity because the rest of the world looked to Wilson to be the man who could bring peace. Readers of his egotistical postwar retrospective, *All in a Lifetime,* published in 1924, come away with the unmistakable impression that it was Morgenthau alone who rescued the 1916 campaign for Woodrow Wilson — and, in turn, saved humanity.

Morgenthau by then had been anointed treasurer of the National Democratic Campaign Committee, the fund-raising job he had had during the previous election. The party's chief public-relations guru, George Creel, publicity director of the Democratic National Committee, was turned loose on Morgenthau. Like Morgenthau, he was counting on a Wilson victory and a prestigious appointment. In fact, Creel would be rewarded for his faithfulness with the powerful chairmanship of the Committee on Public Information, the nation's first propaganda agency, once America was into the war.

Two months after his second inauguration, Wilson — whose main campaign slogan had been "He kept us out of war" — went before the Congress and asked for a declaration of war against Germany. This meant there were immediate opportunities for everyone able to leap onto the giant carousel and grab for a big brass ring, and the indefatigable Morgenthau smoothly eased himself aboard. Staunch patriots were in demand, especially those who had recent first-hand experiences with America's new enemies.

Morgenthau and his aides promptly conjured up a brand-new diplomatic position appropriate to his experience. He would promote himself as a special emissary of the president to broker a separate peace with Turkey. Secretary of State Robert Lansing agreed that the idea, while a long shot, was worth a try. Morgenthau would go to Egypt to begin the secret negotiations. The "cover" for the clandestine mission was that the former ambassador to Turkey was off to Egypt to help alleviate the wartime trials of Jews in Palestine.

But serious diplomatic roadblocks were being put in the way of Morgenthau's mission behind the scenes. U.S. Zionist pressure was being exerted against Morgenthau, who had earlier clearly indicated in numerous campaign speeches that he opposed a Jewish state in Palestine; Britain's conniving diplomacy encouraging a Jewish presence in Palestine to aid that imperialist nation's hold on the Suez Canal at the same they placated the Arabs; and France's equally conspiratorial special interests in the region, based on the secret Sykes-Picot agreement in 1915 that called for Palestine to be divided between France and England.

In mid-June 1917, the Morgenthau party departed New York for an intermediate stop in Gibraltar. There, Morgenthau met with Chaim Weizmann, the Zionist leader who had left from England to counter what he considered interference in the Zionist push for a Jewish state, especially from the confirmed anti-Zionist Morgenthau. To his last days, Morgenthau would remain an unrelenting and outspoken critic of Zionism. In his negotiations with the shrewd and experienced Weizmann, Morgenthau found himself beyond his depth. After two days of meetings during which he exhibited no firm ideas of his beliefs, Morgenthau decided to abandon his diplomatic mission. In Washington, critics labeled him a loose cannon and an incompetent one to boot.

The *New York Times* used a full page in its *Magazine* on September 30 to showcase their hero's latest exploits and his views on the war. The theme of Morgenthau's essay was that the Kaiser must go if the war was to end — and he left no doubt who history's most dangerous man was. "For close to thirty years he has been laying his schemes to conquer the world. Neither Caesar nor Napoleon ever conceived the dream, or plotted with such care, to conquer the world as has this man. In all history he has reared the greatest international menace the world has had to face."

Morgenthau then turned his considerable energies to a new patriotic project, one that would earn him short-term plaudits from his apologists but everlasting criticism by others for his calculated "big lie" with its portentous consequences. He would chronicle his 26 months in Constantinople, tailoring his story so it would become powerful propaganda for the Americans in Paris who were composing sections of the Versailles Treaty.

In late November, Morgenthau wrote to the President that he was considering writing a book about his experiences in Constantinople and was looking for Wilson's approval. Morgenthau made his proposal irresistible by appealing to the ward politician in Woodrow Wilson: he suggested that profits from the book be directed to a committee to assist "all Congressional candidates whose loyalty and support to the Administration there can be no doubt." Americans were by no means unanimous in support of their nation's entry into the war — and the president actively sought buttressing from every source. Morgenthau's letter struck a responsive chord in Wilson and he responded affirmatively the next day, writing that he considered the plan which he hoped would expose German intrigue an excellent one and that he supported the idea.

Morgenthau's book, with its infamous theme of premeditated German perfidy, would be ghostwritten by journeyman writer Burton C. Hendrick,[3] The book would be titled *Ambassador Morgenthau's Story*. Starting with its May 1918 issue, *World's Work* serialized Morgenthau's book, in six monthly installments. It was the third installment, with its subtitle —"*Wangenheim's Account of the Potsdam Conference at which Germany decided to Begin a War*"— that attracted national attention and an impressive editorial in the *New York Times*, painting Morgenthau as an American knight in shining armor. "History would be written differently if Mr. Henry Morgenthau had not been American Ambassador at Constantinople when Turkey, vassal to the Kaiser, entered the war," the paper began. One encomium followed another: "...by reasoning shrewdly with the Young Turk leaders and checkmating Baron Wangenheim ... met Oriental wile with parry and thrust without giving ground ... Mr. Morgenthau was not to be hoodwinked or bluffed by the German Ambassador, whose self-importance never impressed him."

On November 13, the day before the Armistice was signed in France, the *Times*' Book News section led off with an enthusiastic review of the book, titled "Mr. Morgenthau's Luminous Story," written by Columbia University history professor Charles Downer Hazen. Hazen was one of Creel's many court historians, a stout defender of U.S. intervention, and the author of skewed modern-history propaganda pamphlets printed by the millions by Creel's committee. Hazen cut to the heart of Morgenthau's book, to "the most important fact of contemporary history, the responsibility for the beginning of the war." He wrote glowingly that "the evidence furnished by the conversation with Wangenheim is likely to prove the most important single contribution of Mr. Morgenthau to an understanding of the history of our times...."

In his preface, Morgenthau wrote — almost conspiratorially — that he was passing on "inside information" about Germany's undoubted guilt for starting the war and "deliberately planning the conquest of the world." Americans, he went on, "hesitate to convict on circumstantial evidence and for this reason all eye witnesses to this, the greatest crime in modern history, should volunteer their testimony."[7] Morgenthau's incriminating "testimony" was based wholly on what he called his "private conversations" with Baron Hans von Wangenheim, the German ambassador to Turkey. In a chapter entitled "Wangenheim Tells the American Ambassador How the Kaiser Started the War," Morgenthau and Hendrick wove an intricate fiction. The stage was set in June 1914, when Wangenheim suddenly left for Germany. When he returned in July, according to Morgenthau, Wangenheim told him that he had been summoned to Potsdam to participate in a Crown Council meeting that convened on July 5. The Kaiser had presided at the high-level conference that included nearly all the important foreign emissaries, army and navy heads, the great bankers, and captains of industry.

According to Morgenthau's account of what Wangenheim had confided to him, the Kaiser had soberly asked each man in turn: "Are you ready for war?" All replied "yes," except for the financiers. They said they needed two weeks to sell their foreign securities and to make loans. The conference decided to give the bankers time to adjust their finances for the coming war, and then the conferees went quietly back to work or started vacations. Kaiser Wilhelm II, to cover up his nation's war preparations, boarded his royal yacht for his usual summertime cruise.

It was not until 1928, when the noted historian Sidney Bradshaw Fay's authoritative *The Origins of the World War,* was published, that fresh light was shed on the issue.[4] Fay had studied postwar documents unavailable to historians earlier, chiefly the credible *Kautsky Documents* that dealt with the period immediately preceding August 1914, and were taken from the German archives by the distinguished German Socialist Karl Kautsky. Fay concluded that the "Potsdam Council" was a myth. "It is an interesting example of the way legend will grow up, flourish, and receive the widest currency in an atmosphere of war propaganda and readiness to believe anything about an enemy." In Fay's learned view, "Germany did not plot a European War, did not want one, and made genuine, though too belated efforts, to avert one."[5]

Regarding Morgenthau's claim that Wangenheim had told him that "nearly all the important ambassadors" had attended the supposed meeting, Fay's evidence was to the contrary. Concerning the "army and navy heads" whom Morgenthau alleged had been at the meeting, again Fay points to documentation that refutes his contention. What about the big industrialists? Had they been at Potsdam on July 5? Records show that the most powerful arms-maker of all, Krupp von Bohlen-Halbach, had met the Kaiser in Kiel en route to his vacation cruise to Norway. Albert Ballin, head of the Hamburg-Amerika Line, was also absent from Berlin in the early part of July at a health resort.

A reader suspicious of Morgenthau's account is impelled to ask questions of his own. How could a veteran diplomat like Wangenheim, so well respected in Potsdam that he was in line for a higher office, divulge information obviously detrimental to his nation? Germany's stance was that she was fighting a defensive war forced on her by a revengeful France and a rapacious Russia, supported by "perfidious Albion," and so early in the war was trying hard to win American public opinion over to its side.

Why had Morgenthau neglected to report to the Secretary of State what was unquestionably the most important discussion he had had while in Constantinople? In his book he makes no mention of communicating this information to anyone. Fay states that his "careful search through the State Department at Washington shows that there is no dispatch or telegram recounting this interesting information."[6]

Fortunately for Morgenthau, Wangenheim never lived to rebut the intricate fable. He died in Constantinople in August 1915, Morgenthau attending the funeral. Or perhaps it was *because* Baron von Wangenheim was dead that Morgenthau and Hendrick could safely collaborate on the fictitious yarn.

Appendix E

Conspiracy in President Woodrow Wilson's White House, 1919–1920

It was at Pueblo, Colorado, on the way back to Washington, on September 25, 1919, that Woodrow Wilson was hit with the early symptoms of the stroke from which he would never recover. He had been on a speaking tour of the Far West, promoting the League of Nations. The last speech Wilson would ever deliver was to a big crowd that day in the auditorium at the fairgrounds in that tiny city. Wilson began to speak. "Germany must never be allowed…" He stopped in mid-sentence and remained silent. After a long pause, "A lesson must be taught to Germany…" Another long pause. "The world will not allow Germany…"[1] Wilson managed to continue, uncharacteristically mumbling his delivery, with long pauses between phrases. It was as if he was unable to carry through normal thought processes. In fact, the president had begun to show loss of motor control which was the result of a transient ischemic attack — a vascular spasm often presaging a stroke.

As the president's special train rumbled east that night, Wilson was unable to sleep because of an agonizing headache. His omnipresent personal physician, Dr. Cary Grayson, and his wife, Edith, could do nothing to relieve his pain. Grayson woke Joseph Tumulty, Wilson's press secretary, to tell him that the president was seriously ill and unless the trip was cancelled immediately Wilson might die. The two men then told the reporters in the press car that because of the president's illness the remainder of the trip had been cancelled. In response to questions about the nature of Wilson's ailment, Grayson chose to lie. The cover-up was underway. He told the journalists that the president was suffering from "nervous exhaustion" due to the stresses of the previous three weeks' campaigning and that he would not permit the president to exert any effort until he had recovered. This latter restriction was to forestall the reporters from talking to the president, a scenario Grayson and Tumulty viewed as disastrous. It would be nine months before a newspaperman would be given access to Wilson by his three diligent gatekeepers. The reporters could get nothing more from Grayson nor could they observe Wilson waving through the window to nearly empty streets as if to a big crowd, as the train slowed passing through small towns.

By the time the train reached Washington's Union Station, Wilson's condition had improved. He managed to walk unaided to his limousine and was driven to the White House. Then, on the night of October 2, "the crash came," according to "Ike" Hoover, the White House Chief Usher. Wilson had suffered a major cerebral thrombosis, which caved in the lower left side of his face, paralyzed the left side of his body, and reduced the fields of vision in both his eyes.[2] As one authoritative chronicler of the period wrote: "So began the greatest deception in the history of American politics."[3]

From that day throughout the remaining 18 months of his presidency and until his death in 1924, Wilson would remain a cripple. He was scarcely able to walk unaided, his useless left leg dragging behind; he was unable to sustain any prolonged discussion or thought process; he could barely sign his name and speak intelligibly; his near-blindness made it impossible for him to read with any measure of comprehension. He was consumed with prolonged and severe periods of depression. In consequence, as president he certainly was unable to fulfill the requirements of his high office. In his stead, his minimally educated, politically adolescent wife — in connivance with Dr. Grayson and Tumulty — covered up his illness and brazenly assumed the role and functions of president of the United States.[4]

At first Edith Wilson barred all visitors to the sickroom, including members of Wilson's Cabinet and political cronies. Cabinet members were eventually received by the First Lady in her sitting room adjacent to Wilson's room. Then began a formal ritual. She would tell the visitor what the president wanted done; her instructions, she insisted, precisely reflected her husband's wishes. If the visitor had questions, she would excuse herself and go into the president's room (always alone, and punctiliously latching the door securely behind her) and return with an answer. But she was more likely to say imperiously that she could not disturb the president.

No visitor saw Wilson and no one saw a single word in his handwriting except for a very few signatures — all unfamiliar looking to those who recognized his signature. Was his signature distorted because he signed his name in bed or slumped in his boardwalk chair? Had his signature been forged by Edith or by her brother, John Randolph Bolling, who lived in the White House? White House staff now and then glimpsed him outdoors on nice days on the mansion's south portico, bundled up to his chin in blankets in his boardwalk chair, attended by his wife and physician. If the president had been dead, a wax dummy could easily have been seated in the chair in his stead, with no one the wiser.

The extent of Wilson's crippled condition was finally revealed to his Cabinet on April 13, 1920, the first formal meeting since his stroke. White House Chief Usher "Ike" Hoover wheeled him into the room first. Then, as members came in the door — one at a time — Hoover loudly announced them by name. Wilson's near-blindness precluded him from recognizing his cabinet members. Wilson opened the meeting with several inane jokes and initially appeared to be able to transact some routine business. Secretary of Agriculture David Houston recalled that Wilson had "looked old, worn, and haggard.... One of his arms was useless.... His jaw tended to drop on one side. His voice was very weak and strained.... The President seemed at first to have some difficulty in fixing his mind on what we were discussing. Finally, Mrs. Wilson came in, looking rather disturbed, and suggested that we had better go."[5]

Many if not most of the letters addressed to the president of the United States were never answered. When Edith Wilson's papers were deposited in the Library of Congress three decades later, numerous unopened letters were discovered. Those letters that were acted on arrived back at the sender in a form certainly unique in American history. In a barely decipherable script of gigantic proportions that might have been written by an elementary school student with particularly poor handwriting — starting in the left margin, down to the bottom margin, up the right margin, then left across the top, sometimes preposterously continuing on the envelope itself — was the answer the writer sought.

Where was the vice president these months after Wilson was literally swallowed up inside the White House? Thomas Riley Marshall was completing his second term as vice president and was next in line for the presidency, according to Article 2, Section 1 of the Constitution (Appendix J). Marshall wanted no part of the presidency. Small and thin, he matched his stature with an equivalent lifestyle; he and his wife lived in a suite of rooms in the unpretentious Willard Hotel close to the Senate over which he presided.

Senators from both sides of the aisle tried unsuccessfully to persuade Marshall to assume the presidency. The Democrats had the most to lose; their party was leaderless. Even a weakling like Marshall at the helm would be better than a cripple like Wilson. The Republicans, for their part, felt that Marshall would be easier to deal with than with the always intransigent Wilson. He was more than content to draw his $12,000 annual salary and sit out his term on the sidelines as a passive observer to the decline of Wilson's presidency and the liberal issues he had championed.

What was the cost to the nation of Woodrow Wilson's infirmities in his final months as president? In fact, Wilson's physical and mental incapacity during the Paris negotiations earlier — less well known than even his last 18 months in the White House — had profound political implications. He signed an unworkable peace treaty with Germany (and with Austria-Hungary as well) and either acceded to or compromised almost every sensible principle about which he had initially stood firm. He had told his associates that his Fourteen Points should be the basis of a humane treaty, and that he would work to that end. Wilson never discussed the Fourteen Points at any time with Clemenceau, Lloyd George, or Vittorio Emanuele Orlando. Yet he fervently believed at the end of the conference that his idealistic concepts had been adopted.

There is also significant evidence of a president unable to perform even the minimum requirements of his office based on analysis of Wilson's inaction on bills passed by Congress during his illness. Wilson had not been a president who permitted bills to become laws without his signature; he either signed them or vetoed them. Yet 28 bills became law without his signature between September 30 and November 18, 1919. An example was the Volstead Act to enforce prohibition that passed the Congress and was sent to the White House on October 16. The president had 10 days to sign or veto it; he did neither and it automatically became law.

After his stroke, Wilson lived on for four years and four months, a pitiful invalid. Once retired to his new home on S Street in Washington, he managed to participate in a single public function, when he made a brief appearance in 1921 at a Washington commemoration of Armistice Day. Earlier, Wilson had stubbornly insisted that he play his complete part in the inauguration ceremonies for incoming President Warren Harding.[6] But a report from a Secret Service agent who had stepped out the walking required — 190 steps from an elevator in the Capitol to the president's room in the Senate wing, 270 steps through the rotunda to the top of the steps going down to the dignitaries' stand, down 16 steps, and finally 50 steps to his seat — showed this task was far beyond the invalid's capabilities.

Even during his last day in office, the veil of secrecy was not lifted. Wilson entered the Capitol through a freight entrance, after first being screened from photographers by a phalanx of policemen as he was assisted into the limousine for the short ride from the White House. Harding was dropped off in front of the building. Then the car drove to a side entrance door Wilson would use. Again, his transfer was screened from the public, this time with mounted cavalry, as he was carefully lifted from the car and gently stood on his feet. Cane tapping, and invisible to the public, he made his way indoors unassisted, taking an elevator up to the president's room where a distinguished group of well-wishers had gathered. There he was helped into a chair to sign the final bills into law of the Congress that was about to adjourn.

There was one last formality that added a tense note of drama to the scene. A Senate committee had arrived to ask permission of the president to adjourn the Congress. Its impeccably dressed spokesman said sharply and without emotion: "Mr. President, we have come as a committee of the Senate to notify you that the Senate and the House are about to adjourn and await your pleasure." The voice was that of the distinguished senator from Massachusetts, chairman of the powerful Senate Foreign Relations Committee, Henry Cabot Lodge. Tumulty recalled that he intently studied Wilson's face as he met Lodge's gaze. It was Lodge — vindictively and personally by Wilson's lights, more than any other individual who had thwarted Wilson's great dream of a League of Nations nurtured to maturity by the United States. Hatred was mutual. Tumulty expected Wilson to thrash out one last time. But the president's flame had long since sputtered low. Almost inaudibly, Wilson responded: "Senator Lodge, I have no further communication to make. I thank you. Good morning."

Appendix F
Key Excerpts from the Nye "Munitions Hearings" Report, February 24, 1936

Special Committee on Investigation of the Munitions Industry," U.S. Congress, Senate, 74th Congress, 2nd sess.

I. Nature of the Munitions Companies

The committee finds, under the head of "the nature of the industrial and commercial organizations engaged in the manufacture of or traffic in arms, ammunitions, or other implements of war" that almost none of the munitions companies in this country confine themselves exclusively to the manufacture of military materials. Great numbers of the largest suppliers to the Army and Navy (Westinghouse, General Electric, du Pont, General Motors, Babcock & Wilcox, etc.) are predominantly manufacturers of materials for civilian life. Others, such as the aviation companies and Colt's Patent Firearms Co., supply the greatest portion of their output to the military services. In addition to the manufacturers there are several sales companies which act as agents.... There are also brokers dealing largely in old and second-hand supplies.

The Army manufactures its own rifles, cartridges, and field artillery. The Navy manufactures most of its own propellant powder, its own guns, and half of the battleships.

II. The Sales Methods of the Munitions Companies

The committee finds ... that almost without exception, the American munitions companies investigated have at times resorted to such unusual approaches, questionable favors and commissions, and methods of "doing the needful" so as to constitute, in effect, a form of bribery of foreign government officials or of their close friends in order to secure business.

The committee realizes that these were field practices by the agents of the companies ... and that the heads of the American companies were ... apparently unaware of their continued existence and shared the committee's distaste and disapprobation of such practices.

The committee accepts the evidence that the same practices are resorted to by European munitions companies, and that the whole process of selling arms abroad thus ... has "brought into play the most despicable side of human nature; lies, deceit, hypocrisy, greed, and graft occupying a most prominent part in the transactions.

The committee finds, further, that not only are such transactions highly unethical, but that they carry within themselves the seeds of disturbance to the peace and stability of those nations in which they take place.

The committee finds, further, that the intense competition among European and American munitions companies with the attendant bribery of government officials tends to create a corrupt officialdom.

The committee finds, further, that the constant availability of munitions companies with competitive bribes ready in outstretched hands does not create a situation where the officials involved can ... be as much interested in peace as they are in increased armaments.

III. Their Activities Concerning Peace Efforts

The committee finds ... that there is no record of any munitions company aiding any proposals for limitations of armaments, but that, on the contrary, there is a record of their active opposition by some to all such proposals, of resentment toward them, of contempt for those responsible for them, and of violation of such controls whenever established, and of rich profiting whenever such proposals failed.

The first great peace effort after the war was incorporated in the Treaty of Versailles and in the treaty of peace between the United States and Germany in the form of a prohibition on the manufacture, import, and export of arms by Germany. The manufacture and export of military powder by German companies in violation of these treaty provisions first took place in 1924 and was known to the Nobel Co. (predecessors of Imperial Chemical Industries) and to the du Pont Co., but was not brought to the attention of the Department of State. The du Pont officials explained that the violation was allowed because of the close commercial relations between the British and German chemical companies. Later, United Aircraft licensed a German company for the manufacture of airplane engines. Sperry Gyroscope also licensed a German company for the manufacture of its equipment.

The second peace effort was made in 1922, when the Washington Disarmament Conference took place.... The naval part of that conference succeeded in stopping a naval race. There was, however, no effective action taken in regard to checking the use of poison gas, which was the other main subject for consideration.

The Geneva Arms Control Conference of 1925 was watched carefully by the American and European munitions makers. They knew the American military delegates to the conference several weeks before the public was informed of their names.

The influence of American naval shipbuilding companies at the Geneva Disarmament Conference of 1927 has been described by the committee's report

Excerpts from the Nye "Munitions Hearings" Report 197

on Naval Shipbuilding (74th Congress, Report 94). Their agent at Geneva claimed credit for the failure of that conference. An arms embargo resolution was introduced in 1928 by the chairman of the American delegation to that conference The munitions manufacturers, cocky with their success at Geneva, consulted with the Sporting Arms and Ammunition Manufacturers Institute, and found it unnecessary to appear in the front ranks of opposition to this resolution. The munitions people were active in opposition to the arms embargo proposal which was adopted in the Senate without opposition.

In 1932, another disarmament conference was held in Geneva. By this time the failure to prevent the rearmament of Germany had resulted in great profits to the French steel industry which had received large orders for the building of the continuous line of fortifications across the north of France [the Maginot Line], to the French munitions companies, and profits were beginning to flow into the American and English pockets from German orders for aviation material. This in turn resulted in a French and English aviation race, and with Germany openly rearming the much-heralded disarmament conference had failed completely.

In 1934, Congress adopted a joint resolution prohibiting sales of munitions to Bolivia and Paraguay, then engaged in the Chaco War, for a period of almost 6 years. The Chaco embargo, according to indictments issued by a Federal grand jury, was violated by the Curtiss-Wright Export Corporation and the Curtiss Aeroplane Motor Co. The lower court has held the embargo unconstitutional on the ground of delegation of power to the President.

In 1935, a neutrality bill was passed including an embargo on ammunition and implements of war in the event of a state of war between two or more foreign states, and including a munitions-control board with power to issue export licenses. In 1936 an attempt was made to amend the neutrality law by holding the exports of necessary war materials (oil, copper, steel, etc.) to belligerents to normal quotas. This was defeated.

IV. The Effect of Armaments on Peace

The committee finds that some of the munitions companies have occasionally had opportunities to intensify the fears of people for their neighbors and have used them to their own profit.

The committee finds, further, that the very quality which in civilian life tends to lead toward progressive civilization, namely the improvements of machinery, has been used by the munitions makers to scare nations into a continued frantic expenditure for the latest improvements in devices of warfare. The constant message of the traveling salesmen of the munitions companies to the rest of the world has been that they now had available for sale something new, more dangerous and more deadly than ever before and that the potential enemy was or would be buying it.

The committee finds, further, that munitions companies engaged in bribery find themselves involved in the civil and military policies of other nations, and that this is an unwarranted form of intrusion into the affairs of other nations and undesirable representation of the character and methods of the people of the United States.

V. Their Relations with the United States Government

The committee finds that the Navy contractors, subcontractors, and suppliers constitute a very large and influential financial group and that the matter of national defense should be above and separated from lobbying and the use of political influence by self-interested groups and that it has not been above or separated from either of them.

The committee finds, further, that the munitions companies have secured the active support of the War, Navy, Commerce, and even State Departments in their sales abroad, even when the material to be produced is in England or Italy.

The committee finds that the War Department encourages the sale of modern equipment abroad in order that the munitions companies may stay in business and be available in the event of another war, and that this consideration outranks the protection of secrets.

The committee finds that the Army Ordnance Association, consisting of personnel from the munitions companies, constitutes a self-interested organization and has been involved in War Department policies and promotions.

The committee finds that the Navy League of the United State has solicited and accepted contributions from steamship companies, the recipients of subsidy benefits, and that it has solicited contributions from companies with large foreign investments on the ground that these would profit from a large navy and that its contributors have at time been persons connected with Navy suppliers. The committee also finds that the Navy League together with various Navy officials have engaged in political activity looking forward to the defeat of Congressmen unfavorable to the Navy League and Navy views.

VI. International Agreements of Munitions Companies

The committee finds that among the companies investigated, the following have the most extensive foreign arrangements: E. I. du Pont de Nemours Co., Colt's Patent Firearms Co., Electric Boat Co., Sperry Gyroscope Co., Pratt & Whitney Aircraft Co.

The committee finds that the usual form of arrangement is a license to a foreign ally involving rights to manufacture and sell in certain parts of the world, together with more or less definite price-fixing agreements and occasionally profit-sharing arrangements, and that in effect the world is partitioned by parties at interest.

The committee finds that the international commercial interests of such large organizations as du Pont and Imperial Chemical Industries may precede in the minds of those companies the importance of national policy as described publicly by the foreign office of the State Department, and that such considerations of commercial interest were apparently foremost in the rearming of Germany beginning in 1924 and in the sale of a process which could be used to manufacture cheaper munitions in Japan in 1932, shortly after Secretary of State Stimson had taken steps to express the disapproval of this nation for Japan's military activities in Manchuria.

VII. The Chemical Industry and Munitions

The committee finds a general acknowledgement of the importance of the commercial chemical industry to the manufacture of such instruments of warfare as high explosives and gases, that most of the large industrial nations have granted their chemical companies considerable measures of protection in the interests of national defense, and that no effective control has to date been established over these large military resources.

Appendix G
America First Committee: Principles and Membership, 1940

Wayne S. Cole, America First: The Battle Against Intervention, 1940–1941 *(New York: Octagon Books, 1971)*

1. Our first duty is to keep America out of foreign wars. Our entry would only destroy democracy, not save it.
2. We must build a defense, for our own shores, so strong that no foreign power or combination of powers can invade our country by sea, air or land.
3. Not by acts of war, but by preserving and extending democracy at home can we aid democracy and freedom in other lands.
4. In 1917 we sent our ships into the war zone; and this led us to war. In 1941 we must keep our naval convoys and merchant vessels on this side of the Atlantic.

Membership of America First as of September 4, 1940: National Director, R. Douglas Stuart, Jr. Members of the National Committee: Gen. (Ret.) Robert E. Wood, president and chairman of Sears, Roebuck and Company; William H. Regnery; Gen. (Ret.) Thomas S. Hammond, president of the Whiting Corporation; Jay C. Hormel, president of Hormel Meat Packing Company; Hanford MacNider, former national commander of the American Legion; Mrs. Janet Ayer Fairbank, author and former national Democratic committeewoman from Illinois; Edward L. Ryerson, Jr., board member of Inland Steel Corporation; Sterling Morton, secretary of the Morton Salt Company; Mrs. Alice Roosevelt Longworth, daughter of Theodore Roosevelt; John T. Flynn, author and advisor to the Nye Committee investigating the munitions industry; Edward Rickenbacker; Louis Tabor, Master of the National Grange; Bishop Wilbur E. Hammaker, head of the Methodist Church in Denver; Thomas N. McCarter, president of the Public Service Corporation of New Jersey; Avery Brundage, president of the American Olympic Association; Dr. Albert W. Palmer, president of the Chicago Theological Seminary; Mrs. Burton K. Wheeler; Dr. George H. Whipple, joint winner of the Nobel Prize for medicine in 1934; Oswald Garrison Villard, former editor of the *Nation*; and Ray McKaig, head of the Grange in Boise, Idaho.

Appendix H
The Atlantic Charter, August 14, 1941

Argentia Bay, Newfoundland. Foreign Relations,
1941, I, 367–369

The President of the United States of America and the Prime Minister, Mr. Churchill, representing His Majesty's Government in the United Kingdom, being met together, deem it right to make known certain common principles in the national policies of their respective countries on which they base their hopes for a better future for the world.

First, their countries seek no aggrandizement, territorial or other;

Second, they desire to see no territorial changes that do not accord with the freely expressed wishes of the peoples concerned;

Third, they respect the right of all peoples to choose the form of government under which they will live; and they wish to see sovereign rights and self government restored to those who have been forcibly deprived of them;

Fourth, they will endeavor, with due respect for their existing obligations, to further the enjoyment by all States, great or small, victor or vanquished, of access, on equal terms, to the trade and to the raw materials of the world which are needed for their economic prosperity;

Fifth, they desire to bring about the fullest collaboration between all nations in the economic field with the object of securing, for all, improved labor standards, economic advancement and social security;

Sixth, after the final destruction of the Nazi tyranny, they hope to see established a peace which will afford to all nations the means of dwelling in safety within their own boundaries, and which will afford assurance that all the men in all the lands may live out their lives in freedom from fear and want;

Seventh, such a peace should enable all men to traverse the high seas and oceans without hindrance;

Eighth, they believe that all of the nations of the world, for realistic as well as spiritual reasons must come to the abandonment of the use of force. Since no future peace can be maintained if land, sea or air armaments continue to be employed by nations which threaten, or may threaten, aggression outside of their frontiers, they believe, pending the establishment of a wider and permanent system of general security, that the disarmament of such nations is essential. They will likewise aid and encourage all other practicable measures which will lighten for peace-loving peoples the crushing burden of armaments.

Franklin D. Roosevelt
Winston S. Churchill

Appendix I

Key Excerpts from a Charles A. Lindbergh Speech, September 11, 1941

"Who Are the War Agitators?"

Delivered at the America First Committee's Rally in Des Moines, Iowa. New York Times, *September 12, 1941*

... When this war started in Europe, it was clear that the American people were solidly opposed to entering it. Why shouldn't we be? We had the best defensive position in the world; we had a tradition of independence from Europe; and the one time we did take part in a European war left European problems unsolved, and debts to America unpaid. National polls showed that when England and France declared war on Germany, in 1939, less than ten percent of our population favored a similar course for America.

But there were various groups of people, here and abroad, whose interests and beliefs necessitated the involvement of the United States in the war. I shall point out some of these groups tonight, and outline their methods of procedure. In doing this, I must speak with the utmost frankness, for in order to counteract their efforts, we must know exactly who they are....

The three most important groups who have been pressing this country toward war are the British, the Jewish and the Roosevelt administration....

As I have said, these war agitators comprise only a small minority of our people; but they control a tremendous influence. Against the determination of the American people to stay out of war, they have marshaled the power of their propaganda, their money, their patronage. Let us consider these groups, one at a time.

First, the British: It is obvious and perfectly understandable that Great Britain wants the United States in the war on her side. England is now in a desperate position. Her population is not large enough and her armies are not strong enough to invade the continent of Europe and win the war she declared against Germany. Her geographical position is such that she cannot win the war by the use of aviation alone, regardless of how many planes we send her.... If England can draw this country into the war, she can shift to our shoulders a large potion of the responsibility for waging it and for paying its cost....

England has devoted, and will continue to devote every effort to get us into the war. We know that she spent huge sums of money in this country during the last war in order to involve us. Englishmen have written books about the cleverness of its use. We know that England is spending great sums of money for propaganda in America during the present war. If we were Englishmen, we would do the same. But our interest is first in America; and as Americans, it is essential for us to realize the effort that British interests are making to draw us into their war.

The second major group I mentioned is the Jewish. It is not difficult why Jewish people desire the overthrow of Nazi Germany. The persecution they suffered in Germany would be sufficient to make bitter enemies of any race. No person with a sense of the dignity of mankind can condone the persecution of the Jewish race in Germany. But no person of honesty and vision can look on their pro-war policy here today without seeing the dangers involved in such a policy, both for us and for them. Instead of agitating for war, the Jewish groups in this country should be opposing it in every possible way for they will be among the first to feel its consequences.

Tolerance is a virtue that depends upon peace and strength. History shows that it cannot survive war and devastation. A few far-sighted Jewish people realize this and stand opposed to intervention. But the majority still do not. Their greatest danger to this country lies in their large ownership and influence in our motion pictures, our press, our radio and our government.... We cannot blame them for looking out for what they believe to be their own interests, but we must look out for ours. We cannot allow the natural passions and prejudices of other peoples to lead our country to destruction.

The Roosevelt administration is the third powerful group which has been carrying this country toward war. Its members have used the war emergency to obtain a third presidential term for the first time in American history. They have used the war to add unlimited billions to a debt which was already the highest we have ever known. And they have used the war to justify the restriction of congressional power, and the assumption of dictatorial procedures on the part of the president and his appointees.... The danger of the Roosevelt administration lies in its subterfuge. While its members have promised us peace, they have led us to war heedless of the platform upon which they were elected....

When hostilities commenced in Europe, in 1939, it was realized by these groups that the American people had no intention of entering the war. They knew it would be worse than useless to ask us for a declaration of war at that time. But they believed that this country could be entered into the war in very much the same way we were entered into the last one. They planned: first, to prepare the United States for foreign war under the guise of American defense; second, to involve us in the war, step by step, without our realization; third, to create a series of incidents which would force us into the actual conflict.

Excerpts from a Charles A. Lindbergh Speech

These plans were, of course, to be covered and assisted by the full power of their propaganda.

Our theaters soon became filled with plays portraying the glory of war. Newsreels lost all semblance of objectivity. Newspapers and magazines began to lose advertising if they carried anti-war articles. A smear campaign was instituted against individuals who opposed intervention. The terms "fifth column," "traitor," "Nazi," "anti–Semitic" were thrown ceaselessly at any one who dared to suggest that it was not in the best interests of the United States to enter the war. Men lost their jobs if they were frankly anti-war. Many others dared no longer to speak....

We are on the verge of war, but it is not too late to stay out. It is not too late to show that that no amount of money, or propaganda, or patronage can force a free and independent people into war against its will.... The entire future rests upon our shoulders. It depends upon our actions, our courage, and our intelligence. If you oppose our intervention in the war, now is the time to make your voice heard....

Appendix J
United Nations Declaration, January 1, 1942

Foreign Relations, *1942, I, 25–26*

A Joint Declaration by the United States, the United Kingdom, the Union of Soviet Socialist Republics, China, Australia, Belgium, Canada, Costa Rica, Cuba, Czechoslovakia, Dominican Republic, El Salvador, Greece, Guatemala, Haiti, Honduras, India, Luxemburg, Netherlands, New Zealand, Nicaragua, Norway, Panama, Poland, South Africa, Yugoslavia.

The Governments signatory hereto,

Having subscribed to a common program of purposes and principles embodied in the Joint Declaration of the President of the United States of America and the Prime Minister of the United Kingdom of Great Britain and Northern Ireland dated August 14, 1941, known as the Atlantic Charter. Being convinced that complete victory over their enemies is essential to defend life, liberty, independence and religious freedom, and to preserve human rights and justice in their own lands as well as in other lands, and that they are now engaged in a common struggle against savage and brutal forces seeking to subjugate the world,

Declare:

(1) Each Government pledges itself to employ its full resources, military and economic, against those members of the Triparte Pact and its adherents with which such governments is at war.

(2) Each Government pledges itself to cooperate with the Governments signatory hereto and not to make a separate armistice or peace with the enemies.

The foregoing declaration may be adhered to by other nations which are, or which may be, rendering material assistance and contributions in the struggle for victory over Hitlerism.

Done at Washington
January First, 1942

Appendix K
U.S. Mustard Gas at Bari, Italy, 1943

On December 2, 1943, the harbor of Bari, Italy was crowded with over 30 Allied ships unloading their cargoes in support of the U.S. advance up the western side of the Italian Peninsula and of the British advance up the Adriatic coast. Bari was an important port on the Adriatic coast east of Naples. The British had captured Bari easily following the bloody battle to capture Salerno in September.

While the Allies knew that the Luftwaffe was still a force to be reckoned with in Italy, for some reason that has never been explained, as darkness fell that night, lights were turned on to assist incoming vessels and to help in the offloading of cargo. The brightly illuminated port, as events transpired, greatly simplified the job of the approximately 100 Ju-88 bombers that attacked just as the sun went down. Furthermore, the port was completely undefended; there were no anti-aircraft guns and no Allied fighter planes.

German pathfinder aircraft arrived first and sowed the area with chaff to confuse Allied radar, and in turn to confuse the non-existent anti-aircraft defense. Then the Ju-88s came in to drop their bombs. "Although the raid lasted only 20 minutes, the results were spectacularly successful for the Germans. Not since Pearl Harbor had the allies lost so many ships at one time."[1] Almost immediately two ammunition ships were hit, resulting in explosions which shattered windows seven miles away. Then an oil pipeline was cut and the fuel quickly ignited. Adding to the growing inferno were the cargoes of oil and gasoline tankers that had also been struck. In total 16 ships and 38,000 tons of vital cargo were destroyed. Loss of life among American seamen was heavy — and "it would be weeks before the port could resume normal operations."[2]

A far more ominous tragedy was unfolding at the same time in the burning harbor. The freighter *John Harvey* carried a mixed cargo of munitions and about 100 tons of unfuzed 100-pound bombs filled with liquid mustard gas, "to be used in retaliation if the Germans initiated toxic warfare."[3] The *Harvey* took a direct hit and exploded, rupturing the thin casings of the gas bombs and spreading liquid mustard across the harbor. Some sank, some burned on the surface, some mixed with floating oil, and some evaporated to intersperse with the dense clouds of smoke from the burning oil. A fortuitous offshore breeze carried the deadly fumes away from the beaches.

But because the gas shells had been cloaked in security — and the crew of the *Harvey*, some of whom knew their ship's cargo, had all been killed in the explosion — it was many hours before the injured with their unusual symptoms were diagnosed correctly as victims of mustard gas. "All told, there were 617 known mustard casualties ... of which 83 persons or 13.6 per cent died."[4] The "incident" was kept under wraps, classified TOP SECRET until 1959.

Mustard gas, considered a "harassing agent," is a pale yellow gas with the distinct odor of garlic. It causes severe burns to eyes and lungs, and blisters exposed skin. In heavy concentrations, mustard can kill. Mustard is not volatile and is generally effective for days after its use. During the Great War, it caused about one-quarter of U.S. gas casualties. — Seymour M. Hersh, *Chemical and Biological Warfare — America's Hidden Arsenal* (New York: Bobbs-Merrill, 1968).

Appendix L

Memorandum by Henry Morgenthau, Jr., on the Scorched-Earth Plan

As reproduced in Germany Is Our Problem *(New York: Harper, 1945) by Henry Morgenthau, Jr., in the form of a memorandum which President Franklin D. Roosevelt took to his second Quebec conference with Winston Churchill in September 1944.*

TOP SECRET

Program to Prevent Germany from Starting a World War III

1. *Demilitarization of Germany.*
   It should be the aim of the Allied Forces to accomplish the complete demilitarization of Germany in the shortest period of time after surrender. This means completely disarming the German Army and people (including the removal or destruction of all war material).
2. *New Boundaries of Germany*
   a) Poland should get that part of East Prussia which doesn't go to the U.S.S.R. and the southern portion of Silesia.
   b) France should get the Saar and the adjacent territories bounded by the Rhine and Moselle Rivers.
   c) As indicated in 4 below an International Zone should be created containing the Ruhr and the surrounding industrial areas.
3. *Partitioning of New Germany.*
   The remaining portion of Germany should be divided into two autonomous, independent states, 1) a South German state comprising Bavaria, Wurtemberg, Baden and some smaller areas and 2) a North German state comprising a large part of the old state of Prussia, Saxony, Thuringia and several smaller states.
   There shall be a customs union between the new South German state and Austria, which will be restored to her pre–1938 political borders.

4. *The Ruhr Area.* (The Ruhr, surrounding industrial areas including the Rhineland, the Kiel Canal, and all German territory north of the Kiel Canal.)

Here lies the heart of German industrial power. This area should not only be stripped of all presently existing industries but so weakened and controlled that it cannot in the foreseeable future become an industrial area. The following steps will accomplish this:

   a) Within a short period, if possible not longer than 6 months after the cessation of hostilities, all industrial plants and equipment not destroyed by military action shall be completely dismantled and transported to Allied Nations as restitution. All equipment shall be removed from the mines and the mines closed.

   b) The area should be made an international zone to be governed by an international security organization to be established by the United Nations. In governing the area the international organization should be guided by policies designed to further the above stated objective.

5. *Restitution and Reparation.*

Reparations, in the form of future payments and deliveries, should not be demanded. Restitution and reparation shall be effected by the transfer of existing German resources and territories, e.g.,

   a) by restitution of property looted by the Germans in territories occupied by them;

   b) by transfer of German territory and German private rights in industrial property situated in such territory to invaded countries and the international organization under the program of partition;

   c) by the removal and distribution among devastated countries of industrial plants and equipment situated within the International Zone and the North and South German states delimited in the section of partition;

   d) by forced German labor outside Germany; and

   e) by confiscation of all German assets of any character whatsoever outside of Germany.

6. *Education and Propaganda.*

   a) All schools and universities will be closed until an Allied Commission of Education has formulated an effective reorganization program. It is contemplated that it may require a considerable period of time before any institutions of higher learning are reopened. Meanwhile the education of German students in foreign universities will not be prohibited. Elementary schools will be reopened as quickly as appropriate teachers and textbooks are available.

   b) All German radio stations and newspapers, magazines, weeklies, etc. shall be discontinued until adequate controls are established and an appropriate program formulated.

7. *Political Decentralization.*

The military administration in Germany in the initial period should be carried out with a view toward the eventual partitioning of Germany. To facil-

itate partitioning and to assure its permanence the military authorities should be guided by the following principles:
   a) Dismiss all policy-making officials of the Reich government and deal primarily with local governments.
   b) Encourage the reestablishment of state governments in each of the states corresponding to 18 states into which Germany is presently divided and in addition make the Prussian provinces separate states.
   c) Upon the partition of Germany, the various state governments should be encouraged to organize a federal government for each of the newly partitioned areas. Such new governments should be in the form of a confederation of states, with emphasis on states' rights and a large degree of local autonomy.
8. *Responsibility of Military for Local German Economy.*

The sole purpose of the military in control of the German economy shall be to facilitate military operations and military occupation. The Allied Military Government shall not assume responsibility for such economic problems as price controls, rationing, unemployment, production, reconstruction, distribution, consumption, housing, or transportation, or take any measures designed to maintain or strengthen the German economy, except those which are essential for military operations. The responsibility for sustaining the German economy and people rests with the German people with such facilities as may be available under the circumstances.

9. *Controls over Development of German Economy.*

During a period of at least twenty years after surrender adequate controls, including controls over foreign trade and tight restrictions on capital imports, shall be maintained by the United Nations designed to prevent in the newly-established states the establishment or expansion of key industries basic to the German military potential and to control other key industries.

10. *Agrarian program.*

All large estates should be broken up and divided among the peasants and the system of primogeniture and entail should be abolished.

11. *Punishment of War Crimes and Treatment of Special Groups.*

A program for the punishment of certain war crimes and for the treatment of Nazi organizations and other special groups is contained in section 11.

12. *Uniforms and Parades.*
   a) No German shall be permitted to wear, after an appropriate period of time following the cessation of hostilities, any military uniform or any uniform of any quasi-military organizations.
   b) No military parades shall be permitted anywhere in Germany and all military bands shall be disbanded.

13. *Aircraft.*

All aircraft (including gliders), whether military or commercial, will be confiscated for later disposition. No German shall be permitted to operate any aircraft, including those owned by foreign interests.

14. *United States Responsibility.*

Although the United States would have full military and civilian representation on whatever international commission or commissions may be established for the execution of the whole German program, the primary responsibility for the policing of Germany and for civil administration in Germany should be assumed by the military forces of Germany's continental neighbors. Specifically, these include Russian, French, Polish, Czech, Greek, Yugoslav, Norwegian, Dutch and Belgian soldiers.

Under this program United States troops should be withdrawn within a relatively short time.

Appendix M
The Potsdam Declaration, July 26, 1945

Signed by President Harry Truman and Prime Minister Winston Churchill, with the concurrence of Chiang Kai-shek, President of the National Government of China. U.S. Senate, Surrender of Italy, Germany and Japan.

1. We — the President of the United States, the President of the National Government of the Republic of China, and the Prime Minister of Great Britain, representing the hundreds of millions of our countrymen, have conferred and agree that Japan shall be given the opportunity to end this war.
2. The prodigious land, sea and air forces of the United States, the British Empire and of China, many times reinforced by their armies and air fleets from the west, are poised to strike the final blows upon Japan. This military power is sustained and inspired by the determination of all the Allied Nations to prosecute the war against Japan until she ceases to resist.
3. The result of the futile and senseless German resistance to the might of the aroused free peoples of the world stands forth in awful clarity as an example to the people of Japan. The might that now converges on Japan is immeasurably greater than that which, when applied to the resisting Nazis, necessarily laid waste to the lands, the industry and the method of life of the whole German people. The full application of our military power, backed by our resolve, will mean the inevitable and complete destruction of the Japanese armed forces and just as inevitably the utter destruction of the Japanese homeland.
4. The time has come for Japan to decide whether she will continue to be controlled by those self-willed militaristic advisers who unintelligent calculations have brought the Empire of Japan to the threshold of annihilation, or whether she will follow the path of reason.
5. Following are our terms. We will not deviate from them. There are no alternatives. We shall brook no delay.
6. There must be eliminated for all time the authority and influence of those who have deceived and misled the people of Japan into embarking on world conquest, for we insist that a new order of peace, security and justice will be impossible until irresponsible militarism is driven from the world.

7. Until such a new order is established and until there is convincing proof that Japan's war-making power is destroyed, points in Japanese territory shall be designated by the Allies to be occupied to secure the achievement of the basic objectives we are here setting forth.
8. The terms of the Cairo Declaration shall be carried out and Japanese sovereignty shall be limited to the islands of Honshu, Hokkaido, Kyushu, Shikoku and such minor islands as we determine.
9. The Japanese military forces, after being completely disarmed, shall be permitted to return to their homes with the opportunity to lead peaceful and productive lives.
10. We do not intend that the Japanese shall be enslaved as a race or destroyed as a nation, but stern justice shall be meted out to all war criminals, including those who have visited cruelties upon our prisoners. The Japanese Government shall remove all obstacles to the revival and strengthening of democratic tendencies among the Japanese people. Freedom of speech, of religion, and of thought, as well as respect for fundamental human rights shall be established.
11. Japan shall be permitted to maintain such industries as will sustain her economy and permit the exaction of just reparations in kind, but not those which would enable her to re-arm for war. To this end, access to, as distinguished from control of, raw materials shall be permitted. Eventual Japanese participation in world trade relations shall be permitted.
12. The occupying forces of the Allies shall be withdrawn from Japan as soon as these objectives have been accomplished and there has been established in accordance with the freely expressed will of the Japanese people a peacefully inclined and responsible government.
13. We call upon the government of Japan to proclaim now the unconditional surrender of all Japanese armed forces, and to provide proper and adequate assurances of their good faith in such action. The alternative for Japan is prompt and utter destruction.

Notes

Preface

1. *New York Times*, September 12, 1940.
2. Robert E. Sherwood, *Roosevelt and Hopkins: An Intimate History* (Harper & Brothers Publishers, New York) 1948, 191.
3. John Toland, *Infamy: Pearl Harbor and Its Aftermath* (Doubleday & Company, Garden City NY) 1982, 134.

Introduction

1. Charles Callan Tansill, *Back Door to War* (Henry Regenry, Chicago) 1952, 588–589.
2. Warren F. Kimball, *The Juggler — Franklin Roosevelt as Wartime Statesman* (Princeton University Press, Princeton NJ) 1991, 7.
3. Thomas A. Bailey, *The Man in the Street — The Impact of American Public Opinion on Foreign Policy* (Macmillan, New York) 1948, 11.
4. Robert B. Stinnett, *Day of Deceit — The Truth About FDR and Pearl Harbor* (The Free Press, New York) 2000, xiii.
5. The term "fireside chat" originated with Harry C. Butcher, manager of the CBS Washington office. FDR had said he wanted to catch the spirit of a person in his home talking informally to neighbors in their home. William Manchester, *The Glory and the Dream: A Narrative History of America, 1932–1972* (Little, Brown and Company, Boston) 1973, 81.
6. On October 13, 1944, Republican Congresswoman from Connecticut Clare Booth Luce excoriated Roosevelt "as the only American president who ever lied us into a war because he did not have the political courage to lead us into it. Although a majority of the American people may forgive him, history never will ... the president was not only untrustworthy but also incompetent. Shall we trust the making of a new peace to the tired and shaking hands of a man who could not keep the one he inherited when he was young and strong?" She also said that during seven peacetime years he did not seek to achieve greater collective security in the world and that "New Dealers" often presented "extenuating circumstances," among them "that the United States was the victim of an unprovoked attack by Japan." Luce then quoted Oliver Lyttleton, British Minister of Production: "Japan was provoked into attacking America at Pearl Harbor. It is a travesty on history to say that America was forced into the war. It is incorrect to say that America was ever truly neutral." "No," Luce concluded, "the theory of the unprovoked attack will not wash." *New York Times*, October 14, 1944.
7. Viscount James Bryce, before 1914, was an internationally respected British scholar, historian, and former ambassador to the United States. Kaiser Wilhelm II had awarded him the *Pour le Merite,* the highest honor that could be bestowed on a foreigner. After 1914 he was chairman of his country's infamous committee that cataloged supposed German army atrocities in Belgium. Could such a noble man be swayed by simple patriotic exigencies? Most Americans thought not. They were wrong. Stewart Halsey Ross, *Propaganda for War — How America Was Conditioned to Fight the Great War of 1914–1918)* (McFarland & Company, Inc., Publishers, Jefferson NC) 1996, 52.
8. James Duane Squires, *British Propaganda at Home and in the United States — from 1914 to 1917* (Harvard University Press, Cambridge MA) 1935, 67.
9. Ross, *Propaganda for War*, 145.
10. John T. Flynn wrote that until 1956 the origin of the Neutrality Act had never been made public. He stated that he had been "acting as one of the advisers of the Nye Committee (Appendix F) ... and was in a position to know the facts." He pointed out that on March 20, 1935, Senator Gerald P. Nye informed an executive session of the Committee that the president wanted to meet with "as many members as possible" of the Committee. FDR first lectured the group on the causes of war, adding his own personal experiences as Assistant Secretary of the Navy during the Great War. He

then suggested it would be "a wise thing for the Committee to prepare an act which would guarantee, in the event of a European war, the absolute neutrality of the American people." After consultation with his colleagues, Nye prepared the first draft of what became the Neutrality Act. John T. Flynn, *The Roosevelt Myth* (Devan-Adair Company, New York) 1956, 168–169.
 11. *New York Times*, October 6, 1937.
 12. Bruce Bartlett, *Cover-Up: The Politics of Pearl Harbor, 1941–1946* (Arlington House Publishers, New Rochelle NY) 1978, 15.
 13. *Ibid.*, 25.
 14. Saul Friedlander, *Prelude to Downfall* (Alfred A. Knopf, New York) 1967, 209.
 15. Robert E. Sherwood, *Roosevelt and Hopkins — An Intimate History* (Harper & Brothers) 1948, 83.
 16. Richardson was adamant that the Pacific Fleet should be based on the West Coast, that its presence in the mid–Pacific was more than an irritant to the concerned Japanese, it was an obvious incentive for war.
 17. Robert B. Stinnett, *Day of Deceit: The Truth About FDR and Pearl Harbor* (Simon & Schuster, New York) 2000, 9.
 18. *Ibid.*, 10.
 19. *Ibid.*
 20. Kemp Tolley, *Cruise of the Lanakai — Incitement to War* (Naval Institute Press, Annapolis MD) 1973, 162–163.
 21. A "leak" is properly defined as "an unofficial release of confidential information, usually to the media."
 22. *The New York Times*, October 30, 1940. The Rainbow Series was based on five hypothetical war scenarios. Rainbow One was a defensive war that would protect the U.S. and the Western Hemisphere north of 10 degrees south latitude. In such a war, the planners assumed the United States had no major allies. Rainbow Two assumed that the U.S. would be supported by Great Britain and France as allies. This arrangement would permit an immediate offensive in the Pacific against the most likely enemy, Japan. Rainbow Three was a modified Plan Orange (the original war plan against Japan), with the stipulation that defense of the hemisphere would first be secured, as proposed in Rainbow One. Rainbow Four was the same as Rainbow One but extended the defenses to include the entire Western Hemisphere. Rainbow Five, America's strategy during World War II, assumed that Britain and France would be U.S. allies, which would allow for offensive operations by U.S. forces in Europe, Africa, and the Pacific. Ronald H. Spector, *Eagle Against the Sun: The American War with Japan* (Free Press, New York) 1984, 59.
 23. *New York Times,* October 30, 1940.

Chapter 1

 1. Thomas A. Bailey and Paul B. Ryan, *Hitler vs. Roosevelt — The Undeclared Naval War* (The Free Press, New York) 1979, 184.
 2. Charles A. Beard, *President Roosevelt and the Coming of the War 1941— A Study in Appearances and Realities* (Yale University Press, New Haven) 1948, 155.
 3. John Terraine, *The U-Boat Wars — 1916–1945* (G. P. Putnam's Sons, New York) 1989, 342.
 4. On December 11, 1941, Japanese land-based torpedo planes based in Formosa sank the *Prince of Wales* and her accompanying battle cruiser HMS *Repulse* off the Malay coast.
 5. Harry Elmer Barnes, ed., *Perpetual War for Perpetual Peace — A Critical Examination of the Foreign Policy of Franklin Delano Roosevelt and Its Aftermath* (The Caxton Printers, Caldwell ID) 1953, 218.
 6. John T. Flynn., *The Roosevelt Myth* (Devan-Adair Company, New York) 1956, 385.
 7. *Ibid.*, 386.
 8. Postwar all of the logs of German submarines, except those that were lost at sea, were available to U.S. and British researchers. Except for one (the log of U-30 which sank the British passenger liner *Athenia* ten hours after Great Britain declared war on Germany and was "corrected" at the order of Admiral Doenitz) all can be accepted as accurate accounts.
 9. German submarines had separate periscopes with optics suited to their function; one could survey ships on the surface through an arc of 360-degrees, and a second aimed at the sky with large magnification could pick up aircraft.
 10. Bailey and Ryan, *Hitler vs. Roosevelt*, 172–173.
 11. *New York Times,* September 12, 1941.
 12. Wilson had connived to involve the U.S. in the Great War after having been reelected on the strength of the slogan "He Kept Us Out of War." He had taken an untenable stance that mistook human rights for neutral rights, including a rejection of repeated German proposals of guaranteed safe conduct for American ships. Wilson, too, was a champion dissembler; testifying before a Senate committee in 1919, he insistently denied he had known about the infamous secret treaties among the Allies before he went to the Paris Peace Conference. There is now irrefutable evidence that Wilson knew about them beforehand.
 13. The "freedom of the seas" clause never stood a chance of acceptance at Versailles. The British, who had historically relied on their high-seas navy to expand and defend their empire, were not about to yield this vital right.

14. *New York Times,* September 12, 1941.
15. Harry Elmer Barnes, Ed., *Perpetual War for Perpetual Peace* (The Caxton Printers, Caldwell ID) 1953, 219.
16. Terraine, *The U-Boat Wars,* 351.
17. *Ibid.,* 219.
18. Submarine commanders preferred surface attacks, preferably in the dark of night or just at dusk or before the sun rose. On the surface submarines were considerably faster and more maneuverable. They sat low in the water and when bows-on or stern-on, had a narrow silhouette. They also presented confusing radar targets in heavy seas.
19. Bailey and Ryan, *Hitler vs. Roosevelt,* 207.
20. Beard, *President Roosevelt and the Coming of the War,* 149.
21. Bailey and Ryan, *Hitler vs. Roosevelt,* 186. These four men were identified as such by the strongly isolationist and anti–Roosevelt *Chicago Tribune.*

Chapter 2

1. Winston Churchill, *Their Finest Hour* (Houghton Mifflin Company, Boston) 1949, 400.
2. *Ibid.,* 406.
3. Philip Goodhart, *Fifty Ships That Saved the World — The Foundation of the Anglo-American Alliance* (Doubleday & Company, Inc., Garden City NY) 1965, 236–237.
4. For example, to meet the insatiable demands of Churchill for weaponry the United States had clandestinely cleaned out its armories of relics of the Great War: "some half-a-million bolt-action Springfields and Krag-Jorgensen 30/40s, 900 75 mm field guns, 80,000 machine guns, much ammunition, an assortment of bombs, TNT, and smokeless powder" and shipped the materials to Great Britain — gratis." Frederic Rockwell Sanborn, *Design for War — A Study of Secret Power Politics, 1937–1941* (The Devin-Adair Company, New York) 1951, 127.
5. Asdic: Allied Submarine Detection Investigating Committee.
6. Goodhart, *Fifty Ships,* 88.
7. *Ibid.,* 89.
8. John Terraine, *The U-Boat Wars — 1916–1945* (G. P. Putnam's Sons, New York) 1989, 277.
9. Goodhart, *Fifty Ships,* 145–146.
10. *Ibid.,* 84.
11. Churchill, *Their Finest Hour,* 406.
12. *Ibid.,* 558.
13. Sanborn, *Design for War,* 179.
14. Thomas A. Bailey and Paul B. Ryan, *Hitler vs. Roosevelt: The Undeclared Naval War* (The Free Press, New York) 1979, 86.

15. Churchill, *Their Finest Hour,* 404.
16. Bailey and Ryan, *Hitler vs. Roosevelt,* 91.
17. *Ibid.,* 96.
18. *Ibid.,* 97.
19. Terraine, *The U-Boat Wars,* 279–280.
20. Goodhart, *Fifty Ships,* 237.
21. Terraine, *The U-Boat Wars,* 281.
22. Goodhart, *Fifty Ships,* 213.

Chapter 3

1. Warren F. Kimball, *The Most Unsordid Act — Lend-Lease, 1939-1941* (The Johns Hopkins Press, Baltimore MD) 1969, Vi.
2. Thomas A. Bailey and Paul B. Ryan, *Hitler vs. Roosevelt — The Undeclared Naval War* (The Free Press, New York) 1979, 109.
3. Henry L. Stimson and McGeorge Bundy, *On Active Service in Peace and War* (Harper & Brothers, New York) 1947, 361. In the book's Introduction, Stimson immediately wrote: "The writing of the book has been the work of Mr. McGeorge Bundy. Its style and composition are his...." xi.
4. Winston Churchill, *Their Finest Hour* (Houghton Mifflin Company, Boston) 1949, 569.
5. Ten days after the start of World War II, FDR wrote for the first time to Winston Churchill, then First Lord of the Admiralty, suggesting he reply with "anything you want me to know about." The two leaders subsequently exchanged over 1,700 messages, an average of almost one a day until Roosevelt died on April 12, 1945. Dust jacket, *Roosevelt and Churchill — Their Secret Wartime Correspondence.*
6. *Ibid.,* 567.
7. Francis L. Loewenheim, Harold D. Langley, and Manfred Jonas, *Roosevelt and Churchill — Their Secret Wartime Correspondence* (E. P. Dutton & Co., New York) 1975, 123.
8. *Ibid.*
9. *Ibid.,* 124.
10. *Ibid.,* 125.
11. *Ibid.*
12. The Johnson Debt-Default Act of 1934 required nations at war to pay cash for American military supplies.
13. Churchill, *Their Finest Hour,* 568.
14. *New York Times,* December 30, 1940.
15. *Ibid.,* January 7, 1941.
16. Thomas Fleming, *The New Dealers' War — F.D.R. and the War Within World War II* (Basic Books, New York) 2001, 82.
17. *Ibid.,* 82–83.
18. Kimball, *The Most Unsordid Act,* 190.
19. *Ibid.*
20. Stimson was a former Secretary of War in the cabinet of President William Howard

Taft from 1911 to 1913. President Calvin Coolidge had named him Governor General of the Philippines in 1927 and President Herbert Hoover appointed him Secretary of State in 1929.
21. *New York Times,* January 18, 1941.
22. Kimball, *The Most Unsordid Act,* 167.
23. Winston Churchill, *Blood, Sweat, and Tears* (G. P. Putnam's Sons, New York) 1941, 453.
24. Fleming, *The New Dealers' War,* 83.
25. Bailey and Ryan, *Hitler vs. Roosevelt,* 109.
26. Ted Morgan, *FDR — A Biography* (Simon and Schuster, New York) 1985, 579.
27. Churchill, *Their Finest Hour,* 569.
28. Saul Friedlander, *Prelude to Downfall* (Alfred A. Knopf, New York) 1967, 297.
29. James V. Compton, *The Swastika and the Eagle — Hitler, the United States, and the Origins of World War II* (Houghton Mifflin Company, Boston) 1967, 158.
30. *Ibid.*

Chapter 4

1. Wayne S. Cole, *Charles A. Lindbergh and the Battle Against Intervention in World War II* (Harcourt Brace Jovanovich, New York) 1974, 128.
2. Charles A. Lindbergh, *The Wartime Journals of Charles A. Lindbergh* (Harcourt Brace Jovanovich, New York) 1970, 567.
3. Leonard Mosley, *Lindbergh: A Biography* (Doubleday & Company, Garden City NY) 1976, xi.
4. A. Scott Berg, *Lindbergh* (G. P. Putnam's Sons, New York) 1998, 15.
5. In 1928, he presented his *Spirit of St. Louis* to the Smithsonian Institution in Washington for permanent exhibition, where it hangs today at the museum's main entrance next to the Wright Brothers' Kitty Hawk biplane. *Spirit,* specially built to Lindbergh's specifications at the small Ryan Aeronautical Company in San Diego, California, was financed by a group of businessmen in St. Louis, Missouri. Interestingly, the *Spirit* had no conventional transparent windscreen; to save weight Lindberg used a forward-facing periscope instead. Lindbergh felt that the only time he needed forward vision was when he was landing, and then he could poke his head out a side window.
6. Charles A. Lindbergh, *The Spirit of St. Louis* (Charles Scribner's Sons, New York) 1953, 495.
7. His official flight time was 33 hours, 30 minutes, 29.8 seconds from Roosevelt Field on Long Island, New York. For the feat he was awarded the Orteig Prize of $25,000, named after the New York hotelier who established these requirements: "to any flier or group of fliers who shall cross the Atlantic in a land or water aircraft (heavier than air) from Paris or the shores of France to New York, or from New York to Paris or the shores of France, without stop." Mosely, *Lindbergh,* 73.
8. Albert Fried, *FDR and His Enemies,* (St. Martin's Press, New York) 1999, 95.
9. Berg, *Lindbergh,* 247.
10. *Ibid.,* 273.
11. *Ibid.,* 277.
12. Mosley, *Lindbergh,* 190.
13. Berg, *Lindbergh,* 334. Lindbergh's certainty regarding Hauptmann's guilt has not been matched by numerous historians who have questioned the court's verdict, for example: George Waller, *Kidnap* (Dial Press, New York) 1961; Ludovic Kennedy, *The Airman and the Carpenter: The Lindbergh Kidnapping and the Framing of Richard Hauptmann* (Viking, New York) 1985. Jim Fisher, *The Ghosts of Hopewell: Setting the Record Straight in the Lindbergh Case* (Southern Illinois University Press, Carbondale IL) 1999.
14. Bruno Richard Hauptmann went to the electric chair on April 3, 1936. He never admitted his guilt, although by doing so the governor of New Jersey offered to commute his sentence to life imprisonment.
15. Fried, *FDR* , 92.
16. *Ibid.*
17. *New York Times,* March 15, 1934.
18. Cole, *Charles A. Lindbergh,* 33.
19. *Ibid.,* 34.
20. *Ibid.,* 37.
21. *Ibid.,* 39. The Messerschmitt Bf-109 was everything Lindbergh thought it was and more, and during the war in Europe, even when it was superseded by the newer Focke-Wulf Fw-190, it remained a mainstay of the Luftwaffe's fighter-plane force. Bf-109s were supplied to many air forces, and Messerschmitt licensed production of its *Gustav* model to Avia in Prague and IAR in Romania. In 1948, Israel flew Czech-built Bf-109 *Gustavs* against the Egyptian air force. These remarkable airplanes remained in active service until the 1960s, when turbojet-engine powered aircraft made them obsolete. David Donald, Ed., *Warplanes of the Luftwaffe* (Barnes & Noble Books, New York) 1994, 196–209.
22. *Ibid.,* 41.
23. Berg, *Lindbergh,* 377–378. The medal itself was a gold cross embellished with four small swastikas, on a white enamel background. It was strung on a red silk ribbon with black and white borders. Accompanying the decoration was a proclamation on parchment signed by Hitler. The same medal had recently

been awarded to the French Ambassador and Henry Ford. As for the medal's presenter, Reichsmarschal Hermann Göring, who had been considerably slimmer during the Great War, had been a flier and a genuine ace (five or more confirmed aerial victories). On July 14, 1918, when he had accumulated twenty-one confirmed "kills" and eight days after *Rittmeister* Manfred von Richthofen (The Red Baron) was killed, Lieutenant Göring was handed the ceremonial walking stick—or *Geschwaderstock*—as commander of the famous "Flying Circus," *Jagdgeschwader 1*. Göring was also decorated with the *Pour le Merite*, the highest distinction possible to a soldier of his rank. William E. Burrows, *Richthofen: A True History of the Red Baron* (Harcourt, Brace & World, Inc., New York) 1969, 206. By the late 1930s Göring was proud of his powerful Luftwaffe, and relished a chance to talk airplanes with an expert like Lindbergh and to demonstrate Germany's latest aircraft.

24. Cole, *Charles A. Lindbergh*, 43.

25. Berg, *Lindbergh*, 381. Lindbergh subsequently donated the medal and proclamation to the Missouri Historical Society, where from time to time the two items are put on display along with his other awards.

26. Hamilton Fish, *FDR: The Other Side of the Coin: How We Were Tricked into World War II* (Vantage Press, New York) 1976, 32.

27. *New York Times*, October 22, 1940.

28. Berg, *Lindbergh*, 411.

29. *Ibid.*, 412.

30. Warren F. Kimball, *The Most Unsordid Act: Lend-Lease, 1939–1941* (John Hopkins Press, Baltimore MD) 1969, 202.

31. *New York Times*, September 16, 1941. During the first 18 months of World War II in Europe, prior to his joining The America First Committee, Lindbergh "had already made five nationwide radio broadcasts, addressed two public meetings, published three articles in popular national magazines, testified before two major legislative committees, and consulted with numerous noninterventionist leaders.... He had become the most praised, the most damned, the most controversial, and most tenaciously independent of the major opponents of the Roosevelt administration's policies toward the European war." Cole, *Lindbergh*, 76–77.

32. Berg, *Lindbergh*, 397.

33. *New York Times*, October 14, 1940.

34. Berg, *Lindbergh*, 412–413.

35. *New York Times*, January 24, 1941.

36. Berg, *Lindbergh*, 418.

37. Lindbergh, *The Wartime Journals*, 478.

38. *Ibid.*, 480. After Pearl Harbor, Lindbergh felt his place was in the USAAF, and he sought reinstatement of his commission. But Roosevelt took the opportunity to frustrate him and vengefully directed War Secretary Stimson to turn him down. Lindbergh subsequently spent World War II as a civilian, first as an adviser to Henry Ford at his River Rouge plant manufacturing B-24 bombers, and then as a test pilot for Chance-Vought aircraft's F4U Corsair. As a civilian "adviser" in the Pacific Lindbergh flew more than 50 combat missions in USAAF-marked aircraft, shooting down one Japanese plane; all were gross violations of international law.

39. Berg, *Lindbergh*, 423–424.

40. *New York Times*, April 18, 1941.

41. *Ibid.*, September 12, 1941.

42. *Ibid.* The latest example of a "wartime emergency" was a "manufactured" emergency by the George W. Bush administration. Following the September 11, 2001, hijackings and the subsequent destruction of New York City's World Trade Center towers and the damage to the Pentagon in Washington, White House propaganda operatives skillfully morphed the tragedies into a war with Iraq and a war on "terrorism."

43. Lindbergh, *Wartime Journals*, 538.

44. Berg, *Lindbergh*, 385.

45. *Ibid.*, 386.

46. *Ibid.*, 393.

47. *Ibid.*, 402.

Chapter 5

1. Kemp Tolley, *Cruise of the Lanakai—Incitement to War* (Naval Institute Press, Annapolis MD) 1973, 19–20.

2. *Ibid.*, 18.

3. *New York Times*, December 2, 1941.

4. Frederic Rockwell Sanborn, *Design for War—A Study of Secret Power Politics, 1937–1941* (The Devin-Adair Company, New York) 1951, 515–518.

5. Tolley, *Cruise of the Lanakai*, 268.

6. *Ibid.*, 269.

7. *Ibid.*

8. The third "small vessel," another schooner, the *Molly Moore*, needed more extensive fitting-out, and time ran out before she could be commissioned and sent on *her* mission.

9. It has never been explained why Hart did not provision his submarines and order them to sea to attack the coming invasion forces. Hart himself retreated to Australia, an admiral with no ships to command. He was then ordered back to Washington to sit behind an unimportant desk. Never formally relieved of command of his defunct Asiatic Fleet, Hart never again was given a combat command. Robert B. Stinnett, *Day of Deceit: The Truth*

About FDR and Pearl Harbor (The Free Press, New York) 2000, 147. "Perhaps the question has been muted," wrote Rear Admiral Kemp Tolley, "because the subs, unlike the Pearl Harbor ships, were not lost in surprise attack. Actually, had they been on offensive stations at sea, their effectiveness would have been minimal through faulty torpedoes. But nobody knew that then." Tolley, *Cruise of the Lanakai*, 58.
 10. Tolley, *Cruise of the Lanakai*, 19–20.
 11. *Ibid.*, 46.
 12. *Ibid.*, 47.

Chapter 6

 1. Edward L. Beach, *Scapegoats: A Defense of Kimmel and Short at Pearl Harbor* (Naval Institute Press, Annapolis MD) 1995, 159.
 2. California Committee on Pacific Friendship, November 1937. *Perpetual War for Perpetual Peace*, Harry Elmer Barnes, ed. (The Caxton Printers, Ltd., Caldwell ID) 1953, 231.
 3. John Toland, *The Rising Sun: The Decline and Fall of the Japanese Empire, 1936–1945* (Random House, New York) 1970, 146.
 4. Robert B. Stinnett, *Day of Deceit: The Truth About FDR and Pearl Harbor* (Simon & Schuster, New York) 2000, Dust Jacket.
 5. John Costello, *Days of Infamy: MacArthur, Roosevelt, Churchill: The Shocking Truth Revealed* (Pocket Books, New York) 1994, 241.
 6. John Toland, *Infamy: Pearl Harbor and Its Aftermath* (Berkely Books, New York) 1982, 256.
 7. William H. Honan, *Visions of Infamy: The Untold Story of How Journalist Hector C. Bywater Devised the Plans That Led to Pearl Harbor* (St. Martin's Press, New York) 1991, 251.
 8. *Ibid.*,14–15.
 9. *Ibid.*, 18–19.
 10. *Ibid.*, 126.
 11. *Ibid.*, 71.
 12. Toland, *Infamy*, 249–250.
 13. *New York Times,* September 13, 1925.
 14. Since the Imperial Japanese Navy regarded the United States as its likeliest future adversary, it sent its most promising young naval officers there on various tours of duty. Yamamoto visited several ports of call on America's west coast aboard a training ship in 1909, spent one year at Harvard studying English, returned as a delegate to the Washington Naval Conference in 1921, and then was naval attaché at the Japanese embassy in Washington. Honan, *Visions of Infamy*, 179.
 15. Operation Z, Admiral Yamamoto's Pearl Harbor plan, was named in honor of the famous Z signal given by Admiral Togo at the start of battle of Tsushima in 1905 when he sank the Russian fleet: ON THIS ONE BATTLE RESTS THE FATE OF OUR NATION. LET EVERY MAN DO HIS UTMOST.
 16. Toland, *Infamy*, 250–251.
 17. There was Winston Churchill's recent amphibious-landing debacle at Gallipoli in 1915–1916 to contemplate — in which Allied forces before withdrawing suffered fifty percent casualties, some 250,000 men, and their navies lost three battleships. It was generally concluded that modern weapons such as airplanes, submarines and mines gave every advantage to the defenders. For example, off Gallipoli a single U-boat had significantly disrupted the orderly landing of troops; observers agreed that if more than one German submarine had been on the scene, no landings would have take place.
 18. Stinnett, *Day of Deceit,* 147.
 19. Lt. Commander McCollum's proposed eight steps, designed to incite Japan into committing an overt act of war, were discovered by historian Robert B. Stinnett "in Box 6 of a special US Navy collection in RG 38 in the Military Reference Branch of Archives H, January 24, 1995." Stinnett, *Day of Deceit,* 271.
 20. Japan, after overrunning the Malay Peninsula, Singapore, and the Philippines in 1942, immediately declared those former colonies free.
 21. Stinnett, *Day of Deceit,* 273.
 22. *Ibid.*, 275. On the day after Hitler's invasion of Russia, Secretary of the Interior Harold Ickes wrote Roosevelt: "To embargo oil to Japan would be as popular a move in all parts of the country as you could make. There might develop from the embargoing of oil to Japan such a situation as would make it, not only possible but easy, to get into this war in an effective way. And if we should thus indirectly be brought in, we would avoid the criticism that we had gone in as an ally of communistic Russia." John Toland, *The Rising Sun: The Decline and Fall of the Japanese Empire 1936–1945* (Random House, New York) 1970, 85.
 23. John G. Winant, *A Letter from Grosvenor Square* (Hodder & Stoughton, London) 1947, 198–199.
 24. Toland, *Infamy,* 317–318.
 25. Barnes, Ed., *Perpetual War,* 242.
 26. Geoffrey C. Ward, *Before the Trumpet: Young Franklin Roosevelt 1882–1905* (Harper & Row, New York) 1985, 87–88.
 27. Barnes, ed., *Perpetual War,* 241–242.
 28. *Ibid.*, 243.
 29. *Ibid.*, 638–639.
 30. See Anthony Cave Brown, *Bodyguard of Lies*, Vol. I and II (Harper & Row, New York) 1975: "The extraordinary true story of the clandestine war of intricate deceptions that hid the secrets of D-Day from Hitler and sealed the Allied victory."

31. Stinnett, *Day of Deceit*, 60.
32. *Ibid.*, 69.
33. *Ibid.*, 71.
34. *Ibid.*, 47. Chief Radioman Homer Kisner was the Pacific Fleet's radio intercept traffic chief and a storehouse of vital information. Yet, "neither Kisner nor any of the sixty-five men reporting to him nor the remaining hundred-odd intercept operators were ever called before any of the [then] nine Pearl Harbor investigations.... The reason, our government would still claim after the fact, was that their testimony could compromise our national security." Stinnett, *Day of Deceit*, 55.
35. *Ibid.*
36. *Ibid.*, 48.
37. Niitakyama is a 13,000-foot peak in Formosa, the highest mountain in what was then part of Japan. Scaling it was considered a significant mountaineering feat. In this instance it was final confirmation that the First Air Fleet should attack Pearl Harbor.
38. James Rusbridger and Eric Nave, *Betrayal at Pearl Harbor: How Churchill Lured Roosevelt into World War II* (Summit Books, New York) 1991, 146.
39. *Ibid.*, 138.
40. *Ibid.*, 139.
41. Stinnett, *Day of Deceit*, 46.
42. The aura of omnipotence surrounding the Boeing B-17 *Flying Fortress* was a product of the collaborative propaganda generated by both the airplane's builder and the U.S. Army Air Forces, an early example of the "military-industrial complex" in action. The qualities of the optical Norden bombsight, supposedly capable of dropping bombs into pickle-barrels from 20,000 feet, were also extravagantly promoted. In fact, the B-17 and its Norden were a woefully inadequate anti-shipping weapons. Over cloud-covered Europe, against *stationary* targets many times larger than even the biggest man-of-war, the B-17/Norden was also ineffective. Throughout the war, U.S. "precision bombing" was a hoax. The B-17 furthermore was no "fortress"; without fighter escorts, it was extremely vulnerable to fighter-plane attacks. Luftwaffe fighter pilots referred to the *Flying Fortresses* as "Flying Coffins." Stewart H. Ross, *Strategic Bombing by the United States in World War II: The Myths and the Facts* (McFarland & Company, Inc., Jefferson NC) 2003.
43. To prevent their aerial torpedoes from burying themselves in the mud of the shallow harbor, dredged to 40 feet deep, the Japanese came up with a simple fix. They attached wooden box fins that slipped over the noses of the torpedoes configured to raise the nose during the run-in.
44. Walter J. Boyne, ed., *Today's Best Military Writing* (Tom Doherty Associates, New York) 2004.
45. The 14-part message was the Japanese response to Secretary of State Cordell Hull's ten-point ultimatum to Japan on November 26 which had been vetted by FDR. The memorandum was essentially the maximum terms of an American policy for the entire Orient. It demanded that Japan withdraw all military, naval, air, and police forces from China and Indochina, and to recognize only Chiang Kai-shek's Chungking government; to make additional concessions of a similar nature; to observe in China the political and economic practices once covered by the "Open Door," which was the old imperialistic formula for America's own intervention in China. Charles A. Beard has concluded: "At no time in the history of American diplomatic relations with the Orient, if public records are to be trusted, had the Government of the United States proposed to Japan such a sweeping withdrawal from China under a veiled threat of war and under the pressure of economic sanctions likely to lead to war." Roosevelt and Hull were so certain that the Japanese government would refuse to accept the crushing proposals that, without waiting for a reply, they issued a war warning to U.S. commanders in the Pacific *the next day.* Charles A. Beard, *President Roosevelt and the Coming of the War 1941: A Study in Appearance and Realities* (Yale University Press, New Haven CT) 1948, 132, 238.
46. Costello, *Days of Infamy*, 202.
47. Rusbridger, *Betrayal at Pearl Harbor*, 26.
48. Frederic Rockwell Sanborn, *Design for War: A Study of Secret Power Politics, 1937–1941* (The Devin-Adair Company, New York) 1951, 541.
49. Second only to the photograph of six U.S. marines raising the American flag atop Mount Suribachi on Iwo Jima, the dramatic photograph of the explosion of the forward magazines of the battleship *Arizona* inside Pearl Harbor on December 7, 1941, remains the fixed image of World War II. A high-ranking marine officer who observed the posed flag raising and civilian Joseph Rosenthal's picture-taking is alleged to have said to a fellow officer that the photograph would ensure a Marine Corps "for the next 200 years." The *Arizona* memorial floats atop the wreck of the barely submerged battleship, and is a principal tourist attraction in Oahu.
50. The first wave lost five torpedo *Kates* bombers, one *Val*, and three *Zeros*. The second wave lost fourteen Vals and six *Zeros*. In addition to these twenty-nine missing aircraft, seventy-four had sustained some damage. Gordon W. Prange with Donald M. Goldstein and Katherine V. Dillon, *At Dawn We Slept: The*

Untold Story of Pearl Harbor (McGraw-Hill, New York) 1986, 544–545.
51. Costello, *Days of Infamy*, 240.
52. Toland, *Infamy*, 311.
53. Richard N. Current, "How Stimson Meant to 'Maneuver' the Japanese." The Mississippi Valley Historical Review, Vol. 40, No.1 (June 1953), 67–74.
54. Beard, *President Roosevelt and the Coming of the War*, 517–569.
55. *Ibid.*, 518.
56. Toland, *The Rising Sun*, 146.
57. Toland, *Infamy*, 16–17.
58. *New York Times*, December 9, 1941.
59. John Toland, *Adolf Hitler* (Doubleday & Company, Garden City NY) 1976, 695.
60. *Ibid.*, 696.
61. Stinnett, *Day of Deceit*, 256.
62. Toland, *Infamy*, 321.
63. Knox's report was locked away and never made public until it "was discovered by accident years later by Senator Homer Ferguson." Ferguson had been one of the Republican members of the Congressional Committee of 1945–1946. Bruce Bartlett, "The Pearl Harbor Cover-Up," *Reason*, February 1976, 25.
64. The ten Pearl Harbor investigations: 1.—Secretary of the Navy Frank Knox's Investigation, December 8 to December 14, 1941.2.—The Roberts Commission, December 18, 1941 to January 23, 1942. 3.—The Hart Inquiry, February 12, 1944 to June 15, 1944. 4.—The Army Pearl Harbor Board, July 20, 1944 to October 20, 1944. 5.—The Naval Court of Inquiry, July 24, 1944 to October 19, 1944. 6.—The Clarke Investigation, August 4 to September 20, 1944. 7.—The Clausen Investigation, January 24 to September 12, 1945. 8.—The Hewitt Inquiry, May 14, 1945 to July 11, 1945. 9.—The Joint Congressional Committee, November 15, 1945 to May 31, 1946. 10.—Senator Strom Thurmond's Capitol Hill Hearing, April 27, 1995.
65. Toland, *Infamy*, 21–22.
66. *New York Times*, January 24, 1942.
67. Stinnett, *Day of Deceit*, 255.
68. Toland, *Infamy*, 42.
69. *Ibid.*, 321.
70. *Ibid.*, 36.
71. Costello, *Days of Infamy*, 247.
72. Stinnett, *Day of Deceit*, 257.
73. Costello, *Days of Infamy*, 258.
74. Harry Elmer Barnes, ed., *Perpetual War for Perpetual Peace: A Critical Examination of the Foreign Policy of Franklin Delano Roosevelt and Its Aftermath* (The Caxton Printers, Ltd., Caldwell ID) 1953, 466.
75. Toland, *Infamy*, 320–321.
76. *Ibid.*, 319.
77. *Ibid.*, 324.
78. John T. Flynn, *Country Squire in the White House* (Doubleday, Doran and Company, Inc., New York) 1940, 7.
79. *Ibid.*, 105.
80. *New York Times*, May 26, 1999.

Chapter 7

1. J.F.C. Fuller, *The Second World War, 1939–1945* (Duell, Sloan, Pearce, New York) 1948, 355.
2. Thomas Fleming, *The New Dealers' War: FDR and the War Within World War II* (Basic Books, New York) 2001, 176. Paul Josef Goebbels was unimpressive physically, just over five feet tall and slight of build. Like FDR, he had been wracked by polio, leaving him with a clubfoot. He compensated for his deformity with a powerful drive to excel. He graduated from Heidelberg University in 1921 with a Ph.D. in literature. Like Hitler, Goebbels was a fiery speaker.
3. William Henry Chamberlain, *America's Second Crusade* (Henry Regnery, Chicago) 1950, 292–293.
4. Kai Bird and Lawrence Lifschultz, eds., *Hiroshima's Shadow* (The Pamphleteer's Press, Stony Creek CT) 1998, 136.
5. David MacIsaac, *Strategic Bombing in World War II: The Story of the United States Strategic Bombing Survey* (Garland Publishing Company, New York) 1976, 54.
6. Monica Braw, *The Atomic Bomb Suppressed: American Censorship in Occupied Japan* (M. E. Sharpe, Armonk NY) 1991, ix.
7. Harry Elmer Barnes, ed., *Perpetual War for Perpetual Peace: A Critical Examination of the Foreign Policy of Franklin Delano Roosevelt* (The Caxton Printers, Ltd., Caldwell ID) 1953, 653.
8. British misgivings about the lack of readiness of U.S. soldiers seemed justified when the previous month the U.S. Eighth Army was stalled by the numerically inferior Afrika Korps. Then more ammunition was given the British when Field Marshal Erwin Rommel's veteran army attacked American troops near the Kasserine Pass in Tunisia. Under heavy pressure, and for the first time experiencing demoralizing Luftwaffe dive bombing, some units retreated without being ordered to do so. This quickly escalated into a panic-stricken rout of over 50 miles. Pleased with themselves, the British commanders in Africa used the debacle as proof of their suspicions. General Harold Alexander, soon to be theater commander, wrote General Alan Brooke, chief of the Imperial General Staff, that the GI's were "soft, green, and quite untrained ... is it surprising they lack the will to fight? ... If this handful of divisions here are their best, the

value of the rest may be imagined." Matthew Parker, *Monte Cassino: The Hardest-Fought Battle of World War II* (Doubleday, New York) 1993, 8.

9. R. Ernest Dupuy and Trevor N. Dupuy, *The Encyclopedia of Military History from 3500 B.C. to the Present* (Harper & Row, New York) 1970, 955.

10. Fuller, *The Second World War*, 274.

11. Cordell Hull later wrote: "I was told that the Prime Minister was dumbfounded" at Roosevelt's pronouncement of unconditional surrender. Cordell Hull, *The Memoirs of Cordell Hull*, Vol. II (Macmillan, New York) 1948, 1570. In 1948, Robert E. Sherwood wrote to Winston Churchill asking him if he had discussed the unconditional surrender statement with FDR before the press conference in Casablanca. Churchill replied: "I heard the words 'Unconditional Surrender' for the first time from the President's lips at the Conference. It must be remembered that at that moment no one had a right to proclaim that victory was assured. Therefore, defiance was the note. I would not myself have used these words, but I immediately stood by the President and have frequently defended the decision. It is false to suggest that it prolonged the war. Negotiation with Hitler was impossible. He was a maniac with supreme power to play his hand out to the end, which he did, and so did we." Robert E. Sherwood, *Roosevelt and Hopkins: An Intimate History* (Harper & Brothers, New York) 1948, 664.

12. John Slessor, *The Central Blue* (Praeger, New York) 1957, 434.

13. The Casablanca formula had an earlier parallel in the Great War. As the war wound down in the fall of 1918, former President Theodore Roosevelt, itching to make another run for the nation's top office, positioned himself and the Republican Party four-square against Woodrow Wilson's offer of an armistice based on his Fourteen Points (Appendix C). As far as jingo Roosevelt was concerned only Germany's unconditional surrender of its army was acceptable. General John J. Pershing, commander of the American Expeditionary Force, agreed and wanted to parade his victorious troops down Berlin's Unter der Linden to convince the German people that they had lost the war. Pershing's vigorous stance was dismissed by America's principal allies: British Prime Minister David Lloyd George barked that "someone had put him up to it" and Georges Clemenceau, the French premier, rejected the idea as "theatrical." Thomas Fleming, *The New Dealers' War: F.D.R. and the War Within World War II* (Basic Books, New York) 2001, 182–183.

14. Lord Hankey, *Politics, Trials and Errors* (Henry Regnery, Chicago) 1950, 29.

15. *Ibid.*, 35–36.

16. *Ibid.*, 46–47.

17. James MacGregor Burns, *The Lion and the Fox* (Harcourt Brace Jovanovich, New York) 1956, 18.

18. Anne Armstrong, *Unconditional Surrender: The Impact of the Casablanca Policy upon World War II* (Rutgers University Press, New Brunswick NJ) 1961, 150.

19. Albert Wedemeyer, *Wedemeyer Reports* (Holt, New York) 1958, 96.

20. *Ibid.*, 169.

21. Fleming, *The New Dealers' War*, 175.

22. *Ibid.*, 176.

23. Gordon A. Craig, *Germany 1866–1945* (Oxford University Press, New York) 1978, 760–761.

24. *Ibid.*, 761.

25. Anthony Cave Brown, Vol. I, *Bodyguard of Lies: The Extraordinary True Story of the Clandestine War of Intricate Deceptions That Hid the Secrets of D-Day from Hitler and Sealed the Allied Victory* (Harper & Row Publishers, New York) 1975, 277.

26. Robert E. Sherwood, *Roosevelt and Hopkins: An Intimate History* (Harper & Brothers, New York) 1948, 665.

27. Fuller, *The Second World War*, 258.

28. Chamberlain, *America's Second Crusade*, 290.

29. Armstrong, *Unconditional Surrender*, 43–44.

30. *The Franco-Prussian War.* Had Prussia been the instigator? No, if the views of the American and British people *at that time* are assessed. In 1870, public opinion in the United States considered the war a defensive one on the part of Prussia, and it was well known that France had declared war first. Furthermore, the cause of German national unification was regarded sympathetically by all the great powers. Following the war and until 1914, a unified Reich was — unique among the great powers — a peaceful nation. By comparison, in the period 1871 to 1914, the United States went to war against Mexico and Spain; Russia fought Turkey and then Japan; England fought the Boers; and France was involved in continuous "small" wars with rebels in her colonies.

The Great War. At the end of the Great War in 1918, the victors pointed the finger of sole guilt — Kriegsschuldfrage — directly at Germany for provoking the conflict, with the infamous Article 231 of the equally infamous (to the Germans) Versailles Treaty. Since then many objective analyses by diplomatic historians apportion guilt differently. Sidney Bradshaw Fay, Professor of History at Harvard University, wrote that as a result of the accumulation of credible documentary evidence by the mid-1920s, "no serious historians any longer accept the dictum of the Allied victors of 1919 that Germany and her allies were solely responsible. They are all agreed that the responsibility is a divided one; they differ merely as to the relative responsibility of each of the Great Powers." Sidney Bradshaw Fay, *The Origins of the World War* (Macmillan, New York) 1928, 4. Furthermore, "Germany did not plot a European War, did not want one, and made genuine, though too belated efforts, to avert one.... The forty years following the Franco-Prussian War ... there developed a system of alliances which divided Europe into two hostile groups. This hostility was accentuated by the increase of armaments, economic rivalry, nationalist ambitions and antagonisms, and newspaper incitement. But it is very doubtful whether all these dangerous tendencies would have actually led to war had it not been for the assassination of Franz Ferdinand.... But the verdict of the Versailles Treaty that Germany and her allies were responsible for the war ... is historically unsound. It should therefore be revised." *Ibid.*, 552–558.

World War II. On September 1939, England declared war on Germany the day Wehrmacht Panzers crossed the Polish borders. At the same time the Red Army marched into eastern Poland and the Baltic states. Yet, Great Britain did not declare war on the Soviet Union for violating the sanctity of small states—only on Germany. This indicates that Britain's entry into the war was not intended to be a response to aggression. Rather, it was aimed at the restoration of the balance-of-power equilibrium in Europe at the expense of German hegemony.

31. Hull, *The Memoirs*, 1570.

32. Matthew Parker, *Monte Cassino: The Hardest-Fought Battle of World War II* (Doubleday, New York) 1993, 42.

33. Hull, *The Memoirs*, 1571.

34. Parker, *Monte Cassino*, xvi.

35. Eric Morris, *Circles of Hell: The War in Italy 1943–1945* (Crown Publishers, Inc., New York) 1993, 436.

36. *Ibid.*, 437.

37. Fuller, *The Second World War*, 355.

38. Morris, *Circles of Hell*, 212.

39. Armstrong, *Unconditional Surrender*, 131.

40. R. Ernest Dupuy and Trevor N. Dupuy, *Military Heritage of America* (McGraw-Hill, New York) 1956, 466.

41. Fuller, *The Second World War*, 349.

42. *New York Times*, August 6, 1944.

43. B. H. Liddell Hart, *The German Generals Talk* (William Morrow & Co., New York) 1948, 304.

44. *Ibid.*, 29.

45. *Ibid.*, 307.

46. *Ibid.*, 308.

47. B. H. Liddell Hart, ed., *The Rommel Papers* (Harcourt, Brace, New York) 1953, 427–428.

48. *Ibid.*

49. Hans Guderian, *Panzer Leader* (Dutton, New York) 1952, 142.

50. Karl Doenitz, *Memoirs: Ten Years and Twenty Days* (World Publishers, Cleveland OH) 1960, 142.

51. *Ibid.*, 307–308.

52. Erich Raeder, *My Life* (Naval Institute Press, Annapolis MD) 1960, 380.

53. Armstrong, *Unconditional Surrender*, 262.

54. Fuller, *The Second World War*, 390.

55. The Japanese did not know of the secret agreement at the Yalta Conference in which Stalin agreed to declare war on Japan three months after Germany's formal defeat in Europe. The Soviet dictator was as good as his word, punctually declaring war on the agreed-upon date and sending Red Army troops storming into Manchuria.

56. Fuller, *The Second World War*, 391.

57. John Toland, *The Rising Sun: The Decline and Fall of the Japanese Empire 1936–1945* (Random House, New York) 1970, 764.

58. Bird and Lifschultz, eds., *Hiroshima's Shadow*, 137.

59. *Ibid.*, 523.

60. Robert J. C. Butow, *Japan's Decision to Surrender* (Stanford University Press, Stanford CA) 1954, 130.

61. During the Great War, despite an understanding by all the belligerents that use of poison gas gave the first side using it only a temporary advantage, the usage of gas saw steady increases in potency. Chlorine replaced tear gas, phosgene replaced chlorine, and mustard (Appendix K) superseded chlorine. By the end of the conflict, the United States had developed more toxic lewisite. Following the war, there was a world-wide aversion to the use of poison gases, which led to the Geneva Conference of 1925. Use of all poisonous and asphyxiating gases was henceforth outlawed. The U.S. delegation signed the treaty but the Senate Foreign Relations Committee refused to ratify it. The so-called Geneva protocol was eventually endorsed by thirty-two nations, but not by the United States. During the 1930s, Germany secretly developed a new class of super chemical killers, the family of nerve gases: tabun, sarin, and soman. Odorless and invisible, these agents were nearly one hundred times more lethal than the mustard gas that caused most of the gas casualties during the Great War. These gases kill in minutes. Adolf Hitler, who had been gassed on the Western Front in 1918, was strongly opposed to their use and stated that

Germany would not be the first to use poison gas.

62. Mark Weber, "American Leaders Planned Poison Gas Attack Against Japan," *Journal of Historical Review*, vol. 16, No. 3, May/June 1997, 12.

63. Bird and Lifschultz, eds., *Hiroshima's Shadow*, 138.

64. Three years after the war, Henry Stimson (and McGeorge Bundy) finally acknowledged, but limply, "that history might find that the United States, by its delay in stating its position [regarding unconditional surrender] had prolonged the war." Henry L. Stimson and McGeorge Bundy, *On Active Service in Peace and War* (Harper, New York) 1948, 629.

65. Robert Jay Lifton and Greg Mitchell, *Hiroshima in America: Fifty Years of Denial* (G. P. Putnam's Sons, New York) 1995, 332.

Chapter 8

1. Anthony Cave Brown, *Bodyguard of Lies*, Vol. I (Harper & Row, New York) 1975, 423.

2. *Ibid.*, Vol. II, 918.

3. *Ibid.*, Vol. I, 349.

4. Louis P. Lochner, *Always the Unexpected* (Macmillan, New York) 294.

5. Allen W. Dulles, *Germany's Underground: The Anti–Nazi Resistance* (Da Capo Press, New York) 1947, 37–38.

6. Hans Rothfels, *The German Opposition to Hitler* (Henry Regnery, Chicago) 1948, 16.

7. Anne Armstrong, *Unconditional Surrender: The Impact of the Casablanca Policy upon World War II* (Rutgers University Press, New Brunswick NJ) 1961, 158.

8. German time-fuses could not be used because they made an audible hissing sound when triggered. British time-fuses, on the other hand, were silent and small. The Wehrmacht knew all about British pyrotechnics because the Royal Air Force regularly parachuted supplies of them along with plastic explosives to their agents in France and Germany. Just as regularly, German patrols gathered them up. They were available in three color-coded time-delay versions: one ignited the charge after ten minutes; another after a half hour; and the third, after two hours. They seemed foolproof.

9. Joachim Fest, *Planning Hitler's Death: The Story of the German Resistance* (Henry Holt and Company, New York) 1996, 257.

10. Peter Hoffmann, *Stauffenberg: A Family History, 1905–1944* (Cambridge University Press, Cambridge) 1995, 266. In 1937, Major Albert C. Wedemeyer had met Stauffenberg in Berlin who was in his class in the German War College. He recalled him as "a very handsome man — a fine military bearing, courteous, considerate and sensitive." Anton Gill, *An Honourable Defeat: A History of German Resistance to Hitler, 1933–1945* (Henry Holt and Company, New York) 1994, 230.

11. *Ibid.*, 277.

12. Peter Hoffmann, *The History of the German Resistance 1933–1945* (MIT Press, Cambridge MA) 1977, 404.

13. Hoffmann, *Stauffenberg*, 278. On July 20, not a single enemy soldier had as yet set foot in Germany. American and British troops were held by stubborn defenses in Italy; in France they had just broken out of their Normandy beachheads and the pivotal capture of Avranches, which Eisenhower declared had decided the war, took place on July 25. The Red Army had only just begun fighting its way into Rumania and Poland. Eberhard Zeller, *The Flame of Freedom: The German Struggle Against Hitler* (University of Miami Press, Coral Gables FL) 1969, 385.

14. Dulles, *Germany's Underground*, 1–2.

15. Fest, *Planning Hitler's Death*, 292.

16. Brown, *Bodyguard of Lies*, Vol. II, 893.

17. Zeller, *The Flame of Freedom*, 445.

18. *New York Times*, July 24, 1944.

19. Theodore Hamerow, *On the Road to the Wolf's Lair: German Resistance to Hitler* (Harvard University Press, Boston) 1997, 354.

20. Lochner, *Always the Unexpected*, 210–211.

21. John Toland, *Adolf Hitler* (Doubleday & Company, Garden City NY) 1976, 737.

22. Lochner, *Always the Unexpected*, 211.

23. Toland, *Adolf Hitler*, 592.

24. *Ibid.*

25. Brown, *Bodyguard of Lies*, 333.

26. Soon after the Focke-Wulf Fw-200 *Condor* first flew in 1937, it was recognized as the best long-range airliner in Europe, if not the world. On August 10, 1938, it took off from Berlin-Tempelhof airport and made a record-setting non-stop flight against headwinds to Floyd Bennett Field in New York. During the war, the Luftwaffe took advantage of the plane's great range and used it as a convoy-spotter for U-boats in the Atlantic; some were fitted with bomb racks for anti-shipping operations. In late 1943, the main role of the *Condor* was to interdict Allied convoys from Gibraltar and variants were fitted with wing pylons to carry anti-ship missiles. By 1944, the lumbering Fw-200, far from being the "scourge of the Atlantic," as Winston Churchill described the plane, was vulnerable to patrolling fighters or even to Allied maritime reconnaissance aircraft. David Donald, ed., *Warplanes of the Luftwaffe* (Barnes & Noble Books, New York) 1994, 85–92.

27. Hoffmann, *The History of the German Resistance*, 202–203.
28. Dulles, *Germany's Underground*, xi.
29. Rothfels, *The German Opposition*, 20.
30. Hoffmann, *The History of the German Resistance*, 215.
31. Dulles, *Germany's Underground*, 132–133.
32. Brown, *Bodyguard of Lies*, 333.
33. Toland, *Adolf Hitler*, 732. Few of Nazi Germany's top generals survived the war. Those who managed to escape Hitler's fury were unable to avoid retribution by the Allies. They were either shot, committed suicide, were compelled to commit suicide, or were jailed. What was most significant, was the large number of suicides, "the ultimate signal of fear and despair," which totaled ninety-seven. During and after the Great War, only three German generals died by their own hands. Brown, *Bodyguard of Lies*, Vol. II, 897.
34. *Ibid.*, 346. The infamous Night of the Long Knives, June 30, 1934, was Hitler's ruthless purge of all those he considered a threat to his assumption of supreme power in Germany. Among those murdered was General Kurt von Schleicher, the former German Chancellor, and his wife.
35. Toland, *Adolf Hitler*, 176.
36. *Ibid.*, 420–421.
37. Dulles, *Germany's Underground*, 38.
38. Brown, *Bodyguard of Lies*, Vol. II, 656.
39. Hamerow, *On the Road*, 6.
40. Rothfels, *The German Opposition*, 84.
41. *Ibid.*
42. Anton Gill, *An Honourable Defeat: A History of German Resistance to Hitler, 1933–1945* (Henry Holt and Company, New York) 1994, 77.
43. Hoffmann, *Stauffenberg*, 254.
44. Rothfels, *The German Opposition*, 17.
45. Fest, *Planning Hitler's Death*, 296.
46. U.S. war planners "had not a clue that Germany, until 1944, was operating on an almost peacetime-economy footing with enormous surplus capacity to be exploited when necessary." They "would erroneously characterize Germany's economy as operating under 'heavy stress,' with the needs of war production adversely impacting the social and industrial fabric of the country." Stewart H. Ross, *Strategic Bombing by the United States in World War II: The Myths and the Facts* (McFarland & Company, Jefferson NC) 2003, 48.
47. Rothfels, *The German Opposition*, 18.
48. Fest, *Planning Hitler's Death*, 367.
49. Hans Guderian, *Panzer Leader* (Dutton, New York) 1952, 344.
50. *Ibid.*, 44–345.
51. *Ibid.*, 349.
52. Rothfels, *The German Opposition*, 160.
53. Hamerow, *On the Road*, 215.
54. Fest, *Planning Hitler's Death*, 3–4.
55. *Ibid.*, 367.

Chapter 9

1. Harry Elmer Barnes, Ed., *Perpetual War for Perpetual Peace* (Caxton Printers, Ltd., Caldwell ID) 1953, 519. Historian F. J. P. Veale wrote in *Advance to Barbarism — The Development of Total Warfare From Sarajevo to Hiroshima* (Mitre Press, London) 1962, 224: "In a nutshell the Morgenthau Plan was designed to bring about, artificially, in Germany the conditions of poverty, distress, and degeneration existing at that time in parts of the American South as a result of natural economic causes, which have been so graphically described by Erskine Caldwell in *Tobacco Road*." William Henry Chamberlain in his book *America's Second Crusade* (Henry Regnery, Chicago) 1950, 306: "It is no exaggeration to say that the Morgenthau Plan, accepted by Mr. Roosevelt and Mr. Churchill at the Quebec Conference in September 1944, if applied, would have been an indiscriminating sentence to death for millions of Germans. The area in which it was proposed to forbid all heavy industries and mining is one of the most urbanized and thickly populated in Europe."
2. Michael Beschloss: *The Conquerers: Roosevelt, Truman and the Destruction of Hitler's Germany, 1941–1945* (Simon & Schuster, New York) 2002, 103.
3. Henry Morgenthau III, *Mostly Morgenthaus — A Family History* (Ticknor & Fields, New York) 1991, 365.
4. Beschloss, *The Conquerers*, 249.
5. John Morton Blum, *From the Morgenthau Diaries: Years of War 1941–1945* (Houghton Mifflin, Boston) 1967, 334.
6. Morgenthau III, *Mostly Morgenthaus*, 245.
7. Beschloss, *The Conquerers*, 49.
8. Morgenthau III, *Mostly Morgenthaus*, 354.
9. Dwight D. Eisenhower, *Crusade in Europe* (Doubleday & Company, Garden City NY) 1948, 287.
10. David Eisenhower, *Eisenhower at War 1943–1945* (Random House NY) 1986, 402.
11. Beschloss, *The Conquerers*, 95–96.
12. *Ibid.*, 103.
13. *Ibid.*, 104.
14. *Ibid.* Surprisingly, in Morgenthau's draft of his plan (Appendix L) there was no reference to what was the keystone of his program: the conversion of industrialized Germany into a totally agrarian society. The only tie, and a tenuous one at that, was the document's demand

that large estates be fragmented into small parcels and redistributed "among the peasants." The draft also avoided using the pejorative word "flooding" of the Ruhr's coal mines, which Morgenthau frequently used in his private discussions; instead, the mines were simply to be "closed."

15. In 1947, McGeorge Bundy, whom Stimson acknowledged in the second sentence of his memoir as the ghost of his book, *On Active Service in Peace and War* (Harper, New York) 1948, 567, wrote that the Secretary of War "had wrestled with the results of that economically impossible treaty [Versailles]. He hoped for a settlement [of World War II] which would involve no burden of debts, no barriers to the internal trade of Central Europe...." At a special exhibition titled "Doomed Youth: The Poetry and the Pity of the First World War" at the Yale Center for British Art, New Haven, in the summer of 1999, one of the artifacts shown was a bound volume of the Versailles Treaty, explicitly displaying page 101: PART VIII. REPARATIONS. SECTION I. GENERAL PROVISIONS. The first article of SECTION I was 231. The accompanying caption was as follows: "The Treaty of Versailles included the Covenant of the League of Nations and the point-by-point demands made of a defeated Germany, including a provision that Germany accept all responsibility for the war. The formulation and implementation (in principle, if not completely in fact) of the Treaty of Versailles was clearly one of the monumental acts of modern politics. While the treaty-makers envisioned a new Europe and a world at peace at the end of its conditions, it [is] clear that the Treaty sowed the seeds for the Second European War, the rise of Adolf Hitler following an almost step-by-step denunciation and violation of its provisions."

16. Beschloss, *The Conquerers*, 105.
17. *Ibid.*, 106–107.
18. Knox, who had been appointed to be the moderator of the committee, had absented himself from the first day's discussions and never again showed up.
19. Stimson, *On Active Service*, 571–572.
20. William Manchester, *The Arms of Krupp — 1587-1968* (Little, Brown and Company, Boston) 1964, 141.
21. Stimson, *On Active Service*, 573.
22. Beschloss, *The Conquerers*, 115.
23. *Ibid.*, 118.
24. Morgenthau had not been invited to attend the meeting initially, but Roosevelt decided in Quebec that he should come to the conference and personally unveil his plan to Churchill. Neither Stimson nor Hull had been invited to attend nor had any idea that Morgenthau had been in Quebec. In outline, the Morgenthau Plan (Appendix L) could be summarized as follows:.
 1. Reduce Germany's size by cession of border areas to neighboring nations.
 2. Divide a smaller Germany into three parts; one area, consisting of the Ruhr, the Saar, and Kiel, would be governed by an international agency and would not be permitted to trade with the rest of Germany.
 3. Carve two new states out of the remaining areas, a "southern" state economically tied to Austria and a "northern'" state inside Prussia.
 4. Destroy or dismantle and deliver to the victors all manufacturing plants and facilities in all three areas of the "new" Germany.
 5. Pay special attention to the Ruhr's and the Saar's coal and iron mines, which would be stripped of all equipment and the mines themselves wrecked. Cordell Hull, *The Memoirs of Cordell Hull*, Vol. II (Macmillan, New York) 1948, 72.

25. Beschloss, *The Conquerers*, 125.
26. Morgenthau III, *Mostly Morgenthaus*, 386.
27. *Ibid.*, 387–388.
28. *Ibid.*, 388.
29. Stimson, *On Active Service*, 578.
30. Hull, *The Memoirs*, Vol. II, 1617.
31. *Ibid.*, 1618.
32. Beschloss, *The Conquerers*, 160.
33. *Ibid.*, 161.
34. Anne Armstrong, *Unconditional Surrender: The Impact of the Casablanca Policy upon World War II* (Rutgers University Press, New Brunswick, NJ) 1961, 216–217.
35. William Chamberlain, *America's Second Crusade* (Henry Regnery, Chicago) 1950, 291.
36. Beschloss, *The Conquerers*, 126.
37. Hull's successor was Edward Stettinius, impeccably groomed to give the appearance of an imposing Secretary of State, but considered a lightweight by all who knew him. One of his associates derided him "as much a Secretary of State as I was King of Spain," and Stimson, a history buff, considered him "pretty ignorant of international history." Ickes wrote in his diary that Stettinius' appointment had depressed him (Beschloss, *The Conquerors*, 167). But FDR wanted a reliable front man to head the State Department so he could continue to be his own Secretary of State, and the handsome Stettinius filled the bill.
38. Truman was right! High-level Nazi generals had banded together to negotiate an armistice with the western allies. They were in agreement that the battle of Stalingrad meant the war was lost and were hoping to avoid another blood-bath on D-Day. FDR wanted no

part of a negotiated settlement, American casualties be damned (Chapter 8).
39. Beschloss, *The Conquerors,* 248–249.
40. Henry Morgenthau, Jr., *Germany Is Our Problem* (Harper & Brothers Publishers, New York) 1945, 10–12.
41. Henry Morgenthau, Jr.'s depiction of a cabal of German industrialists meeting to plan a coming war is, *almost unbelievably,* a reprise of his father's fabrication of an earlier meeting that had never taken place (Appendix D). In 1918, Henry Morgenthau, Sr., recently resigned U.S. Ambassador to Turkey, published a book that alleged a high-level Crown Council Meeting on July 5, 1914, that had been convened by Kaiser Wilhelm II to prepare the Second Reich for its forthcoming preemptive war. Morgenthau, Sr.'s book was intended as anti–German propaganda for the forthcoming Paris Peace Conference. The book and its fable was proved a hoax by Historian Sidney Bradshaw Fay in his authoritative *The Origins of the World War* (Macmillan, New York) 1928, 167–182.
42. Morgenthau, *Germany Is Our Problem,* 11. Henry Morgenthau, Jr.'s virulent Germanophobia, like fellow Cabinet officer Harold Ickes,' became a symbol of American perfidy in the eyes of highest-level Nazi officials. Karl Doenitz, former Grand Admiral in the Kriegsmarine and commander of the submarine fleet—and for a short time after Hitler's suicide, his replacement as Reich Chancellor—was interviewed in his cell in Spandau Prison: Leon Goldensohn, *The Nuremberg Interviews* (Alfred A. Knopf, New York) 2004, 10. In a conversation regarding the legality of the tribunal holding him guilty of conspiracy, Doenitz asked rhetorically: "How can a foreign court try a sovereign government of another country? Could we have tried your President Franklin Delano Roosevelt and Secretary Henry Morgenthau ... if we had won the war?" Doenitz was sentenced to and served 10 years at Spandau Prison. U.S. Admiral Chester L. Nimitz provided testimony in his behalf during the trial, saving him from a more severe sentence, by stating that U.S. Navy submarines in the Pacific also engaged in unrestricted submarine warfare.
43. Morgenthau, *Germany Is Our Problem,* 12.
44. Beschloss, *The Conquerors,* 252.

Chapter 10

1. John T. Flynn, *The Roosevelt Myth* (The Devan-Adair Company, New York) 1956, 396.
2. Robert H. Ferrell, *The Dying President: Franklin D. Roosevelt 1944–1945* (University of Missouri Press, Columbia MO) 1998, 10.
3. Hugh Gregory Gallagher, *FDR's Splendid Deception: The Moving Story of Roosevelt's Massive Disability and the Intense Efforts to Conceal It from the Public* (Vandamere Press, Arlington VA) 1985, 202–203.
4. Bert Park, *The Impact of Illness on World Leaders* (University of Pennsylvania Press, Philadelphia) 1980, xix.
5. Ferrell, *The Dying President,* 10.
6. Kenneth Crispell and Carlos Gomez, *Hidden Illness in the White House* (Duke University Press, Durham NC) 1988, 96.
7. Gallagher, *FDR's Splendid Deception,* 97. 179.
8. James A. Farley, *Jim Farley's Story* (McGraw-Hill, New York) 1948, 109.
9. Jim Bishop, *FDR's Last Year: April 1944–April 1945* (William Morrow & Company, Inc., New York) 1974, 270.
10. Ferrell, *The Dying President,* 11.
11. Ferrell poses a provocative "what if." If his daughter Anna had not finally forced McIntire into the consultation in Bethesda, and if McIntire stayed in charge, it is possible that FDR would have died in 1944. "The then vice president, Henry A. Wallace, would have become president ... and who later was seen to have had very limited understanding of American politics...." But Anna had intervened, and Roosevelt lived long enough for a wiser politician, Harry S. Truman, to move into the presidency. Ferrell, *The Dying President,* 35.
12. Ferrell, *The Dying President,* 32.
13. McIntire wrote that the president frequently had such examinations. However, in the absence of Roosevelt's hospital chart, which "mysteriously" disappeared, and similar records that might have given evidence, there is no way of knowing for sure. It is certainly possible, if not likely, that in his previous eleven years as president of the United States, Roosevelt had not had a single such thorough examination.
14. Park, *The Impact of Illness,* 226.
15. Ferrell, *The Dying President,* 37.
16. Park, *The Impact of Illness,* 227.
17. Ferrell, *The Dying President,* 37.
18. Crispell and Gomez, *Hidden Illness,* 180–181.
19. Ferrell, *The Dying President,* 38.
20. Robert E. Gilbert, *The Mortal Presidency: Illness and Anguish in the White House* (Basic Books, New York) 1992, 48.
21. Crispell and Gomez, *Hidden Illness,* 117–118.
22. *Ibid.,* 121.
23. Gilbert, *The Mortal Presidency,* 57.
24. Ross McIntire, *White House Physician* (G. P. Putnam's Sons, New York) 1946, 193.
25. Bishop, *FDR's Last Year,* 378.
26. *Ibid.*

27. Ferrell, *The Dying President*, 151.

28. Roosevelt needed a retreat close to Washington. He had built for his personal use in the close-by Catoctin Mountains in Maryland a rustic facility with three cabins, a mess hall, and a pool for his water therapy sessions. It was called appropriately *Shangri-La*, from the book and the movie, *Lost Horizon* by James Hilton. *Shangri-La* was a mystical lamasery high and deep in the Himalayas, where its meditating Buddhist residents lived extraordinarily long lives, yet retained their youthful looks. How often Roosevelt went there to rest was unknown to the public. President Dwight D. Eisenhower later during his two terms as president used the facility, not only for his convalescence from his heart attack, but as a relaxing get-away. He renamed it Camp David after his grandson.

29. Gallagher, *FDR's Splendid Deception*, 179.

30. Ferrell, *The Dying President*, 105.

31. Gilbert, *The Mortal Presidency*, 57.

32. Robert E. Sherwood, *Roosevelt and Hopkins: An Intimate History* (Harper & Brothers, New York) 1948, 815.

33. *Ibid.*, 816.

34. William D. Leahy, *I Was There: The Personal Story of the Chief of Staff to Presidents Roosevelt and Truman Based on His Notes and Diaries Made at the Time* (Whittlesey House, New York) 1950, 322–323.

35. Gallagher, *FDR's Splendid Deception*, 195.

36. John Toland, *The Rising Sun: The Decline and Fall of the Japanese Empire 1936–1945* (Random House, New York) 1970, 634.

37. Robert E. Gilbert, *The Mortal Presidency: Illness and Anguish in the White House* (Basic Books, New York) 1992, 62.

38. Ibid, 61.

39. Ferrell, *The Dying President*, 108.

40. Sixty years later the debate on the Yalta Conference goes on between political conservatives and liberals in the United States. In the view of many conservatives, the failing Roosevelt did nothing less at Yalta than sell out Eastern Europe to Soviet control for the next half-century. Liberals, on the other hand, point out that Roosevelt conceded Poland and parts of Eastern Europe to Stalin because the Red Army controlled the territory anyway, and Yalta changed no realities on the ground. Yalta agreements also called for free elections in Poland, which Stalin later ignored.

41. MacArthur's reconquest of the Philippines cost 60,628 U.S. casualties, killed, wounded and missing. Fuller, J. F. C., *The Second World War, 1939–1945: A Strategical and Tactical History* (Duell, Sloan, Pearce, New York) 1948, 387.

42. John Costello, *Days of Infamy: MacArthur, Roosevelt, Churchill — The Shocking Truth Revealed* (Pocket Books, New York) 1994, 268.

43. *Ibid.*, 269.

44. The title page lists George Creel as "collaborator," which to the author was a strong indication of the kind of book McIntire's memoir would be. There are no Notes and no Index, in keeping with the sort of superficial book Creel was comfortable writing. Creel had been Chairman of the Committee on Public Information during the Great War, when Woodrow Wilson appointed him head of government propaganda. The author wrote of Creel in his 1996 book *Propaganda for War — How the United States Was Conditioned to Fight the Great War of 1914–1918*, 23: "George Creel was a journalist of modest repute with a penchant for controversy. While some historians casually credit him with being a 'muckraker' — a crusading, progressive journalist — CPI's chairman did not quite make the grade. Creel was far more a 'muckslinger,' less willing to support his often wild contentions with facts than to capture his readers with sensationalism. He was an opportunist, most of all — the very personification of a fast-growing breed of American hucksters, the public relations counsel."

45. McIntire, *White House Physician*, 16.

46. Ferrell, *The Dying President*, 13.

47. McIntire, *White House Physician*, 110–111.

48. *Ibid.*, 159.

49. Flynn, *The Roosevelt Myth*, 397.

Chapter 11

1. Harry Elmer Barnes, *Perpetual War for Perpetual Peace — A Critical Examination of the Foreign Policy of Franklin Delano Roosevelt and Its Aftermath* (The Caxton Printers, Ltd., Caldwell ID) 1953, 191.

2. Holger H. Herwig, *Politics of Frustration: The United States in German Naval Planning, 1889–1941* (Little, Brown and Company, Boston) 1976, 182.

3. *Ibid.*, 214.

4. James V. Compton, *The Swastika and the Eagle: Hitler, the United States, and the Origins of World War II* (Houghton Mifflin Company, Boston) 1967, 244.

5. Hans Rothfels, *The German Opposition to Hitler* (Henry Regnery, Chicago) 1948, 25.

6. Japanese Vice Admiral Chuichi Nagumo and his First Air Fleet (six aircraft carriers and their complements of over 400 aircraft, two high-speed battleships, and supporting surface ships and submarines) had steamed

some 3,000 miles from the Kurile Islands to Pearl Harbor, November 26 to December 7, 1941, without being visually detected by surface ships or aircraft. Through RDF (Radio Detection Finding) the British, Dutch, Chinese, and Americans had tracked the task force from the day it left its anchorage in Hitokappu Bay (Chapter VI).

7. Herwig, *Politics of Frustration*, 14.
8. *Ibid.*, 15–16.
9. *Ibid.*, 16.
10. *Ibid.*, 33–34.
11. *Ibid.*, 30.
12. *Ibid.*, 94.
13. *Ibid.*, 37.
14. *Ibid.*, 38.
15. G. J. A O'Toole, *The Spanish War: An American Epic, 1898* (W. W. Norton, New York) 1984, 389.
16. Harry Elmer Barnes, *The Genesis of the World War* (Alfred A. Knopf, New York) 1929, 15–16.
17. Martin Gilbert, *The First World War: A Complete History* (Henry Holt and Company, New York) 1994, 251–252.
18. *Ibid.*, 252.
19. *Ibid.*, 329.
20. *Ibid.*, 435.
21. *Ibid.*, 503.
22. *Ibid.*, 541.
23. The United States finally signed a peace treaty with Germany on August 25, 1921, which was ratified by a Senate vote of 72–23 on October 18, 1921. This agreement was far briefer than that reached at Versailles two years earlier. There were only three articles, compared to 440 in the pact rejected by the United States. But the key element was a joint Congressional resolution made a part of the treaty that stipulated that the U.S. expressly reserved to itself: "all rights, privileges, indemnities, reparations, or advantages, together with the right to enforce the same, to which it or they have become entitled under the terms of the armistice signed November 11, 1918, or any extensions or modifications thereof; or which were acquired by or are in the possession of the United States of America by reason of its participation in the war or to which its nationals have thereby become entitled; or which, under the Treaty of Versailles, have been stipulated for its or their benefit; or to which it is entitled as one of the principal Allied and Associated powers; or to which it is entitled by virtue of any Act or Acts of Congress; or otherwise." Four days earlier, in Vienna, the United States signed a treaty of peace with Austria, with similar modifications to the Allied treaty of St. Germain (September 10, 1919). And four days later, a peace treaty was signed with Hungary in Budapest, again with similar modifications made to the original Treaty of Trianon. Since America had never formally gone to war against Bulgaria or Turkey, no additional treaties were required for the United States to officially be at peace with the former Central Powers.

24. Warren F. Kimball, *The Most Unsordid Act: Lend-Lease, 1939–1941* (John Hopkins Press, Baltimore MD) 1969, 48.
25. Winston Churchill, *Blood, Sweat, and Tears* (G. P. Putnam's Sons, New York) 1941, 297.
26. B. H. Liddell Hart, *The German Generals Talk* (William Morrow & Co., New York) 1948, 134.
27. *Ibid.*, 134.
28. *Ibid.*, 135. Under Adolf Hitler, the Third Reich made significant gains in foreign affairs, effectively dismantling all of the oppressive provisions of the Versailles Treaty. Just before he came to power in 1933, the reparations issue, which had caused friction between France and Germany during the 1920s, was settled amicably at the Lausanne Conference with the cancellation of all future payments. Major steps followed: in October 1933, the Nazi government withdrew from the League of Nations; in January 1935, the Saar region which had been excised from Germany voted in a plebiscite to reunify with Germany; in March of that year Hitler denounced the disarmament clauses of the Versailles Treaty, and reintroduced conscription and, more ominously, increased the Wehrmacht to 36 divisions. The following March came the remilitarization of the Rhineland, clearly reasserting the sovereignty of Germany's military. In October 1936, Hitler reached "an understanding" with Italy, forming what became known as the Rome-Berlin Axis. A month later, Germany and Japan formed the Anti-Comintern Pact that was intended to counter international communism and was a clear signal to the Soviet Union.
29. *Ibid.*, 136.
30. *Ibid.*, 136.
31. Adolf Hitler, *The Testament of Adolf Hitler* (Cassell & Company Ltd., London) 1961, 96.
32. Heinz Guderian, *Panzer Leader* (Dutton, New York) 1952, 117.
33. William Chamberlain, *America's Second Crusade* (Henry Regnery, Chicago) 1950, 83.
34. Kaiser Wilhelm II had thought so much of Mahan's book that he ordered copies put aboard every *Reichsmarine* man-of-war.
35. Chamberlain, *America's Second Crusade*, 50.
36. Ernst Hanfstaengl, *Hitler — The Missing Years* (Arcade Publishing, New York) 1957, 40.
37. Chamberlain, *America's Second Crusade*, 50.
38. Alton Frye, *Nazi Germany and the West-*

ern Hemisphere — 1933–1941 (Yale University Press, New Haven CT) 1967, 177.

39. Ibid., 178.

40. Wayne S. Cole, *America First: The Battle Against Intervention 1940–1941* (Octagon Books, New York) 1971, 120.

41. Norman Rich, *Hitler's War Aims: The Establishment of the New Order* (W.W. Norton & Company, New York) 1974, 417. The four-engine Messerschmitt Me-264 — the *Amerika-Bomber*— with a specified range of 9,000 miles and a bomb load of two tons, never went into operation; only a single prototype was manufactured. Another long-range bomber was the Heinkel He-177, which was plagued with engine fires. It had two nacelles, with two paired engines in each nacelle. Some 1,500 He-177s were built and went into service; they were only moderately successful.

42. Herwig, *Politics of Frustration*, 223.

43. The May 1941 Luftwaffe plan was discovered by East German historian Olaf Groehler in 1971. Herwig, *Politics of Frustration*, 241.

44. Ibid., 226–227.

45. Chamberlain, *America's Second Crusade*, 83.

46. Frye, *Nazi Germany*, 184.

47. Hermann Rauschning, *The Voice of Destruction* (G. P. Putnam's Sons, New York) 1940, 61.

48. Ibid., 64.

49. Adolf Hitler, *Mein Kampf* (Houghton Mifflin Company, New York) reprint 1999, xv.

50. Rauschning, *The Voice of Destruction*, 68–69.

51. Ibid., 109–110.

52. Ibid., 122.

53. Ibid., 134.

54. Ibid., 135.

55. Compton, *The Swastika and the Eagle*, 133.

56. Ibid., 135.

57. Adolf Hitler, Gerhard L. Weinberg, ed., *Hitler's Second Book: The Unpublished Sequel to Mein Kampf* (Enigma Books, New York) 2003, 110.

58. Gerhard L. Weinberg, "Hitler's Image of the United States," American Historical Association, 1962, 1009.

59. In August 1924, the Dawes Plan produced a report on the question of German reparations as spelled out in the Treaty of Versailles. Payments were to begin at 1 billion gold marks in the first year and rise to 2.5 billion gold marks by 1928. The plan provided for the reorganization of the Reichbank and for an initial loan of 800,000 marks to Germany. By 1929 it was believed that the strict controls over Germany could be removed and total reparations fixed. This was accomplished by the Young Plan, which revised the Dawes Plan, and went into effect in September 1930. It reduced the amount due from Germany to 121 billion Reichmarks in 59 annuities. Hardly had the Young Plan begun operations than the depression of the 1930s began and Germany's ability to pay disappeared. In 1932. the Laussane Conference proposed a reduction to 3 billion marks, but the proposal was never ratified. Within a few years of coming to power in 1933, Hitler repudiated all important obligations under the Treaty of Versailles.

60. Weinberg, "Hitler's Image of the United States," 1010. *The Grapes of Wrath* was a 1940 motion picture based on the John Steinbeck novel of the same name. It told the story of a dirt-poor, share-cropping family in Oklahoma, driven from their home by greedy landowners during the height of the depression. To survive, they bought a rickety old truck with their life savings, loaded it with their meager possessions, and headed west to California where phony handbills had told them "there was work." Enroute and once they crossed the Colorado River into California, local police intent on driving off the flood of "Okies" were extravagantly depicted as lawless, cruel bullies. Fruitgrove managers were portrayed as pitiless Simon Legrees paying below a living wage to the hungry itinerants who had no options. There were plenty of scenes with hungry, ill-clad children, quietly begging for food. While the story and the cinematography were typical of a small segment of the population of the United States during the 1930s, they were not characteristic of the nation as a whole. Adolf Hitler chose to interpret the film otherwise, as but one example of America's and the New Deal's failure to extricate itself from the depression.

61. Karl May was a prolific German author of adventure stories. He wrote more than 70 books, many of which have been translated into over 30 languages. In the last quarter of the 19th century, May was the most popular author of boys' books in Germany. Many of his books were stories of the post–Civil War American West, yet May did not travel to the United States until late in life. He patterned his books after those of James Fenimore Cooper, ennobling Native Americans and at the same time condemning the "palefaced" interlopers who massacred their people, laid waste to their settlements, and stole their land. May's admiration for Indian culture and customs was an early denunciation of American racism. In his recollections, *Spandau: The Secret Diaries* (347–348), Albert Speer wrote that Hitler used May as proof that "it was not necessary to know the desert to direct troops in the African theater of war ... it wasn't necessary to travel

in order to know the world." Speer wrote further that "any account of Hitler as a commander of troops should not omit references of Karl May.... Hitler was wont to say that he had always been deeply impressed by the tactical finesse and circumspection that Karl May conferred upon his [Indian] character Winnetou. Such a man was the very model of a company commander." During World War II, Hitler ordered 300,000 copies of May's *Winnetou* to be distributed among Wehrmacht troops. As a devoted reader of May, Adolf Hitler was in good company: Konrad Adenauer, Albert Einstein, Albert Schweitzer, Helmut Kohl and Arnold Schwarzenegger were also his fans. Karl May, *Winnetou* (Washington State University Press, Pullman WA) 1999, xii.

62. Compton, *The Swastika and the Eagle*, 8.

63. Hanfstaengl, *Hitler — The Missing Years*, 31–33. Ernst Hanfstaengl became the head of Nazi Germany's foreign press bureau, where he doubled as a goodwill ambassador. It was a post he held until 1938, when he fled to England, learning that members of Hitler's Elite Guard sought him out. He arrived back in the United States on the *Ile de France* in April of that year, slipping ashore after the other passengers had debarked, to avoid the press. He had last been in America in 1934.

64. *Ibid.*, 36.

65. *New York Times*, October 6, 1937.

66. Finland, Estonia, Latvia, Lithuania, Sweden, Norway, Denmark, the Netherlands, Belgium, Great Britain and Ireland, France, Portugal, Spain, Switzerland, Liechtenstein, Luxemburg, Poland, Hungary, Rumania, Yugoslavia, Russia, Bulgaria, Greece, Turkey, Iraq, the Arabias, Syria, Palestine, Egypt, and Iran.

67. *New York Times*, April 16, 1939.

68. Thomas A. Bailey and Paul B. Ryan, *Hitler vs. Roosevelt — The Undeclared Naval War* (The Free Press, New York) 1979, 23.

69. *Ibid.*, 23.

70. Compton, *The Swastika and the Eagle*, 244.

71. *Ibid.*, 245.

72. *New York Times*, April 28, 1939.

73. Chamberlain, *America's Second Crusade*, 88.

74. Michael Gannon, *Operation Drumbeat* (Harper & Row, New York) 1990, 70.

75. The V-1 was a subsonic pulse-jet powered missile with a 1,000 Kg warhead. Its maximum speed was 350–400 mph, with a range of 150 miles. Between October 1944 and March 1945, 7,800 V-1s were launched against continental targets, mainly Antwerp. After D-Day and until the launching sites in France were overrun by the Allies in 1945, about 7,400 were launched against targets in England. Casualties in England: 5,649 killed, 16,194 injured. The more sophisticated V-2 was a liquid-fueled rocket that traveled at supersonic speed, a true ballistic missile; it also carried a 1,000 Kg warhead. Its range was 200 miles. The first V-2 fell in England on September 8, 1944 and the last on March 27, 1945. Casualties in England: 2,754 killed, 6,524 injured.

76. Albert Speer, *Spandau — The Secret Diaries* (Macmillan New York) 1976, 50.

77. *Ibid.*, 56.

78. *Ibid.*, 58.

79. Ibid, 80.

80. *Ibid.*, 345.

81. Adolf Hitler, *The Testament of Adolf Hitler* (Cassell & Company Ltd., London) 1961, 45.

82. *Ibid.*, 46.

83. *Ibid.*, 76.

84. *Ibid.*, 87–89.

85. Adolf Hitler, *Hitler's Secret Conversations: 1941–1944* (Farrar, Straus, and Young, New York) 1953, 12.

86. *Ibid.*, 149.

87. *Ibid.*, 155.

88. *Ibid.*, 181.

89. *Ibid.*, 206.

90. *Ibid.*, 228.

91. *Ibid.*, 245.

92. *Ibid.*, 257.

93. *Ibid.*, 351.

94. *Ibid.*, 470–471.

95. *Ibid.*, 490–492.

96. Compton, *The Swastika and the Eagle*, 73.

97. Albert Speer, *Inside the Third Reich: Memoirs of Albert Speer* (Collier Books, New York) 1981, 356.

98. This "far better to fight our enemies over there rather than here" mantra has a long and troubling history in the United States. Even before America went to war in 1917, one famous recruitment poster carried this message: "If this War is not fought to a finish in Europe, it will be fought on the soil of the United States." Its illustration was a fanged gorilla with a Pickelhaube on his head, holding a club labeled Kultur, and wading ashore cradling a bare-breasted maiden. It was so repugnant to Germans that in 1939, Josef Goebbels reprinted the poster with a new caption: "When they assaulted us 25 years ago, they wrote on their rotten slanderous poster: 'Destroy this mad beast'— They meant the German people." See frontispiece illustration in author's *Propaganda for War — How the United States Was Conditioned to Fight the Great War of 1914–1918* (McFarland & Company, Jefferson NC) 1996. While the Atlantic Ocean in the 1940s represented a nearly insurmountable defense rampart for the United States, a complete

victory in Europe by Germany in 1940–1941 would have freed Nazi engineers and scientists to perfect advanced weapons. Rapid progress in rocket propulsion in both the United States and the Soviet Union in the immediate postwar years is directly attributable to the work begun earlier in Nazi Germany. At war's end, both the Americans and the Soviets swiftly rounded up as many as they could of these former enemy weapons experts and transported them and their families to their respective countries where they could continue their work — under new masters. George W. Bush, in both presidencies, has regularly invoked the fears of waves of terrorists originating in Iraq swarming into the United States, as justification for his war.

99. Thomas A. Bailey, *The Man in the Street — The Impact of American Public Opinion on Foreign Policy* (Macmillan New York) 1948, 61.

Epilogue

1. Charles A. Beard, *President Roosevelt and the Coming of the War 1941* (Yale University Press, New Haven CT) 1948, 598.
2. *New York Times*, January 3, 2003.
3. John Bartlett, *Familiar Quotations: A Collection of Passages, Phrases and Proverbs Traced to Their Sources in Ancient and Modern Literature* (Little, Brown and Company, Boston) 1980, 355.

Appendix A

1. Alyn Brodsky, *Grover Cleveland — A Study in Character* (St. Martin's Press, New York) 2000, 312.
2. W.W. Keen, "The Surgical Operations on President Cleveland in 1893," *Saturday Evening Post*, September 22, 1917.
3. Ibid.

Appendix D

1. Henry Morgenthau, *Ambassador Morgenthau's Story* (Doubleday Page, New York) 1918, 86.
2. Morgenthau, *Ambassador Morgenthau's Story*, 385–386.
3. Earlier, Hendrick had worked with such prominent writers as Lincoln Steffens, Ida Tarbell, and Ray Stannard Baker. In 1920, he wrote *Victory at Sea*, a biography of Vice Admiral William S. Sims, commander of U.S. naval forces in Europe during the war, which brought him his first Pulitzer Prize. Two years later, he published a three-volume work, *Life and Letters of Walter Hines Page*, for which he was awarded his second Pulitzer. In 1928, he received yet another Pulitzer Price for a second Page biography, *The Training of an American*.
4. Fay's successful book was reissued three times in 1929. A second edition was printed in 1930, and reprinted in 1931, 1932, 1935, 1938, 1939, 1941, 1942, 1947, and 1948. The book went into its 22nd printing in 1964.
5. Sidney Bradshaw Fay, *The Origins of the World War* (Macmillan, New York) 1928, 552.
6. Ibid., 182.

Appendix E

1. Public Papers of Woodrow Wilson, Baker and Dodds, editors, VI, 413–414.
2. Sixty years later, Dr. Edwin A. Weinstein, professor of Neurology Emeritus at Mount Sinai Medical School, published his detailed analyses of Woodrow Wilson's health in a landmark book, *Woodrow Wilson: A Medical and Psychological Biography* (Princeton University Press, Princeton NJ) 1981. He stated that the symptoms pointed unequivocally to "an occlusion of the right middle cerebral artery, which resulted in a complete paralysis of the left side of his body, a loss of sensation on that side, and a left homonymous hemianopie — a loss of vision in the left half fields of both eyes. Because he had already lost central vision in his left eye from his stroke in 1906, he had clear vision only in the temporal (outer) half field of his right eye. The weakness of the muscles of the left side of his face, tongue, jaw, and pharynx accounted for his difficulty in swallowing and his impairment of his speech. His voice was weak and dysarthic, and his speech never regained its modulation, resonance, fluency, and melody. It was especially affected by emotion." 357.
3. Thomas Fleming, *The Illusion of Victory — America in World War I* (Basic Books, New York) 2003, 419.
4. In her memoir, Edith Wilson admitted she had never voted and had never planned to do so. Before she met Wilson, she had been totally apolitical, unknown to anyone in Washington's political or diplomatic community. She wrote that in 1912, a presidential election year: "...so little was my interest in political affairs that I could hardly have told who the candidates were." Edith Bolling Wilson, *My Memoir* (The Bobbs-Merrill Company, New York) 1938, 33.
5. David F. Houston, *Eight Years with Wilson's Cabinet, Vol II* (Doubleday, Page & Company, Garden City NY) 1926, 70.

6. Gene Smith, *When the Cheering Stopped — The Last Years of Woodrow Wilson* (William Morrow and Company, New York) 1964, 181.

Appendix K

1. U.S. Naval Institute *Proceedings*, 36, September 1967, Captain D. M. Saunders, U.S. Navy, 36.
2. *Ibid.*, 4/26/2005.
3. *Ibid.*, 38.
4. *Ibid.*, 39.

Bibliography

Abbazia, Patrick. *Mr. Roosevelt's Navy: The Private War of the U.S. Atlantic Fleet, 1939–1942*. Annapolis MD: Naval Institute Press, 1975.
Allison, Graham. *Nuclear Terrorism: The Ultimate Preventable Catastrophe*. New York: Henry Holt, 2004.
Armstrong, Anne. *Unconditional Surrender: The Impact of the Casablanca Policy upon World War II*. New Brunswick NJ: Rutgers University Press, 1961.
Bailey, Thomas A. *The Man in the Street: The Impact of American Public Opinion on Foreign Policy*. New York: Macmillan, 1948.
____, and Paul B. Ryan, *Hitler vs. Roosevelt: The Undeclared Naval War*. New York: Free Press, 1979.
Baldwin, Hanson. *Great Mistakes of the War*. New York: Harper & Brothers, 1949.
Balfour, Michael. *Propaganda in War, 1939–1945: Organisations, Policies and Publics in Britain and Germany*. London: Routledge & Kegan Paul, 1979.
Barnes, Harry Elmer. *Perpetual War for Perpetual Peace: A Critical Examination of the Foreign Policy of Franklin Delano Roosevelt and its Aftermath*. Caldwell IA: Caxton Printers, 1953.
Bartlett, Bruce. *Cover-Up: The Politics of Pearl Harbor, 1941–1946*. New Rochelle NY: Arlington House, 1978.
____. "The Pearl Harbor Coverup," *Reason*, February 1976, pp. 24–27.
Beach, Edward L. *Scapegoats: A Defense of Kimmel and Short at Pearl Harbor*. Annapolis MD: Naval Institute Press, 1995.
Beard, Charles A. *The Navy: Defense or Portent*. New York: Harper & Brothers, 1932.
____, *President Roosevelt and the Coming of the War 1941*. New Haven CT: Yale University Press, 1948.
Belgion, Montgomery. *Victors' Justice*. Hinsdale IL: Henry Regnery, 1949.
Ben-Zvi, Abraham. *The Illusion of Deterrence: The Roosevelt Presidency and the Origins of the Pacific War*. Boulder CO: 1987.
Beschloss, Michael. *The Conquerers: Roosevelt, Truman and the Destruction of Hitler's Germany, 1941–1945*. New York: Simon & Schuster, 2002.
Bird, Kai, and Lawrence Lifschultz, eds. *Hiroshima's Shadow*. Stony Creek CT: Pamphleteer's Press, 1998.
Bishop, Jim. *FDR's Last Year: April 1944-April 1945*. New York: William Morrow, 1974.
Blum, John Morton. *From the Morgenthau Diaries: Years of War 1941–1945*. Boston: Houghton Mifflin, 1967.
Bond, Brian. *The Pursuit of Victory: From Napoleon to Saddam Hussein*. New York: Oxford University Press, 1996.
Braw, Monica. *The Atomic Bomb Suppressed: American Censorship in Occupied Japan*. Armonk NY: M. E. Sharpe, 1991.
Brodsky, Alyn. *Grover Cleveland: A Study in Character*. New York: St. Martin's, 2000.

Brown, Anthony Cave. *Bodyguard of Lies.* two vols. Harper & Row, New York: 1975.
Brownlow, Donald Grey. *The Accused: The Ordeal of Rear Admiral Husband Edward Kimmel, U.S.N.* New York: Vantage, 1968
Burtness, Paul S., and Warren U. Ober. *The Puzzle of Pearl Harbor.* Evanston IL: Row, Peterson, 1962
Butow, Robert J. C. *Japan's Decision to Surrender.* Stanford CA: Stanford University Press, 1954.
Bywater, Hector C. *The Great Pacific War: A History of the American-Japanese Campaign of 1931–1933.* Boston: Houghton Mifflin, 1925. Novel.
_____. *Sea-Power in the Pacific: A Study of the American-Japanese Naval Problem.* New York: Houghton Mifflin, 1921.
Chamberlain, William. *America's Second Crusade.* Chicago: Henry Regnery, 1950.
Churchill, Winston. *Their Finest Hour.* Boston: Houghton Mifflin, 1949.
Cole, Wayne S. *America First: The Battle Against Intervention 1940–1941.* New York" Octagon, 1971.
_____. *Charles A. Lindbergh and the Battle Against Intervention in World War II.* New York: Harcourt Brace Jovanovich, 1974.
Compton, James V. *The Swastika and the Eagle: Hitler, the United States, and the Origins of World War II.* Boston: Houghton Mifflin, 1967.
Costello, John. *Days of Infamy: MacArthur, Roosevelt, Churchill: The Shocking Truth Revealed.* New York: Pocket Books, 1994
Craig, Gordon A. *Germany 1866–1945.* New York: Oxford University Press, 1978.
Crispell, Kenneth, and Carlos Gomez. *Hidden Illness in the White House.* Durham NC: Duke University Press, 1988.
Current, Richard N. "How Stimson Meant to 'Maneuver' the Japanese," *Mississippi Valley Historical Review,* Vol. 40, No. 1, June 1953, 67–74.
Deutsch, Harold. *The Conspiracy Against Hitler In the Twilight War.* Minneapolis: University of Minnesota Press, 1968.
Dobson, Alan P. *US Wartime Aid to Britain, 1940–1946.* New York: St. Martin's, 1986.
Doenecke, Justus D., ed. *In Danger Undaunted: The Anti-Interventionist Movement of 1940–1941 as Revealed in the Papers of the America First Committee.* Stanford CA: Hoover Institution Press, 1990.
Doenitz, Karl. *Memoirs: Ten Years and Twenty Days.* Cleveland OH: World, 1960.
Dower, John W. *War Without Mercy: Race and Power in the Pacific War.* New York: Pantheon, 1986.
Dulles, Allen Welsh. *Germany's Underground: The Anti-Nazi Resistance.* New York: DaCapo, 2000.
Dupuy, R. Ernest, and Trevor N. Dupuy. *The Encyclopedia of Military History from 3500 B.C. to the Present.* New York: Harper & Row, 1970.
_____. *Military Heritage of America.* New York: McGraw-Hill, 1956.
Eisenhower, David. *Eisenhower at War, 1943 to 1945.* New York: Random House, 1986.
Eisenhower, Dwight D. *Crusade in Europe.* Garden City NY: Doubleday, 1948.
Eiler, Keith E. *Wedemeyer on War and Peace.* Stanford CA: Hoover Institution Press, 1987.
Farley, James A. *Jim Farley's Story.* New York: McGraw-Hill, 1948.
Fay, Sidney Bradshaw. *The Origins of the World War.* New York: Macmillan, 1928.
Feis, Herbert. *The Road to Pearl Harbor: The Coming of the War Between the United States and Japan.* Princeton NJ: Princeton University Press, 1950.
Ferrell, Robert, H. *The Dying President: Franklin D. Roosevelt 1944–1945.* Columbia: University of Missouri Press, 1998.
Fest, Joachim. *Planning Hitler's Death: The Story of the German Resistance.* New York: Henry Holt, 1996.

Fish, Hamilton. *FDR: The Other Side of the Coin: How We Were Tricked into World War II*. New York: Vantage, 1976.
____. *Tragic Deception: FDR and America's Involvement in World War II*. Old Greenwich CT: Devin-Adair, 1983.
Fleming, Thomas. *The New Dealers' War: F.D.R. and the War Within World War II*. New York: Basic Books, 2001
Flynn, John T. *Country Squire in the White House*. New York: Doubleday, Doran and Company, 1940.
____. *The Final Secret of Pearl Harbor*. New York: Privately Printed, 1950.
____. *The Roosevelt Myth*. New York: Devan-Adair, 1956.
Freud, Sigmund, and William C. Bullitt. *Thomas Woodrow Wilson: A Psychological Study*. (Boston: Houghton Mifflin, 1967.
Fried, Albert. *FDR and His Enemies*. New York: St. Martin's, 1999.
Friedlander, Saul. *Prelude to Downfall*. New York: Alfred A. Knopf, 1967.
Fuller, J.F.C. *The Second World War, 1939–1945: A Strategical and Tactical History*. New York: Duell, Sloan, Pearce, 1948.
Frye, Alton. *Nazi Germany and the Western Hemisphere: 1933–1941*. New Haven: Yale University Press, 1967.
Galbraith, John Kenneth. *A Life in Our Times*. Boston: Houghton Mifflin, 1981.
Gallagher, Hugh Gregory. *FDR's Splendid Deception*. New York: Dodd, Mead, 1985.
Gannon, Michael. *Operation Drumbeat*. New York: Harper & Row, 1990.
____. U.S. Naval Institute *Proceedings*, December 1994.
Gaevernitz, Gero, ed. *They Almost Killed Hitler*. New York: Macmillan, 1947.
Gilbert, Martin. *The First World War: A Complete History*. New York: Henry Holt, 1994.
Gilbert, Robert E. *The Mortal Presidency: Illness and Anguish in the White House*. New York: Basic, 1992.
Gill, Anton. *An Honourable Defeat: A History of German Resistance to Hitler, 1933–1945*. New York: Henry Holt, 1994.
Goodhart, Philip. *Fifty Ships That Saved the World: The Foundation of the Anglo-American Alliance*. Garden City NY: Doubleday, 1965.
Goodwin, Doris Kerns. *No Ordinary Time: Franklin and Eleanor Roosevelt: The Home Front in World War II*. New York: Simon & Schuster, 1994.
Greaves, Percy L. "FDR's Watergate: Pearl Harbor." *Reason*, February 1976, 16–23.
Guderian, Hans. *Panzer Leader*. New York: Dutton, 1952.
Hamerow, Theodore. *On the Road to the Wolf's Lair: German Resistance to Hitler*. Boston: Harvard University Press, 1997.
Hanfstaengl, Ernst. *Hitler: The Missing Years*. New York: Arcade Publishing, 1957.
Hankey, Lord. *Politics, Trials and Errors*. Chicago: Henry Regnery, 1950.
Harman, Nicholas. *Dunkirk: The Patriotic Myth*. New York: Simon & Schuster, 1980.
Hart, B. H. Liddell. *The German Generals Talk*. New York: William Morrow, 1948.
____, ed. *The Rommel Papers*. New York: Harcourt, Brace, 1953.
Heiden, Konrad. *Der Fuehrer: Hitler's Rise to Power*. Boston: Houghton Mifflin, 1944.
Hersh, Seymour M. *Chemical and Biological Warfare: America's Hidden Arsenal*. New York: Bobbs-Merrill, 1968.
Herwig, Holger H. *Politics of Frustration: The United States in German Naval Planning, 1889–1941*. Boston: Little, Brown, 1976.
Hilton, James. *Lost Horizon*. New York: William Morrow, 1933. Novel.
Hitler, Adolf. *Hitler's Second Book: The Unpublished Sequel to Mein Kampf*. Gerhard L. Weinberg, ed. New York: Enigma, 2003.
____. *Hitler's Secret Conversations: 1941–1944*. New York: Farrar, Straus, and Young, 1953.
____. *Mein Kampf*. New York: Houghton Mifflin, 1999.

_____. *The Testament of Adolf Hitler*. London: Cassell, 1961.
Hoffmann, Peter. *The History of the German Resistance 1933–1945*. Cambridge MA: MIT Press, 1977.
_____. *Stauffenberg: A Family History, 1905–1944*. Cambridge UK: Cambridge University Press, 1995.
Honan, William H. *Visions of Infamy: The Untold Story of How Journalist Hector C. Bywater Devised the Plans That Led to Pearl Harbor*. New York: St. Martin's, 1991.
Hull, Cordell. *The Memoirs of Cordell Hull, Vol. II*. New York: Macmillan, 1948.
Ickes, Harold L. *The Secret Diary of Harold L. Ickes*. Vol. 3: *The Lowering Clouds 1939–1941*. New York: Simon & Schuster, 1955.
Jones, Alfred Haworth. *Roosevelt's Image Brokers*. Port Washington NY: Kennikat, 1974.
Keen, W.W., "The Surgical Operations on President Cleveland in 1893," *Saturday Evening Post*, September 22, 1917.
Kennedy, Robert F., Jr. *Crimes Against Nature: How George W. Bush and His Corporate Pals Are Plundering the Country and Hijacking Our Democracy* (New York: HarperCollins, 2004.
Kimball, Warren F. *The Juggler: Franklin Roosevelt as Wartime Statesman*. Princeton NJ: Princeton University Press, 1991.
_____. *The Most Unsordid Act: Lend-Lease, 1939–1941*. Baltimore MD: Johns Hopkins Press, 1969
_____. *Swords or Plowshares? The Morgenthau Plan for Defeated Nazi Germany, 1943–1946*. New York: J. B. Lippincott, 1976.
Kimmel, Husband E. *Admiral Kimmel's Story*. Chicago IL: Henry Regnery, 1955.
Langer, William L., and S. Everett Gleason. *The Undeclared War 1940–1941*. New York: Harper & Brothers, 1953.
Larrabee, Eric. *Commander in Chief: Franklin Delano Roosevelt, His Lieutenants and Their War*. New York: Harper & Row, 1987.
Leahy, William D. *I Was There: The Personal Story of the Chief of Staff to Presidents Roosevelt and Truman Based on His Notes and Diaries Made at the Time*. New York: Whittlesey House, 1950.
Lifton, Robert Jay, and Greg Mitchell. *Hiroshima in America: Fifty Years of Denial*. New York: G. P. Putnam's Sons, 1995.
Lindbergh, Charles A. *Of Flight and Life*. New York: Charles Scribner's Sons, 1948.
_____. *The Spirit of St. Louis*. New York: Charles Scribner's Sons, 1953.
_____. *The Wartime Journals of Charles A. Lindbergh*, New York: Harcourt Brace Jovanovich, 1970.
Lindqvist, Sven. *A History of Bombing*. New York: New Press, 2000.
Lochner, Louis P. (ed. and trans.). *The Goebbels Diaries: 1942–1943*. Garden City NY: Doubleday, 1948.
_____. *Always the Unexpected*. New York: Macmillan, 1956.
Love, Robert W., Jr., ed. *Pearl Harbor Revisited*. New York: St. Martin's, 1995
Lowenheim, Francis L., Harold D. Langley, and Manfred Jonas, eds. *Roosevelt and Churchill: Their Secret Wartime Correspondence*. New York: E. P. Dutton & Co., 1975.
MacArthur, Douglas. *Reminiscences*. New York: McGraw-Hill, 1964.
Manchester, William. *American Caesar: Douglas MacArthur, 1880–1964*. Boston: Little, Brown, 1978.
_____. *The Arms of Krupp: 1587–1968*. Boston: Little, Brown, 1964.
Manvell, Roger, and Heinrich Fraenkel. *Dr. Goebbels: His Life and Death*. New York: Simon and Schuster, 1960.
May, Karl. *Winnetou*. Pullman: Washington State University Press, 1999.
McIntire, Ross. *White House Physician*. New York: G. P. Putnam's Sons, 1946.
Miles, Sherman. "Pearl Harbor in Retrospect," *Atlantic Monthly*, July 1948. pp. 65–72.

Morgan, Ted. *FDR: A Biography*. New York: Simon & Schuster, 1985.
Morgenstern, George. *Pearl Harbor: The Story of the Secret War*. New York: Devin-Adair, 1947.
Morgenthau, Henry, Jr. *Germany Is Our Problem*. New York: Harper & Brothers, 1945.
Morgenthau, Henry III. *Mostly Morgenthaus: A Family History*. New York: Ticknor & Fields, 1991.
Morris, Eric. *Circles of Hell: The War in Italy 1943–1945*. New York: Crown, 1993.
Mosley, Leonard. *Lindbergh: A Biography*. Garden City NY: Doubleday, 1976.
O'Connor, Raymond G. *Diplomacy for Victory: FDR and Unconditional Surrender*. New York: W. W. Norton, 1971.
Park, Bert. *The Impact of Illness on World Leaders*. Philadelphia: University of Pennsylvania Press, 1980.
Parker, Matthew. *Monte Cassino: The Hardest-Fought Battle of World War II*. New York: Doubleday, 1993.
Petersen, Neal H., ed. *From Hitler's Doorstep: The Wartime Intelligence Reports of Allen Dulles, 1942–1945*. University Park: Pennsylvania State University Press, 1996.
Pond, Hugh. *Salerno*. Boston: Little, Brown, 1961.
Prange, Gordon W., with Donald M. Goldstein, and Katherine V. Dillon. *At Dawn We Slept: The Untold Story of Pearl Harbor*. New York: McGraw-Hill, 1986.
Raeder, Erich. *My Life*. Annapolis MD: U.S. Naval Institute Press, 1960.
Rauschning, Hermann. *The Voice of Destruction*. New York: G. P. Putnam's Sons, 1940.
Regis, Ed. *The Biology of Doom: The History of America's Secret Germ Warfare Project*. New York: Henry Holt, 1999.
Rich, Norman. *Hitler's War Aims: Ideology, the Nazi State, and the Course of Expansion*. New York: W. W. Norton, 1973.
_____. *Hitler's War Aims: The Establishment of the New Order*. New York: W. W. Norton, 1974.
Richardson, James O. *On the Treadmill to Pearl Harbor: The Memoirs of Admiral James O. Richardson*. Washington DC: Naval History Div., Dept. of the Navy, 1973.
Ross, Bill D. *Iwo Jima: Legacy of Valor*. New York: Vanguard, 1985.
Ross, Stewart Halsey. *Strategic Bombing by the United States in World War II: The Myths and the Facts*. Jefferson NC: McFarland, 2003.
_____. *Propaganda for War: How America Was Conditioned to Fight the Great War of 1914–1918*. Jefferson NC: McFarland, 1996.
Rothfels, Hans. *The German Opposition to Hitler*. Chicago: Henry Regnery, 1948.
Rusbridger, James, and Eric Nave. *Betrayal at Pearl Harbor: How Churchill Lured Roosevelt into World War II*. New York: Summit, 1991.
Saunders, D. M. "The Bari Incident" *Proceedings of the U.S. Naval Institute*, September 1967.
Sanborn, Frederic Rockwell. *Design for War: A Study of Secret Power Politics, 1937–1941*. New York: Devin-Adair, 1951.
Sayers, Michael, and Albert E. Kahn. *Sabotage: The Secret War Against America*. New York: Harper & Brothers, 1942.
Schlabrendorff, Fabian von. *They Almost Killed Hitler*. New York: Macmillan, 1947.
Sheehan, Fred. *Anzio: Epic of Victory*. Norman: University of Oklahoma Press, 1964.
Sherry, Michael S. *The Rise of American Air Power: The Creation of Armageddon*. New Haven CT: Yale University Press, 1987.
Sherwood, Robert E. *Roosevelt and Hopkins: An Intimate History*. New York: Harper & Brothers, 1948.
Skates, John Ray. *The Invasion of Japan: Alternative to the Bomb*. Columbia: University of South Carolina Press, 1994
_____. *Spandau: The Secret Diaries*. New York: Macmillan, 1976.

Speer, Albert. *Inside the Third Reich: Memoirs of Albert Speer.* New York: Collier, 1981.
Steinberg, Rafael. *Return to the Philippines.* Alexandria VA: Time-Life Books, 1980.
Stettinius, Edward R., Jr. *Lend-Lease: Weapon for Victory.* New York: Macmillan, 1944.
Stimson, Henry L., and McGeorge Bundy. *On Active Service in Peace and War.* New York: Harper, 1948.
Stinnett, Robert B. *Day of Deceit: The Truth About FDR and Pearl Harbor.* New York: Free Press, 2000.
Stapfer, Hans-Henri, and Gino Kunzle. *Strangers in a Strange Land.* Vol. 2: *Escape to Neutrality.* Carrollton TX, Squadron-Signal Publishing Co., 1992.
Tansill, Charles Callan. *Back Door to War.* Chicago: Henry Regenry, 1952.
Taylor, A.J.P. *The Origins of the Second World War.* New York: Atheneum, 1961.
Theobold, Robert A. *The Final Secret of Pearl Harbor.* Old Greenwich CT: Devin-Adair, 1954.
Thompson, Robert Smith. *A Time for War: Franklin D. Roosevelt and the Path to Pearl Harbor.* New York: Prentice Hall, 1991.
Toland, John. *Adolf Hitler.* Garden City NY: Doubleday, 1976.
_____. *But Not in Shame: The Six Months After Pearl Harbor.* New York: Random House, 1961.
_____. *The Rising Sun: The Decline and Fall of the Japanese Empire, 1936–1945.* New York: Random House, 1970.
_____. *Infamy: Pearl Harbor and Its Aftermath*, New York: Berkley, 1982.
Tolley, Kemp. *Cruise of the Lanakai: Incitement to War.* Annapolis MD: Naval Institute Press, 1973.
Trevor-Roper, H. R., Introduction and Preface. In Rauschning, Hermann. *Hitler's Table Talk 1941–1944: His Private Conversations.* New York: Enigma, 2000.
Wedemeyer, Albert. *Wedemeyer Reports.* New York: Henry Holt, 1958.
Weinberg, Gerhard L. "Hitler's Image of the United States." Paper presented at the 1962 meeting of the American Historical Association.
Wilson, Edith Bolling. *My Memoir*, New York: Bobbs-Merrill, 1938.
Winslow, W. G. *The Fleet the Gods Forgot: The U.S. Asiatic Fleet in World War II.* Annapolis MD: Naval Institute Press, 1982.
Yahara, Hiromichi. *The Battle for Okinawa.* New York: John Wiley, 1995.
Young, Desmond. *Rommel: The Desert Fox.* New York: Harper, 1951.
Zeller, Eberhard. *The Flame of Freedom: The German Struggle Against Hitler.* Coral Gables FL: University of Miami Press, 1969.

Index

Abwehr 90
Adams, Henry 152
Adams, John 19
Aichi D3A *Val* 72, 73
airmail controversy 38, 41, 42, 48, 49, 51, 52, 53, 136, 204
Alexander, Gen. Harold 87, 222
America First Committee 47, 49, 51, 52, 53, 200; principles and membership 1940 200
anti–Semitism 38, 45, 52, 53, 122, 125, 186
Anzio 95
Ardennes Offensive (Battle of the Bulge) 96, 104
Argentia Bay 16, 29, 201
USS *Arizona* 75, 79, 221
Armstrong, Anne 3
Army Ordnance Association 198
Arnold, Gen. Henry Harley "Hap" 48, 99
Atlantic Charter 17, 127, 201, 202, 206
Atlantic Conference 17
atomic bomb 47
Avranches 96, 103, 104, 120
Avro *Lancaster* 171
Azore Islands 17, 161

Badoglio, Marshall Pietro 169
Bailey, Thomas A. 5, 28, 169
Baldwin, Hanson 26
Ballin, Albert 190
BARBAROSSA (Germany's attack on Russia) 20
Barkley, Sen. Albin 34, 82
Barnes, Harry Elmer 3, 46, 154
Baruch, Bernard 141
Beard, Charles Austin 3, 22, 76, 334, 46, 76, 221
Beck, Gen. Ludwig 113, 115, 116, 163, 164
Bermuda 29
Birse, A. H. 145
Bismarck, Chancellor Otto von 151
Blum, John Morton 134
Blumentritt, Gen. Gunther 157, 158
Boeing B-17 *Flying Fortress* 71, 110, 171, 221
Boeing B-29 *Superfortress* 100
Boeing P-26 72
Boettiger, Anna Roosevelt (daughter) 138, 146

Bolling, John Randolph 192
Boone, Dr. Joel E. 137
Bosch, Robert 116
Brewster, Owen 81
Brooke, Gen. Alan 222
Bruenn, Dr. Howard G. 136, 137, 138, 143
Brundage, Avery 46
Bryan, William Jennings 66
Bryce, James 215; Bryce Report 6
Bundy, McGeorge 215, 217, 227
HMS *Burnham* 28
Burns, James MacGregor 101, 102, 123
Bush, Pres. George W. 177, 219, 233
Byrnes, James F. 102
Bywater, Hector C. 62, 63

Cadogan, Alexander 17
Caesar, Gaius Julius 113
HMS *Campbeltown* 28
Canada 28
Canaris, Adm. Wilhelm 90, 91
Canary Islands 161
Carter, Pres. Jimmy 71
Casino 95
Castle, William R. 53
Chaco War 197
Chance Vought F4U *Corsair* 72, 219
Chance Vought SB2U *Vindicator* 72
Chase, Stuart 47
Cherwell, Lord (Frederick Lindemann) 128, 129
Chiang Kai-chek 40, 136
Christian Front 45
Churchill, Prime Minister Winston S. 5, 8, 17, 23, 24, 27, 30, 31, 35, 36, 65, 77, 128, 150, 156, 162; 4,000-word letter 138; reaction to Morgenthau Plan 128
Citizens' Keep America Out of War Committee 46
Clark, Gen. Mark 95
Clausewitz, Carl von 159
Clemenceau, Georges 155, 193, 223
Cleveland, Pres. Grover 141, 179
Cole, Wayne S. 200
Colt's Patent Firearms Co. 198

Committee to Defend America by Aiding the Allies 38, 45
Connally, Sen. Tom 34
Consolidated B-24 *Liberator* 171, 219
Consolidated PBY *Catalina* 72
Costello, John 3
Coughlin, Charles E., Father 45, 53
Cox, James M. 122
Creel, George 139, 140, 149, 187, 229
Cudahy, Amb. John 170
Curtiss Aeroplane Motor Co. 197
Curtiss P-36 *Hawk* 72
Curtiss P-40 *Warhawk* 72
Curtiss-Wright Export Co. 197

Daniels, Jonathan 147
Dawes Plan 156, 231
De Gaulle, Gen. Charles 86
Delano, Warren 66
Denmark 45
Dern, Sec. of War George H. 42
Destroyers-for-Bases deal 23, 27, 28, 35, 36
Dewey, Adm. George 62, 152
Dewey, Thomas E. 34, 131, 144
Dieckhoff, Amb. Hans 42, 169
Diederichs, Adm. Otto von 3, 151, 152, 153
Doenitz, Adm. Karl 98, 228
Dolittle, Jimmy 96
Donovan, William 111
Douglas A-20 *Havoc* 71
Douglas SBD *Dauntless* 72, 73
Dulles, Allen Welsh 111, 112
Dunkirk 157, 158

Eaker, Gen. Ira C. 90, 99
Early, Stephen T. 12, 18, 143
E.I. du Pont de Nemours Co. 196, 198
Eight-action memorandum 64
Eisenhower, David (grandson) 123
Eisenhower, Gen. Dwight D. 87, 89, 93, 102, 103, 122, 123
Electric Boat Co. 198
Elliott, Pvt. George E. 74
USS *Enterprise* 70, 73, 75, 76

Farley, Post Gen. James 41, 137
Fay, Sidney Bradshaw 189, 223
Ferguson, Sen. Homer 81, 122
Ferrell, Robert H. 137, 149
Fest, Joachim 119
Fifty-destroyers deal 26, 27, 28, 31
Fireside chats 19, 32, 215
First Air Fleet (*Kido Butai*) 70, 71, 72, 75
Fish, Hamilton 46
Flynn, John T. 47, 142, 149, 215
Focke-Wulf Fw-190 218
Focke-Wulf Fw-200 *Condor* 110, 161, 225
Ford, Henry 47, 53, 165, 219
Forrestal, Sec. of State James V. 101
Four Freedoms 33
Fourteen-part message 82, 221

Fourteen Points (Woodrow Wilson's) 19, 182, 183
Franco-Prussian War of 1870–1871 223
Frankfurter, Felix 80
Frederick the Great of Prussia 159
Freedom of Information Act 2
Fritsch, Gen. Werner von 113
Fuchida, Com. Mitsuo 75
Fuller, Gen. J.F.C. 95

Gallagher, Hugh Gregory 137
Gallipoli 87, 220
Gannon, Michael 171
"garden hose" press conference 32
Geneva Arms Control Conference (1925) 196
Geneva Disarmament Conference (1927) 196, 197
Geneva Disarmament Conference (1932) 197
George, David Lloyd 155, 175, 193, 223
George VI, King 25
German-American Bund 45
Giraud, Gen. Henri 86
Goebbels, Paul Josef 78, 85, 90, 108, 109, 150, 222, 232
Goerdler, Carl Friedrich 114, 116
Göring, Gen. Hermann 42, 51, 159, 160, 170, 219; gives Lindbergh medal 44
Grant, Gen. Ulysses S. 89
The Grapes of Wrath 166, 231
Grayson, Dr. Cary Travers 136, 137, 191; cover-up of Woodrow Wilson's stroke 137, 140, 191
Great War (1914–1918) 15, 46, 156, 223
Greater East Asian Co-Prosperity Sphere 11, 64, 77
Greenland to come
USS *Greer* 15, 18, 19
Grew, Amb. Joseph 11, 69, 99
Grieffenberg, Gen. Hans von 157
Grumman F4F *Wildcat* 69, 70, 72
Grumman F6F *Hellcat* 72
Grunspan, Herschel 169
Guam 69
Guderian, Gen. Heinz 98, 118, 157, 158
Gunther, John 144
Gustav Line 94

Haegawa, Capt. Kiichi 69
Halder, Gen. Franz 114
Halifax 24
Halsey, Rear Adm. William F. "Bull" 69
Hamerow, Theodore S. 119
Hanfstaengl, Ernst F.S. 159, 166, 167
Hankey, Lord 88, 89
Hannibal 92
Harding, Pres. Warren 122, 194
Harriman, Averill 65
Harriman, E.H. 126
Harrison, Pres. Benjamin 152
Harrison, Maj. Eugene 76
Hart, Basil Liddell 97, 157

Index

Hart, Adm. Thomas C. 55, 56, 58, 59, 219
Hauptmann, Bruno Richard 40, 41, 218
Hay, Amb. John 153
Hazen, Charles Downer 189
Heinkel, Ernst 44
Heinkel He-111 106, 159
Heinkel He 177 161, 231
Helfrich, Adm. Conrad E.L. 65, 66
Henderson, Neville 159
Hendrick, Burton C. 184, 188, 190, 233
Hersh, Seymour M. 208
Herwig, Holger H. 3, 150, 151
Hess, Rudolph 170
Himmler, Heinrich 106
Hirohito, Emperor 64, 69, 73, 78, 83, 101, 102
Hiroshima 22, 83, 102
Hitler, Adolf 11, 21, 106, 107, 110, 111, 150, 157, 160, 161, 163; a compelling speaker 167, 169, 170; interest in automobiles 166; interest in U.S. 166, 174, 175; interprets attack on Pearl Harbor 172; order to stop advance of Panzers 157, 159; plots on his life 105, 106, 107, 108, 110, 114; seeks peace with Britain 157
Hitlers's *Second Book* 164, 165
Hitler's Table Talk 1941–1944: His Private Conversations 164, 172, 173
Hitokappu Bay 69, 70, 71
Hoffmann, Peter 111
Honan, William H. 63
Honolulu Conference (1944) 148
Hoover, Pres. Herbert 40, 137
Hoover, "Ike" 192
Hopkins, Harry 30, 36, 56, 91, 125
Hossbach, Col. Friedrich 164
House, Col. Edward M. 7, 154
Houston, Sec. of Agriculture David F. 192, 193
Hull, Cordell 17, 56, 67, 92, 93, 129; reaction to Morgenthau Plan 130; ten-point ultimatum to Japan 221
HUSKY (Invasion of Sicily) 87

Iceland 16
Ickes, Harold L. 22, 26, 44, 50, 51, 175, 220
International law 24, 26, 35, 36
USS *Isabel* 56, 57, 76
Islands for War Debts Committee 46

Java 70
Jefferson, Pres. Thomas 19
Jews in America 38, 51, 52, 53, 136, 204
JN-25 (Japanese Naval Code) 61, 70, 71
Johnson, Hugh 47
Jovanovich, William 52
Judson, Clay 47
Junkers Ju-87 *Stuka* 159
Junkers Ju-88 43, 207
Jutland, Battle of 155

Kasserine Pass debacle 222
Kaufman, Samuel H. 82
Kautsky Documents 189
USS *Kearny* 20
Keep America Out of the War Congress 45
Keitel, Gen. Wilhelm 105
Kennedy, Joseph, Sr. 131
Kessel, Gen. Albrecht von 112
Kesselring, Field Marshal Albert 92, 94, 97
Keynes, John Maynard 125
Kimmel, Adm. Husband 11, 23, 65, 69, 79, 80, 84
King, Adm. Ernest 63, 79, 86, 99
Kirk, Adm. Alan 63, 69
Kisner, Homer 221
Kleist, Field Marshal Ewald von 157
Kluge, Gen. Gunther von 114
Knox, Sec. of Navy Frank 10, 22, 79, 80
Koiso, Gen. Kuniaki 99
Konoye, Fuminaro 61
Korean War 22, 84
Kristallnacht 169
Krock, Arthur 130, 131
Krupp, Bohlen-Halbach von 190
Krupp, Friedrich 116
Krupp 88 mm cannon 95, 159
Krupp steel 126
Kurile Islands 70

LaGuardia, Fiorello 175
Lamour, Dorothy 59
USS *Lanakai* 58, 59, 76
Lansing, Robert 184, 187
Layton, Com. Edwin T. 68
Lea, Homer 62
League of Nations 7
Leahy, Adm. William D. 99, 100, 145
Lee, Gen. Robert E. 89
Lend-lease 9, 30, 32, 33, 34, 35, 36, 37, 161
Lenin 62, 113
Lewis, Fulton, Jr. 53
USS *Lexington* 63, 70, 72, 76
Lilienthal Aeronautical Society 45
Lindbergh, Anne 40, 44
Lindbergh, Charles A. 34, 38, 48, 49, 52, 203, 219; accepts medal from Goring 44; admires German society 43; Charles, Jr., kidnapped 39, 40; flies across Atlantic 38, 39, 218; speech in Des Moines, Iowa 51, 203; spokesman for America First Committee 49, 50, 51, 203
Lindbergh, Jon (son) 41
Lochner, Louis P. 109
Lockhard, Spec. Joseph L. 74
Lodge, Sen. Henry Cabot 153, 194
Lothian, Lord 25
Lucas, Scott 82
Luce, Clare Booth 215
Ludendorff, Gen. Erich 3, 151
Luther, Hans 175

MacArthur, Gen. Douglas 85, 135, 148; corrupt relationship with Manuel Quezon 148
Mahan, Adm. Alfred Thayer 66, 153, 159
Make Europe Pay War Debts Committee 46
Malaya 69
Manila 70
Manstein, Gen. Fritz Erich von 97
Manteuffel, Gen. Hasso von 97
Marshall, Gen. George C. 82, 86, 99
Marshall, Vice Pres. Thomas Riley 193
May, Karl 66, 174, 231, 232
McCloy, John J. 99, 125
McCollum, Lt. Com. Arthur H. 64, 65, 69, 220
McIntire, Dr. Ross T. 82, 135, 149; covers up FDR's cardiovascular illness 137, 139, 142, 147; medical incompetence 137, 138
McKinley, Pres. William 153
Mein Kampf 162, 164, 165
Messerschmitt, Willi 44
Messerschmitt Bf-109 42, 43, 110, 218
Messerschmitt Me-262 *Swallow* 159
Messerschmitt Me-264 *Amerika-Bomber* 161, 176, 231
Midway Island 3, 69, 70
Mikawa, Vice Adm. Gunichi 69
Milch, Gen. Erhard 42
Mitsubishi A6M *Zero* 72, 73, 74
Moran, Lord 144, 145
Morgenthau, Henry, Jr. 22, 32, 120, 121, 128, 132, 134, 135, 175, 226; Morgenthau Plan 96, 121, 127, 133, 209; relationship with FDR 121, 122
Morgenthau, Henry, Sr. 7, 184, 185, 186, 187, 188, 189, 190
Morgenthau, Henry, III 121, 122
Murphy, John W. 82
Mussolini, Benito 40, 93

Nagasaki 100, 101
Nagumo, Rear Adm. Chiuchi 69, 75, 229
Nakajima B5N *Kate* 72, 73
Napoleon 92, 113
National Committee of Free Germans 91
National Congress to Keep America Out of Foreign Wars 46
National Council for the Prevention of War 45
Navy League 198
Neurath, Konstantin von 113
Neutrality Acts 7, 8, 16, 27, 32, 37, 216
New York Times 24, 63, 108, 188, 186
Newton, Rear Adm. John H. 70
Night of the Long Knives 113, 226
Niitakyama 221
Nimitz, Adm. Chester M. 61, 148
Ninety-nine year leases 23
No Foreign Wars Committee 46, 47
Noiseless bomb fuses 105, 106, 114, 115, 225
North American P-51 *Mustang* 94
Norway 45

Noyes, Rear Adm. Leigh 78
Nuremberg War Crimes Trial 114, 150, 170, 171
Nye, Sen. Gerald P. 15, 47, 170, 215, 216; "Munitions Hearings" 15, 195

Ochs, Adolph 186
Office of Strategic Services (OSS) 111
Office of War Information (OWI) 18
OLYMPIC (Invasion of Kyushu) 100
Operation Z 63, 70, 71, 220
Orlando, Vittorio Emanuele 193
Oshima, Hiroshi 77, 161

Page, Amb. Walter Hines 26
Panama Canal 26
Park, Dr. Bert E. 137, 139
Patton, Gen. George 120
Paulus, Field Marshal Friedrich von 113
Payne, Lt. John W., Jr. 57
Pearl Harbor Investigations 76, 79, 80, 81, 222
Pegler, Westbrook 66
Pelley, William Dudley 45
Pepper, Sen. Claude 34, 50
Pershing, Gen. John J. 155, 223
Poison gas: German 224; U.S. 100, 101, 207, 208, 224
Polls 8, 45, 54
"Pop up cruisers" scheme 11, 56, 65, 82
Pope Pius XII 98
Porsche, Ferdinand 166
Potsdam Conference (1945) 101, 133
Potsdam Declaration 101, 102, 213, 214
Pratt & Whitney Aircraft Co. 198
HMS *Prince of Wales* 17, 46, 216
Propaganda: British 1, 6, 48, 92, 93, 118; German 36, 90, 131, 132, 160; Soviet 91; U.S. 6, 32, 46, 47, 48, 49, 93, 102, 103, 117, 118, 219, 221, 228, 232
Purple (Japanese Diplomatic Code) 68, 69, 81

Quebec Conference I (OCTAGON) 127
Quebec Conference II (QUADRANT) 209
Quezon, Pres. Manuel 148

Raeder, Adm. Erich 36, 98, 161, 171, 216
Rainbow Five (War Plans) 12, 164, 216
Rauschning, Hermann 162, 163, 173
Regnery, William H. 47
Reinhardt, Gen. Hubert Lans 157
HMS *Repulse* 216
USS *Reuben James* 21, 22
Ribbentrop, Joachim von 77, 78, 160, 170, 171
Richardson, Adm. James O. 10, 80
Richthofen, *Rittmeister* Manfred von 219
Rickenbacker, Eddie 47
Roberts, Owen J. 80
Rommel, Field Marshal Erwin 98, 103, 164, 222

Index

Roosevelt, Eleanor (wife) 66, 138
Roosevelt, Elliott (son) 91
Roosevelt, Franklin Pres. Delano 1, 2, 5, 6, 10, 20, 221, 23, 25, 27, 332, 33, 35, 37, 50, 55, 56, 65, 73, 76, 77, 83, 89, 93, 120, 123, 135, 136, 177, 178; corresponds with Winston Churchill 217; covers up cardiovascular illness 141, 142, 143, 144; covers up polio paralysis 140, 141; declares war on Japan 129; history lessons 19, 50, 89; loses cognition 129, 147, 148; love of ships 22, 83; "quarantine-the-aggressors" speech 8, 168; relations with press 141, 143
Roosevelt, James (son) 142
Roosevelt, Theodore 66, 223
Roth, Rep. William V. 84
Rothfels, Hans 118
Royal Navy 25, 33, 45, 64
Rundstedt, Field Marshal Gerd von 157, 158
Rusbridger, James 70
Russo-Japanese War 62
Ryan, Paul B. 28, 169

Salereno 95
Samoan Islands 152, 153
Sampson, Adm. William 62
USS *Saratoga* 63, 72
Sato, Naotake 100
Schlabrendorff, Fabian von 114, 115
Schlieffen, Gen. Alfred von 3, 151
Die Schwarze Kapelle (Anti-Nazi movement in Germany) 97, 98, 103, 104, 109, 110, 112, 113, 115
Selective Service Act (1940) 65
Shangri-La 143, 229
Shirer, William L. 16
Short, Gen. Walter C. 23, 80
Sicily 87, 92
Silver Shirts 45
Singapore 69
Slessor, John, Air Marshal 88
Smith, Lt. Col. Truman 42, 43, 44, 48
Spandau — The Secret Diaries 171, 172
Spanish-American War 63
Speer, Albert 171, 175
Sperry Gyroscope Co. 196, 198
Spirit of St. Louis 38, 39, 218
Stalin, Josef 91, 92, 145, 146
Stalingrad 104, 113.
Standley, Adm. William 80
Stark, Adm. Harold "Betty" 11, 24, 55, 56, 69, 82
Stauffenberg, Col. Claus von 104, 105, 106, 107, 115
Stettinius, Sec. of State Edward R. 227
Stilwell, Gen. Joseph 136
Stimson, Sec. of War Henry L. 22, 34, 35, 76, 80, 125, 126; reaction to Morgenthau Plan 130
Stinnett, Robert E. 2, 3, 5, 68, 69, 220
Stuart, Douglas, Jr. 47, 49

Submarine warfare 15, 18, 19, 20, 21, 28, 35, 87, 94, 120, 155, 159, 171, 217
Sutherland, Richard 148
Suzuki, Gen. Teiichi 99, 101
Swanson, Claude A. 67
Sykes-Picot Agreement 187
SYMBOL (Casablanca Conference) 86, 87, 88

Taylor, Myron 98
Teheran Conference (1943) 17
Testament of Adolf Hitler 164, 172
USS *Texas* 20
Thomas, Norman 45
Thompson, Dorothy 49
Tirpitz 3, 28, 151, 153
Tirpitz, Adm. Alfred von 151, 153
Togo, Shinegoro 100
Toland, John 3, 60
Tolley, Rear Adm. Kemp 58, 59, 220
Tovey, Lord 23
Town-Class destroyers 24
Tresckow, Gen. Henning von 114
Trevor-Roper, H.R. 173
Triparte Pact 27, 78
Truman, Pres. Harry S. 37, 99, 100, 101, 102, 120, 123, 132, 133; reaction to Morgenthau Plan 133
Tuchman, Barbara W. 181
Tumulty, Joseph 194; covers up Woodrow Wilson's stroke 140, 191
Tyler, Lt. Kermit A. 74

Udet, Gen. Ernst 42, 44
Unconditional Surrender edict 85, 86, 88, 89, 91, 92, 93, 95, 96, 97, 101, 102, 112, 117, 133, 223
United Nations Declaration (Jan. 1, 1942) 17, 206

V-1 and V-2 guided missiles 129, 171, 232
Vallandigham, Clement L. 50
Vandenberg, Sen. Arthur 34, 79, 227
Verdienstkreuz Deutscher Adler Medal 44, 218, 219
Versailles Treaty 7, 156, 162, 196; Article 231 7, 184, 223, 187
Vian, Philip 28
Victoria, Queen 159
Vietnam War 22, 84, 136
Villard, Oswald Garrison 46
Volkswagen 165
Volstead Act (Prohibition) 194

Wake Island 69, 70
Wallace, Vice Pres. Henry A. 228
Walsh, David I. 27
Wangenheim, Amb. Hans von 186, 188, 189
War Debts Committee 46
War Plan Orange (Japan) 59
Warlimont, Gen. Walter 105

Washington Disarmament Conference (1922) 196
Wedemeyer, Gen. Albert C. 13, 65, 66, 89
Weigand, Karl von 170
Weinberg, Gerhard L. 165
Weinstein, Dr. Edwin A. 233
Weizmann, Chaim 187
Welles, Sumner 17
Wheeler, Sen. Burton K. 47
White, Harry Dexter 124
White, William Allen 33
Wilhelm, Kaiser, II 150, 153, 159, 189,
Willkie, Wendell L. 48
Wilson, Edith Bolling 191, 193, 233; covers up Woodrow Wilson's stroke 140, 191, 192, 194; Woodrow Wilson's Fourteen Points 189, 193; Woodrow Wilson's incapacity 192 193, 194

Wilson, Hugh R. 43, 44, 169
Wilson, Pres. Woodrow 1, 2, 7, 15, 19, 66, 78, 154, 171, 185, 188, 191
Winant, Amb. John 65
Wood, Robert E. 47
Woodin, William 122

Yalta Conference (ARGONAUT) 136, 134, 145, 146, 229
Yamamoto, Adm. Isoruku 3, 22, 61, 69, 70, 220
Yarnell, Adm. H.E. 63
Young Plan 156, 166, 231

Zimmermann Telegram 1, 154, 181
Zionism 185, 187

www.ingramcontent.com/pod-product-compliance
Lightning Source LLC
Chambersburg PA
CBHW051217300426

44116CB00006B/612